CRISIS *Intervention*
THEORY AND METHODOLOGY

CRISIS
Intervention
THEORY AND METHODOLOGY

Donna C. Aguilera
Ph.D., F.A.A.N., M.F.C., F.I.A.E.P.

Consultant and Private Practice
Beverly Hills and Sherman Oaks, California

SEVENTH EDITION
with 32 illustrations

 **Mosby**

St. Louis Baltimore Boston Chicago London Madrid Philadelphia Sydney Toronto

Publisher: Alison Miller
Editor: Jeff Burnham
Developmental Editor: Jolynn Gower
Project Manager: Barbara Bowes Merritt
Editing and Production: Graphic World Publishing Services
Manufacturing Supervisor: Betty Richmond
Cover Design: Renee Duenow

SEVENTH EDITION

Printed in the United States of America
Composition by Graphic World, Inc.
Printing/binding by R.R. Donnelley & Sons Company, Crawfordsville

Mosby–Year Book, Inc.
11830 Westline Industrial Drive
St. Louis, Missouri 63146

Library of Congress Cataloging-in-Publication Data

Aguilera, Donna C.
    Crisis intervention: theory and methodology   /   Donna C. Aguilera.
    —7th ed.
        p.   cm.
    Includes bibliographical references and index.
    ISBN 0-8016-6936-7
    1.   Crisis intervention (Psychiatry)   2.   Crisis intervention
    (Psychiatry)—Case studies.   I.   Title.
    [DNLM: 1.   Crisis Intervention—methods.   2.   Stress Disorders, Post-
Traumatic—therapy.   3.   Psychotherapy—methods.   4.   Life Change
Events.   WM 401 A283c   1993]
    RC480.6.A38   1993
    616.89'025—dc20
    DNLM/DLC   93-24181
    for Library of Congress   CIP

94   95   96   97   98   /   9   8   7   6   5   4   3   2   1

To

all from whom I have learned

and

all who will yet forever teach me

Foreword

Biologic evolution has prepared man to survive even in the most challenging of life's threats and trauma, both physical and psychological. We have learned, however, that the *alarm reaction,* first described in full detail by Hans Selye during the 1940s, is associated with trauma and threats of trauma by the flow of stress hormones and neurotransmitters, and other rapidly changing bodily physiology which, if unmodulated, can produce illness (physical or emotional) from *over-reaction* to trauma. We now also know that trauma and threat of trauma can lead to changes in the immune system, which may operate against survival if such changes are unmodulated. Oftentimes, the threat of trauma can be more devastating than the actual trauma itself, especially in the case of children (for example, in the witnessing of home violence) and anyone else who is helpless and is without well-timed social and psychological support at the time that the trauma threat occurs.

Man's physical and psychic survival requires both physical and emotional support from others in the environment. This modulating influence from the environment is a part of man's biological and social heritage. Humans are social mammals and are predisposed toward social responses toward others and integrated joint activity, ensuring survival of the species. This social predisposition toward shared experience in humans makes it possible for an individual suffering pain, trauma or distress, or threats of these trauma to be understood and acknowledged directly or intuitively by another person. Thus, one person's pain and trauma or threat becomes a shared threat or a shared trauma for others in the community.

Even before the days of technically equipped emergency services, "911," the paramedics, mountain rescue teams, as well as the crisis intervention hotlines and professional societies mobilized to respond to massive trauma in the community (referred to in this volume), the lives of many men, women, and children were saved because someone noticed and responded to them and provided a safe haven and a protective environment for the person in trouble or threat. What was provided prior to our more sophisticated methods of life saving technology was primarily psychological together with warmth and protection. Such support provided by our unsophisticated ancestors worked then and still works now. We now know *why* it works, and that is because a supportive psychological and physical environment actually does modulate the over-reactive response of the body and the mind to a trauma or threat; thus, the feeling of helplessness is diminished and does not escalate into an exaggerated, non-adaptive illness-producing response. For example, during a recent backpacking trip to the high Sierras, one of our party was stung on the finger by a wasp. Her whole hand began to swell, and she was frightened of dying and not easily reassured, even after she received some Benadryl and cold packs were applied to the hand. Luckily, we met a pleasant, uniformed forest ranger who had himself been attacked by a swarm of wasps when he inadvertently disturbed their nest on the forest floor. He told us of his experience and of his recovery and reaffirmed the correctness of the treatment given and indicated further that the danger period for more complicated events had now passed.

Appropriate response to a crisis in the present helps individuals clearly distinguish between a minor stress and an impending catastrophe in the future. Learning to make this distinction is extremely important for each individual and can be helped by an understanding person who is knowledgeable and helpful to a person who has been traumatized. Making this distinction then prepares the person to truly emerge from the present situation with knowledge and understanding such that the anxiety signal that alerts the person to a danger then also brings to mind the appropriate response to the danger, taking into account its magnitude. Not all dangers are of equal magnitude. A modulated response is required.

The helping professions must have, and must be able to convey to others, their presence and emotional availability in a timely fashion to the person in crisis. The professional must be able to understand the peculiar nature of each individual in crisis and out of such understanding, help the patient gain hope and increased confidence in being able to survive the crisis. Another important asset of the professional is the capacity to understand that the person himself contains the forces that can lead to recovery. The implication is that the helping person helps the traumatized individual see and understand how to make use of their most strongly developed coping capacities. Well-timed warmth, caring, love, information leading to understanding, good communication, and the capacity of the injured party to distinguish between a minor transient incident and a more serious long-term incapacity provide a powerful holding environment that allows the individual to recover, even though temporarily overwhelmed with feelings of helplessness.

Many people have gone through traumatic experiences during their formative years without remembering such experiences. Over-reactions later on to a faintly similar experience can be understood as a maladaptive response to the actual present reality, including the tendency to provoke and repeat the traumatic experience. Unrecognized post-traumatic effects coming late on the heels of earlier trauma are a source of considerable pain, suffering, and maladaptation in adolescent and adult life. They are the result of poorly resolved early traumatic experience, inadequately responded to by the environment and with an inadequate convalescence of the person from the traumatic experience. Convalescence following any illness or trauma is the most important variable that determines whether the illness becomes chronic or whether it becomes fully resolved. It is worth pointing out here that life if full of eu traumas (health-producing traumas), which were fully incorporated in Selye's theory of adaptation in the fifties. A recent well-controlled study by Andrews et al, 1993, showed that students going to foreign countries under AFS International Exchange programs showed a long-term decline in vulnerability to neurotic symptoms as compared to a well-matched control group. Parmalee has written on the importance of helping families of young acute and chronically ill children adapt to situations in the hospital, to crisis, to potentially traumatic surgeries, etc., emphasizing that successfully traversing these rather common potentially traumatic situations in childhood actually leaves the child and family in a stronger, more resilient psychological state.

Human beings inherently strive to attain new understandings and new meanings in every life experience. New meaning is critical for recovery from trauma and helps prevent the long-term consequences of repressed traumatic experience. Many cases of post-traumatic stress disorder have been hidden by this repression for many years.

This book will be of considerable aid to helping those who help or who want to help. It will soon be learned and acknowledged by anyone in the field, however, that helping is not as simple as it might seem on the surface. Sometimes "help" can add to distress and trauma rather than lead to a resolution of it. The complexity of both conscious and unconscious motivations of the persons providing help should be required as a part of the training of anyone espousing skills in helping others. This book will help individuals achieve that kind of understanding. Insight, however, is a long, hard, and difficult road. The working through of insight in the helping professions requires constant vigilance and continuing psychological work.

Justin D. Call, M.D.
Newport Beach, California
University of California, Irvine

REFERENCES

Andrews G, Page AC, Neilson M: Sending your teenagers away: controlled stress decreases neurotic vulnerability, *Arch Gen Psychiatr* 50:585-589, 1993.
Parmalee AH: Children's illnesses and normal behavioral development: the role of care giver, *Zero to Three* 13(4):1-9, 1993.

Preface

The seventh edition of this textbook recognizes the need for an overview as well as an introduction and guide to crisis intervention from its historical development to its current utilization. Although the techniques and skills of a therapist must be learned and practiced under professional supervision, knowledge and an awareness of the basic theory and principles of crisis intervention are of value to all who are involved in the helping professions. It should be of special interest and value to all who are involved in the helping professions. This book should be of particular importance as a guideline to those in the mental health field who are in constant proximity to persons in stressful situations who seek help because they are unable to cope alone.

Chapter 1 deals with the historical development of crisis intervention methodology. Its intent is to create awareness of the broad base of knowledge incorporated into current practice.

Chapter 2 discusses the differences between the psychotherapeutic techniques of psychoanalysis and psychoanalytic psychotherapy and between brief psychotherapy and crisis intervention methodology in the major areas of their goals, foci, activities of the therapists, indications for treatment, the average length of treatment, and the approximate cost to the individual.

Chapter 3 focuses on the problem-solving process and introduces the reader to basic terminology used in this method of treatment. A paradigm of intervention is shown for the purpose of clarifying the sequential steps of crisis development. Two other case studies, with paradigms, illustrate its application as a guide to the case studies in subsequent chapters.

Chapter 4 is a new chapter that discusses the legal and ethical issues inherent in psychotherapy. Discussed are the legal aspects of malpractice. Sexual harassment is discussed as it relates to psychotherapy, and a case study is included to demonstrate the use of crisis intervention techniques in a case of sexual harassment.

A new Chapter 5 has been included because the content is currently applicable; it explores posttraumatic stress disorder. It is presented with emphasis on diagnostic problems, definitions, elements of stress (the victims, reactions of stress, and assessing symptoms of stress). The Desert Shield families at risk, children's needs, and the problems of the homeless are also discussed.

Chapter 6 deals with stressful events that could precipitate a crisis in individuals regardless of socioeconomic or sociocultural status. These events include prematurity, child abuse, status and role change, abortion, rape, physical illness, Alzheimer's disease, abuse of the elderly, chronic mental illness, wife abuse, divorce, cocaine abuse, suicide, and death and the grief process. Hypothetical case studies based on factual experience are presented to illustrate the techniques used by therapists in crisis resolution. Theoretical material preceding each case study is presented as an overview relevant to the crisis situation.

Chapter 7 is devoted to those changes that occur during concomitant physiological and social transitions, such as birth, puberty, young adulthood, marriage, illness or death of a family member, the climacteric, and old age. Maturational crises have been described as normal processes of growth and development; they differ from situational crises in that they usually evolve over an extended period of time and frequently require more characterological changes of the individual. Case studies are included with appropriate theoretical material.

Chapter 8 delineates the concerns of AIDS patients. It has been expanded and updated to 1993. It includes the most current definition and understanding of the disease and all of its ramifications. Four case studies are presented with appropriate theoretical material. The case studies presented include homosexual, heterosexual, male, female, adult, and adolescent clients.

Chapter 9 focuses on the burn-out syndrome that occurs so frequently in high-stress situations. Theoretical material includes the impact of AIDS on staff members. A case study is presented to illustrate the utilization of the crisis model. Theoretical content and a case study are also presented on burn-out that can occur in a hospice staff.

I am indebted to many people who have been of direct and indirect assistance in writing this edition. I wish to thank specifically the following individuals for their roles in bringing this manuscript to fruition: my editors, Jeff Burnham and Jolynn Gower, for their patience and understanding; Tim Waddell and Suzanne Ferrell for their friendship, help, and encouragement (may it last forever); and Janice M. Messick, former co-author, for her moral support and continued friendship. For the seventh edition it is an honor to have Justin Call, M.D., write the foreword. Our collegial friendship goes back many happy years. To my family, who are my kindest critics and strongest supporters, I owe a very special debt—my eternal love.

Donna C. Aguilera

Contents

CRISIS *Intervention*
THEORY AND METHODOLOGY

Chapter 1

Historical Development of Crisis Intervention Methodology

Prior to 1970, when the first edition of this book was published, the word *crisis* could not be found in any psychological dictionary. In medical dictionaries, *crisis* referred to the change in a disease process that meant either life or death. Today, the media has made the word *crisis* a household word that can refer to any tense or stressful event.

A psychological crisis refers to an individual's inability to solve a problem. We all exist in a state of emotional equilibrium, a state of balance, or homeostasis. When something that is different (either positive or negative), a change, or a loss that creates a state of disequilibrium occurs, we strive to regain and maintain our previous level of equilibrium. A person in crisis is at a turning point. He* faces a problem that he cannot readily solve by using the coping mechanisms that have worked before. As a result, his tension and anxiety increase, and he becomes less able to find a solution. A person in this situation feels helpless—he is caught in a state of great emotional upset and feels unable to take action *on his own* to solve the problem.

Crisis intervention can offer the immediate help that a person in crisis needs to reestablish equilibrium. It is an inexpensive, short-term therapy that focuses on solving the immediate problem. Increasing awareness of sociocultural factors that could precipitate crisis situations has led to the rapid evolution of crisis intervention methodology. Therefore, these factors are discussed first, to clarify their social and cultural implications.

Everywhere today we hear talk of the changes in our lives that have been made by "urbanization" and "technology." A closer study of these changes will add to our understanding of what they have meant to families and to individuals.

Before the revolution in technology and industrialization, most people lived on farms or in small rural communities. They were chiefly self-employed, either on farms or in small, associated businesses. When sons and daughters married, they were likely to remain near their parents and work in the same occupations, and in this way trades and occupations were a link between generations. Families tended to be large and, because family members lived and worked together and relied

---

*For the sake of clarity, male pronouns have been used throughout this book except where the name of the patient or therapist denotes female gender.

chiefly on each other for social interaction, they developed strong loyalties and a sense of responsibility for other family members. Contemporary urban life, however, does not encourage or allow this kind of sheltered, close-knit family relationship. People who live in cities are likely to be employed by a company and paid a wage. They work with business associates and live within a neighborhood rather than working and living with just their immediate family. Because of housing conditions and the necessity of living on a wage, families in cities usually consist of parents and unmarried children.

These differences between rural and urban life have important repercussions to individual security and stability. The extended rural family offered a large and relatively constant group of associates. Family size and the varying strength of blood ties meant that there was always someone to talk to, even about a problem involving two family members. By contrast, urban life is highly mobile. There is often a rapid turnover in business associates and neighbors, and there is no certainty that these relative strangers will share the same values, beliefs, and interests. All these factors make it difficult for people to develop real trust and interdependence outside the small immediate family. In addition, urban life requires that people meet each other only superficially, in specific roles and in limited relationships rather than as total personalities.

All these factors taken together mean that people in cities are more isolated than ever from the emotional support provided by the family and by close and familiar peers. As a result, there are no role models to follow—yet the demands of urban life are constantly changing, and coping behavior that was appropriate and successful several years before may be hopelessly ineffective today.

This situation provides a favorable environment for the development of crises. As defined by Caplan (1961), *crisis* may occur when the individual faces a problem that he cannot solve, which causes a rise in inner tension and signs of anxiety and creates an inability to function in extended periods of emotional upset.

Historical Development

The origin of modern crisis intervention dates back to the work of Eric Lindemann and his colleagues following the Coconut Grove fire in Boston on November 28, 1942. In what was at that time the worst single-building fire in the country's history, 493 people perished when flames swept through the crowded Coconut Grove night-club. Lindemann and others from the Massachusetts General Hospital played an active role in helping survivors who had lost loved ones in the disaster. His clinical report (Lindemann, 1944) on the psychological symptoms of the survivors became the cornerstone for subsequent theorizing on the grief process, a series of stages through which a mourner progresses on the way toward accepting and resolving loss. Lindemann came to believe that clergy and other community caretakers could play a critical role in helping bereaved people through the mourning process and thereby head off later psychological difficulties. This concept was further opera-tionalized with the establishment of the Wellesley Human Relations Service (Boston) in 1948, one of the first community mental health services noted for its focus on short-term therapy in the context of preventive psychiatry.

Lindemann's (1956) initial concern was to develop approaches that might contribute to the maintenance of good mental health and the prevention of emotional disorganization on a community wide level. He chose to study bereavement reactions in his search for social events or situations that would predictably be followed by emotional disturbances in a considerable portion of the population. In his study of bereavement reactions among the survivors of those killed in the Coconut Grove nightclub fire, he described both brief and abnormally prolonged reactions occurring in different individuals as a result of the loss of a significant person in their lives.

In his experiences of working with grief reactions, Lindemann concluded that a conceptual frame of reference constructed around the concept of an emotional crisis, as exemplified by bereavement reactions, might be profitable for investigation and useful for the development of preventive efforts. Certain inevitable events in the course of the life cycle of every individual can be described as hazardous situations, for example, bereavement, the birth of a child, and marriage. He postulated that in each of these situations emotional strain would be generated, stress would be experienced, and a series of adaptive mechanisms would occur that could lead either to mastery of the new situation or to failure with more or less lasting impairment to function. Although such situations create stress for all people who are exposed to them, they become crises for those individuals who by personality, previous experience, or other factors are especially vulnerable to this stress and whose emotional resources are taxed beyond their usual adaptive resources.

Lindemann's theoretical frame of reference led to the development of crisis intervention techniques, and in 1946 he and Caplan established a community wide program of mental health in the Harvard area, the Wellesley Project.

According to Caplan (1961), the most important aspects of mental health are the state of the ego, the stage of its maturity, and the quality of its structure. Assessment of the ego's state is based on three main areas: (1) the capacity of the person to withstand stress and anxiety and to maintain ego equilibrium, (2) the degree of reality recognized and faced in solving problems, and (3) the repertoire of effective coping mechanisms the person can employ in maintaining a balance in his biopsychosocial field.

Sigmund Freud was the first to demonstrate and apply the principle of causality as it relates to psychic determinism (Bellak and Small, 1965). Simply put, this principle states that every act of human behavior has its cause, or source, in the history and experience of the individual. It follows that causality is operative, whether or not the individual is aware of the reason for the behavior. Psychic determinism is the theoretical foundation of psychotherapy and psychoanalysis. The free association technique, dream interpretation, and assignment of meaning to symbols are based on the assumption that causal connections operate unconsciously.

A particularly important outcome of Freud's deterministic position was his construction of a developmental or "genetic" psychology (Ford and Urban, 1963). Present behavior is understandable in terms of the life history or experience of the individual, and the crucial foundations for all future behavior are laid down in infancy and early childhood. The most significant determinants of present behavior are the "residues" of past experiences (learned responses), particularly those developed during the earliest years to reduce biological tensions.

Freud assumed that a reservoir of energy that exists in the individual initiates all behavior. Events function as guiding influences, but they do not initiate behavior; they only serve to help mold behavior in certain directions.

Since the end of the nineteenth century, the concept of determinism, as well as the scientific bases from which Freud formulated his ideas, have undergone many changes. Although the ego-analytic theorists have tended to subscribe to much in the Freudian position, they differ in several respects that seem to be extensions of Freudian theory rather than direct contradictions. As a group, they concluded that Freud neglected the direct study of normal or healthy behavior.

Heinz Hartmann was an early ego analyst who was profoundly versed in Freud's theoretical contributions (Loewenstein, 1966). He postulated that the psychoanalytic theories of Freud could prove valid for normal as well as pathological behavior. Hartmann began with the study of ego functions and distinguished between two groups: those that develop from conflict and those that are "conflict-free," such as memory, thinking, and language, which he labeled "primary autonomous functions of the ego." He considered these important in the adaptation of the individual to the environment. Hartmann's conception of the ego as an organ of adaptation required further study of the concept of reality. Hartmann emphasized that a person's adaptation in early childhood as well as his ability to maintain adaptation to the environment in later life had to be considered. He also described the search for an environment as another form of adaptation—the fitting together of the individual and society. He believed that, although the behavior of the individual is strongly influenced by culture, a part of the personality remains relatively free of this influence.

Sandor Rado developed the concept of adaptational psychodynamics, providing a new approach to the unconscious as well as new goals and techniques of therapy (Salzman, 1962). Rado saw human behavior as being based on the dynamic principle of motivation and adaptation. An organism achieves adaptation through interaction with culture. Behavior is viewed in terms of its effect on the welfare of the individual, not just in terms of cause and effect. The organism's patterns of interaction improve through adaptation, with the goal being the increase of possibilities for survival. Freud's classical psychoanalytic technique emphasized the developmental past and the uncovering of unconscious memories, and he attached little if any importance to the reality of the present. Rado's adaptational psychotherapy, however, emphasizes the immediate present without neglecting the influence of the developmental past. Primary concern is with failures in adaptation "today," what caused them, and what the patient must do to learn to overcome them. Interpretations always begin and end with the present; preoccupation with the past is discouraged. As quickly as insight is achieved, it is used as a beginning to encourage the patient to enter into the present, real-life situation repeatedly. Through practice, the patient automatizes new patterns of healthy behavior. According to Rado, this automatization factor—not insight—is ultimately the curative process. He believes that it takes place not passively, in the therapist's office, but actively, in the reality of daily living (Ovesy and Jameson, 1956).

Erik H. Erikson further developed the theories of ego psychology, which complement those of Freud, Hartmann, and Rado, by focusing on the epigenesis of the ego and on the theory of reality relationships (Rappaport, 1959). Epigenetic development is characterized by an orderly sequence of development at particular stages, each depending on the previous stage for successful completion. Erikson perceived eight stages of psychosocial development, spanning the entire life cycle of the individual and involving specific developmental tasks that must be solved in each phase. The solution achieved in each phase is applied in subsequent phases. Erikson's theory is important in that it offers an explanation of the individual's social development as a result of encounters with the social environment. Another significant feature is his elaboration on the normal rather than the pathological development of social interactions. He dealt in particular with the problems of adolescence and saw this period in life as a "normative crisis," that is, a normal maturational phase of increased conflicts, and one with apparent fluctuations in ego strength (Pumpian-Mindlin, 1966). Erikson integrated the biological, cultural, and self-deterministic points of view in his eight stages of human development and broadened the scope of traditional psychotherapy with his theoretical formulations concerning identity and identity crises. His theories have provided a basis for the work of others who further developed the concept of maturational crises and began serious consideration of situational crises and individual adaptation to the current environmental dilemma.

Caplan believes that all the elements that compose the total emotional milieu of the person must be assessed in an approach to preventive mental health. The material, physical, and social demands of reality, as well as the needs, instincts, and impulses of the individual, must all be considered important behavioral determinants. As a result of his work in Israel (1948) and his later experiences in Massachusetts with Lindemann and with the Community Mental Health Program at Harvard University, he evolved the concept of the importance of *crisis* periods in individual and group development (Caplan, 1951).

Caplan defined crisis as occurring "when a person faces an obstacle to important life goals that is, for a time, insurmountable through the utilization of customary methods of problem solving. A period of disorganization ensues, a period of upset, during which many abortive attempts at solution are made" (Caplan, 1961, p.18). In essence, the individual is viewed as living in a state of emotional equilibrium, with the goal always to return to or to maintain that state. When customary problem-solving techniques cannot be used to meet the daily problems of living, the balance or equilibrium is upset. The individual must either solve the problem or adapt to nonsolution. In either case, a new state of equilibrium develops, sometimes better and sometimes worse insofar as positive mental health is concerned. There is a rise in inner tension, there are signs of anxiety, and there is disorganization of function, resulting in a protracted period of emotional upset. This he refers to as "crisis." The outcome is governed by the kind of interaction that takes place during that period between the individual and the key figures in his emotional milieu.

Evolution of Community Psychiatry

Community psychiatry has emerged as a new field. New concepts and new bio-psychosocial problems arise continually in rapidly changing cultures so that it is a broad, fluid field. A difference is now perceived between long-term, psychoanalytic therapy of the individual and short-term, reality-oriented psychotherapy as practiced in community psychiatry. In the middle 1960s, the term *crisis intervention* was not yet included in psychiatric dictionaries. In 1970, the fourth edition of Hinsie and Campbell's *Psychiatric Dictionary* listed crisis intervention as one of several modes of community psychiatry: "In the crisis intervention model, the focus is on transitional-situational demands for novel adaptational responses. Because minimal intervention at such times tends to achieve maximal and optimal effects, such a model is more readily applicable to population groups than the medical model" (1970, p.606).

According to Bellak (1964), community psychiatry evolved from multiple disciplines and is intrinsically bound to the development of psychoanalytic theory. The social and behavioral sciences that advanced during the first half of the century were predicated on psychodynamic hypotheses. At the same time, concepts of public health and epidemiology were advancing in community health programs.

After World War II, the general public's increasing awareness and acceptance of the high incidence of psychiatric problems created changes in attitudes and demands for community action. The discovery and use of psychotropic drugs were important steps forward; they resulted in opportunities for open wards and rehabilitation of the hospitalized patient in his home milieu.

It would be incorrect to assume that all these factors merged spontaneously, creating a successful, structured cure for mental illness. Rather, it was a slow process of trial and error. Widely different programs—each striving to meet problems involving different cultures, interests, knowledge, and skills—were communicated and related to other programs similarly initiated. Disciplines once separated in their goals became cognizant of their interdependence in attaining mutually recognized goals. New allied disciplines developed; roles changed and expanded. Tasks were diffused, and lines between disciplines became more flexible.

The origin of day hospitals for the care of psychiatric patients grew out of a shortage of hospital beds (Ross, 1964), which forced premature discharges of patients to their homes, rather than out of a treatment innovation. The first reported day hospital was associated with the First Psychiatric Hospital in Moscow in 1933. As Dzhagarov (1937) states, "The need to continue treatment and for special observation in a setting similar to that of a hospital suggested a practical solution in the form of admission to the preventive section of the hospital. In a time a transformation took place, the day hospital was created, proving to be adequately prepared to meet the new needs." In referring to this day hospital in Moscow, Kramer, as quoted by Ross (1964, p.190), says: "While this day center is little known and probably had little effect on later developments in the Western world, it is accurate to say that this was the first organized Day Hospital for individuals with severe mental illness."

In the late 1930s Bierer, (1964) began the Marlborough Experiment in England. Patients, as members of a "therapeutic social club," lived outside the hospital and were treated at day hospitals or part-time facilities. According to Bierer, the primary goal of the program was to change the patient's role concept from that of a passive object of treatment to one of an active participant-collaborator. At the same time, the psychiatrist and staff had to reconceptualize the patient as a human being accessible to reason and emphasize his assets rather than concentrating on his psychopathology and conflicts. The reality of here and now was the focus of attention.

These innovations in attitude gave rise to the concept of "therapeutic community." The patient became a partner and collaborator with the staff and was granted equal rights, opportunities, and facilities. The medical staff and their assistants functioned as advisors.

The patient group assumed responsibility for the behavior of its members, as well as for planning for activities, planning their futures, and offering support to each other. Group and social methods were used that encouraged the constant interaction of the members.

Other complementary projects developed in the Marlborough Program were the Day Hospital, the Night Hospital, the Aftercare Rehabilitation Center, the Self-Governed Community Hotel, Neurotics Nomine, and the Weekend Hospital.

Linn (1964) describes Cameron's first day hospital in Montreal, Canada, in 1946, in which he and others were responsible for defining and giving formal structure to the program as a treatment innovation.

With this frame of reference, it was only natural that the general hospital added to the various roles in which it serves the community that of becoming a focal point of preventive medicine and public health functions in psychiatry.

In 1958, a "Trouble Shooting Clinic" was initiated by Bellak (1960) as part of City Hospital of Elmhurst, New York, a general hospital with 1000 beds. The clinic was designed to offer first aid for emotional problems and was not limited to urgent crises. It combined two aspects of service on a walk-in basis around the clock: major emergencies as well as minor problems involving guidance, legal problems, and marital relations.

After the passage of the California Community Mental Health Act in 1958, the California Department of Mental Hygiene established the first state agency in the country (1961) to undertake the training of specialists in community psychiatry. It was recognized that clinics were needed to accommodate those individuals in the community who were unfamiliar with established forms of psychiatric treatment. The cause for these individuals' exclusion from treatment conceivably could have been divergence in social or cultural background, lack of communication, or lack of recognition of the need for services by both the population and the existing agencies.

In January 1962, the Benjamin Rush Center for Problems of Living, a division of the Los Angeles Psychiatric Service, was opened as a no-wait, unrestricted intake, walk-in crisis intervention center. The center is currently under the aegis of the Didi Hirsch Community Mental Health Center. After more than 30 years of operation, the Benjamin Rush Center has accumulated considerable evidence that persons who come to the Center are often those who would not typically seek treatment in a traditional clinic. The approach has been to attract persons who, while judged to be genuinely in need of psychiatric treatment, would not have sought traditional treatment because of reluctance to consider themselves "sick," to assume the patient role, or to accept the stigma of psychiatric treatment.

In 1967, crisis intervention replaced emergency detention at the San Francisco General Hospital. On each of the psychiatric units, interdisciplinary teams were established whose primary goal was to reestablish independent functioning of the clients as soon as possible. In a follow-up study, Decker and Stubblebine (1972) concluded that the crisis intervention program achieved the anticipated reduction in psychiatric inpatient treatment.

In the early 1970s, the Bronx Mental Health Center (Centro de Hygiene Mental del Bronx) (Morales, 1971) was created for crisis intervention for Spanish-speaking people of low socioeconomic status; it was staffed by Spanish-speaking psychiatrists.

At about the same time, suburban churches in Montreal, Canada, offered brief crisis intervention services on an experimental basis (Lecker and others, 1971). The goal of the program was to reach families undergoing a variety of stresses through a roving walk-in clinic. The clinics served to facilitate delivery of these services to a latent population at risk, not reached by other means, and at a point early in the evolution of a life crisis.

The first hot line was started at Children's Hospital in Los Angeles in 1968. Hot lines and youth crisis centers have been created in recognition of the failure of traditional approaches to make contacts among adolescents. Twenty-four–hour crisis telephones, free counseling with a minimum of red tape, walk-in contacts, crash pads, and young people serving as volunteer staff in such services continue to be increasingly attractive to youth who have emerged as the locus of a counterculture.

Trends such as these are being repeated around the country as community mental health programs recognize the value of providing services in primary and secondary prevention unique to the needs of their particular clients. Increasing recognition is also being given to the need to provide more services for those clients whose needs are for continuing support in rehabilitation after resolution of the immediate crisis. The major concern confronting community mental health centers is no longer that of discerning just what services are appropriate to the needs of potential clients. It is not even that of recruiting clients for the services provided. The centers are being faced with the problem of obtaining an adequate supply of human resources to meet demands for their services, as well as the finances to pay for services. Professionals and nonprofessionals alike have been recruited and trained to fill the gap between supply and demand for these services. This has led to the deprofessionalization of many mental health functions previously considered to be solely within the scope of the professional's skills. Role boundaries have undergone increasing diffusion as the needs of the individual client and his community have become the determining factors in establishing the appropriateness of services.

REFERENCES

Bellak L: A general hospital as a focus of community psychiatry, *JAMA* 174:2214, 1960.
Bellak L, editor: *Handbook of community psychiatry and community mental health*, New York, 1964, Grune & Stratton.
Bellak L, Small L: *Emergency psychotherapy and brief psychotherapy*, New York, 1965, Grune & Stratton.

Bierer J: *The Marlborough experiment*. In Bellak L, editor: *Handbook of community psychiatry and community mental health*, New York, 1964, Grune & Stratton.

Caplan G: A public health approach to child psychiatry, *Ment Health* 35:235, 1951.

Caplan G: *An approach to community mental health*, New York, 1961, Grune & Stratton.

Caplan G: *Principles of preventive psychiatry*, New York, 1964, Basic Books.

Decker JB, Stubblebine JM: Crisis intervention and prevention of psychiatric disability; a follow-up study, *Am J Psychiatry* 129:101, 1972.

Dzhagarov MA: Experience in organizing a day hospital for mental patients, *Neurapathologia Psikhiatria* 6:147, 1937 (Translated by G Wachbrit).

Ford D, Urban H: *Systems of psychotherapy*, New York, 1963, John Wiley & Sons.

Hinsie LE, Campbell RJ: *Psychiatric dictionary*, ed 4, New York, 1970, Oxford University Press.

Lecker S and others: Brief interventions: a pilot walk-in clinic in suburban churches, *Can Psychiatr Assoc J* 16:141, 1971.

Lindemann E: Symptomatology and management of acute grief, *Am J Psychiatry* 101:101-148, Sept 1944.

Lindemann E: The meaning of crisis in individual and family, *Teachers Coll Rec* 57:310, 1956.

Linn L: *Psychiatric program in a general hospital*. In Bellak L, editor: *Handbook of community psychiatry and community mental health*, New York, 1964, Grune & Stratton.

Loewenstein RM: *Psychology of the ego*. In Alexander F, Eisenstein S, Grotjahn M, editors: *Psychoanalytic pioneers*, New York, 1966, Basic Books, Inc.

Morales HM: Bronx Mental Health Center, NY State Division, *Bronx Bull* 13:6, 1971.

Ovesy L, Jameson J: *Adaptational techniques of psychodynamic therapy*. In Rado S, Daniels G, editors: *Changing concepts of psychoanalytic medicine*, New York, 1956, Grune & Stratton.

Pumpian-Mindlin E: *Contributions to the theory and practice of psychoanalysis and psychotherapy*. In Alexander F, Eisenstein S, Grotjahn M, editors: *Psychoanalytic pioneers*, New York, 1966, Basic Books.

Rappaport D: *A historical survey of psychoanalytic ego psychology*. In Klein GS, editor: *Psychological issues*, New York, 1959, International Universities Press.

Ross M: *Extramural treatment techniques*. In Bellak L, editor: *Handbook of community psychiatry and community mental health*, New York, 1964, Grune & Stratton.

Salzman L: *Developments in psychoanalysis*, New York, 1962, Grune & Stratton.

Sifneos PE: A concept of emotional crisis, *Ment Hyg* 44:169, 1960.

ADDITIONAL READINGS

Anderson L, Thobaben M: Clients in crisis: when should the nurse step in? *J Gerontol Nurse* 10:6-10, 1984.

Bachrach LL: Community psychiatry's changing role, *Hosp Community Psychiatry* 42:573-574, 1991.

Baird SF: Helping the family through a crisis, *Nursing* 17:66, 1987.

Battegay R, Klaui C: Analytically oriented group psychotherapy with borderline patients as long-term crisis management, *Crisis* 7:94-110, 1986.

Baumann DJ and others: Citizen participation in police crisis intervention activities, *Am J Community Psychol* 15:459-471, 1987.

Bayuk LL: Nursing families in crisis: protecting yourself, *Wash State J Nurs* 54:17-20, 1983.

Beard P: Nursing Mirror community forum: health visiting in a crisis, *Nurs Mirror* 158:i-iii, 1984.

Bengelsdorf H, Alden DC: A mobile crisis unit in the psychiatric emergency room, *Hosp Community Psychiatry* 38:662-665, 1987.

Bengelsdorf H and others: A crisis triage rating scale: brief dispositional assessment of patients at risk for hospitalization, *J Nerv Ment Dis* 172:424-430, 1984.

Bishop JB: The university counseling center: an agenda for the 1990s, *J Counsel Dev* 68:408-413, 1990.

Blazyk S, Canavan MM: Managing the discharge crisis following catastrophic illness or injury, *Soc Work Health Care* 11:19-32, 1986.

Blouin J and others: Effects of patient characteristics and therapeutic techniques on crisis intervention outcome, *Psychiatr J Univ Ott* 10:153-157, 1985.

Bonneson ME, Hartsough DM: Development of the Crisis Call Outcome Rating Scale, *J Consult Clin Psychol* 55:612-614, 1987.

Britton J: The crisis home program, *Minn Nurs Accent* 55:45, 1983.

Britton JG, and Mattson-Melcher DM: The crisis home: sheltering patients in emotional crisis, *J Psychosoc Nurs Ment Health Serv* 23:18-23, 1985.

Brownell MJ: The concept of crisis: its utility for nursing, *ANS* 6:10-21, 1984.

Bryce G, Baird D: Precipitating a crisis: family therapy and adolescent school refusers, *J Adolesc* 9:199-213, 1986.

Chansky ER: Reducing patients' anxieties: techniques for dealing with crises, *AORN J* 40:375-377, 1984.

Cheifetz DI, Salloway JC: Crisis intervention: interpretation and practice by HMOs, *Med Care* 23:89-93, 1985.

Christensen S, Harding M: Integrating theories of crisis intervention into hospice home care teaching, *Nurs Clin North Am* 20:449-455, 1985.

Comstock BS and others: Crisis treatment in a day hospital: impact on medical care-seeking, *Psychiatr Clin North Am* 8:483-500, 1985.

Davidhizar R: An experience in crisis intervention for nursing students, *Can J Psychiatr Nurs* 25:9-11, 1984.

Dougherty MB: Emergency room: fighting a state of crisis, *Nurs Manage* 15:11-13, 1984.

Dulcan MK: Brief psychotherapy with children and their families: the state of the art, *J Am Acad Child Adolesc Psychiatry* 23:544-551, 1984.

Eastman K, Coates D, Allodi F: The concepts of crisis: an expository review. *Can Psychiatr Assoc J* 15:463, 1970.

Ellison JM, Wharff EA: More than a gateway: the role of the emergency psychiatry service in the community mental health network, *Hosp Community Psychiatry* 36:180-185, 1985.

Fontes LA: Constructing crises and crisis intervention theory, *J Strat Syst Ther* 10:59-68, 1991.

Golan N: When is a client in crisis? *Soc Casework* 50:389, 1969.

Goldney RD: Survivor-victims and crisis care, *Crisis* 6:4-9, 1985.

Gordy HE: Crisis aspects of test taking: how the teacher can help, *Nurs Health Care* 5:100-105, 1984.

Gray-Price H, Szczesny S: Crisis intervention with families of cancer patients: a developmental approach, *Top Clin Nurs* 7:58-70, 1985.

Hansson L and others: The use of treatment contracts in short-term psychiatric care, *Acta Psychiatr Scand* 70:180-190, 1984.

Hart D: Helping the family of the potential organ donor: crisis intervention and decision making, *JEN* 12(4):210-212, 1986.

Hobbs M: Crisis intervention in theory and practice: a selective review, *Br J Med Psychol* 57:23-24, 1984.

Hollenkamp M, Attala J: Meeting health needs in a crisis shelter: a challenge to nurses in the community, *J Community Health Nurs* 3:201-209, 1986.

Janis L: *Psychological stress*, New York, 1958, John Wiley & Sons.

Jillings C: The concept of crisis and the care of the critically ill patient, *Crit Care Nurs* 5:8-10, 1985.

Johnson J: Psychiatric nursing in a crisis center: standards and practice, *Nurs Manage* 17:81-82, 1986.

Kalafat J: Training community psychologists for crisis intervention, *Am J Community Psychol* 12:241-251, 1984.

Keane SM: Challenge within the community: crisis intervention for society's unemployed, *Nurs Forum* 21:138-142, 1984.

Kennedy B: Gold award: stabilizing teens in crisis and fortifying their support network, *Hosp Community Psychiatry* 38:1211-1214, 1987.

Kostrzewa L: Nurturing parents in crisis, *Can Nurs* 81:20-22, 1985.

Kraiker F: Crisis as a corollary of cancer diagnosis, *Can Nurs* 79:37-39, 1983.

Kresky-Wolff M and others: Crossing Place: a residential model for crisis intervention, *Hosp Community Psychiatry* 35:72-74, 1984.

Kupchock S: The client, the situational crisis, the nurse, *J Ophthal Nurs Technol* 3:13-15, 1984.

Lampkin N and others: Crisis intervention: when the client is a nursing student, *J Nurs Educ* 24:148-150, 1985.

Lawler TG, Yount EH: Managing crises effectively: an intervention model, *J Nurs Adm* 17:39-43, 1987.

Leaman K: A hospital alternative for patients in crisis, *Hosp Community Psychiatry* 38:1221-1223, 1987.

Lipson JG: Crises intervention techniques for the ET nurse, *J Enterostomal Ther* 12:18-26, 1985.

Manglass L: Psychiatric interventions you can use in an emergency, *RN* 49:38-39, 1986.

Margetts D: Crisis intervention: the myth of expertise, part 1, *Aust Nurses J* 14:45-47, 1984.

Margetts D: Crisis intervention: the myth of expertise, part 2, *Aust Nurses J* 14:46-48, 1984.

Marvin JA: Crisis management for patients/families experiencing acute physiological crisis (burn/trauma), *Wash State J Nurs* 54:8-11, 1983.

Mayo DJ: Confidentiality in crisis counseling: a philosophical perspective, *Suicide Life Threat Behav* 14:96-112, 1984.

McCarthy PR, Knapp SL: Helping styles of crisis interveners, psychotherapists, and untrained individuals, *Am J Community Psychol* 12:623-627, 1984.

McGee RF: Hope: a factor influencing crisis resolution, *ANS* 6:34-44, 1984.

Merker MS: Psychiatric emergency evaluation, *Nurs Clin North Am* 21:387-396, 1986.

Miller WR and others: The helpful responses questionnaire: a procedure for measuring therapeutic empathy, *J Clin Psychol* 47:444-448, 1991.

Mitchell PH: Crisis management for families living with chronic illness, *Wash State J Nurs* 54:2-8, 1983.

Murdach AD: Decision making in psychiatric emergencies, *Health Soc Work* 12:267-274, 1987.

Paschal JH, Schwahn L: Intensive crisis counseling in Florida, *Child Today* 15:12-16, 1986.

Perlmutter RA, Jones JE: Assessment of families in psychiatric emergencies, *Am J Orthopsychiatry* 55:130-139, 1985.

Pruett HL, Brown VB: Present and future issues, *New Directions for Student Services* Spring, 75-81, 1990.

Rapoport L: The state of crisis: some theoretical considerations, *Soc Service Rev 36:211, 1962.*

Rice ME and others: Crisis prevention and intervention training for psychiatric hospital staff, Am J Community Psychol 13:289-304, 1985.

Rickel LM: Making mountains manageable: maximizing quality of life through crisis intervention, *Oncol Nurs Forum* 14:29-34, 1987.

Rivera A: Nursing intervention in a disaster, *Int Nurs Rev* 33:140-142, 1986.

Rix G: An admission of crisis, *Nurs Times* 81:28-29, 1985.

Rosenfeld MS: Crisis intervention: the nuclear task approach, *Am J Occup Ther* 38:382-385, 1984.

Ryan J: The neglected crisis, *Am J Nurs* 84:1257-1258, 1984.

Salome A: Crisis counseling, *Nurs J India* 75:106,-107, 1984.

Scherl EK, Schmetzer AD: CMHC emergency services in the 1980s: effects of funding changes, *Community Ment Health J* 25:267-275, 1989.

Schram PC, Burti L: Crisis intervention techniques designed to prevent hospitalization (clinical conference), *Bull Menninger Clin* 50:194-204, 1986.

Slaby AE: Crisis-oriented therapy, *New Dir Ment Health Serv* 12:21-34, 1985.

Stein DM, Lambert MJ: Telephone counseling and crisis intervention: a review, *Am J Community Psychol* 12:101-126, 1984.

Sullivan-Taylor L: Policemen and nursing students: crisis intervention team, *J Psychosoc Nurs Ment Health Serv* 23:26-30, 1985.

Szmukler GI: The place of crisis intervention in psychiatry, *Aust N Z J Psychiatry* 21:24-34, 1987.

Tavani-Petrone C: Psychiatric emergencies, *Prim Care* 13:157-167, 1986.

Viney LL and others: An evaluation of three crisis intervention programmes for general hospital patients, *Br J Med Psychol* 58:75-86, 1985.

Von Broembsen F: Separation crisis in a family with a borderline adolescent, *Am J Psychoanal* 46:62-75, 1986.

Waldron G: Crisis intervention: is it effective? *Br J Hosp Med* 31:283-287, 1984.

Weisman GK: Crisis-oriented residential treatment as an alternative to hospitalization, *Hosp Community Psychiatry* 36:1302-1305, 1985.

Winter DA and others: Explorations of a crisis intervention service, *Br J Psychiatry* 151:232-239, 1987.

Wolterman MC, Miller M: Caring for parents in crisis, *Nurs Forum* 22:34-37, 1985.

Wyka GT, Caraulia AP: Crisis intervention: stopping push before it comes to shove, *Nursing* 16:44-45, 1986.

Chapter 2

Differentiation Between Psychotherapeutic Techniques

Psychotherapy as a form of treatment has had many definitions, some conflicting and others concurring. Areas of divergence are generally those of methodology, therapeutic goals, length of therapy, and indications for treatment. There is general agreement, however, that psychotherapy is a set of procedures for changing behaviors based primarily on the establishment of a relationship between two (or more) people.

Psychoanalysis and Psychoanalytic Psychotherapy

The original theories of Sigmund Freud, the founder of psychoanalysis, passed through several phases as he subjected changing hypotheses to the tests of experience and observation, all directed toward the goal of making the unconscious available to the conscious.

In collaboration with Breuer, Freud first developed the psychotherapeutic technique of "cathartic hypnosis." Recognizing that ego control of the unconscious was released under the influence of hypnosis, Freud used hypnotism to induce the patient to answer direct questions in an effort to uncover the unconscious causes of the symptomatology and to allow free expression of pent-up feelings.

Freud observed, however, that to obtain therapeutic results, the procedure had to be repeated. He recognized that material brought to consciousness during hypnosis returned to the unconscious as the awakening patient regained control over his emotions. The therapeutic task of making the conscious patient recall and face repressed emotions in order to gain insight and increased ego strength was only transiently achieved by this technique.

Freud then experimented with what he referred to as "waking suggestion." Laying his hand on the patient's forehead, he would strongly suggest that the patient could recall the past if he tried. Freud soon learned that a person could not be forced to recall repressed, conflictual emotional events through this approach. He next devised an indirect method of freeing unconsciously repressed material for confrontation by the conscious. Using the process of "free association," the patient was expected to verbalize whatever thoughts came into his mind, freely associating events from his whole life span of experiences, feelings, fantasies, and dreams without concern for logic or continuity. Freud concentrated on gaining an intellectual understanding of the patient's psychogenic past. He insisted on the "basic rule" that the patient tell the therapist everything that came into his mind during each interview. Nothing, no matter how inconsequential the patient might think it was, could be withheld from the analyst. In this process of a search for repressed memories, Freud found that repressed emotions were gradually discharged as they emerged, although not as dramatically as in cathartic hypnosis.

One of the most important discoveries by Freud is considered to be "transference phenomena." He deemed transference to be a valuable therapeutic tool in overcoming the patient's defenses in resisting the release of unconscious, repressed emotional experiences. He thought of transference as an emotional reaction of the patient to the therapist in which the patient would relive his conflicts and emotions as they emerged from the past, from his unconscious. He would transfer to the therapist emotions he had felt toward authority figures in his childhood.

Freud referred to this reliving of the neurotic past in a present relationship with the therapist as *transference neurosis*. The principal factor in this process was that the patient expressed his aggressions against the therapist without any fears of the reprisal or censure that he may have been subjected to by the authority figure in his childhood. Through the therapist's nonjudgmental acceptance, the patient was encouraged to face new material released from his own unconscious with reduced fear and anxiety. As these new experiences were assimilated into the conscious ego, coping skills increased, which in turn facilitated further release of repressed material. Alexander (1956) refers to this process as a "corrective emotional experience."

Psychoanalysis is concerned with theory as well as techniques. Alexander and French (1946) also state that the traditional approach in psychoanalytic therapy has been nondirective. The therapist is a passive observer who follows the lead of the patient's verbal expressions as they unfold. Tarachow (1963) indicates that psychoanalytic therapy is for those whose personalities and ego strengths are relatively intact, despite neurotic symptoms or mild to moderately severe characterological disturbances due to unconscious conflicts.

Stone (1951) lists eight factors in the situation and technique of psychoanalysis from which technical variations have derived:

(1) Practically exclusive reliance during the hour of the patient's free associations for communications; (2) regularity of the time, frequency and duration of appointments and clearly defined financial agreement; (3) three to five appointments a week (originally six), with daily appointments the dominant tendency; (4) recumbent position, in most instances with some impediment against seeing the analyst directly; (5) confinement of the analyst's activity essentially to interpretation or other purely informative interventions such as reality testing, or an occasional question; (6) the analyst's emotional passivity and neutrality (benevolent objectivity), specifically abstention from gratifying the analysand's transference wishes; (7) abstention from advice or any other direct intervention or participation in the patient's daily life; (8) no immediate emphasis on curing symptoms, the procedure being guided largely by the patient's free associations from day to day. In a sense the analyst regards the whole scope of the patient's psychic life as his field of observation.

In psychoanalytic psychotherapy, the therapist is more active than in psycho-analysis. The therapist interacts more with the patient and does not interpret the transference attitudes as completely as in analysis. The most helpful attitude is one of calmness, continued interest, and sympathetic, understanding helpfulness. This differs from the neutral attitude of the analyst in psychoanalysis. The contention is that this calm, helpful, interested attitude of the therapist in psychotherapy provides support for the patient in dealing with tensions, sustains contact with reality, and provides gratifications and rewards in the therapeutic relationship, which provide incentives for the patient to continue to deal with emerging unconscious material.

Freud (1924) expressed the opinion that any digression from classical psycho-analysis that still recognizes the two basic facts of transference and resistance and takes them as the starting point of its work may call itself psychoanalysis, even though it arrives at results other than his own.

Alexander (1956) has noted that in procedures that deviate from the classical psychoanalysis of Freud, one or another of the basic phenomena is emphasized from the standpoint of therapeutic significance and is often being dealt with in isolation from others. For example, Rank centered on life situation, believing that insight into infantile history had no therapeutic significance. Feranczi placed emphasis on the emotional experience in transference (abreaction factor). Reich concentrated on the analysis of the resistances in order to allow, by their removal, the discharge of highly charged emotional experiences. He emphasized the importance of hidden forms of resistance and the understanding of the patient's behavior apart from his verbal communication. Psychoanalytic psychotherapy procedures have customarily been divided into two functional categories based on methodology; these are frequently referred to as *supportive* and *uncovering procedures.*

According to Alexander (1956), the aim of the uncovering procedure is to intensify the ego's ability to handle repressed emotional conflict situations that are unconscious. Through the use of transference, the patient relives his early interpersonal conflicts in relation to the therapist. Supportive and uncovering procedures overlap, but it is not difficult to differentiate between them. Primarily, supportive methods of treatment are indicated when functional impairment of the ego is temporary in nature and caused by acute emotional distress. Alexander designated therapeutic tasks in supportive methodology as follows: (1) gratifying dependency needs of the patient during stress situations, thereby reducing anxiety; (2) reducing stress by giving the patient an opportunity for abreaction; (3) giving intellectual guidance by objectively reviewing with the patient his acute stress situation and assisting the patient in making judgments, thereby enabling him to gain proper perspective of the total situation; (4) supporting the patient's neurotic defenses until the ego can handle the emotional discharges; and (5) actively participating in manipulation of the life situation when this might be the only hopeful approach in the given circumstances.

Psychoanalysis and psychoanalytic psychotherapy require many years of intensive training on the part of the therapist; this in itself has limited the number of therapists available. Both methods may require that the individual remain in therapy over an extended period of time, often for years. The obligation of time as well as expense for such extensive treatment also limits its availability for many.

Brief Psychotherapy

Brief psychotherapy as a treatment form developed as the result of the increased demand for mental health services and the lack of personnel trained to meet this demand. Initially, much of it was conducted by psychiatric residents as part of their training. Later, psychiatric social workers and psychologists became involved in this form of treatment.

Brief psychotherapy has its roots in psychoanalytic theory but differs from psychoanalysis in terms of goals and other factors. It is limited to removing or alleviating specific symptoms when possible. Intervention may lead to some reconstruction of personality, although it is not considered the primary goal. As in more traditional forms of psychotherapy, the therapy must be guided by an orderly series of concepts directed toward beneficial change in the patient. It is concerned with the degree of abatement of the symptoms presented and the return to or maintenance of the individual's ability to function adequately. To attain this goal, the individual may choose to get involved in a longer form of therapy. Another goal is assistance in preventing the development of deeper neurotic or psychotic symptoms after catastrophies or emergencies in life situations.

Free association, interpretation, and the analysis of transference are also used successfully in a modified manner. According to Bellak and Small (1965), free association is not a basic tool in short-term therapy. It may arise in response to a stimulus from the therapist. Interpretation is modified by the time limit and the immediacy of the problem. Although it may occur in brief psychotherapy, it is commonly used with medical or environmental types of intervention.

Bellak and Small also believe that positive transference should be encouraged. It is crucial in brief therapy that the patient sees the therapist as being likeable, reliable, and understanding. The patient *must* believe that the therapist will be able to help. This type of relationship is necessary if treatment goals are to be accomplished in a short period of time. This does not mean that negative transference feelings are to be ignored; it does mean that these feelings are not analyzed in terms of defenses.

The therapist assumes a more active role than in the traditional methods. Trends not directly related to the presenting problem are avoided. The positive is accentuated, and the therapist acts as an interested, helpful person. The difficulties faced by the patient are circumscribed. The environmental position in which the patient finds himself is used by the therapist to help the patient evaluate the reality of his situation in an attempt to modify and change it. Productive behavior is encouraged.

Diagnostic evaluation is extremely important in short-term therapy. Its aim is to understand the symptoms and the patient dynamically and to formulate hypotheses that can be validated by the historical data. The results of the diagnosis enable the therapist to decide which factors are most susceptible to change and to select the appropriate method of intervention. Part of the evaluation should be the degree of discrepancy or accord between the patient's fantasies and reality. The patient's probable ability to tolerate past and future frustrations should also be considered; the adequacy of his past and present relationships is also pertinent. The question "Why do you come now?" must be asked and means not only "What is it that is going on in your life that distresses you?" but "What is it that you expect in the way of help?" It is reasonable to assume that a request for help is motivated by emotional necessities, both external and internal, that are meaningful to the patient. Short-term goals can be beneficial for *all* patients.

After determining the causes of the symptoms, the therapist elects the appropriate intervention. Interpretation in order to achieve insight is used with care. Direct confrontation is used sparingly. An attempt is made to strengthen the ego by increasing the patient's self-esteem. One facet of this approach is to help the patient feel on a level with the therapist and no less worthwhile. Nor are his problems to be seen as being more unusual than those of others. This technique not only relieves the patient's anxiety but also facilitates communication between the patient and the therapist. Other basic procedures used include catharsis, drive repression and restraint, reality testing, intellectualization, reassurance and support, counseling and guidance to move the patient along a line of behavior, and conjoint counseling (Bellak and Small, 1965).

The ending of treatment is an important phase in brief therapy. The patient must be left with a positive transference and the feeling that he may return if the need arises. The learning that has taken place during therapy must be reinforced in order to encourage the patient to realize that he has begun to understand and solve his own problems. This has a preventive effect that helps the patient recognize possible future problems.

As an adjunct, drug therapy may be used in selected cases, in contrast to pure psychoanalysis, where drugs are seldom used. Environmental manipulation is considered when it is necessary to remove or modify an element causing disruption in the patient's life pattern. Included might be close scrutiny of family and friends, job and job training, education, and plans for travel (Bellak and Small, 1965).

Brief psychotherapy is indicated in cases of acutely disruptive emotional pain, in cases of severely destructive circumstances, and in situations endangering the life of the patient or others. Another indication involves the life circumstances of the individual. If the person cannot participate in the long-term therapeutic situation, which implies a stable residence, job, and so forth, brief therapy is advocated to alleviate disruptive symptoms.

It is imperative that the patient feel relief as rapidly as possible, even during the first therapeutic session. The span of treatment can be any reasonable, limited number of sessions but usually is more than six. Most clinics expect the number of visits to be under twenty. Treatment goals can be attained in this short time if the patient is seen quickly and intensively after requesting help. Circumstances associated with disrupted functioning are more easily accessible if they are recent. Only active conflicts are amenable to therapeutic intervention. Disequilibrated states are more easily resolved *before* they have crystallized, acquired secondary gain features, or developed into highly maladaptive behavior patterns.

Crisis Intervention

Crisis intervention extends logically from brief psychotherapy. The minimum therapeutic goal of crisis intervention is psychological resolution of the individual's immediate crisis and restoration to at least the level of functioning that existed before the crisis period. A maximum goal is improvement in functioning above the precrisis level.

Caplan (1964) emphasizes that crisis is characteristically self-limiting and lasts from 4 to 6 weeks. This time constitutes a transitional period, representing both the danger of increased psychological vulnerability and an opportunity for personality growth. In any particular situation, the outcome may depend to a significant degree on the ready availability of appropriate help. On this basis, the length of time for intervention is from 4 to 6 weeks, with the median being 4 weeks (Jacobson, 1965). Because time is at a premium, a therapeutic climate is generated that commands the concentrated attention of both therapist and patient. A goal-oriented sense of commitment develops, in sharp contrast to the more modest pace of traditional treatment modes.

METHODOLOGY

Jacobson and associates (1968, 1980) state that crisis intervention may be divided into two major categories, which may be designated as generic and individual. These two approaches are complementary.

Generic approach. A leading proposition of the generic approach is that there are certain recognized patterns of behavior in most crises. Many studies have substantiated this thesis. For example, Lindemann's (1944) studies of bereavement found a well-defined process that a person goes through in adjusting to the death of a relative. He refers to these sequential phases as "grief work" and found that failure of a person to grieve appropriately or to complete the process of bereavement could potentially lead to future emotional illness.

Subsequent studies of generic patterns of response to stressful situations have been reported. Kaplan and Mason (1960)* and Caplan (1964)* studied the effect on the mother of the birth of a premature baby and identified four phases or tasks that she must work through to ensure healthy adaptation to the experience. Janis (1958) suggests several hypotheses concerning the psychological stress of impending surgery and the patterns of emotional response that follow a diagnosis of chronic illness. Rapoport (1963)* defines three subphases of marriage during which unusual stress could precipitate crises. These are only a few of the broad research studies done in this field.

The generic approach focuses on the characteristic course of the *particular kind of crisis* rather than on the psychodynamics of each individual in crisis. A treatment plan is directed toward an adaptive resolution of the crisis. Specific intervention measures are designed to be effective for all members of a given group rather than for the unique differences of one individual. Recognition of these behavioral patterns is an important aspect of preventive mental health.

Tyhurst (1957) has suggested that knowledge of patterned behaviors in transitional states occurring during intense or sudden change from one life situation to another might provide an empirical basis for the management of these states and the prevention of subsequent mental illness. He cites as examples the studies of

---

* These studies are also discussed in Chapters 6 and 7 of this text.

individual responses to community disaster, migration, and retirement of pensioners.

Jacobson and associates (1968) state that generic approaches to crisis intervention include

direct encouragement of adaptive behavior, general support, environmental manipulation and anticipatory guidance . . . . In brief, the generic approach emphasizes (1) specific situational and maturational events occurring to significant population groups, (2) intervention oriented to crisis related to these specific events, and (3) intervention carried out by non–mental health professionals.

This approach has been found to be a feasible mode of intervention that can be learned and implemented by nonpsychiatric physicians, nurses, social workers, and others. It does not require a mastery of knowledge of the intrapsychic and inter-personal processes of an individual in crisis.

Individual approach. The individual approach differs from the generic in its emphasis on assessment, by a professional, of the interpersonal and intrapsychic processes of the person in crisis. It is used in selected cases, usually those not responding to the generic approach. Intervention is planned to meet the unique needs of the individual in crisis and to reach a solution for the particular situation and circumstances that precipitated the crisis. It differs from the generic approach, which focuses on the characteristic course of a particular kind of crisis.

Unlike extended psychotherapy, the individual approach deals relatively little with the developmental past of the individual. Information from this source is seen as relevant only for the clues that may result in a better understanding of the present crisis situation. Emphasis is placed on the immediate causes for disturbed equilib-rium and on the processes necessary for regaining a precrisis or higher level of functioning.

Jacobson (1968, 1970) cites the inclusion of family members or other important persons in the process of the individual's crisis resolution as another area of dif-ferentiation from most individual psychotherapy. In comparison with the generic approach, the individual approach is viewed by Jacobson as emphasizing the need for greater depth of understanding of the biopsychosocial process, intervention oriented to the individual's unique situation, and intervention carried out only by mental health professionals.

Morley and associates (1967) recommend several attitudes that are important adjuncts to the specific techniques. In essence, these attitudes comprise the general philosophical orientation necessary for the full effectiveness of the therapist.

1. It is essential that the therapist view the work being done not as a "second-best" approach but as the treatment of choice with persons in crisis.
2. Accurate assessment of the presenting problem, *not* a thorough diagnostic evaluation, is essential to an effective intervention.
3. Both the therapist and the individual should keep in mind throughout the contacts that the treatment is sharply time-limited and should persistently direct their energies toward resolution of the presenting problem.
4. Dealing with material not directly related to the crisis has no place as an intervention of this kind.
5. The therapist must be willing to take an active and sometimes directive role

in the intervention. The relatively slow-paced approach of more traditional treatment is inappropriate in this type of therapy.
6. Maximum flexibility of approach is encouraged. Such diverse techniques as serving as a resource person or information giver and taking an active role in established liaison with other helping resources are often appropriate in particular situations.
7. The goal toward which the therapist is striving is explicit. Energy is directed entirely toward returning the individual to at least his precrisis level of functioning.

STEPS IN CRISIS INTERVENTION

There are certain specific steps involved in the technique of crisis intervention (Morley and associates, 1967). Although each cannot be placed in a clearly defined category, typical intervention would pass through the following sequence of phases:
1. Assessment: Assessment of the individual and his problem is the first phase. It requires the therapist to use active focusing techniques to obtain an accurate assessment of the precipitating event and the resulting crisis that brought the individual to seek professional help. The therapist may have to judge whether the help-seeking person presents a high suicidal or homicidal lethality. If the patient is thought to show a high level of danger to himself or others, referral is made to a psychiatrist for consideration of hospitalization. If hospitalization is not deemed necessary, the intervention proceeds.

    The initial hour may be spent entirely on assessing the circumstances directly relating to the immediate crisis situation.
2. Planning therapeutic intervention: After accurate assessment is made of the precipitating event(s) and the crisis, intervention is planned. It is not designed to bring about major changes in the personality structure but to restore the person to at least the precrisis level of equilibrium. In this phase, determination is made of the length of time since onset of the crisis. The precipitating event usually occurs from 1 to 2 weeks before the individual seeks help. Frequently, it may have occurred within the past 24 hours. It is important to know how much the crisis has disrupted the person's life and the effects of this disruption on others in his environment. Information is also sought to determine what strengths he has, what coping skills he may have used successfully in the past and is not using presently, and what other people in his life might be used as supports. Search is made for alternative methods of coping that for some reason are not presently being used.
3. Intervention: The nature of intervention techniques is highly dependent on the preexisting skills, creativity, and flexibility of the therapist. Morley suggests some of the following, which have been found useful:
    a. *Helping the individual to gain an intellectual understanding of his crisis.* Often the individual sees no relationship between a hazardous situation occurring in life and the extreme discomfort of disequilibrium that he is experiencing. The therapist could use a direct approach, describing to the patient the relationship between crisis and the event in his life.
    b. *Helping the individual bring into the open his present feelings to which he may not have access.* Frequently the person may have suppressed some very

real feelings, such as anger or other inadmissible emotions toward someone he "should love or honor." It may also be denial of grief, feelings of guilt, or failure to complete the mourning process following bereavement. An immediate goal of intervention is the reduction of tension by providing means for the individual to recognize these feelings and bring them into the open. It is sometimes necessary to produce emotional catharsis and reduce immobilizing tension.

   c. *Exploration of coping mechanisms.* This approach requires assisting the person to examine alternate ways of coping. If for some reason the behaviors used in the past for successfully reducing anxiety have not been tried, the possibility of their use in the present situation is explored. New coping methods are sought, and frequently the person devises some highly original methods that he has never tried before.

   d. *Reopening the social world.* If the crisis has been precipitated by loss of someone significant to the person's life, the possibility of introducing new people to fill the void can be highly effective. It is particularly effective if supports and gratifications provided by the "lost" person in the past can be achieved to a similar degree from new relationships.

4. *Resolution of the crisis and anticipatory planning* are the last phase. The therapist reinforces those adaptive coping mechanisms that the individual has used successfully to reduce tension and anxiety. As coping abilities increase and positive changes occur, they may be summarized to allow the person to reexperience and reconfirm the progress made. Assistance is given as needed in making realistic plans for the future, and there is discussion of ways in which the present experience may help in coping with future crises.

Summary

A differentiation between psychoanalysis, brief psychotherapy, and crisis intervention methodology has been explored. No attempt has been made to state that one type of therapy is superior to another. Table 2-1 provides the reader with a succinct profile of some of their major differences.

In psychoanalysis, the goal of therapy is restructuring the personality, and the focus of treatment is the genetic past and the freeing of the unconscious. Psychoanalytic psychotherapeutic procedures are usually divided into two functional categories: supportive and uncovering procedures. The therapist's role is nondirective, exploratory, and that of a passive observer. This type of therapy is indicated for those individuals with neurotic personality patterns. Length of the therapy is indefinite and depends on the individual and the therapist.

Brief psychotherapy has as its goal removing specific symptoms and aiding in the prevention of deeper neurotic or psychotic symptoms. Its focus is on the genetic past as it relates to the present situation, repression of the unconscious, and restraining of drives. The role of the therapist is indirect, suppressive, and that of a participant observer. Basic tools used are psychodynamic intervention coupled with medical or environmental types of intervention. Indications for brief psychotherapy are acutely disruptive emotional pain, severely disruptive circumstances, and situations endangering the life of the individual or others. It is also indicated for those

Table 2-1   Major Differences Between Psychoanalysis, Brief Psychotherapy, and Crisis Intervention Methodology

	Psychoanalysis	Brief psychotherapy	Crisis intervention
Goals of therapy	Restructuring the personality	Removal of specific symptoms	Resolution of immediate crisis
Focus of treatment	1. Genetic past 2. Freeing the unconscious	1. Genetic past as it relates to present situation 2. Repression of unconscious and restraining of drives	1. Genetic present 2. Restoration to level of functioning prior to crisis
Usual activity of therapist	1. Exploratory 2. Passive observer 3. Nondirective	1. Suppressive 2. Participant observer 3. Indirect	1. Suppressive 2. Active participant 3. Direct
Indications	Neurotic personality patterns	Acutely disruptive emotional pain and severely disruptive circumstances	Sudden loss of ability to cope with a life situation
Average length of treatment	Indefinite	1-20 sessions	1-6 sessions
Cost of treatment	$100-200	$75-100	$0-75

who have problems that do not require psychoanalytic intervention. The average length of treatment is from one to twenty sessions.

The goal of crisis intervention is the resolution of an immediate crisis. Its focus is on the genetic present, with the restoration of the individual to his precrisis level of functioning or possibly to a higher level of functioning. The therapist's role is direct, suppressive, and that of an active participant. Techniques are varied and limited only by the flexibility and creativity of the therapist. Some of these techniques include helping the individual gain an intellectual understanding of the crisis, assisting the individual in bringing his feelings into the open, exploring past and present coping mechanisms, finding and using situational supports, and anticipatory planning with the individual to reduce the possibility of future crises. This type of therapy is indicated when a person (or family) suddenly loses the ability to cope with a life situation. The average length of treatment is from one to six sessions. The cost of each therapy is dependent on the geographic region.

REFERENCES

Alexander F: *Psychoanalysis and psychotherapy,* New York, 1956, WW Norton & Co.

Alexander F, French TM: *Psychoanalytic therapy,* New York, 1946, Ronald Press.

Bellak L, Small L: *Emergency psychotherapy and brief psychotherapy,* New York, 1965, Grune & Stratton.

Caplan G: *Principles of preventive psychiatry,* New York, 1964, Basic Books.

Freud S: *Collected papers,* vol 1, London, 1924, Hogarth Press (translated by J Riviere, A Strachey, and J Strachey).

Jacobson G: Crisis theory and treatment strategy: some sociocultural and psychodynamic considerations, *J Nerv Ment Dis* 141:209, 1965.

Jacobson G: Crisis theory, *New Dir Ment Health Serv* 6:1, 1980.

Jacobson G, Strickler M, Morley WE: Generic and individual approaches to cirsis intervention, *Am J Public Health* 58:339, 1968.

Janis IL: *Psychological stress, psychoanalytical and behavioral studies of surgical patients,* New York, 1958, John Wiley & Sons.

Kaplan DM, Mason EA: Maternal reactions to premature birth viewed as an acute emotional disorder, *Am J Orthopsychiatry* 30:539, 1960.

Lindemann E: Symptomatology and management of acute grief, *Am J Psychiatry* 101:101, 1944.

Mason EA: Method of predicting crisis outcome for mothers of premature babies, *Public Health Rep* 78:1031, 1963.

Morley WE, Messick JM, Aguilera DC: Crisis: paradigms of intervention, *J Psychiatr Nurs* 5:537, 1967.

Rapoport R: Normal crises, family structure, and mental health, *Fam Process* 2:68, 1963.

Stone L: Psychoanalysis and brief psychotherapy, *Psychoanal Q* 20:217, 1951.

Tarachow S: *An introduction to psychotherapy,* New York, 1963, International Universities Press.

Tyhurst JA: *Role of transition states—including disasters—in mental illness.* Paper presented at Symposium on Preventive and Social Psychiatry, sponsored by Walter Reed Institute of Research, Walter Reed Medical Center, and National Research Council, Washington, DC, April 15-17, 1957, US Government Printing Office.

ADDITIONAL READINGS

Alleway L: Disasters: Hungerford's nightmare, *Nurs Times* 83:25-27, 1987.

Armstrong J: Meeting the mental health needs of victims of crime, *Can J Psychiatr Nurs* 28:4-5, 1987.

Arnstein RL: A student mental health service as a place to work: what is its role in the university, and how does that affect the therapeutic effort? *J College Student Psychotherapy* 5:19-33, 1990.

Bachrach LL: Continuity of care, *New Dir Ment Health Serv* 28:63-73, 1987.

Ballweg JA, Bray RM: Smoking and tobacco use by US military personnel, *Milit Med* 154:165-168, 1989.

Barker GA, Hillard JR: The patient on the ledge: evaluation and intervention, *Hosp Community Psychiatry* 38:992-994, 1987.

Bartone PT, and others: The impact of a military air disaster on the health of assistance workers, *J Nerv Ment Dis* 177:317-328, 1989.

Bergman AS and others: Clinical social work in a medical setting, *Soc Work Health Care* 9:1-12, 1984.

Bosse LA: A disaster with few survivors, *Am J Nurs* 87:918-919, 1987.

Bray RM and others: Prevalence, trends, and correlates of alcohol use, nonmedical drug use, and tobacco use among US military personnel, *Milit Med* 154:1-11, 1989.

Brodsky L, Pieczynski B: The use of antidepressants in a psychiatric emergency department, *J Clin Psychopharmacol* 5:35-38, 1985.

Clarkin JF, Frances A: Selection criteria for the brief psychotherapies, *Am J Psychother* 36:166-180, 1982.

Cowen EL: Person-centered approaches to primary prevention in mental health: situation-focused and competence-enhancement, *Am J Community Psychol* 13:31-48, 1985.

Cozza KL, Hales RE: Psychiatry in the Army: A brief historical perspective and current developments, *Hosp Community Psychiatry* 42:413-418, 1991.

Cutler DL: Community residential options for the chronically mentally ill, *Community Ment Health J* 22:61-73, 1986.

Donovan CM: Problems of psychiatric practice in community mental health centers, *Am J Psychiatry* 139:456-460, 1982.

Dudley HA: The case for acute intervention, *Med J Aust* 141:662-663, 1984.

Ellis A: Using rational emotive therapy (RET) as crisis intervention: a single session with a suicidal client, *J Adlerian Theory Res Pract* 45:75-81, 1989.

Erickson GD: A framework and themes for social network intervention, *Fam Process* 23:187-204, 1984.

George J, George A: Help in the home, *Nurs Times* 83:37-38, 1987.

Goldberg RL, Green S: Medical psychotherapy, *Am Fam Physician* 31:173-178, 1985.

Gordon JS: Alternative mental health services and psychiatry, *Am J Psychiatry* 139:653-656, 1982.

Hersch JB and Lathan C: The Mental Health Walk-In Clinic: the University of Massachusetts experience, *J Am Coll Health* 34:15-17, 1985.

Hoffman JA, Forssmann-Falck R: Emergency psychiatry training: the new old problem, *Gen Hosp Psychiatry* 6:143-146, 1984.

Hose MA, Hirschman R: Psychological training of emergency medical technicians: an evaluation, *Am J Community Psychol* 12:127-131, 1984.

Hugill S and others: Prevention is better than referral, *J Support Learning* 2:27-35, 1987.

Iveson-Iveson J: The disasters copers, *Nurs Mirror* 157:18, 1983.

Jensen PS and others: Father absence: effects on child and maternal psychopathy, *J Am Acad of Child and Adolesc Psychiatry* 28:171-175, 1989.

Kaforey EC: Crisis intervention and the new unemployed, *Occup Health Nurs* 32:154-157, 1984.

Kahn EM, White EM: Adapting milieu approaches to acute inpatient care for schizophrenic patients, *Hosp Community Psychiatry* 40:609-614, 1989.

Kaskey GB, Ianzito BM: Development of an emergency psychiatric treatment unit, *Hosp Community Psychiatry* 35:1220, 1984.

Lamb HR and others: Psychiatric needs in local jails: emergency issues, *Am J Psychiatry* 141:774-777, 1984.

Lukas L: Self help and crisis intervention, *Int Forum Logotherapy* 13:24-31, 1990.

Maloney JJ: Control theory psychology and crisis intervention counseling, *J Real Therapy* 9:50-52, 1990.

Meltzer ML: Community psychology as a model for the new private practice of psychology, *J Clin Psychol* 42:392-398, 1986.

Murphy SA: After Mount St. Helens: disaster stress research, *J Psychosoc Nurs Ment Health Serv* 22:8-11, 1984.

Nader K: Hungerford's aftermath, *Nurs Times* 83:20-21, 1987.

Olarte SW, Lenz R: Learning to do psychoanalytic therapy with inner city population, *J Am Acad Psychoanal* 21:89-99, 1984.

Pang J Jr: Partial hospitalization: an alternative to inpatient care, *Psychiatr Clin North Am* 8:587-595, 1985.

Petersen GA: Psychological effects of disasters and guidelines for their management, *Nurs RSA* 2:32-34, 1987.

Peterson LC: Attribution theory and its application in crisis intervention, *Perspect Psychiatr Care* 22:133, 1984.

Prerost FJ: Intervening during crisis of life transitions: promoting a sense of humor as a stress moderator, *Counsel Psychol Q* 2:475-480, 1983.

Raphael B, Middleton W: Mental health responses in a decade of disasters: Australia, 1974-1983, *Hosp Community Psychiatry* 38:1331-1337, 1987.

Saravay SM: Psychoanalytic concepts in the general hospital and the transference cure, *Int J Psychoanal Psychother* 10:549-566, 1984-85.

Stefansson CG, Cullberg J: Introducing community mental health services: the effects on a suburban patient population, *Acta Psychiatr Scand* 74:368-378, 1986.

Szmukler GI: The place of crisis intervention in psychiatry, *Aust N Z J Psychiatry* 21:24-34, 1987.

Takaviche-Grad O, Zavasnik A: Comparison between counselor's and caller's expectations and their realization on the telephone crisis line, *Crisis* 8:162-177, 1987.

Talley S, Chiverton P: The psychiatric clinical specialist's impact on psychiatric emergency services, *Gen Hosp Psychiatry* 5:241-245, 1983.

Terr LC: Treating psychic trauma in children: a preliminary discussion, *J Traum Stress* 2:3-20, 1989.

Ursano RJ and others: Psychiatric care in the military community: family and military stressors, *Hosp Community Psychiatry* 40:1284-1289, 1989.

VanRybroek GJ and others: Preventive aggression devices (PADS): ambulatory restraints as an alternative to seclusion, *J Clin Psychiatry* 48:401-405, 1987.

Weinberg RB: Consultation and training with school-based crisis teams, *Prof Psychol Res Pract* 20:305-308, 1989.

Chapter 3

Problem-Solving Approach to Crisis Intervention

According to Caplan (1964), a person is constantly faced with a need to solve problems in order to maintain equilibrium. When he is confronted with an imbalance between the difficulty (as he perceives it) of a problem and his available repertoire of coping skills, a crisis may be precipitated. If alternatives cannot be found or if solving the problem requires unusual amounts of time and energy, disequilibrium occurs. Tension rises and discomfort is felt, with associated feelings of anxiety, fear, guilt, shame, and helplessness.

One purpose of the crisis approach is to provide the consultation services of a therapist skilled in problem-solving techniques. The therapist will not have an answer to every problem; however, he will be expected to have a ready and knowledgeable competency in problem solving, guiding and supporting his client toward crisis resolution. The therapeutic goal for the individual seeking help is the establishment of a level of emotional equilibrium equal to or better than the precrisis level.

Problem solving requires that a logical sequence of reasoning be applied to a situation in which an answer is required for a question and in which there is no immediate source of reliable information (Black, 1946). This process may take place either consciously or unconsciously. Usually the need to find an answer or solution is felt more strongly where such a resolution is most difficult.

The problem-solving process follows a structured, logical order of steps, each depending on the one preceding. In the routine decision making required in daily living, this process is rarely necessary. Most people are unaware that they may follow a defined, logical sequence of reasoning in making decisions; often they only remark that some solutions seem to have been reached more easily than others. Finding out the time or deciding which shoe to put on first rarely calls for long, involved reasoning, and more often than not the question arises and the answer is found without any conscious effort.

Factors Affecting the Problem-Solving Process

Depending on past experience related to the immediate problem, some people are more adept at finding solutions than others. Both internal and external factors affect the process at any given time, although initially there may be a temporary lack of concrete information. For example, when a driver finds himself lost because of a missing road sign, how much finding the right directions means to him in terms of his physical, psychological, and social well-being could affect the ease with which he finds an answer to the problem. Anxiety will increase in proportion to the value he places on finding a solution. If he is out driving for pleasure, for example, he may feel casually concerned, but if he is under stress to be somewhere on time, his anxiety may increase according to the importance of his arrival at his immediate goals.

When anxiety is kept within tolerable limits, it can be an effective stimulant to action. It is a normal response to an unknown danger, experienced as discomfort, and helps the individual mobilize his resources in meeting the problem. As anxiety increases, however, perceptual awareness narrows and all perceptions are focused on the difficulty. When problem-solving skills are available, the individual is able to use this narrowing of perceptions to concentrate on the problem at hand.

If a solution is not found, anxiety may become more severe. Feelings of discomfort intensify, and perceptions are narrowed to a crippling degree. The ability to understand what is happening and to make use of past experiences gives way to concentration on the discomfort itself. The individual becomes unable to recognize his own feelings, the problem, the facts, the evidence, and the situation in which he finds himself (Peplau, 1952).

Although problem solving involves a logical sequence of reasoning, it is not *always* a series of well-defined steps. According to Myer and Heidgerken (1962), it usually begins with a feeling that something has to be done. The problem area is generalized rather than specific and well defined. Next, the memory is searched in an attempt to come up with ideas or solutions from similar problems in the past. March and Simon (1963) refer to this as "reproductive problem solving," and its value greatly depends on past successes in finding solutions.

When no similar past experiences are available, the individual may next turn to "productive problem solving." Here he is faced with the need to construct new ideas from more or less raw data. He will have to go to sources other than himself to get his facts. For example, the driver looking for the road sign may find someone nearby who can give him the needed new data—directions to the right road. If no one is nearby, he will have to find some other source of information. He may resort to trial and error and with luck and patience find the way himself. Finding a solution in this way may meet a present need, but the information gained may not always be applicable to solving a similar problem in the future.

Problem Solving in Crisis Intervention

John Dewey (1910) proposed the classical steps or stages represented in different episodes of problem solving: (1) a difficulty is felt; (2) the difficulty is located and defined; (3) possible solutions are suggested; (4) consequences are considered; and (5) a solution is accepted. With minor modifications, this approach to the steps in problem solving has persisted over the years. Johnson (1955) simplified problem solving by reducing the number of steps to three: preparation, production, and judgment.

In 1962, Merrifield and associates conducted extensive research on the role of intellectual factors in problem solving. They advocated return to a five-stage model: preparation, analysis, production, verification, and reapplication. The fifth term was included in recognition of the fact that the problem solver often returns to earlier stages in a kind of revolving fashion.

According to Guilford (1967), the general problem-solving model involves the following processes: (1) *input* (from environment and soma), (2) *filtering* (attention aroused and directed), (3) *cognition* (problem sensed and structured), (4) *production* (answers generated), (5) *cognition* (new information obtained), (6) *production* (new answers generated), and (7) *evaluation* (input and cognition tested, answers tested; new tests of problem structure, new answers tested).

ASSESSMENT OF THE INDIVIDUAL AND THE PROBLEM

When professional help is sought because a person is in crisis, the therapist must use logic and background knowledge to define the problem and plan intervention. The model for problem solving in the crisis approach will be readily familiar to mental health professionals.

The crisis approach to problem solving involves an assessment of the individual and the problem, planning of therapeutic intervention, intervention, and resolution of the crisis and anticipatory planning (Morley, Messick, and Aguilera, 1967).

The first therapy session is directed toward finding out what the crisis-precipitating event was and what factors are affecting the individual's ability to solve problems.

It is important that both therapist and client be able to define a situation clearly before taking any action to change it. Questions such as "What do I need to know?" and "What must be done?" are asked. The more specifically the problem can be defined, the more likely it is that the "correct" answer will be sought.

Clues are investigated to point out and explore the problem or what is happening. The therapist asks questions and uses observational skills to obtain factual knowledge about the problem area. It is important to know what has happened within the immediate situation. How the individual has coped in past situations may affect his present behavior. Observations are made to determine his level of anxiety, expressive movements, emotional tone, verbal responses, and attitudinal changes.

It is important to remember that the therapist's task is to focus on the immediate problem. There is not enough time and *no need* to go into the patient's past history in depth.

One of the therapist's first questions usually is "Why did you come for help today?" The word *today* should be emphasized. Sometimes the individual will try to avoid stating why he came by saying, "I've been planning to come for some time." The usual reply is "Yes, but what happened that made you come in *today?*" Other questions to ask are "What happened in your life that is *different? When* did it happen?"

In crisis, the precipitating event usually occurs 10 to 14 days before the individual seeks help. Frequently, it is something that happened the day before or the night before. It could be almost anything: threat of divorce, discovery of extramarital relations, finding out that a son or daughter is taking drugs, loss of boyfriend or girlfriend, loss of job or status, an unwanted pregnancy, and so forth.

The next area on which to focus is the individual's perception of the event: What does it mean to him? How does he see its effect on his future? Does he see the event realistically, or does he distort its meaning?

The patient is then questioned about available situational supports: Who in the environment can the therapist find to support the person? With whom does he live? Who is his best friend? Whom does he trust? Is there a member of the family to whom he feels particularly close? Crisis intervention is sharply time-limited, and the more people involved in helping the person, the better. Also, if others are involved and familiar with the problem, they can continue to give support when therapy is terminated.

The next area of focus is ascertaining what the person usually does when he has a problem he cannot solve: What are his coping skills? Has anything like this ever happened to him before? How does he usually abate tension, anxiety, or depression? Has he tried the same method this time? If not, why not, if it usually works for him? If his usual method was tried and it did not work, why did it not work? What does he feel would reduce his symptoms of stress? The patient usually thinks of something; coping skills are so very individual. Methods of coping with anxiety that have not been used in years may be remembered. One man recalled that he used to "work off tensions" by playing the piano for a few hours, and it was suggested that he try this method again. Because he did not have a piano, he rented one; by the next session his anxiety had reduced enough to enable him to begin problem solving.

One of the most important parts of the assessment is to find out whether the person is suicidal or homicidal. The questions must be very *direct* and *specific:* Is he planning to kill himself or someone else? How? When? The therapist must find out and assess the lethality of the threat. Is the person merely thinking about it or does he have a method selected? Is it a lethal method—a loaded gun? Has he picked out a tall building or bridge? Can he tell you when he plans to do it, for example, after the children are asleep?

If the threat does not seem too imminent, the person is accepted for crisis therapy. If the intent is carefully planned and details are specific, hospitalization and psychiatric evaluation are arranged in order to protect the person or others in the community.

PLANNING THERAPEUTIC INTERVENTION

After identifying the precipitating event and the factors that are influencing the individual's state of disequilibrium, the therapist plans the method of intervention. Determination must be made as to how much the crisis has disrupted the individual's life. Is he able to work? Go to school? Keep house? Care for his family? Are these activities being affected? This is the first area to examine for the degree of disruption. How is his state of disequilibrium affecting others in his life? How does his wife (or husband, boyfriend, girlfriend, roommate, or family) feel about this problem? What do they think he should do? Are they upset?

This is basically a search process in which data are collected. It requires the use of cognitive abilities and recollection of past events for information relative to the present situation. The last phase of this step is essentially a thinking process in which alternatives are considered and evaluated against past experience and knowledge as well as in the context of the present situation.

Tentative solutions are advanced about *why* the problem exists. This step requires familiarity with theoretical knowledge and anticipation of more than one answer. In the study of behavior, it is important to seek causal relationships. Clues observed in the environmental conditions are examined and related to theories of psychosocial behavior to suggest reasons for the individual's disturbed equilibrium.

INTERVENTION

In the third step, intervention is initiated. Action is taken with the expectation that if the *planned action* is taken, the *expected result* will occur.

After the necessary information is collected, the problem-solving process is continued to initiate intervention. The therapist defines the problem from the information that has been given and reflects it back to the individual. This process clarifies the problem and encourages focusing on the immediate situation. The therapist then explores possible alternative solutions to the problem to reduce the symptoms produced by the crisis. At this time, specific directions may be given as to what should be tried as tentative solutions. Then the individual can leave the first session with some positive guidelines for going out and testing alternative solutions. At the next session, the individual and therapist evaluate the results. If none of these solutions has been effective, they work toward finding others.

The therapist may validate observations and tentative conclusions by reviewing the case with another therapist when he thinks it may be helpful or necessary. Briefly, the therapist identifies the crisis-precipitating event, symptoms that the crisis has produced in the individual, degree of disruption evident in the individual's life, and plan for intervention. Planned intervention may include one technique or a combination of several techniques. It may be helping the individual to gain an intellectual understanding of the crisis or helping him to explore and ventilate his feelings. Other techniques may be helping the individual to find new and more effective coping mechanisms or utilizing other people as situational supports. Finally, a plan is presented for helping the person establish realistic goals for the future.

ANTICIPATORY PLANNING

An evaluation determines whether the planned action has produced the expected results. Appraisal must be objective and impartial to be valid. Has the individual returned to his usual level or a higher level of equilibrium in his functioning? The problem-solving process is continued as the therapist and the individual work toward resolution of the crisis.

Paradigm of Intervention

According to Caplan (1964), a crisis has four developmental phases:
1. There is an initial rise in tension as the stimulus continues and more discomfort is felt.

2. There is a lack of success in coping as the stimulus continues and more discomfort is felt.
3. A further increase in tension acts as a powerful internal stimulus that mobilizes internal and external resources. In this stage, emergency problem-solving mechanisms are tried. The problem may be redefined, or there may be resignation and the giving up of certain aspects of the goal as unattainable.
4. If the problem continues and can be neither solved nor avoided, tension increases and a major disorganization occurs.

Whenever a stressful event occurs, certain recognized balancing factors can effect a return to equilibrium; these factors are perception of the event, available situational supports, and coping mechanisms, as shown in Figure 3-1. The upper portion of the paradigm illustrates the "normal" initial reaction of an individual to a stressful event.

A stressful event is seldom so clearly defined that its source can be determined immediately. Internalized changes occur at the same time as the externally provoked stress; as a result, some events may cause a strong emotional response in one person, yet leave another apparently unaffected. Much is determined by the presence or absence of factors that can effect a return to equilibrium.

In column *A* of Figure 3-1, the balancing factors are operating and crisis is avoided. However, in column *B* the absence of one or more of these balancing factors may block resolution of the problem and thus increase disequilibrium and precipitate crisis.

Figure 3-2 demonstrates the use of the paradigm for presentation of subsequent case studies. Its purpose is to serve as a guideline to help the reader focus on the problem areas. An example of its applicability is presented in the cases of two people affected by the same stressful event. One resolved the problem and avoided crisis; the other did not.

Balancing Factors Affecting Equilibrium

Between the perceived effects of a stressful situation and the resolution of the problem are three recognized balancing factors that may determine the state of equilibrium. Strengths or weaknesses in any one of the factors can be directly related to the onset of crisis or to its resolution. These factors are perception of the event, available situational supports, and coping mechanisms.

Why do some people go into crisis when others do not? This is illustrated in Figure 3-2 by the case of two men, Mr. A and Mr. B. Both men have possible symptoms of cancer and are told of the need for diagnostic tests. Mr. A is upset but does not go into crisis, whereas Mr. B *does* go into crisis. Why does Mr. A react one way and Mr. B another? What "things" in their lives make the difference?

PERCEPTION OF THE EVENT

Cognition, or the subjective meaning, of a stressful event plays a major role in determining both the nature and degree of coping behaviors. Differences in cognition, in terms of the event's threat to an important life goal or value, account for large differences in coping behaviors. The concept of *cognitive style* (Cropley and

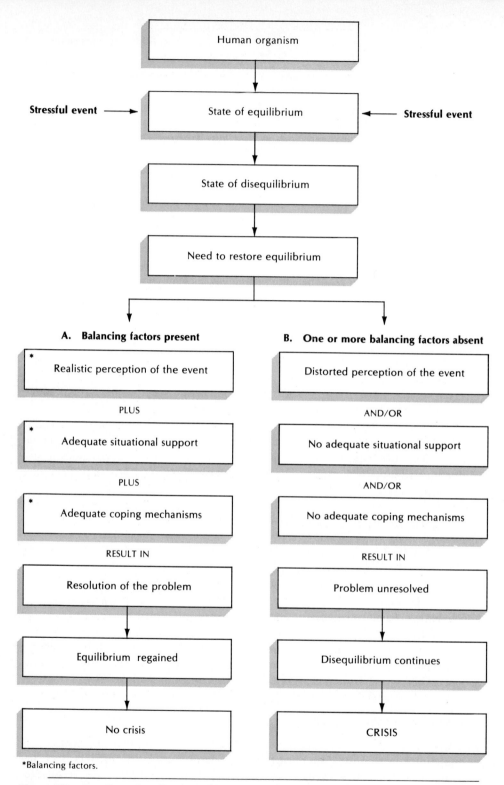

*Balancing factors.

Figure 3-1   Paradigm: the effect of balancing factors in a stressful event.

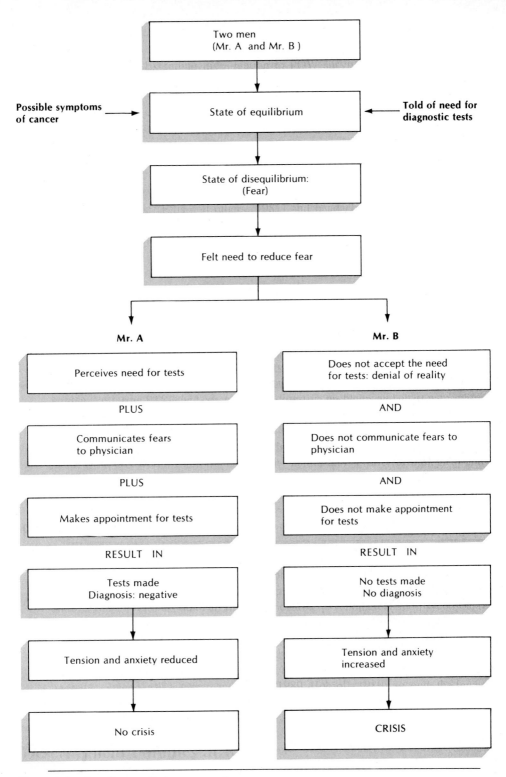

Figure 3-2   Paradigm applied to case study.

Field, 1969) suggests uniqueness in the way people take in, process, and use information from the environment.

Cognitive styles, or the characteristic modes for organizing perceptual and intellectual activities, play an important role in determining an individual's coping responses to daily life stresses. According to Inkeles (1966), cognitive style helps to set limits on information seeking in stress situations. It also strongly influences perceptions of others, interpersonal relationships, and responses to various types of psychiatric treatment.

For example, in stressful situations a person whose cognitive style is identified as "field-dependent" is very dependent on external objects in the environment for orientation to reality. This type of individual tends to use such coping mechanisms as repression and denial. In contrast, the "field-independent" person tends to prefer intellectualization as a defense mode.

If the event is perceived realistically, the relationship between the event and feelings of stress is recognized. Problem solving can be appropriately oriented toward reduction of tension, and successful solution of the stressful situation is more probable.

Lazarus (1966) and colleagues (1974) focused on the importance of the mediating cognitive process, *appraisal,* to determine the various coping methods used by individuals. This approach recognizes that coping behaviors always represent an interaction between the individual and the environment, and that environmental demands of each unique situation initiate, form, and limit coping activities that may be required in the interaction. As a result, people engage in widely diverse behavioral and intrapsychic activities to meet actual or anticipated threats.

Appraisal, in this context, is an ongoing perceptual process by which a potentially harmful event is distinguished from a potentially beneficial or irrelevant event in one's life.

When a threatening situation exists, first a *primary* appraisal is made to judge the perceived outcome of the event in relation to one's future goals and values. This is followed by a *secondary* appraisal whereby one perceives the range of coping alternatives available either to master the threat or to achieve a beneficial outcome. As coping activities are selected and initiated, feedback cues from changing internal and external environments lead to ongoing *reappraisals* or to changes in the original perception.

As a result of the appraisal process, coping behaviors are never static. They change constantly in both quality and degree as new information and cues are received during reappraisal activities. New coping responses may occur whenever new significance is attached to a situation.

If, in the appraisal process, the outcome is judged to be too overwhelming or too difficult to be dealt with by using available coping skills, an individual is more likely to resort to use of intrapsychic defensive mechanisms to repress or distort the reality of the situation. An appraisal of a potentially successful outcome, however, more likely leads to the use of direct action modes of coping such as attack, flight, or compromise.

If the perception of the event is distorted, a relationship between the event and feelings of stress may not be recognized. Thus, attempts to solve the problem are ineffective, and tension is not reduced.

In other words, what does the event mean to the individual? How is it going to affect his future? Can he look at it realistically or does he distort its meaning? In the example, Mr. A perceived the need for diagnostic tests; his perception of the event was realistic. Mr. B was unable to accept the need for tests to confirm or refute the possibility of having cancer; his perception was distorted, and he used denial.

SITUATIONAL SUPPORTS

By nature, human beings are social and dependent on others in their environment to supply them with reflected appraisals of their own intrinsic and extrinsic values. In establishing life patterns, certain appraisals are more significant to the individual than others because they tend to reinforce the perception the individual has of himself.

Dependency relationships may be more readily established with those whose appraisals tend to support the individual against feelings of insecurity and with those who reinforce feelings of ego integrity.

These meaningful relationships with others provide a person with nurturance and support, resources vital for coping with a wide variety of stressors. Social isolation, whatever the cause, denies a person availability of social interactions and opportunities to develop meaningful relationships. Sudden or unexpected social isolation results in the loss of usual resource supports. With these lacking, a person is much more vulnerable to daily living stressors.

Loss, threatened loss, or feelings of inadequacy in a supportive relationship may also leave a person in a vulnerable position. Confrontation with a stressful situation, combined with a lack of situational support, may lead to a state of disequilibrium and possible crisis.

Appraisal of self varies across ages, sexes, and roles. The belief system that forms the basis of the self-concept and self-esteem develops out of experiences with significant others in a person's life. Although self-esteem is fairly static within a certain range, it does fluctuate according to internal and external environmental variables that impinge on it at a specific time and in a specific situation. In order to achieve and maintain a sense of value and self-worth, a person must feel loved by others and capable of achieving an ideal self, one that is strong, capable, good, and loving of others.

When self-esteem is low or when a situation is perceived as particularly threatening, the person is strongly in need of and seeks out others from whom positive reflective appraisals of self-worth and ability to achieve can be obtained. The lower the self-esteem or the greater the threat, the greater the need to seek situational supports. Conversely, a person avoids or withdraws from contacts with those he perceives as threatening to his self-esteem, whether the threat is real or imagined. Any potentially stressful situation can set off questions of self-doubt about how one is perceived by others, the kind of impression being made, and the real or imagined inadequacies that might be disclosed (Mechanic, 1974).

Success or failure of a coping behavior is always strongly influenced by the social context in which it occurs. The environmental variable most centrally identified is the person's significant others. From them, a person learns to seek advice, support, and so forth in solving daily problems in living. Confidence in being liked and respected by these peers is based on past testing and reaffirmation of their expected supportive responses.

Any perceived failure to obtain adequate support to meet psychosocial needs may provoke, or compound, a stressful situation. The receipt of negative support could be equally detrimental to a person's self-esteem.

Situational supports are those persons who are available in the environment and who can be depended on to help solve the problem. In the example Mr. A talked to his physician and told him of his fear of having cancer. He asked about the tests that would be conducted and what would be done if the tests did reveal that he had cancer. He talked with his wife and children about the possibility of having cancer. He received reassurance from his family and his physician. In effect, he had strong support during this stressful event. Mr. B did not feel close enough to his physician to discuss his fears about the possibility of having cancer, and he did not talk to his family or friends about his symptoms. His denial made him isolate himself. He did not have anyone to turn to for help; therefore he felt overwhelmed and alone.

COPING MECHANISMS

Through the process of daily living, people learn to use many methods to cope with anxiety and reduce tension. Life-styles are developed around patterns of response, which in turn are established to cope with stressful situations. These life-styles are highly individual and quite necessary to protect and maintain equilibrium.

The early work of Cannon (1929, 1939) provided a basis for later systematic research on the effects of stress on the human organism. According to Cannon's "fight or flight" theory, reactions of acute anxiety, similar to those of fear, are vital to readying the individual physiologically to meet any real or imagined threat to self. From his studies of homeostasis, Cannon described the mechanisms whereby human and other animal life systems maintain steady life states, with the goal always to return to such states whenever conditions force a temporary departure.

Over the years, it has been unusual to find the term *coping* used interchangeably with such similar concepts as adaptation, defense, mastery, and adjustive reactions. Coping activities take a wide variety of forms, including all the diverse behaviors that people engage in to meet actual or anticipated challenges. In psychological stress theory, the term *coping* emphasizes various strategies used, consciously or unconsciously, to deal with stress and tensions arising from perceived threats to psychological integrity. It is not synonymous with mastery over problematical life situations; rather, it is the *process* of attempting to solve them (Lazarus, 1966).

Coleman (1950) defined *coping* as an adjustive reaction made in response to actual or imagined stress in order to maintain psychological integrity. Within this concept human beings are perceived as responding to stress by either attack, flight, or compromise reactions. These reactions become complicated by various ego-defense mechanisms whenever the stress becomes ego-involved.

Attack reactions usually attempt to remove or overcome the obstacles seen as causing stress in life situations. They may be primarily constructive or destructive in nature. Flight, withdrawal, or fear reactions may be as simple as physically removing the threat from the environment (such as putting out a fire) or removing oneself from the threatening situation (running away from the fire area). They might also involve much more complex psychological maneuvering, depending on the perceived extent of the threat and the possibilities for escape.

Compromise or substitution reactions occur when either attack or flight from the threatening situation is thought to be impossible. This method is most commonly used to deal with problem solving and includes accepting substitute goals or changing internalized values and standards.

Masserman (1946) demonstrated that, in situations of extended frustration, individuals find it increasingly possible to compromise for substitute goals. This often involves use of *rationalization,* a defense mechanism whereby "half a loaf" does indeed soon appear to be "better than none."

Tension-reducing mechanisms can be overt or covert and can be consciously or unconsciously activated. They have been generally classified into such behavioral responses as aggression, regression, withdrawal, and repression. The selection of a response is based on tension-reducing actions that successfully relieved anxiety and reduced tension in similar situations in the past. Through repetition, the response may pass from conscious awareness during its learning phase to a habitual level of reaction as a learned behavior. In many instances, the individual may not be aware of *how,* let alone *why,* he reacts to stress in given situations. Except for having vague feelings of discomfort, the individual may not notice the rise and consequent reduction in tension. When a novel stress-producing event arises and learned coping mechanisms are ineffectual, discomfort is felt on a conscious level. The need to "do something" becomes the focus of activity, narrowing perception of all other life activities.

Normally, defense mechanisms are used constructively in the process of coping. This is particularly evident whenever there is danger of becoming psychologically overwhelmed. Almost all defense mechanisms are seen as important for survival. None is equated with a pathological condition unless it interferes with the process of coping, such as being used to deny, to falsify, or to distort perceptions of reality.

According to Bandura and others (1977), the strength of the individual's conviction in his own effectiveness in overcoming or mastering a problematical situation determines whether coping behavior is even attempted in the first place. People fear and avoid stressful, threatening situations that they believe exceed their ability to cope. They behave with assurance in those situations where they judge themselves able to manage and they expect eventual success. It is the perceived ability to master that can influence the choice of coping behaviors as well as the persistence used once one is chosen.

Available coping mechanisms are what people *usually* do when they have a problem. They may sit down and try to think it out or talk it out with a friend. Some cry it out or try to get rid of their feelings of anger and hostility by swearing, kicking a chair, or slamming doors. Others may get into verbal battles with friends. Some may react by temporarily withdrawing from the situation in order to reassess the problem. These are just a few of the many coping methods people use to relieve their tension and anxiety when faced with a problem. Each has been used at some time in the developmental past of the individual, has been found effective in maintaining emotional stability, and has become part of his life-style in meeting and dealing with the stresses of daily living.

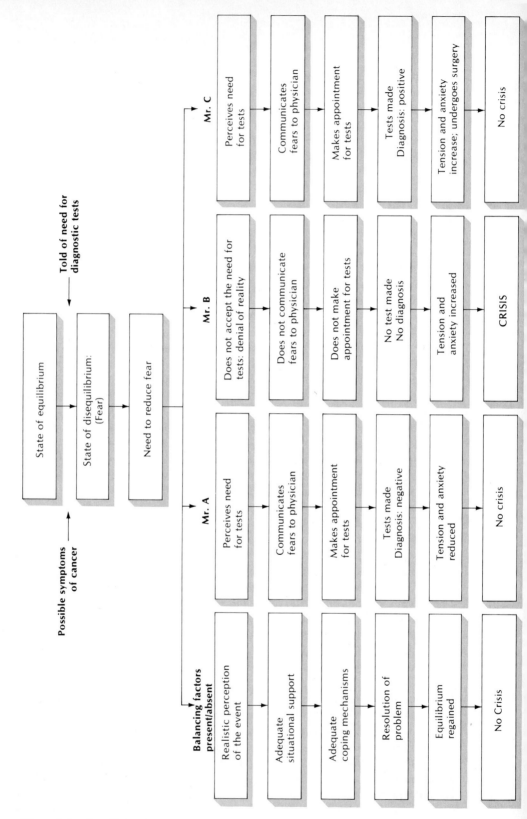

Figure 3-3 Paradigm of comparative cases.

Continuing with the example, Mr. A made an appointment for the tests recommended by his physician. The tests were conducted; the diagnosis was negative for cancer. His tension and anxiety were reduced, equilibrium was restored, and he did not have a crisis. Mr. B withdrew; he had no coping skills. He did not make an appointment for the needed tests, no tests were made, and, as a result, he had no definitive diagnosis, and his tension and anxiety increased. Unable to solve the problem and to function, Mr. B went into crisis.

The balancing factors that affect equilibrium were demonstrated in Figure 3-2. Mr. A had a *realistic* perception of the events and returned to his original state of equilibrium. He did not have a crisis. Mr. B had a *distorted* perception of the event, used denial, remained in a state of disequilibrium, and went into crisis.

What if Mr. A's tests had been *positive* instead of negative? Figure 3-3 presents a new paradigm of comparative cases and introduces Mr. C, whose balancing factors are identical to Mr. A's with one exception: Mr. C had the diagnostic tests for cancer and his results were *positive*. His tension and anxiety increased, and he had surgery that successfully removed the cancer. He did not have a crisis. The balancing factor that made the difference was his realistic perception of the event. The relationship between the event and his feelings of stress was recognized. His problem solving was appropriately oriented toward reduced tension, and his stressful situation was resolved successfully.

REFERENCES

Bandura A and others: Cognitive processes mediating behavioral change, *J Pers Soc Psychol* 35:125, 1977.

Black M: *Critical thinking: an introduction to logic and scientific method,* Englewood Cliffs, NJ, 1946, Prentice-Hall.

Cannon WB: *Bodily changes in pain, hunger, fear, and rage,* New York, 1929, D Appleton.

Cannon WB: *The wisdom of the body,* ed 2, New York, 1939, WW Norton.

Caplan G: *Principles of preventive psychiatry,* New York, 1964, Basic Books.

Coleman JC: *Abnormal psychology and modern life,* Chicago, 1950, Scott, Foresman.

Cropley A, Field T: Achievement in science and intellectual style, *J Appl Psychol* 53:132, 1969.

Dewey J: *How we think,* Boston, 1910, Heath.

Guilford JP: *The nature of human intelligence,* New York, 1967, McGraw-Hill.

Inkeles A: Social structure and the socialization of competence, *Harv Ed Rev* 36:265-283, 1966.

Johnson DM: *The psychology of thought and judgment,* New York, 1955, Harper & Row.

Lazarus RS: *Psychological stress and the coping process,* New York, 1966, McGraw-Hill.

Lazarus RS and others: *The psychology of coping: issues in research and assessment.* In Coehlo GV and others, editors: *Coping and adaptation,* New York, 1974, Basic Books.

March JG, Simon HA: *Organizations,* New York, 1963, John Wiley & Sons.

Masserman JH: *Principles of dynamic psychology,* Philadelphia, 1946, WB Saunders.

Mechanic D: *Social structure and personal adaptation: some neglected dimensions.* In Coehlo GV and others, editors: *Coping and adaptation,* New York, 1974, Basic Books.

Merrifield PR and others: The role of intellectual factors in problem-solving, *Psychol Monogr* 76:1-21, 1962.

Morley WE, Messick JM, Aguilera DC: Crisis: paradigms of intervention, *J Psychiatr Nurs* 5:538, 1967.

Myer B, Heidgerken LE: *Introduction to research in nursing,* Philadelphia, 1962, JB Lippincott.

Peplau HE: *Interpersonal relations in nursing,* New York, 1952, GP Putnam's Sons.

ADDITIONAL READINGS

Alexander J: Discussion of Gilbar's paper, *Clin Soc Work J* 19:305-307, 1991.

Arand JU, Harding CG: An investigation into problem solving in education: a problem-solving curricular framework, *J Allied Health* 16:7-17, 1987.

Battegay R, and others: Trends in group psychotherapy with borderline patients. Special section: group psychotherapy with borderline personalities, *Group Analysis* 25:61-73, 1992.

Beker J: Back to the future: effective residential group care and treatment for children and youth and the Fritz Redl legacy, *Residential Treatment for Children and Youth* 8:57-71, 1991.

Cella DF and others: Ego identity status, identification, and decision-making style in late adolescents, *Adolescence,* 22:849-861, 1987.

Clement CA, Palmagne RJ: Logical reasoning, world knowledge, and mental imagery: interconnections in cognitive processes, *Mem Cognit* 14:299-307, 1986.

Corcoran SA: Task complexity and nursing expertise as factors in decision making, *Nurs Res* 35:107-112, 1986.

Cozza KL, Hales RE: Psychiatry in the army: a brief historical perspective and current developments, *Hosp Community Psychiatry,* 42:413-418, 1991.

Dazord A and others: Pretreatment and process measures in crisis intervention as predictors of outcome, *Psychother Res* 1:135, 1991.

DeGroot HA: Scientific inquiry in nursing: a model for a new age, *ANS* 10:1-21, 1988.

Dubin SE and others: Three day crisis resolution unit, *Indian J Psychiatry* 32:30-34, 1990.

Duckworth DH: Information requirements for crisis intervention after disaster work. *Stress Med* 7:19-24, 1991.

Duffy M, Iscoe I: Crisis theory and management: the case of the older person, *J Ment Health Counsel* 12:303-313, 1990.

Emerson JD, Tritchler D: The three-decision problem in medical decision making, *Stat Med* 6:101-112, 1987.

Farrelly J, Joseph A: Expressive therapies in a crisis intervention service, *Arts Psychother* 18:131-137, 1991.

Field E: Neurolinguistic programming as an adjunct to other psychotherapeutic/hypnotherapeutic interventions, *Am J Clin Hypn* 32:174-182, 1990.

Fullerton AM: Adult age differences in solving series problems requiring integration of new and old information, *Int J Aging Hum Dev* 26:147-154, 1988.

Geller JL: Anyplace but the state hospital: examining assumptions about the benefits of admission diversion, *Hosp Community Psychiatry* 42:145-152, 1991.

Gilbar O: Model for crisis intervention through group therapy for women with breast cancer, *Clin Social Work J* 19:293-304, 1991.

Gustafson DH and others: Computer-based health promotion: combining technological advances with problem-solving techniques to effect successful health behavior changes, *Annu Rev Public Health* 8:387-415, 1987.

Haber LC: The effect of gender role preference on decision-making strategies of married couples, *Arch Psychiatr Nurs* 1:341-349, 1987.

Hains AA, Hains AH: The effects of a cognitive strategy intervention on the problem-solving abilities of delinquent youths, *J Adolesc* 10:399-413, 1987.

Harris CJ: A family crisis intervention model for the treatment of post-traumatic stress reaction, *J Trauma Stress* 4:195-207, 1991.

Haskett ME and others: Factors associated with successful entry into therapy in child sexual abuse cases, *Child Abuse Negl* 15: 467-475, 1991.

Headlee R, Kalogjera IJ: A critical analysis of the process of human choice, *Psychiatr J Univ Ott* 12:16-20, 1987.

Hershey JC, Baron J: Clinical reasoning and cognitive processes, *Med Decis Making* 7:203-211, 1987.

Holbert CM, Abraham C: Reflections on teaching generic thinking and problem solving, *Nurse Educ* 13:23-27, 1988.

Hoyt M, Austad CS: Psychotherapy in a staff model health maintenance organization: providing and assuring quality care in the future, *Psychotherapy* 29:119-129, 1992.

Hurn J and others: Treatment intervention in child abuse emergency shelters: the crucial needs, *Child and Youth Care Forum* 29:133-141, 1991.

Jones JA: Clinical reasoning in nursing, *J Adv Nurs* 13:185-192, 1988.

Juhasz AM, Sonnenshein-Schneider M: Adolescent sexuality: values, morality and decision making, *Adolescence* 22:579-590, 1987.

Keinan G: Decision making under stress: scanning of alternatives under controllable and uncontrollable threats, *J Pers Soc Psychol* 52:639-644, 1987.

Ketefian S: Education for ethical decision making, *NLN Publ* 15:135-146, 1986.

Klingman A: The effects of parent-implemented crisis intervention: a real-life emergency involving a child's refusal to use a gas mask, *J Clin Child Psychol* 21: 70-75, 1992.

Klinteberg BA and others: Cognitive sex differences: speed and problem-solving strategies on computerized neuropsychological tasks, *Percept Mot Skills* 65:683-697, 1987.

Lachnit H: Convergent validation of information processing constructs with Pavlovian methodology, *J Exp Psychol [Hum Percept]* 14:143-152, 1988.

Lewis JM: The changing face of adolescent inpatient psychiatric treatment, *Psychiatr Hosp* 22:165-173, 1991.

Long NJ: What Fritz Redl taught me about aggression: understanding the dynamics of aggression and counteraggression in students and staff, *Residential Treatment for Children and Youth* 8:43-55, 1991.

Lukas E: Self-help and crisis intervention, *Int Forum Logotherapy* 13:24-31, 1990.

MacCarthy B and others: Task motivation and problem appraisal in long-term psychiatric patients, *Psychol Med* 16:431-438, 1986.

Maier HW: What's old is new: Fritz Redl's teaching reaches into the present, *Residential Treatment for Children and Youth* 8:15-30, 1991.

Maloney JJ: Control therapy psychology and crisis intervention counseling, *J Ment Real Ther* 9:50-52, 1990.

Mancuso CA, Rose DN: A model for physicians' therapeutic decision making, *Arch Intern Med* 147:1281-1285, 1987.

Marson DC and others: Psychiatric decision making in the emergency room: a research overview, *Am J Psychiatry* 145:918-925, 1988.

Metcalfe J, Wiebe D: Intuition in insight and noninsight problem solving, *Mem Cognit* 15:238-246, 1987.

Morse WC: A brief orientation to Redl's writing, *Residential Treatment for Children and Youth* 8:101-103, 1991.

Newman RG: Consultation: Redl's influence: crisis intervention in residential treatment, *Residential Treatment for Children and Youth* 8:83-92, 1991.

Nezu AM: Cognitive appraisal of problem solving effectiveness: relation to depression and depressive symptoms, *J Clin Psychol* 42:42-48, 1986.

Nezu AM, Carnevale GJ: Interpersonal problem solving and coping reactions of Vietnam veterans with posttraumatic stress disorder, *J Abnorm Psychol* 96:155-157, 1987.

Pardue SF: Decision-making skills and critical thinking ability among associate degree, diploma, baccalaureate, and master's-prepared nurses, *J Nurs Educ* 26:354-361, 1987.

Perlmutter RA, Jones JE: Problem solving with families in psychiatric emergencies, *Psychiatr Q* 57:23-32, 1985.

Rabinovitch RD: Fritz Redl and residential treatment at Hawthorn Center, *Residential Treatment for Children and Youth* 8:73-92, 1991.

Radford MH and others: Psychiatric disturbance and decision-making, *Aust N Z J Psychiatry* 20:210-217, 1986.

Renna R: The use of control therapy and reality therapy with students who are "out of control", *J Real Therapy* 11:3-13, 1991.

Sautter FJ, Heaney C, O'Neill P: A problem-solving approach to group psychotherapy in the inpatient milieu, *Hosp Community Psychiatry* 42:814-817, 1991.

Strip C, Swassing R, Kidder R: Female adolescents: a first step in emotional crisis intervention, *Roeper Rev* 13:124-128, 1991.

Talbot A, Manton M, Dunn PJ: Debriefing the debriefers: an intervention strategy to assist psychologists after a crisis, *J Traum Stress* 5:45-62, 1992.

Tanner CA: Teaching clinical judgement, *Annu Rev Nurs Res* 5:153-173, 1987.

Terr LC: Mini-marathon groups: psychological "first aid" following disasters, *Bull Menninger Clin* 56:76-86, 1992.

Tiessen JB: Critical thinking and selected correlates among baccalaureate nursing students, *J Prof Nurs* 3:118-123, 1987.

Tsai LS: Overt vs covert problem solving, transfer effects, and programming sequence. I. Inverted triangles, *Percept Mot Skills* 65(1):313-314, 1987.

Turner J, Parsons DA: Verbal and nonverbal abstracting-problem-solving abilities and familial alcoholism in female alcoholics, *J Stud Alcohol* 49:281-287, 1988.

Watts FN and others: Associations between phenomenal and objective aspects of concentration problems in depressed patients (part 2), *Br J Psychol* 79:241-250, 1988.

Webley P: The relationship between physical and social reasoning in adolescents, *J Genet Psychol* 148:375-384, 1987.

Whitman N, Schwenk TL: Problem solving in medical education: can it be taught? *Curr Surg* 43:453-459, 1986.

Wineman D: Fritz Redl: matchmaker to child and environment: a retrospective, *Residential Treatment for Children and Youth* 8:31-42, 1991.

Wright G, Ayton P: Decision time, subjective probability, and task difficulty, *Mem Cognit* 16:176-185, 1988.

Chapter 4

Legal and Ethical Issues in Psychotherapy

Therapist-patient sexual involvement is increasingly being acknowledged as a problem for all mental health professions. It should be noted here that the term *psychotherapist* refers to *any* licensed therapist, including psychologists, psychiatrists, psychiatric social workers, psychiatric nurses, and marriage, family, and child (MFC) therapists. The harm that may occur for a patient has become a focus for clinical inquiry (Pope and Vetter, 1991).

Psychotherapists can obtain information relevant to ethical practice and standards from a large number of sources. These sources include the American Psychiatric Association, the American Psychological Association, the formal ethics committees of all major health disciplines, and published research, clinical, and theoretical works (Conte and others, 1989).

The Legal Aspects of Malpractice

Case law (*Roy v Hartogs*, 1976; Kardener and others, 1976) has reflected agreement with the ethical codes of all mental professional societies that sexual relations between clinicians and their patients are at the least unethical and under rare circumstances criminal. Such relations represent a deviation from the standard of care and a basis for the finding of malpractice if the other requisite elements (damages, for example) are present (Gutheil, 1982). Case law dramatically fails, however, to reflect the actual scope of the problem (Gartrell, 1986) because of the large number of episodes never reported at all and the substantial number of filed legal cases—probably but not provably the majority—that are settled out of court. An unknowable but probably small fraction of these cases might have been settled for legal strategic reasons even though the clinician was not culpable (Gutheil, 1989; Gutheil and Appelbaum, 1982).

Patients with borderline personality disorders are particularly likely to evoke boundary violation of various kinds, including sexual acting out in the transference-countertransference. Patients with borderline disorder apparently constitute the majority of those patients who falsely accuse therapists of sexual involvement. (False accusations represent a minuscule fraction of total allegations; the accusation is usually true.) Therapists can benefit from awareness of certain repeating patterns of errors in therapy and countertransference responses. With this awareness, they can avert the serious outcomes that result from such errors, such as trauma to the patient and/or highly destructive litigation.

One caveat is necessary to prevent misunderstanding. To study the patient-therapist dyad in clinical terms is not the same as indicting the patient (blaming the victim) for some malfeasance, nor is it the same as explaining away, exonerating, or excusing the therapist's behavior. Sex with a patient is never acceptable (Gutheil, 1989).

Codes of ethics covering the practice of professional psychotherapists have been adopted by at least 18 of the 45 national members of the International Union of Psychological Science, and by all but 1 of the 16 members of the European Federation of Professional Psychologists' Associations. These codes cover basic values such as the protection and promotion of human dignity and welfare, assumption of responsibility for professional action, restriction of practice to areas of competence, confidentiality, and honesty in all matters. In most countries, the codes are implemented by ethics committees and usually enforced by appropriate sanctions (Pope and Vetter, 1991).

Differences among nations in the definition of those qualified to provide psychological services make the estimation of human resources in psychotherapy a very uncertain endeavor. However, certain broad differences in the employment patterns of psychological health service providers can be noted among the industrialized countries of the West, the socialist countries, the dynamically developing countries, and the less developed countries.

In the United States, for which data are most readily available, 31% of doctoral-level psychotherapists work full-time in independent practice, followed by 20% in hospitals, and 14% in clinics. Another 19% work in academic or educational settings, with the remainder distributed among business, government, and other human service settings (Stapp and Fulcher, 1983). Counseling therapists are found in the same general fields, but in greater concentration in academic settings (40%), where they counsel students in addition to teaching and performing research.

Throughout Europe, the great majority of professional psychotherapists are salaried employees of public agencies. Private practice is practically nonexistent in the socialist countries and fairly rare in many countries of the industrialized West (e.g., in the United Kingdom), where high-quality public health and welfare services may be available. There are wide variations in the specialties in which psychotherapists may be employed.

When examining urban areas and rural towns throughout the world, it is important to keep in mind the heterogeneity of communities. Many cities require people of different backgrounds to live close together and independently. This heterogeneity may involve language, race, religion, social class, nationality, or a preferred lifestyle. Stress is sometimes associated with this diversity, and with pressures and conflicts that may accompany acculturation. Factors such as national policies that force assimilation or historical and economic factors that generate intergroup conflict are predictive of high stress, and their absence is predictive of low stress (Berry and others, 1987). The weakening of traditional support systems makes such stress especially difficult to handle.

Increases in the rates of divorce, child abuse, crime, and mental illness within urban centers of the world are requiring more services from psychotherapists than has been typical in the past. To be effective, such services must take the cultural background of the client into account. Psychotherapists who are competent to deal with cross-cultural issues in health and human development have developed techniques for measuring and reducing personal alienation, for adapting psychotherapy to local conditions, and for improving the mental health of diverse populations (Triandis and Draguns, 1980).

Crisis intervention is a relatively recent "frontline" mental health specialty with obvious implications for physical health. Experience acquired in providing assistance to ordinary well-functioning individuals on occasions of intense stress (e.g., rape, assault, combat shock or panic, transitory episodes of depression related to changes in personal relationships or circumstances of employment) has enabled psychotherapists to become involved in large-scale efforts to mitigate the harmful effects of human-created and natural disasters.

Therapist-patient sexual involvement confronts us with a pressing question and far-reaching implications for the professions. It may also involve increased understanding of the sexualization of teaching relationships and the ways in which training programs provide education and modeling regarding sexual issues (Pope and Vetter, 1991).

SEXUAL HARASSMENT

The effect of role modeling on the development of professional ethics and behavior cannot be dismissed (Pope, Levenson, and Schover, 1980). According to Sandler (1990),

> One of the most striking aspects of sexual harassment is that the victim feels quite powerless in the situation. Students rely on the professors not only for grades, but future recommendations as well as academic and career opportunities. In a very real sense, a female student's life chances are at stake.

It is rare, then, that a victim exhibits the courage and willingness to take the risk to confront the harasser and, once the complaint process is complete, to share the experience with others.

The Thomas-Hill case (October 1991) attracted the attention not only of the nation but also of the world. The media had a proverbial field day. The results are still being debated today. In Las Vegas, September 1991, the "Tailhook" reunion for carrier pilots was another graphic example of blatant sexual harassment.

Institutional administrators, managers, and supervisors attempting to formulate strategies for the prevention and remediation of sexual harassment may feel caught in a similar muddle: How are we to prevent what we cannot clearly define? How can we be responsible for that which we did not know was occurring? The confusion proceeds less from Kopp's (1972) conundrum (riddle or intricate problem) and more from the range of possible behaviors and judicial findings that the student of sexual harassment will find while researching the topic. Determinations as to whether sexual harassment has taken place necessarily proceed on a case-by-case basis as courts and enforcement agencies consider circumstances ranging from the outright demand for sexual favors at one extreme to complaints about sexual innuendo at the other. Interpretation of such behavior is closely related to context (Padgitt and Padgitt, 1986) so that the finding in one case is unlikely to predict the finding in another. In addition, the fact that institutions and supervisors can be liable for sexual harassment, that "they anticipated or reasonably should have anticipated" (Wetherfield, 1990) is not reassuring.

Although an honest case can be made for the difficulty of crafting an absolute definition of sexual harassment (Walker and Woolsey, 1985), neglecting to formulate institutional policy is hazardous, and disciplinary employment decisions made without pertinent written policy may not be defensible. Apart from concern about legal liability, schools and human service providers should be as eager as they are obligated to provide working and learning environments that are not hostile to students and employees. Resorting to definitional difficulties to explain the absence of policies and procedures concerning sexual harassment neither protects nor empowers its potential victims, and the institutional climate may be expected to remain unchanged.

Blanshan (1982) defined *sexual harassment* as "the unwanted imposition of sexual requirements in the context of a relationship of unequal power." A wide range of behaviors constitutes sexual harassment including the verbal (jokes, innuendos, and catcalls), the nonverbal (winks, leers, and the presence of sexual visual materials), and the physical (patting, stroking, and blocking one's path). In *Sexual Harassment* (1978), the Project on the Status and Education of Women described and elaborated on the varieties of such behavior, and the 1980 guidelines of the U.S. Equal Employment Opportunities Commission include representative examples. What all working definitions have in common is the emphasis in such behavior on the sex of the recipient and the unwelcomeness of the attention (Cammaert, 1985).

Specifically, the guideline definition of the EEOC (1980) is:

Unwelcome sexual advances, requests for sexual favors, and other verbal or physical conduct of a sexual nature constitute sexual harassment when

(1) submission to such conduct is made either explicitly a term or condition of employment,
(2) submission to or rejection of such conduct by an individual is used as a basis for employment decisions affecting such individuals,
    or
(3) such conduct has the purpose or effect of unreasonably interfering with an individual's work performance or of creating an intimidating, hostile or offensive working environment. (29 C.F.R. Part 1604, 1980)

Definitions 1 and 2 are quid pro quo harassment; definition 3 is hostile environment harassment.

In 1986, the U. S. Supreme Court adopted the EEOC definition and found sexual harassment to be a violation of the victim's civil rights as protected by Title VII of the 1964 Civil Rights Act (Meritor Savings bank v Vinson; Aguilera BA, 1993). The Court also alerted employers (and, by extension, educational institutions) to their potential liability not only for quid pro quo harassment in the workplace but also for acts of hostile environment harassment under certain circumstances. This finding and related decisions applying it in lower courts have stimulated growing numbers of employers and educational institutions to formulate sexual harassment policies and to establish pertinent grievance procedures.

Thoughtfully written sexual harassment policies and procedures, widely disseminated, arguably constitute the best legal protection that may be available and may reasonably be expected to provide a preventive influence as well. Organizations lacking such policies should be guided by their affirmative action personnel and legal counsels in formulating appropriate statements.

An adequate sexual harassment policy includes all relevant conduct of a sexual or gender-based nature that may be visited upon an unwilling person. The examples that come most readily to mind, especially with respect to quid pro quo harassment, tend to involve persons of unequal status (e.g., the harassment of students by faculty or workers by their supervisors). It is also important, however, to anticipate those relationships in which the inequality of power is less apparent. Although less obvious, the power of graduate teaching assistants over their students should be considered in the formulation of an adequate policy, for example.

It is also important to be aware of the growing attention being paid to peer harassment. As with sexual harassment in general, such conduct may range from innuendo and jokes to sexual assault (Project on the Status of Women, 1988). Peer harassment appears to be widespread and can have devastating effects. An adequate policy statement identifies it as a form of prohibited activity along with those previously cited (Aguilera BA, 1993).

Students or others wishing to file a complaint of sexual harassment need easy access to nonthreatening grievance procedures that should be described as part of the policy statement. The procedures may be modeled on other grievance procedures within the organization but should include the proviso that grievants may avoid presenting the complaint to their immediate supervisors, who may be the source of the problem (Van Tol, 1986).

Wagner (1990) suggested that a comprehensive policy and effective procedures feature "informal channels that include mediation, and formal avenues which are impartial and confidential, and protect the complainant and witnesses against retaliation." Most organizations have a designated person or persons, such as an equal opportunity or affirmative action officer, who act in an official capacity to receive and investigate formal complaints. These officers should be specified in the policy.

With respect to informal channels, victims may be encouraged to report the incident to another appropriate individual, such as a personnel officer, a division supervisor, a department chair or dean, a faculty member, health service personnel, or a counselor. For such informal means of resolution to work, persons likely to receive these complaints must be provided with guidelines for resolving them and with easy access to consultation with the organization's equal opportunity or affirmative action officer.

Persons complaining of sexual harassment are entitled to a prompt and impartial investigation, which should both protect the complainant from retaliation and observe the due process rights of the alleged harasser. The complainant should be informed about the progress of the investigation as it proceeds in order to allay fears or misunderstandings that may develop. It is important to put the complainant in touch with, and encourage them to use, supportive resources within the organization such as counseling or women's centers. This will be especially critical for victims who exhibit signs of physical and emotional stress.

Where there is a finding of sexual harassment, the victim should be made as whole as is practically possible (Wagner, 1990), that is, given back whatever was lost as a result of the harassment, such as a grade, a job, or a professional opportunity. Corrections applied to the harasser range from a letter of reprimand through a period of mandatory training, counseling, or dismissal from job. Such sanctions should correspond to the seriousness of the harassment and be consistent with the disciplinary practices of the organization.

The following case study illustrates how a young woman, Karen, responded to repeated sexual harassment in her work situation.

Case Study   *Sexual harassment*

ASSESSMENT OF THE INDIVIDUAL AND THE PROBLEM

Karen was brought to a community crisis center by her father, Jack. The receptionist contacted a therapist and stated that Jack had asked to see the therapist before his daughter.

Jack was asked by the therapist to come to her office. He agreed and then introduced his daughter, Karen, who was a poised, tall, very attractive, and obviously distressed young woman. The therapist shook hands with Karen, whose hand was limp and very damp with perspiration, and told her she would see her soon. Karen nodded affirmatively.

Jack began talking the minute Karen left the office. It was apparent that he was very angry and upset. The therapist asked him to sit down and tell her why he was so upset. Jack continued to pace up and down the office, declined to sit, and started to talk nonstop. He said to the therapist, "I'll kill that bastard . . . how dare he talk to my daughter that way, much less touch her!" The therapist asked him to *please* calm down and tell her what had happened.

Jack sat down, with clenched hands, and began telling her what had happened. Apparently, his daughter, Karen, had been sexually harassed by her boss "an old goat of 53, married, with three children," and he didn't know what to do. Karen loved her job and everyone there *except* Mr. X. The therapist told Jack that she would need to talk to Karen to get all the details. He agreed and said that he would take a walk. She thanked him, and they returned to the reception area. The therapist accompanied Karen back to the office.

The therapist asked Karen to sit down and tell her about her work. Karen's poise seemed to crumble, and she began to cry quietly, with tears running down her cheeks. The therapist handed her tissues and let her cry. Karen looked at the therapist and said, "I don't know what to do. I am so confused." The therapist said, "Start at the beginning, Karen."

Karen began by saying that she truly loved her job, was considered an excellent employee, and had received several awards because she was the top loan officer in a very prestigious and well-known company. She continued by saying that she had graduated from a very good local university with a 3.75 GPA; she had been a cheerleader, on the debating team, a member of one of the best sororities on campus, and homecoming queen when she was a senior.

Karen smiled slightly and continued, noting that she had enjoyed studying at the university but that the time she spent on her studies was with *one* goal: to become the best, most productive loan officer in one of the top three international companies. After she left the university, her father gave her a 3-month trip to Europe. He wanted her to perfect her French and Spanish (She had had three years of Latin in high school and four years of French and Spanish at the university).

Karen said that when she returned from Europe, she prepared her resume and made appointments for job interviews at all three companies. She was offered positions at all three companies, even though the country was in a recession. She decided on the number one company because there was a tremendous opportunity for rapid advancement. She then added wryly, "I had no idea I would have problems with Mr. X."

The therapist said, "Karen, tell me what happened with Mr. X. You mentioned sexual harassment in your chart?"

Karen looked at the therapist: "I had no idea I could be so naive, so stupid. He started on me 2 weeks after I began working there. He would lean over my desk, put his hands . . . put his hands on my shoulders, brush against me, and make some crude sexual remark. I would push his hands off and remind him that I was engaged to be married and to *please* not touch me." She continued, saying, "Two months ago, I was to receive an award at a formal affair and dinner at a resort. It would mean spending the night and everyone—and I mean *everyone*—from New York and Europe was going to be there. I was very thrilled.

"I bought a gorgeous dress. I had my acceptance speech ready; I felt very confident. I came downstairs and went into the anteroom, and the first person I saw was Mr. X. He said, 'Karen,' as he put his arm around my waist, 'let's get you a drink.' I answered him coldly: 'I don't drink.' He then said in front of all the people standing with us (some were from our company), 'Karen, I kicked out my roommate. Now you can spend the night with me—in my bed!'"

Karen said that she gasped and tried to push his arm away, but he would not let go. Three of the men standing with them twisted his arm away from her and told him to leave her alone, that he was making a fool of himself, and they took her away from him. Karen said, "I have never been so embarrassed in my life. I was shaking like a leaf."

The therapist asked her to continue. Karen took a deep breath and went on. The men who had gotten her away from Mr. X took her outside on a patio. They sat down with her and began talking to calm her down. One of them, David, said, "Karen, we know you have done absolutely *nothing* to encourage Mr. X's behavior toward you. Ignore him. He should be fired. You are the third or fourth new loan officer he has 'come on to.' The others quit, but it *has* to be in his personnel file."

Karen asked, "Why hasn't he been fired?" "Didn't you know," David replied, "that he is married to the chairman of the board's daughter? No one wants to get in trouble with him!"

David continued, "Karen, you surely realize that you are extremely attractive, intelligent, and appear to be in control of every situation? We *all* admire you and the way you have ignored Mr. X's approaches to you. We are also aware that you are engaged to a fine, handsome young man. Otherwise, every single man in this office would be asking you out!"

Karen looked at David and the other two men from her office and said, "Why didn't you tell me about this before? I haven't been able to sleep, I can't eat, I thought he would stop if I didn't make a big deal out of all his sexist, crude remarks and his tricking me when he could. And he has done this to *other* loan officers? He won't get away with this with me. I am going to the personnel director when we get back, and I am going to file a case of sexual harassment against him *and* the company, and I don't give a damn who he is married to. I don't have to take this from anyone!"

Karen stood up and said, "I am going back in, have dinner, and receive my award. You three keep him away from me or I will make a public announcement to the audience and the president of the company what I have endured from Mr. X —and let the heads roll." She went in the reception room with a smile on her face and walked over to some friends. The gentlemen stayed within a foot of her until she sat down to have dinner, and they then sat on either side and across from her. They practically had her surrounded! Mr. X was seated at the head table, and he had to be content just to look at her.

Karen went up when her name was called, received her award, and gave her acceptance speech—smiling and calm. She then excused herself and went to her room, accompanied by David and his two friends. They saw her to her room and told her "not to open her door to anyone."

Karen said that she threw herself on the bed and began crying. "I thought I would never stop. Finally I did and I called my father." She explained that he "had been very concerned about her nightmares and lack of appetite." She told him everything that had happened since she had started working at the company. She admitted that she had to stop at intervals to cry. She said that her father had been very supportive and wanted her to quit her job immediately. Karen told him not to worry, that she would, but first she wanted to write an incident report to put in her file and talk to the personnel director. Her father wanted to drive up and get her. She refused, saying that David was going to drive home with her.

Karen said that she drove home with David the next morning. Her father and fiancé, Michael, were waiting for her, and both were furious with Mr. X. Both wanted "to kill him." Karen calmed them down and assured them that she was fine, that she would report him, and that "yes, she would quit." This appeased them somewhat, as did her agreement to come to the crisis center.

PLANNING THE INTERVENTION

Karen needed strong situational support from her father and fiancé. She also needed legal advice regarding her rights in the work situation. She was completely frustrated. She knew that she could have gone "straight up the corporate ladder" if Mr. X had not been there to harass her. She would have to go through the "grief process," mourning her wonderful position and how well she had been doing. She would have to have closure on Mr. X by talking to the personnel director and writing the incident report.

INTERVENTION

Before the first session ended, the assessment of Karen was that, first, she was an intelligent, capable individual; second, that she was naive, mostly because of her very sheltered background; third, that she should be able to handle her crisis when she was more stable and able to look at the reality of her situation.

When Karen returned for her next session the following week, she was much calmer, and her father was not with her. She said that she had discussed her current situation (Mr. X's sexual harassment) with the personnel director and that she had been relieved but angry when the director told her that Mr. X had been formally reported three times for sexual harassment. All three victims had been "young and fairly attractive loan officers and all had a written report in his personnel file— before they had resigned." She said she was angry because he had not been fired. The director reminded her who he was married to—the chairman of the board's daughter. Karen smiled and replied, "I don't care *who* he is married to. I am filing a sexual harassment charge against him *and* this company! Here is my resignation and my attorney's card. If you need to talk to me, talk to my attorney instead." She admitted that it was a lot of "bravado." Inside "I was trembling. But I walked out of her office with my head held high."

The therapist asked her what her current plans were. She slumped in her chair and said in a soft voice, "I was hoping you would tell me." The therapist smiled and replied, "What do *you* want to do, Karen? It's your life, not mine."

Karen looked at the therapist, then sat up straight and said, "You are right. It is my life." She was thoughtful for a few minutes. She started talking. "I know I have been too sheltered in my life. Not because I wanted it, but my father was born in the old country and he has very different ideas. No wonder my sister moved out as soon as she could, and my mother divorced him; he is *so* old-fashioned. My mother is French and he is Greek. He really rules with an iron fist. If he says no, it is no! I want to move in with my fiancé, Michael. Then I want to go back to work at the 'number two' company if I can. I will tell them the truth, why I quit. If they don't want me, then I will go to the 'number three' company. If *they* don't want me, well, I'll cross that bridge when I come to it."

During the next session, the therapist had the pleasure of seeing Karen make sound and mature decisions. After that, she would call the therapist every so often to tell her something she had done and ask, "Was that all right?" The therapist would usually smile and say, "Sounds good to me—how do *you* feel about it?" Karen inevitably would answer, "Great. I just felt I should check with you." She was reassured that she was doing extremely well in therapy and was making very sound decisions.

She told the therapist that her father had been furious when she had moved in with Michael and told her "never to darken his door again." He relented in 2 weeks, invited them to dinner at a Greek restaurant, and tried to question Michael "ad nauseam." Michael was very gracious but refused to answer any his questions with a firm "that's our business." Jack apparently respected Michael for his firmness.

By the fourth session, Karen had been accepted for a position at the "number two" company. She had told them why she had quit "number one" (Mr. X), and their response had been very positive. In addition, her new salary was above what

CASE STUDY: KAREN

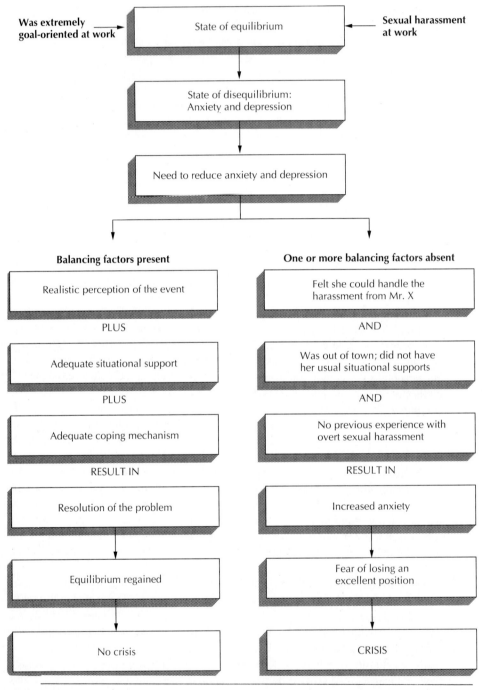

Figure 4-1

she had been making at the first company. She enjoyed her new position and was treated with a great deal of respect.

She had consulted her attorney, who was eager to accept her case of sexual harassment. He was apparently doing a thorough job of getting depositions and subpoenas of Mr. X's personnel file and was also going to file a civil suit.

ANTICIPATORY PLANNING

Karen continued to progress. At her sixth session, she and the therapist reviewed her case from the first session. Karen was amazed at all that had happened and that she "lived through it," with, she quickly added, "your help!" She had stabilized and was able to function at a higher level of equilibrium than before the crisis.

The therapist terminated her and told her that she could come back to the center during any future crises. Karen nodded, her eyes filled with tears, as they gave each other a hug.

SUMMATION OF THE PARADIGM (Figure 4-1)

Karen's crisis was precipitated by overt sexual harassment by her employer in front of others in her company. She was out of town and did not have her usual situational supports. She had no previous experience with sexual harassment. She had been overly protected by her "old-fashioned" father. She was extremely goal oriented in her job and wanted to be the best.

Addendum. Approximately 18 months later, Karen called the therapist. She told her that she was now a vice president. She laughed and said that she had won her case against Mr. X and that he had been fired. She added, "I know you are going to think I am being silly, but in court he looked so old. I felt sorry for him." The therapist replied, "I don't think you are silly. Maybe you have matured, Karen." Karen said softly, "I think you are right. Thank you."

Note: This client was seen before the Thomas-Hill case.

REFERENCES

Aguilera BA, Esq., Senior Vice President and General Counsel, The Mirage, Las Vegas, Nevada. Personal communication, September 1993.

American Psychiatric Association: *The principles of medical ethics with annotations especially applicable to psychiatry,* Washington, DC, 1985, The Association.

American Psychological Association: Report of ethics committee: 1985, *Am Psychol* 41:694, 1986.

Appelbaum PS: Confidentiality: winning for a change, *Hosp Community Psychiatry* 37:334, 1986.

Appelbaum PS: Statutes regulating patient-therapist sex, *Hosp Community Psychiatry* 41:15, 1990.

Appelbaum PS, Jorgenson L: Psychotherapist-patient sexual contact after termination of treatment: an analysis and a proposal, *Am J Psychiatry* 148:1466, 1991.

Berry JW and others: Acculturation and mental health. In Dasen PR, Berry JW, Sartorius NS, editors: *Health and cross cultural psychology.* London, 1984, Sage.

Blanshan S: Activism, research and policy: sexual harassment. *J NAWDAC* 46:16, 1982.

Bond L, Albee G: Training preventionists in the ethical implications of their actions. In Levin G, Tricket E, Hess R, editors: *Ethical implications of primary prevention,* Binghamton, NY, 1990, Haworth.

Brodsky A: Sex between patient and therapist: psychology's data and response. In Gabbard GO, editor: *Sexual exploitation in professional relationships,* Washington, DC, 1989, American Psychiatric Press.

Bulletin of the World Health Organization, vol. 65, Geneva, 1987, The Organization.

Cammaert L: How widespread is sexual harassment on campus? *Int J Women's Studies* 8:388, 1985.

Carr M and others: Fatal attraction: the ethical and clinical dilemma of patient-therapist sex, *Can J Psychiatry* 35:122-127, 1990.

Center for Public Interest Law: *Physician discipline of California,* San Diego, 1989, University of San Diego School of Law.

Conte HR and others: Ethics in the practice of psychotherapy: a survey, *Am J Psychother* 43:32-42, 1989.

Equal Employment Opportunity Commission. *Sexual harassment guidelines 29CFR,* chap XIV, Part 1604.11(a), Washington, DC, 1980, US Government Printing Office.

Ethics Committee of the American Psychological Association: Report of the ethics committee: 1986, *Am Psychol* 42:730, 1987.

Feldman SS: *Sexual contact in fiduciary relationships,* Washington, DC, 1989, American Psychiatric Press.

Gabbard G, editor: *Sexual exploitation in professional relationships,* Washington, DC, 1989, American Psychiatric Association.

Gabbard G, Pope K: *Sexual intimacies after termination: clinical, ethical, and legal aspects.* In Gabbard G, editor: *Sexual exploitation in professional relationships,* Washington, DC, 1989, American Psychiatric Association.

Gartrell N and others: Psychiatrist-patient contact: results of a national survey, *Am J Psychiatry* 143:1126, 1986.

Gutheil TG: Borderline personality disorder, boundary violations and patient-therapist sex: medicolegal pitfalls, *Am J Psychiatry* 146:597, 1989.

Gutheil TG, Appelbaum PS: *Clinical handbook of psychiatry and law,* New York, 1982, McGraw-Hill.

Guthrie GM and others: Small-scale studies and field experiments in family planning in the Philippines, *J Intercultural Relations* 8:391, 1984.

Haas LJ and others: Managed outpatient mental health plans: clinical, ethical and practical guidelines for participation, *Prof Psych Res Pract* 22:45, 1991.

Hamilton JA and others: The emotional consequences of gender-based abuse in the workplaces: new counseling programs for sex discrimination, *J Women Ther* 6:155, 1987.

Holtzman WH and others: Psychology and health: contributions of psychology to the improvement of health and healthcare, *Int J Psychol* 22:221, 1987.

Hotelling K: Special feature: sexual harassment. Introduction to special feature, *J Counseling Dev* 69:495, 1991.

Hotelling K: Sexual harassment: a problem shielded by silence, *J Counseling Dev* 69:497, 1991.

Howard S: Organization resources for addressing sexual harassment, *J Counseling Dev* 69:507, 1991.

Kardener SH: Sex and the physician-patient relationship, *Am J Psychiatry* 131:1134, 1974.

Kardener SH, Fuller M, Mensh IN: Characteristics of "erotic" practitioners, *Am J Psychiatry* 133:1324, 1976.

Kopp S: *If you meet the buddha on the road, kill him,* Palo Alto, 1972, Science and Behavior Books.

Miller RR, Weinstock R: Conflict of interest between therapist-patient confidentiality and the duty to report sexual abuse of children, *Behav Sci Law* 5:161, 1987.

Padgitt S, Padgitt J: Cognitive structure of sexual harassment: implications for university policy, *J College Students Personnel* 27:34, 1986.

Pope K, Levenson H, Schover L: Sexual intimacy training: results and implications of a national survey, *Am Psychologist* 34:682-689, 1980.

Pope KS, Vetter, VA: Prior therapist-patient sexual involvement among patients seen by psychologists, *Psychotherapy* 28:429, 1991.

Project on the Status and Education of Women: *Sexual harassment: a hidden issue,* Washington, DC, 1978, Association of American Colleges.

Project on the Status of Women: *Peer harassment: hassles for women on campus,* Washington, DC, 1988, Association of American Colleges.

Riger S: Gender dilemmas in sexual harassment, policies and procedures, *Am Psychol* 46:497, 1991.

Roy v Hartogs, 366 NYS 2d 297 (Civ Ct, NY, 1975); affirmed on condition of remittitur, 381 NYS 2d587 (Sup Ct, NY, 1976).

Sandler BR: Sexual harassment: a new issue for institutions, *Initiatives* 52:5, 1990.

Shackelford JF: Affairs in the consulting room: a review of the literature on therapist-patient sexual intimacy, *J Psychol Christianity* 8:26, 1989.

Stapp J, Fulcher R: The employment of APA members: 1982, *Am Psychol* 38:1298, 1983.

Tarasoff v Regents of the University of California, et al, 131 Cal Rptr 14, 551 P. 2d 334, 1976.

Triandis HC, Draguns J, editors: *Handbook of cross-cultural psychology,* Boston, 1980, Allyn & Bacon.

Van Tol J, editor: *Sexual harassment on campus: a legal compendium,* 1986, American Council on Education. National Association of College and University Attorneys, pp. 123-128, 1986.

Wagner KC: Programs that work: prevention and intervention: developing campus policy procedures, *Initiatives* 52:37, 1990.

Walker GE, Woolsey L: Sexual harassment: ethical research and clinical implications in the academic setting, *Int J Women's Studies* 8:424, 1985.

Weiner MF: Privilege: a comparative study, *J Psychiatry Law* 12:373, 1989.

Wetherfield A: Sexual harassment: the current state of the law governing educational institutions, *Initiatives* 52:23, 1990.

Williams MH: Therapist-patient sex as sex abuse: six scientific professional and practice dilemmas in addressing victimization and rehabilitation: comment, *Prof Psychol Res Pract* 21:420, 1990.

Wubbolding RE: Professional ethics: intervention in suiciding behaviors, *J Real Ther* 7:13, 1988.

ADDITIONAL READINGS

American Psychological Association: Ethical principles of psychologists (amended June 2, 1989), *Am Psychol* 45:390-395, 1990.

Brett JM, Goldberg SB, Ury WL: Designing systems for resolving disputes in organizations, *Am Psychol* 45:162-170, 1990.

Erhart JK, Sandler B: *Rx for success: improving the climate for women in medical schools and teaching hospitals,* Washington, DC, 1990, Association of American Colleges.

Gabbard G, Pope K: Sexual intimacies after termination: clinical, ethical and legal aspects. In Gabbard GO, editor: *Sexual exploitation in professional relationships,* Washington, DC, 1989, American Psychiatric Press.

Gartrell N and others: Prevalence of psychiatrist-patient sexual contact. In Gabbard GO, editor: *Sexual exploitation in professional relationships,* Washington, DC, 1989, American Psychiatric Press.

Gechtman L: Sexual contact between social workers and their clients. In Gabbard GO, editor: *Sexual exploitation in professional relationships,* Washington, DC, 1989, American Psychiatric Press.

Gilbert L, Scher M: The power of an unconscious belief, *Prof Pract Psychol* 8:94-108, 1989.

Haas LJ, Malouf JL: *Keeping up the good work: a practitioner's guide to mental health ethics,* Sarasota, FL, 1989, Professional Resource Exchange.

Hite M: Sexual harassment and the university community, *Initiatives* 52:11-15, 1990.

Kluft R: Treating the patient who has been sexually exploited by a previous therapist, *Psychiatr Clin North Am* 12:483-500, 1989.

MacKenzie KR: Recent developments in brief psychotherapy, *Hosp Community Psychiatry* 39:742, 1989.

Mason v Marriage and Family Center, California Court of Appeal, Fourth Appellate District, Division One, filed March 14, Daily Journal DAR, pp 3070-3072, 1991.

Mazer DB, Percival EF: Students' experiences of sexual harassment at a small university, *Sex Roles* 20:1-22, 1989.

Mednick MT: On the politics of psychological constructs: stop the bandwagon, I want to get off, *Am Psychol* 44:1118-1123, 1989.

Morgenson G: Watch that leer, stifle that joke, *Forbes,* pp 69-72, May 1989.

Moses YT: *Black women in academe: issues and strategies,* Washington, DC, 1990, Association of American Colleges.

Nelson LJ and others: Taking the train to a world of strangers: health care marketing and ethics, *Hastings Cent Rep* 19:36-43, 1989.

Peters L: A student's experience, *Initiatives* 52:17-21, 1990.

Pope K: How clients are harmed by sexual contact with mental health professionals, *J Counseling* 67:222-226, 1988.

Pope K: Therapist-patient sex syndrome: a guide for attorneys and subsequent therapists to assessing damage. In Gabbard GO, editor: *Sexual exploitation in professional relationships,* Washington, DC, 1989, American Psychiatric Press.

Pope K: Ethical and malpractice issues in hospital practice, *Am Psychol* 45:1066-1070, 1990.

Pope K: Therapist-patient sex as sex abuse: six scientific, professional, and practical dilemmas in addressing victimization and rehabilitation, *Prof Psychol Res Pract* 21:277-239, 1990.

Pope KS: Therapist-patient sex as sex abuse: six scientific, professional, and practical dilemmas in addressing victimization: comment: response, *Prof Psychol Res Pract* 21:421-423, 1990.

Pope K: Therapist-patient sexual involvement: a review of the research, *Clin Psychol Rev* 10:477-490, 1990.

Pope K: Rehabilitation plans and expert testimony for therapists who have been sexually involved with a patient, *Independent Pract* 11:31, 1991.

Pope K, Bouhoutsos J: *Sexual intimacies between therapists and patients,* New York, 1986, Praeger.

Pope K, Garcia-Peltoniemi R: Responding to victims of torture: clinical issues, professional responsibilities, and useful resources, *Prof Psychol Res Pract* 1991.

Pope K, Keith-Spiegel P, Tabachnick B: Sexual attraction to patients: the human therapist and the (sometimes) inhuman training system, *Am Psychol* 41:147-158, 1986.

Pope K, Levenson H, Schover L: Sexual intimacy in psychology training: results and implications of a national survey, *Am Psychol* 34:682-689, 1979.

Pope K, Tabachnick B, Keith-Spiegel P: Ethics of practice: the beliefs and behaviors of psychologists as therapists, *Am Psychol* 42:993-1006, 1987.

Pope K, Vasquez M: *Ethics in psychotherapy and counseling: a practical guide for psychologists,* San Francisco, 1991, Jossey-Bass.

Rhodes FHT: The moral imperative to prevent sexual harassment on campus, *Initiatives* 52:1-4, 1990.

Saal FE, Johnson CB, Weber N: Friendly or sexy? It may depend on whom you ask, *Psychol Women Q* 13:263-276, 1989.

Sandler BR: Sexual harassment: a new issue for institutions, *Initiatives* 52:5, 1990.

Shopland S, VandeCreek L: Sex with ex-clients: theoretical rationales for prohibition, *Ethics Behav* 1:35-44, 1991.

Singer TL: Sexual harassment in graduate schools of social work: provocative dilemmas, *J Social Work Ed* 25:68-76, 1989.

Sonne J: A example of group therapy for victims of therapist-client sexual intimacy. In Gabbard GO, editor: *Sexual exploitation in professional relationships,* Washington, DC, 1989, American Psychiatric Press.

Sonne J, Pope K: Treating victims of therapist-patient sexual involvement, *Psychotherapy* 28:176-184, 1991.

Sperry L: Contemporary approaches to brief psychotherapy: a comparative analysis, *Individ Psychol: J Adlerian Therapy, Research and Practice* 45:3-25, 1989.

Stone A: No good deed goes unpunished, *Psychiatric Times,* p 24, March 1990.

Tabachnick B, Keith-Spiegel P, Pope K: Ethics of teaching: beliefs and behaviors of psychologists as educators, *Am Psychol* 46:506-515, 1991.

Trickett E: *Living an idea,* Cambridge, Mass, 1990, Broadline.

Trickett E, Levin G: *Paradigms for prevention: providing a context for confronting ethical issues.* In Levin G, Trickett E, Hess R, editors: *Ethical implications of primary prevention,* Binghamton, NY, 1990, Haworth.

Vasquez M: Sexual intimacies with clients after termination, *Ethics & Behav* 1:45-61, 1991.

Zimet CN: The mental health care revolution; will psychology survive? *Am Psychol* 44:703-708, 1989.

Chapter 5

Posttraumatic Stress Disorder

In response to a mandate by Congress (Public Law 98-160), a National Vietnam Veterans Readjustment Study (NVVRS) was initiated. A special section was published in *Journal of Consulting and Clinical Psychology*. This chapter is based on the findings of this study, which is fairly new (1991), comprehensive, and relevant, as well as on other journal articles.

DSM-III-R Diagnostic Criteria

The American Psychiatric Association's (1987) DSM-III-R diagnostic criteria contain the following conditions and symptoms that should exist before an individual can be classified as having posttraumatic stress disorder (PTSD). The numeric listing is "309.89 Post-traumatic Stress."

A. The person has experienced an event that is outside the range of usual human experience and that would be markedly distressing to almost anyone, e.g., serious threat to one's life or physical integrity; serious threat or harm to one's children, spouse, or other close relatives and friends, sudden destruction of one's home or community; or seeing another person who has been, or is being seriously injured or killed as the result of an accident or physical violence.

B. The traumatic event is persistently reexperienced in at least one of the following ways:
   (1) recurrent and intensive distressing recollections of the event (in young children, repetitive play in which themes or aspects of the trauma are expressed)
   (2) recurrent distressing dreams of the event
   (3) sudden acting or feeling as if the traumatic event were recurring (includes a sense of reliving the experience, illusions, hallucinations, and dissociative [flashback] episodes, even those that occur upon awakening or when intoxicated)
   (4) intense psychological distress at exposure to events that symbolize or resemble an aspect of the traumatic event, including anniversaries of the trauma

C. Persistent avoidance of stimuli associated with the trauma or numbing of the general responsiveness (not present before the trauma), as indicated by at least three of the following:
   (1) efforts to avoid thoughts or feelings associated with the trauma
   (2) efforts to avoid activities or situations that arouse recollections of the trauma
   (3) inability to recall an important aspect of the trauma (psychological amnesia)
   (4) markedly diminished interest in significant activities (in young children, loss of recently acquired developmental skills such as toilet training or language skills)
   (5) feeling of detachment or estrangement from others
   (6) restricted range of affect, e.g., unable to have loving feelings
   (7) sense of foreshortened future, e.g., does not expect to have a career, marriage, or children, or a long life

D. Persistent symptoms of increased arousal (not present before the trauma) as indicated by at least two of the following:
   (1) difficulty falling or staying asleep
   (2) irritability or outbursts of anger
   (3) difficulty concentrating
   (4) hypervigilance
   (5) exaggerated startle response
   (6) psychological reactivity upon exposure to events that symbolize or resemble an aspect of the traumatic event (e.g., a woman who was raped in an elevator breaks out in a sweat when entering any elevator)
E. Duration of the disturbance (symptoms in B, C and D above of at least one month).

Historical

Victims of posttraumatic stress syndrome who suffer from feelings of powerlessness, helplessness, or the hopelessness beyond that often experienced cannot accept a psychological basis for their trauma. As an escape route, they may search for causes external to themselves to explain their symptoms and pain and act out violently against agencies, society, loved ones, and self (Staudenmayer and Steiner, 1987).

Within the past decade, psychosocial scientists have shown renewed interest in understanding acute and long-term psychological responses to extraordinary and potentially life-threatening stressor events. Although the topic of stress has intrigued researchers and clinicians for many years (Cannon, 1932; Selye, 1950), the influence of stress on such multifaceted outcomes as psychiatric disorders, physical and psychological well-being, and interpersonal functioning has been the focus of recent debate (Dohrenwend and Shrout, 1985; Lazarus and others, 1985). The literature on stress now encompasses articles describing daily hassles (Lazarus and DeLongis, 1983), stressful life events (Holmes and Rahe, 1967), persistent adversity and chronic strains (Rutter, 1986), experiences of transition and multiple losses (Hobfoll, 1989), and other distressing but not unusual circumstances, such as loss of loved ones or physical aspects of self (Horowitz, 1986).

It is not necessary to draw categorical distinctions between extraordinary stressors and more common life event stressors to observe that there appear to be environmental conditions that wreak havoc on living creatures and are appraised almost uniformly as horrendous in terms of threat to life, psychological loss, and devastating consequences, particularly when they fall within one's personal life domain. Paralleling conditions often created to "provoke experimental neuroses" in animals and characterized by features of unpredictability and uncontrollability, these stressors are associated with profound affective, cognitive, and physiological disturbances (Mineka and Kihlstron, 1978). Disasters of this extreme ilk include the traumas of war (Holloway and Ursano, 1984), incarceration in Nazi concentration camps (Eitinger, 1975; Thygesen, Hermann, and Willanger, 1970), and confinement as prisoners of war (Rahe and Genender, 1983) or political prisoners (Goldfeld, and others, 1988). The literature also includes accounts of such natural disasters as volcanic eruption (Shore, Tatum, and Vollmenr, 1986) and bushfire (McFarlane, 1988), the technological calamities of nuclear accident (Baum, Gatchel, and Schaeffer, 1983; Bromet, and others, 1982; Cornely and Bromet, 1986; Kasl, Chisholm, and Eskenazi, 1981), and such violent crimes as kidnapping (Terr, 1983) and rape (Kilpatrick, Resick, and Veronen, 1981).

Survivors of these and other disastrous circumstances have not necessarily been ignored by social scientists for the past few decades, but introduction of posttramatic stress disorder (PTSD) as a distinct category of psychiatric disorder in DSM-III (American Psychiatric Association, 1980) with revisions in the DSM-III-R prompted increased scrutiny of the psychological symptoms and their clustering that may develop after trauma experiences. Although a commonality of stress-related responses may be implied by the DSM-III-R PTSD conceptualization, creation of the category propelled psychosocial scientists to examine victim reactions to discrete stressor circumstances, such as the Vietnam War (Kulka and others, 1990) and the terrors associated with political imprisonment and deliberate torture (Goldfeld and others, 1988; Mollica, Wyshak, and LaVelle, 1987; Mollica and others, 1987). The literature has also expanded to include studies of child (Saigh, 1989) and second-generation victims (Solomon, Kotler, and Mikulincer, 1988), significant others of victims (Matsakis, 1988), and health assistance workers aiding families of victims (Bartone and others, 1989).

Stress Victims

Diverse subpopulations within American society may be seen as potentially suffering the symptoms of PTSD, as well as other stress-related accompanying psychiatric residuals, by reason of their exposure to stressor events of sufficient magnitude or severity to qualify as precursors for development of the disorder. The presence of a stressor is not by definition tantamount to developing PTSD symptoms; however, an environmental antecedent is required for the disorder to be recognized by current nosology. That even the most devastating stressors are not sufficient to elicit symptoms of PTSD in some survivors is a phenomenon of great interest (Grinker and Spiegel, 1945; Sutker, Bugg, and Allain, 1991). It is frequently assumed that with extreme stressor severity, the symptoms of PTSD can potentially develop in almost anyone. Ursano (1981) documented that socially advantaged men who had been selected as aviators for their psychological health and coping abilities developed psychiatric illness subsequent to the stress of POW captivity in North Vietnam and that predisposition to psychiatric illness was neither necessary nor sufficient for development of psychiatric morbidity.

Who in the United States might reasonably be evaluated for assessment of PTSD? There remain alive 11 million veterans of the World War II (WW II) era (Hamilton and Canteen, 1987), 5 million veterans of the Korean Conflict era (Veterans Administration, 1984), more than 3 million survivors of Vietnam combat (Kulka and others, 1990), and more than 500,000 Operation Desert Shield returnees (Department of Veterans Affairs, 1991). National figures document approximately 71,000 living American POW survivors who were held in European and Asian prison camps (Stenger, 1991), and Mollica and others (1990) indicate that since 1975 approximately 1 million refugees have resettled in the United States, many of whom experienced brutal tortures. These figures do not include the millions of Americans victimized by criminal acts, particularly rape, or those exposed to the devastation of earthquake, hurricane, flood, or other natural catastrophes. Recent epidemiological studies cite PTSD prevalence estimates in community samples as being between 1% and 2% (Helzer, Robins, and McEvoy, 1987; Kulka and others, 1990), placing PTSD prevalence at rates consistent with those for schizophrenia (Keane and Penk, 1988) and somewhat less than those for antisocial personality disorder (APD) (Jordan and others, 1989). Current and lifetime PTSD prevalence rates of 15% and 31%, respectively, have been reported in community-based samples of Vietnam combat veterans (Kulka and others, 1990), and assignment of current PTSD diagnoses ranges from 56% among WW II former POWs (Zeiss and Dickman, 1989) to 90% among Korean Conflict POW survivors (Sutker and others, 1990b).

Diagnostic Problems

Some writers have expressed optimism that disagreements regarding the legitimacy and clinical usefulness of PTSD as a diagnostic entity have been largely quelled (Keane, 1989). Questions remain about the unique association of the disorder with stressful events, the definition of type and magnitude of events considered traumatogenic, the specificity of the disorder and its distinctness from other psychiatric diagnoses, and the nature of the disorder as regards clinical and laboratory findings, familial characteristics, predictable clinical course, and expected response to treatment.

From a clinically descriptive standpoint, PTSD may be seen as a multifaceted set of psychological and biological symptoms assumed to be associated with extreme trauma and thought to be exacerbated by stress experiences of various kinds. Kolb (1987) urged classification of the disorder into mild, moderate, and severe forms, depending on the number of symptoms, their expression, and potential for intensification on reexposure to emotional stress. The DSM-III-R nomenclature allowed specification of delayed onset, and its predecessor identified both acute and chronic expression.

There appears to be no overriding agreement regarding the most appropriate theoretical framework for understanding the disorder, particularly in accounting for its etiology, expression, and course. PTSD is the most likely of all psychiatric disorders to be explained by psychological constructs, with specific reference to learning and conditioning processes and changes in behavior as a result of experience. Although there may be biological and perhaps dispositional vulnerabilities and contributors to the disorder, highlighting the role of the trauma in marking disorder onset calls into play the necessity of exploring both stimulus and response aspects of the disorder as well as the afflicted person.

Definitions

The definition of *stress* is contemporary in the psychological literature (Dohrenwend and Shrout, 1985; Hobfoll, 1989; Lazarus and others, 1985), and the issues raised have relevance to development of assessment strategies essential for clinical and research identification of stress-related residuals and PTSD. Lazarus and others (1985) defined *stress* as "a complex rubric consisting of many interrelated variables and processes rather than a simple variable that can be readily measured and correlated with adaptational outcomes." In their view, stress lies not in the environmental input but in the person's appraisal of the relationship between the input and its demands and the person's beliefs and capabilities to meet, mitigate, and alter demands in the interest of his well-being. In this system, there are no environmental events identified as stressful independent of subjective appraisal and no environmental stressors without vulnerable people. There is no definition of stressful events except by reference to properties of individuals that render their well-being vulnerable to those events. It becomes necessary, then, to determine those factors that, in interaction with a given environmental situation, are associated with appraisals of harm or loss, threat, or challenge. Lazarus and others (1985) pointed to target variables that must be assessed, including values and commitments, beliefs about self and others, individual resources, and environmental supports (Sutker and others, 1991).

The definition of PTSD demands evaluation of the nature, severity, and duration of the presumed related stressors, their social and physical properties, and the totality of stressor impact over time. Quantification of environmental factors, such as objective specification of stress parameters, does not preclude determination of cognitive appraisals of stressor events, and measures of objective properties of stress are best combined with those that elicit subjective appraisals of its meaning and substantiate self-reported data by external validation.

Stress has been conceptualized more narrowly by reference to its environmental properties and characteristics (Dohrenwend and Shrout, 1985). Stressful events are identified in the environment by categories with attention to parameters of duration, sequencing, severity, and type. Stimulus definitions of stress demand quantification of event characteristics toward such purposes as creating a taxonomy of stressful events, isolating commonalities among stressful events, and identifying predictable reactions to events in different categories or characterized on specified dimensions of severity. Because stress as a concept implies effects on response systems, whether it can be quantified purely independently of response parameters is a topic for debate. Nevertheless, attempts to apply empirical methods of description to events conceptualized as stressful are integral to advancing an understanding of the etiology and expression of PTSD and other stress-symptom responses. An artificial dichotomy between these positions is not necessarily useful, and measurement of objective properties of discrete stressful circumstances does not preclude efforts to understand the individual meanings of such experiences or to quantify unique responses to stressful events.

Arguments regarding the emphasis allocated to the objective measurement of stress, the role assignment to personal appraisal or meaning, and the characteristics of individuals who make some types of stress imperceptible versus monumental, for example, constituted a major focus of a special series of papers on PTSD and the stressor criterion. Breslau and Davis (1987a) contended that there was insufficient evidence to show that a set of symptoms thought to define PTSD was strongly and uniquely associated with extraordinary stressors or that extreme stressors form a discrete class in terms of probability of psychiatric sequelae or distinct nature of subsequent psychopathology. It has also been suggested that the cumulative effects of multiple losses or severe life events resemble those following an extraordinary stressor (Horowitz, Wilner, and Alvarez, 1979) and that daily hassles may be more predictive of psychological symptoms than more intense life events (Kanner and others, 1981).

Ursano (1987) cautioned against the assumption that extraordinary stressors are equivalent to those of everyday living and emphasized both the quantity and quality of the stressor as influencing subsequent symptom patterns. Although data gathered across diverse traumatized samples almost uniformly point to the magnitude of the stressor experience as predictive of subsequent psychological distress (March, 1990), investigators rarely differentiate quantity versus quality indexes. Specially targeted measures, often tallied cumulatively, are used to characterize the severity of given stressors. For example, measures of combat exposure (Foy and others, 1984; Friedman and others, 1986) are available, most of which are pertinent to military duty in Vietnam. Among others, there are indexes to describe POW trauma (Sutker and others, 1986) and physical atrocities and torture (Goldfeld and others, 1988), measures of rape brutality (Kilpatrick and others, 1989), and frameworks to quantify natural disaster trauma and its typology (Green, 1982). Few data are collected that span stressor types, transcend cohort effects, or are applicable to evaluation of stressful events across a range of experiences.

Elements of Stress

Characterizing stressful events in terms of their salient aspects or pinpointing those psychosocial and biological components of trauma that are most deleterious in terms of psychological residuals is essential. Studies have shown that exposure to abusive violence and participation in atrocities increased the risk of stress-related symptoms among Vietnam combat veterans (Breslau and Davis, 1987b), as did exposure to the grotesque or macabre (Green and others, 1989) and the experience of having been wounded (Pitman, Altman, and Macklin, 1989). Conditions of severe malnutrition and physical torture have been documented as increasing stress severity among survivors of Nazi concentration (Eitinger, 1975; Thygesen, Hermann, and Willanger, 1970), POW (Sutker and others, 1990a), and Southeast Asian refugee (Mollica and others, 1987) camps. Kilpatrick and others (1989) found that rape, as compared with other types of criminal violence, was associated with development of subsequent psychopathology, and that dangerousness in the sense of physical injury and cognitive appraisal of life threat was linked to severity of response. Foa, Stekete, and Rothbaum (1989) also cited loss of controllability, lack of predictability, trauma duration, and number of traumatic events as critical parameters for elaborating the nature of stress.

Progress in conceptualizing and assessing the more ordinary forms of stress and environmental change has yet to find full application in assessment of PTSD and related disorders. Methods for characterizing the nature, severity, duration, and meaning of extreme stressful experiences are relatively primitive. Used primarily to determine whether the DSM-III–defined stressor criterion has been satisfied, measures of stress may be simple yes-no queries with elaboration in clinical interview, or self-report checklists and open-ended unstructured or structured interviews may be administered. In most cases, instruments are focused on discrete experience domains, such as combat specific to a war theater. An exception is the Incident Report Interview (IRI), a structured, behaviorally specific interview schedule developed by Kilpatrick and others (1989) to detect and describe such criminal victimization incidents as sexual molestation, rape, aggravated assault, and robbery.

Available technologies for assessment of the stressor are also limited by failure to distinguish discrete, continuous, sequential, and multiple stressors; lack of relevance to an array of stressors from common to extraordinary events; meager attention to quantifying the stressor from objective and personal perspectives; and inadequate methods for corroborating self-reported information. Additionally, most measures do not distinguish positive and negative events or provide for positive event reporting, and stressor and response properties may be confounded by summary measures. Thygesen, Hermann, and Willanger (1970) and Sutker and others (1990a) found trauma-induced weight loss to be an index of stress severity for Nazi concentration and POW prison camp survivors; that is, the amount of captivity weight loss was shown to be predictive of the severity of psychological maladjustment, psychiatric morbidity, and cognitive impairment. Although capable of validation and reflective of both biological and psychological brutalization, this index confounds the properties of stressor severity with an indication of stressor response (e.g., extent of weight loss).

Assessing Symptoms of Stress

With publication of the DSM-III and DSM-III-R, a new name was created to describe the psychiatric residuals of combat and other severe stressors known earlier as *traumatic neurosis* or *shell shock* (Grinker and Spiegel, 1945; Kardiner, 1959). In the present classification, PTSD is conceptualized as an anxiety-based disorder tied uniquely to an environmental stressor with a complex symptom picture derived from acute, chronic, or delayed expression, phasic fluctuations, potential reactivation, a high degree of symptom overlap, and frequent comorbidities. Although most critics of the revised nomenclature have not challenged the notion of stress-related psychiatric symptoms, they have voiced concerns about whether PTSD constitutes a disorder distinct from established clinical entities and have questioned the adequacy of the defining criteria. Skepticism about its clinical validity was enhanced by the outline of symptoms spanning cognitive, emotional, and behavioral spheres and possible differences between acute combat stress reactions and symptom onset subsequent to trauma cessation. Other concerns were featured in research reports of symptom fabrication and malingering (Fairbank, McCaffrey, and Keane, 1985; Hamilton, 1985) and factitious and delusional phenomena (Lynn and Belza, 1984).

Little effort has been devoted to unraveling the intricacies of disorder cooccurrence and symptom overlap among samples of subjects exposed to identifiable stressor circumstances and appropriate control subjects. Studying a small group of Vietnam War and Korean Conflict combat veterans hospitalized for treatment of PTSD, Sierles and others (1983) found that more than 80% met DSM-III criteria for at least one other mental disorder. Frequent coexisting syndromes included alcoholism, anxiety disorders, major depression, and APD among Vietnam War combat veterans. Extending investigation to POW survivors, Kluznik and others (1986) found that generalized anxiety disorder occurred most frequently among PTSD-diagnosed WW II former POWs, and Sutker and others (1991b) reported high rates of comorbidity for other anxiety disorders (55%) and affective disorders (32%) among PTSD-diagnosed former Korean Conflict POWs. Similarly, Mollica and others (1987) found that diagnosis of PTSD among Southeast Asian refugees was almost always associated with additional psychiatric diagnoses, usually major affective disorders.

Of interest is the common coexistence of PTSD and somatic complaints. Concerns about fatigue (Ellis and others, 1981) and headache (Norris and Feldman-Summers, 1981) have been reported by rape victims, particularly in association with more severe forms of assault. Headache figured prominently among survivor-assistance officers providing support to families of victims of a military air disaster (Bartone and others, 1989). Goldfeld and others (1988) listed headache, impaired hearing, gastrointestinal distress, and joint pain as common among survivors of political confinement, mass violence, and torture; Mollica and others (1990) found worsening of most somatic symptoms, particularly headache, over the course of 6 months of psychiatric treatment. Research with POW survivors of WW II and Korea (Sutker, Allain, and Motsinger, 1988; Sutker and others, 1990b; Sutker and others, 1986) also documented common complaints of fatigue, headaches, gastrointestinal disturbance, problems with respiration, hearing and vision losses, and chronic pain. Soldiers suffering PTSD had complaints of digestive problems and chest pains more frequently than did their non–PTSD-diagnosed counterparts but also reported increased use of alcohol and cigarettes.

More thorough assessment of bodily ailments, incorporating consultation with medical experts who are informed about the nature and severity of biological and psychological aspects of the stressor, represents an important complement to psychological assessment for clinical purposes.

Intervention

As mental health professionals, we have a clear responsibility to concern ourselves with the psychological welfare of the combatants, their loved ones, and the nation as a whole. There is much we can do to prevent psychological distress after war and many interventions that can limit the negative psychological and psychosocial sequelae that often emerge from war.

Two elements emerged in the task force's discussion of risk: First, the greater the threat of loss or the actual loss to which individuals were exposed, the greater their level of risk (threat to life being a principal threat of loss; see also Dohrenwend and Dohrenwend, 1981; Green and others, 1989; Hobfoll, 1989); second, the fewer coping resources an individual had, the more likely that he would be overwhelmed by the losses or threats of losses encountered.

Desert Shield Families at Risk

Service personnel are at risk to the extent that their duty is hazardous and to the extent that they believe they would confront chemical warfare. The more time they spend in the field of operations and the more they are exposed to the dead and wounded, the greater their risk. The feeling that they are deserting their families at a time of need causes some service personnel additional stress. After the war, they continue to be affected by the delayed return home, culture shock due to quick foxhole-to-front porch transitions, pressures of reunion, pressures of meeting their own needs as opposed to work and family needs, reorganizing financial and work responsibilities, and changed social relationships.

Families undergo similar disruptions in their routines. Many spouses and other family members are overburdened with multiple roles, financial pressures, fear for their service person's well-being, and disruption and negative reactions in children's lives. For families, reunions also continue to be stressful. Some of the sources of stress for family members during and after reunions include being second-guessed on important decisions and being challenged in their new, more independent roles. Conflicts may arise over new relationships that emerged in the absence of the service persons. Family members may feel stress when idealized dreams of a glorious return are not realized. Families, employers, and others sometimes have a mistaken expectation that the serviceperson returning from the Persian Gulf conflict should not experience prolonged stress because the war was so brief and "antiseptic," compared with the Vietnam experience. This type of misperception may further exacerbate problems that do arise because the individual may feel unjustified in having difficulty. Family conflicts from before the war do not magically resolve, even if the idealized notions about the family pushed them out of thought. Clearly, children are deeply affected by their parents' prolonged absence and may respond with a mixture of relief and anger that their parents may not understand (Green, and others, 1988, 1990; van der Kolk, 1987).

The risk groups recognized by the task force were as follows:
1. Troops who served in the danger zone, especially those whose duty placed them in particular danger and those who witnessed the death and injury of their comrades, civilians, refugees, or enemy soldiers
2. Troops who served outside the danger zone, but who were at risk of entering the danger zone
3. Reservists who could have been called up
4. Families and loved ones of members of any of these groups
5. Children of service personnel
6. Children in general
7. People who are potential targets of terrorism (those who must frequently fly overseas or those who are based in foreign countries with poor security)
8. People who have had previous exposure to war-related stress or to other traumas that may be associated with war (e.g., assault victims, refugees)
9. People who have a history of psychopathology
10. People who have had other recent, major upheavals in their lives
11. People who are socially isolated

Risk factors, of course, do not necessarily lead to negative psychological or psychosomatic consequences. Indeed, a relatively low rate of serious problems was expected by the task force for even the highest risk group in Desert Shield. There are many reasons for this interpretation. Service personnel were at risk without significant protection for only a short period of time, the ground war ended quickly and with few casualties for allied forces, and there was a large degree of support for soldiers and their families. However, just because the war was won with relative ease, the peace may not be conquered so easily. Service personnel and their families spent significant periods of time apart, many service people saw horrible casualties inflicted on Iraqi soldiers and on Kuwaiti civilians, and fear of chemical warfare was significant. The rapidity of the news media brought the war into American homes. For many, the war was all but forgotten after the cease fire, but for service personnel who were in the Gulf and for their families, the conflict continued. Troops overseas continued to be at risk, financial problems and strains on relationships may have become worse, and the uncertainty of when reunions would actually occur weighed on those affected.

Stress Reactions

A number of common stress reactions were considered by the task force. Most are well known to psychologists, but deserve mention, especially as such lists can be helpful when therapists are communicating with allied professionals, support groups, the media, and other outreach targets.

Some of the expected reactions include (1) guilt about actions; (2) shame over some failure; (3) excessive drinking or drug use; (4) uncontrolled or frequent crying and other extreme reactions to stressful events that would normally be handled more calmly; (5) sleep problems (too much or too little); (6) depression, anxiety, and anger; (7) stress-related physical illness (e.g., headaches, gastrointestinal disorders, upper and lower back pain, poor stamina or resistance); (8) inability to forget scenes of horror from the war; (9) difficulty concentrating or excessive ruminating; (10) uncharacteristic social isolation; (11) blunting of emotions; and (12) suicidal thoughts and plans. In addition to these symptoms that are common for individuals, a number of characteristic symptoms of family stress should be watched: (1) family conflict that does not come to resolution, (2) any signs of verbal or physical violence, (3) family members isolating themselves from one another, (4) extreme dependency and clinging, (5) making one or two family members (often children) scapegoats for the family's difficulties, and (6) children's discipline or academic problems. Many of these symptoms are experienced in mild forms and should not cause much concern if they are not prolonged. Individuals and families may well experience some rough times, but most concerns and problems should be able to be resolved with family and other social support and the activation of personal resources. The problem becomes critical when symptoms are persistent or severe.

Some individuals react in a more severe fashion, but they may be only a small percentage of those who were involved in the conflict. If the stress has become traumatic and individuals develop full-blown PTSD, they are likely to continue to react to current stimuli that are reminiscent of the original trauma, with psychological and physiological reactions appropriate only to the traumatic event. If this occurs, they can be expected to have (1) nightmares, (2) intrusive daytime images and bodily sensations related to the traumatic experience, (3) excessive physiological startle, (4) extreme anxiety states alternating with numbing and anhedonia, (5) difficulty modulating arousal in general and anger in particular, and (6) dissociative reactions (American Psychiatric Association, 1987; van der Kolk, 1987).

In the case of PTSD, professional help is required. The best treatment for PTSD has not been established, but most clinicians agree that traumatized individuals need to put their experience into words and go over the details of the events, including their own actions, their fantasies, and what they think they could have done to alter the outcome of events. Some form of desensitization of the traumatic experience appears to be essential. Depending on the theoretical orientation of the clinician and the exigencies of the situation, assistance may range from classical desensitization and flooding procedures to a psychodynamic working through the events and their subjective meaning. Group psychotherapy with peers is generally considered to be very helpful in allowing people to reconnect emotionally with the actuality of the experience and receive support from people who have gone through the same or similar experiences. Hyperarousal and sleep disturbances in PTSD may in many instances be best treated with psychotropic medications, in addition to individual or group intervention (van der Kolk, 1987). Others have had success with mastery or efficacy enhancing intervention, such as teaching self-defense skills to women traumatized from rape or the threat of rape (Ozer and Bandura, 1990) or allowing soldiers with PTSD the opportunity to return to military boot camp or actual combat to prove to themselves (and perhaps others) that they can master military skills (Milgram and Hobfoll, 1986). These nontraditional treatments warrant further investigation and attention by clinicians.

Guidelines

The task force developed a number of guidelines for therapists to use with individuals at risk for war-related stress or stress after other traumatic events. These guidelines can be loosely divided into individual and social coping efforts. It is important to understand that the individual and social spheres interact. Social support is not just delivered to those in need but is based, in part, on both recipients' social skills and the social skills of their potential supporters (Hansson and others, 1984); how people perceive the social support they receive is also related to their own identity and their social view of themselves (Sarason, Sarason, and Pierce, 1990; Sarason and others, 1986). Similarly, individual coping efforts are aided or impeded by the social milieu. Caplan (1974) defined social support principally as aiding individuals' perceptions of their ability to master their environment. Social ties have also been shown to boost self-esteem and forestall the onset of depression during periods of chronic stress (Pearlin and others, 1981). How effectively social support is used is also moderated by the presence or absence of personal resources—strong personality resources activating and enhancing support and weak resources diminishing the positive effect of support (Hobfoll and Leiberman, 1987).

One of the most effective coping strategies involves breaking down major problems into more manageable subcomponents. Many of the problems that follow major stressful events are not only large but also complex (Folkman and others, 1991). A problem may concern a number of financial aspects, interpersonal difficulties with more than one other person, job problems, and leisure activities. It may affect both physiological and psychological health, involve drinking and over-eating, and produce short-term, mid-term, and long-term problems. Even the experienced therapist may feel overwhelmed when clients so distressed enter therapy, and certainly these problems are overwhelming for the individual suffering them. To the extent that those affected can be aided in the direction of (1) disentangling the intertwined aspects of the problem; (2) setting small, accomplishable tasks and goals; and (3) rewarding themselves for small wins, they usually function more effectively in their coping and experience more positive outcomes. Small wins also lead to a greater sense of mastery and control over the environment, which in turn helps individuals feel and become more effective (Bandura, 1982; Meichenbaum, 1985).

A second method of effective coping is becoming part of the solution to others' problems. By becoming involved in problem solving, individuals avoid the victim role and enter a mastery role. Becoming part of the solution can mean letter writing, helping others in need, and performing other volunteer tasks. Many support groups that need a helping hand, single parents and acting parents who could use a break and demobilized military personnel who need help locating jobs are just a few of the hundreds of other possible volunteer interventions. It is paradoxical that someone who needs help can be helped by aiding others, but many members of support groups find solace and a more positive sense of self when they see that they can be of assistance to others, even while in need themselves.

Early stress theory posited specific stages of coping, but coping is much more individualized in its paths. Emotion-focused coping may be very effective at first when one is combating severe stress events and when some denial can be very positive (Breznitz, 1983). Emotion-focused coping should, however, give way to problem-focused coping; if this is delayed too long, problems can amass and multiply until they are almost unmanageable. Emotion-focused coping can be seen as a means of pausing, taking a different perspective, and planning, and therapists can help people take a step back for this important stage of refueling and developing strategy. Then, individuals can reenter the fray with renewed strength, employing more direct action and problem-solving routines.

Emotion-focused coping may be beneficial in situations in which the individual can do nothing (Folkman, 1984). In these circumstances, the individual should be helped to accept the situation and cope with its aftermath through emotion-focused coping techniques such as cognitive restructuring, relaxation or meditation, appropriate social support, grief work, and diverting attention to other activities.

Children's Needs

The task force gave a great deal of attention to the special needs of children. Many of the principles already outlined are relevant to children (Milgram, 1989; Milgram and others, 1988), but children are not just small adults. A knowledge of developmental differences and the social world of children is important to successful prevention and early intervention work with children. Children are less likely than adults to speak directly about their problems or even to know they are having them. Their stress-related difficulties may instead emerge in their schoolwork, in their relations with peers, or in their interactions with family members. Children are also vulnerable because they have less experience in coping with stressful events. Lack of prior experience may lead them to exaggerate their problems and prevent them from seeing light at the end of the tunnel.

The specific coping patterns described earlier need to be adjusted for children at their age-appropriate level. The following suggestions specifically apply to children:

1. Parents and teachers should be encouraged to listen in a nonjudgmental fashion to children's thoughts, concerns, and ideas about the war and about reunion of the family.

2. Adults should provide warmth and reassurance to children without minimizing their concerns. Children need to feel that there is a safe haven provided by strong adults.

3. Adults should not impose their fears or burdens on children. Children should not be entirely sheltered from family difficulties, but they should not be made to feel that it is up to them to shoulder responsibilities that are beyond their developmental capability.

4. Most adults cope effectively, even if there are rough roads to travel in the process of adjustment. Children, too, need to be given this positive expectation. Because of their limited experience and the length of stressors like separation from parents, it is vital that children gain this perspective.

5. Children's reactions often mirror the reactions of their parents. If their parents are combating stressors effectively, the children gain a sense that they, too, can overcome their difficulties. If, however, their parents are not adjusting successfully, children develop a sense that problems are insurmountable, and they lose their key support link. It is critical that parents see that seeking help for themselves when it is needed is the best therapy for their troubled children.

6. Children need accurate information about what has happened and why, but that information should be appropriate to their developmental stage. This information should be provided before, during, and after stressful events. Children also need to know why certain behaviors are required of them and usually need behavioral examples and sometimes rehearsal of behaviors that are not in their repertoire. It should not be assumed that children do not know the "dark side" of current events. Given that they have seen horrible events on television or have overheard serious discussions, it is incumbent on us to help them work through the meaning and significance of these events through discussion, support, and—in cases in which a child is traumatized—professional treatment.

7. As with adults, children should be involved in helpful behaviors. By being part of the solution in their own classrooms, families, and communities, children develop an enhanced sense of mastery and control over their lives and cope more effectively with war and other severe stressful events.

The overall message must be conveyed to all that adjustment is not a short-term process and the commitment to these individuals cannot be short term. In the case of military personnel, some problems created or exacerbated during their absence may linger or become chronic. It would be expected that the period of crisis would be prolonged. Financial hardship, job problems, and conflict in families may emerge that have a long-term effect. Operation Rescue Hope, although not a war, involved the U.S. Marines leaving their families and going to Somalia. Their objective was to provide food and safety for the Somalis. Some of the same Marines were also in Operation Desert Shield. Once again they will miss holidays with their families and friends. What has been written previously about Operation Desert Shield is applicable for Operation Rescue Hope.

The Homeless

Studies conducted during the 1980s convincingly demonstrated that between one half and one third of the homeless suffer from psychiatric or substance abuse disorders (Breakey and others, 1989; Koegel, Burnham, and Farr, 1989; Rossi, 1989; Susser, Struening, and Conover, 1989; Tessler and Dennis, 1989) and suggested that the homeless mentally ill are clinically underserved and in desperate need of a wide range of health care and social services (Morse and Calsyn, 1985-1986; Mulkern and Bradley, 1986; Robertson and Cousineau, 1986; Roth and Bean, 1986; Wright and Weber, 1987). Many have argued that, because of their profound distrust and social alienation, specialized interventions are needed to engage the homeless mentally ill in treatment. Community outreach, to make contact with the homeless on their "home ground," and residential treatment have been specifically identified as critical services for programs seeking to reach this population (Farr, 1986; Morse and Calsyn, 1985-1986; Talbott and Lamb, 1984). In a study by Rosenheck and Gallup (1991), the top four groups of homeless were (1) those with drug problems, (2) those with psychiatric problems, (3) posthospitalization (psychiatric or substance abuse) patients, (4) adolescents. This study provided basic descriptive data on the operation of a national program for the homeless mentally ill. Also evident was an increase in the number of homeless men and families.

As the number of homeless individuals across the country has grown in recent years (U.S. Conference of Mayors, 1989; U.S. General Accounting Office, 1985, 1988), the presence of a significant subgroup of mentally ill individuals among them has been a source of both professional and lay concern. National Institute of Mental Health (NIMH) program announcements define the homeless mentally ill adult population as individuals aged 18 years or older who have long-term, severe mental illnesses and no fixed place of residence (or who are at imminent risk of becoming homeless). In this context, long-term, severe mental illness is defined as a severe and persistent mental or emotional disorder (e.g., schizophrenia, schizoaffective disorder, or mood disorders) that disrupts functional capacities for such primary aspects of daily life as self-care, household management, interpersonal relationships, and work or school.

Delineating the boundaries and size of the homeless mentally ill population, however, is no simple task. Operational definitions of homelessness vary tremendously from study to study, encompassing a range of variables including lack of shelter, income, social support, or affiliation with others. For many years, the estimates of the number of homeless persons in this nation have ranged from 250,000 to 350,000 on a given night (U.S. Department of Housing and Urban Development, 1984) to as many as 3 million over the course of a year (Hombs and Snyder, 1982). Two more recent studies have offered more reliable, although not definitive, estimates of the total homeless population. In 1988, the National Alliance to End Homelessness estimated that on any given night, the number of homeless individuals is 735,000. The Urban Institute concluded that the number of homeless in the United States is between 567,000 and 600,000 on a given night (Burt and Cohen, 1989).

Despite numerous methodological obstacles and challenges, a number of studies have attempted to discern the proportion of homeless people who have severe mental illnesses.

Historical Overview of NIMH Efforts

The NIMH has been the focal point within the federal government for efforts to understand the mental health dimensions of homelessness. The Institute's activities have been designed to develop knowledge about the characteristics and service needs of the homeless mentally ill population and to disseminate this knowledge to a broad audience of federal, state, and local policymakers, service providers, researchers, and private citizens (Sargent, 1989).

Some of the major findings that have emerged from the early NIMH research efforts include the following (Morrisey and Dennis, 1986; Tessler and Dennis, 1989):

1. Approximately one third of the homeless population have severe mental illnesses such as schizophrenia, schizoaffective disorders, and mood disorders.
2. The homeless mentally ill population is a multinational population; in some studies as many as 50% of homeless mentally ill individuals also have a current alcohol or other substance abuse problem.
3. A sizable number of homeless mentally ill people have had involvements with the criminal justice system; these arrests were often associated with such offenses as theft and loitering.
4. Many homeless mentally ill persons have never received mental health treatment, and many homeless mentally ill persons formerly in treatment are no longer disabled by mental illness.
5. A significant proportion of the population is interested in receiving help, but their perceptions of their own service needs often differ from the perceptions of service providers. Not surprisingly, homeless mentally ill persons tend to place a high priority on meeting their basic subsistence needs first, before addressing their mental health needs, whereas mental health professionals often place a higher priority on providing traditional mental health treatment.

One of the major conclusions that can be drawn from these findings is that a homeless mentally ill individual's housing, health, mental health, and other social welfare needs must be met.

One of the challenges of the future will be to use the information generated by research and evaluation to refine the system of generic mental health, housing, and human services to make it appropriate, acceptable, and accessible to the broad population of severely mentally ill individuals, both homeless and domiciled. These new federal initiatives ought to contribute to that effort.

Case Study   *PTSD: Homeless*

ASSESSMENT OF THE INDIVIDUAL

Todd came to the crisis center to ask for help. He was waiting in the reception area for the therapist, who went to get his chart before she saw him. She noted that he did not have a home address or telephone. He had written, in very neat handwriting, that he was hoping to get some help, but honestly didn't think he would.

The therapist looked into the reception area. Todd was the only person there. She observed a man in his early 40s, very clean, above average height, but below average in weight (approximately 20 pounds underweight). At his feet was a well-worn and very full backpack. He was clean-shaven; his hair was slightly longer than the current style.

The therapist went into the reception area, said, "You must be Todd," and held out her hand. Todd stood up, smiled slightly, and replied as they shook hands, "Yes, I am Todd." The therapist introduced herself and asked him to come to her office. He nodded, picked up his backpack, and followed.

In her office, Todd sat down and looked over at her coffee pot. She asked him if he would like a cup of coffee. Todd eagerly said, "Yes, please, with cream and two sugars." She poured the coffee and handed it to him with the cream and sugar. Todd said, "Thanks" as he put in cream and 3 teaspoons of sugar. He took a quick gulp, sighed, and relaxed in his chair.

He was asked, "Are you cold, Todd?" He looked at the therapist and answered, "Yes, cold and hungry. I qualify as one of your infamous 'homeless.' I never thought I would be homeless."

The therapist asked when he had last eaten. Todd said, "You mean like a 'normal' breakfast, lunch, or dinner?" The therapist nodded affirmatively. He was quiet for a minute or so and then said, "Probably when I left my family, my wife and two daughters, in Michigan when I came out here to find a job. That has to be at least 18 months. Eighteen months without a steady job. I have had a job for a day or two every so often here and there, but never enough to get a place to live, eat regularly, or send for my family."

The therapist asked Todd to excuse her for a few minutes. She took her wallet and left the office and gave one of the center's volunteers some money. She asked her if she would mind going to the nearest fast food restaurant and told her what she wanted her to bring back. The volunteer agreed. The therapist reminded her to bring the food to her office.

The therapist went back to her office, where Todd was waiting for her. She apologized for leaving and picked up Todd's chart to see if there was anything else she needed to know about him.

Todd had written that he had served in the army during the Vietnam War. When he returned to the States, he was hospitalized for 6 months for PTSD.

CASE STUDY: TODD

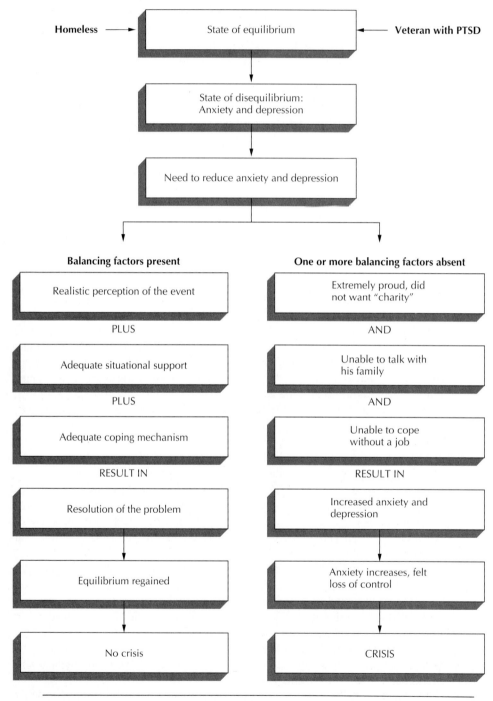

Figure 5-1

The therapist asked how he was feeling now. Todd said, "Not too bad. I occasionally will have a 'flashback' or have trouble sleeping and I don't like being in a place that I can't get out of. Otherwise, it doesn't bother me too much."

There was a knock at the door. The therapist got up and took the food from the volunteer and thanked her. She opened the bags of food and served the meal on the coffee tray. Todd looked amazed; the therapist said, "Eat up." Todd began to eat. He would stop ever so often to smile at the therapist and say thanks. He finished all the food, and he looked very content.

The therapist said to Todd, "You are a veteran who served your country in Vietnam; there must be something they can do for you. Todd said, "Maybe I didn't know where to check."

The therapist said, "Let me talk with someone at the VA." She called someone and told him about Todd's situation. She asked Todd if he would go to the VA for a while if someone picked him up. Todd said, "I don't want charity." The therapist said, "It is *not* charity. It is only what you deserve." Todd answered, "Okay, if I can leave if I want to." He was assured that he could. The therapist then handed the telephone to Todd and said, "Todd, meet Mr. Stone." They talked for 3 or 4 minutes when Todd said, "I'll wait for you here, Mr. Stone. Could you call my wife for me?"

Todd looked up at the therapist and said, "Now I can take a real shower and have a real dinner!" The therapist smiled and said, "Yes." They stood up, and Todd said, "I'll never be able to thank you for everything." He said, "Heck! Can I give you a hug?" The therapist laughed and said, "Yes, keep in touch, Todd." He smiled as he left the office, standing taller and looking much happier.

Because Todd was seen only once, the procedure of planning the intervention and intervention was not carried through. The paradigm has been completed for closure of the case (Figure 5-1).

REFERENCES

American Psychiatric Association: *Diagnostic and statistical manual of mental disorders,* ed 3, Washington, DC, 1980, The Association.

American Psychiatric Association: *Diagnostic criteria: DSM-III-R,* 1987, The Association.

Bandura A: Self-efficacy mechanism in human agency, *Am Psychol* 37:122, 1982.

Bartone PT and others: The impact of a military air disaster on the health of assistance workers: a prospective study, *J Nerv Ment Dis* 177:317, 1989.

Baum A, Gatchel RJ, Schaeffer MA: Emotional, behavioral, and physiological effects of chronic stress at Three Mile Island, *J Consult Clin Psychol* 51:565, 1983.

Breakey W and others: Health and mental health problems of homeless men and women in Baltimore, *JAMA* 262:1352, 1989.

Breslau N, Davis GC: Posttraumatic stress disorder: the stressor criterion, *J Nerv Ment Dis* 175:255, 1987a.

Breslau N, Davis GC: A reply from Naomi Breslau and Glenn C. Davis, *J Nerv Ment Dis* 175:276, 1987b.

Breznitz S: *The seven kinds of denial.* In Breznitz S, editor: *The denial of stress,* 1983, New York, International Universities Press.

Bromet EJ and others: Mental health of residents near the Three Mile Island reactor: a comparative study, *J Prevent Psychiatry* 1:225, 1982.

Burt MR, Cohen BE: *America's homeless: number, characteristics, and programs that serve them,* Washington, DC, 1989, Urban Institute Press.

Cannon WB: *The wisdom of the body,* New York, 1932, Norton.

Caplan G: *Support systems and community mental health: lectures in concept development,* New York, 1974, Behavioral Publications.

Cornely P, Bromet E: Prevalence of behavior problems in three year old children living near Three Mile Island: a comparative study, *J Child Psychol Psychiatry* 27:489, 1986.

Department of Veterans' Affairs, VA Persian Gulf Returnees Working Group (R Rosenheck, Chair): *War zone stress upon returning Persian Gulf troops: a preliminary report,* West Haven, Conn, 1991, Northeast Program Evaluation Center.

Dohrenwend BS, Dowrenwend BP, Socioenvironmental factors, stress, and psychopathology, *Am J Community Psychol* 9:128, 1981.

Dohrenwend BP, Shrout PE: "Hassles" in the conceptualization and measurement of life stress variables, *Am Psychol* 40:780, 1985.

Eitinger L: Jewish concentration camp survivors in Norway, *Israel Ann Psychiatry* 13:321, 1975.

Ellis EM and others: An assessment of short-term reaction to rape, *J Abnorm Psychol* 90:263, 1981.

Fairbank JA, McCaffrey RJ, Keane TM: Psychometric detection of fabricated symptoms of PTSD, *Am J Psychiatry* 142:501, 1985.

Farr RK: A mental health treatment program for the homeless mentally ill in the Los Angeles skid row area. In Jones BE, editor: *Treating the homeless; urban psychiatry's challenge,* Washington, DC, 1986, American Psychiatric Press.

Foa EB, Stekete G, Rothbaum BO: Behavioral/cognitive conceptualizations of post-traumatic stress disorder, *Behav Ther* 20:155, 1989.

Folkman JD: Personal control and stress and coping processes: a theoretical analysis, *J Pers Soc Psychol* 46:839, 1984.

Folkman S and others: *Translating coping theory into intervention,* New York, 1991, Plenum.

Foy DW and others: Etiology of post-traumatic stress disorder in Vietnam veterans: analysis of premilitary, and combat exposure influences, *J Consult Clin Psychol* 52:79, 1984.

Friedman MJ and others: Measurement of combat exposure, posttraumatic stress disorder, and life stress among Vietnam combat veterans, *Am J Psychiatry* 143:537, 1986.

Goldfeld AE and others: The physical and psychological effects of torture: symptomatology and diagnosis, *JAMA* 259:2725, 1988.

Green BL: Assessing levels of psychological impairment following disaster, *J Nerv Ment Dis* 170:552, 1982.

Green BL and others: Long-term coping with combat stress, *J Traum Stress* 1:399, 1988.

Green BL and others: Multiple diagnosis in post-traumatic stress disorder: the role of war stressors, J Nerv Ment Dis 177:329, 1989.

Green BL and others: Risk factors for PTSD and other diagnoses in a general sample of Vietnam veterans, *Am J Psychiatry* 147:729, 1990.

Grinker RR, Spiegel JP: *Men under stress,* New York, 1945, Blakiston.

Hamilton JD: Pseudo-posttraumatic stress disorder, *Milit Med* 150:353, 1985.

Hamilton JD, Canteen W: Posttraumatic stress disorder in World War II naval veterans, *Hosp Community Psychiatry* 38:197, 1985.

Hansson RO and others: Relationship competence and social support. In Shaver P, editor: *Review of personality and social psychology,* Beverly Hills, Calif, 1984, Sage.

Helzer JE, Robins LN, McEvoy L: Post-traumatic stress disorder in the general population: findings of the epidemiologic catchment area survey, *N Engl J Med* 317:1630, 1987.

Hobfoll SE: Conservation of resources: a new attempt at conceptualizing stress, *Am Psychol* 44:513, 1989.

Hobfoll SE, Leiberman Y: Personality and social resource in immediate and continued stress resistance among women, *J Pers Soc Psychol* 52:18, 1987.

Holloway HC, Ursano RJ: The Vietnam veteran: memory, social context, and metaphor, *Psychiatry* 47:103, 1984.

Holmes TH, Rahe RH: The social readjustment ratings scale, *J Psychosom Res* 11:213, 1967.

Hombs ME, Snyder M: *Homelessness in America: a forced march to nowhere,* Washington, DC, 1982, Community for Creative Nonviolence.

Horowitz MJ: *Stress response syndromes,* Northvale, NJ, 1986, Aronson.

Horowitz MJ, Wilner N, Alvarez W: Impact of events scale: a measure of subjective stress, *Psychosom Med* 41:209, 1979.

Jordan BK and others: Antisocial and related disorders in a southern community: an application of grade of membership analysis, *J Nerv Ment Dis* 177:529, 1989.

Kanner AD and others: Comparison of two modes of stress measurement: daily hassles and uplifts versus major life events, *J Behav Med* 4:1, 1981.

Kardiner A: Traumatic neuroses of war. In S. Arieti, editor: *American handbook of psychiatry,* New York, 1959, Basic Books.

Kasl SV, Chisholm RF, Eskenazi B: The impact of the accident at the Three Mile Island on the behavior and well-being of nuclear workers, *Am J Public Health* 71:472, 1981.

Keane TM: Post-traumatic stress disorder: current status and future directions, *Behav Ther* 20:149-153, 1989.

Keane TM, Penk WE: The prevalence of post-traumatic stress disorder, *N Engl J Med* 318:1690, 1988 (letter).

Kilpatrick DG, Resick PA, Veronen LJ: Effects of rape experience: a longitudinal study, *J Soc Iss* 37:105, 1981.

Kilpatrick DG and others: Victim and crime factors associated with the development of crime-related post-traumatic stress disorder, *Behav Ther* 20:199, 1989.

Kluznik JC and others: Forty-year follow-up of United States prisoners of war, *Am J Psychiatry* 143:1443, 1986.

Koegel P, Burnam A, Farr R: The prevalence of specific psychiatric disorders among homeless individuals in the inner-city of Los Angeles, *Arch Gen Psychiatry* 45:1085, 1989.

Kolb LC: A neuropsychological hypothesis explaining post traumatic stress disorder, *Am J Psychiatry* 144:989, 1987.

Kulka RA and others: *The national Vietnam veterans readjustment study: tables of findings and technical appendices,* New York, 1990, Brunner/Mazel.

Lazarus RS, DeLongis A: Psychological stress and coping in aging, *Am Psychol* 38:245, 1983.

Lazarus RS, Folkman S: *Stress, appraisal, and coping,* New York, 1984, Springer.

Lazarus RS, Folkman S, Gruen R: Stress and adaptational outcomes: the problem of confounded measures, *Am Psychol* 40:770, 1985.

Lynn JE, Belza M: Factitious posttraumatic stress disorder; the veteran who never got to Vietnam, *Hosp Community Psychiatry* 35:697, 1984.

McFarlane AC: The phenomenology of posttraumatic stress disorders following a natural disaster, *J Nerv Ment Dis* 176:22, 1988.

March JS: The nosology of posttraumatic stress disorder, *J Anxiety Dis* 4:61, 1990.

Matsakis A: *Vietnam wives,* Kensington, Md, 1988, Woodbine House.

Meichenbaum D: *Stress inoculation training,* New York, 1985, Pergamon Press.

Milgram NA: Social support versus self-sufficiency in traumatic and posttraumatic stress reactions. In Lerer B and Gershon S, editors: *New directions in affective disorders,* New York, 1989, Springer-Verlag.

Milgram NA, Hobfoll SE: Generalization from theory and practice in user-related stress. In Milgram NA, editor: *Stress and coping in time of war,* New York, 1986, Bruner/Mazel.

Milgram NA, Toubiana YH: Bias in identifying and treating high-risk client groups, *Prof Psychol Res Prac* 19:21, 1988.

Milgram NA and others: Situational exposure and personal loss in children's acute and chronic stress reactions to a school bus disaster, *J Traum Stress* 1:339, 1988.

Mineka S, Kihlstron JF: Unpredictable and uncontrollable events: a new perspective on experimental neurosis, *J Abnorm Psychol* 87:256, 1978.

Mollica RF, Wyshak G, LaVelle J: The psychological impact of war trauma and torture on Southeast Asian refugee survivors of mass violence and torture, *Am J Psychiatry* 144:1567, 1987.

Mollica RF and others: Assessing symptom change in Southeast Asian refugee survivors of mass violence and torture, *Am J Psychiatry* 147:83, 1990.

Morrisey JP, Dennis DL: *NIMH-funded research concerning homeless mentally ill persons: implications for public policy and practice,* Rockville, 1986, National Institutes of Health.

Morrisey JP, Dennis DL: *Homelessness and mental illness: toward the next generation of research studies. Proceedings of an NIMH-sponsored conference,* Rockville, Md, 1990, National Institutes of Health.

Morse G, Calsyn RJ: Mentally disturbed homeless people in St. Louis: needy, willing, but underserved, *Int J Ment Health* 14:74, 1985-1986.

Mulkern V, Bradley V: Service utilization and service preferences of homeless persons, *Psychosoc Rehab J* 10:23, 1986.

NIMH awards $3.1M to study homeless mentally ill, *Access,* September 1989.

Norris J, Feldman-Summers S: Factors related to the psychological impacts of rape on the victim, *J Abnorm Psychol* 90:562, 1981.

Ozer EM, Bandura A: Mechanism governing empowerment effects: a self-efficacy analysis, *J Pers Soc Psychol* 58:472, 1990.

Pearlin LI and others: The stress process, *J Health Soc Behav* 2:337, 1981.

Pitman RK, Altman B, Macklin ML: Prevalence of posttraumatic stress disorder in wounded Vietnam veterans, *Am J Psychiatry* 146:667, 1989.

Pitman RK and others: Psychophysiologic assessment of posttraumatic stress disorder imagery in Vietnam combat veterans, *Arch Gen Psychiatry* 44:970, 1989.

Rahe RH, Genender E: Adaptation to and recovery from captivity stress, *Milit Med* 148:577, 1983.

Robertson MJ, Cousineau MR: Health status and access to health services among urban homeless, *Am J Public Health* 76:561, 1986.

Rosenheck R, Gallup P: Involvement in an outreach and residential treatment program for homeless mentally ill veterans, *J Nerv Ment Dis* 179:750, 1991.

Rossi P: *Down and out in America. The causes of homelessness,* Chicago, 1989, University of Chicago Press.

Roth G, Bean GJ: New perspective on homelessness; findings from statewide epidemiological study, *Hosp Community Psychiatry* 37:712, 1986.

Rutter M: Meyerian psychobiology, personality development, and the role of life experiences, *Am J Psychiatry* 143:1077, 1986.

Saigh PA: The validity of the DSM-II posttraumatic stress disorder classification as applied to children, *J Abnorm Psychol* 98:189, 1989.

Sarason BR, Sarason IG, Pierce GR: *Social support: an interactional view,* New York, 1990, Wiley.

Sarason BR, and others: Interrelationships between social support measures: theoretical and practical implications, *J Person Soc Psychol* 52:813, 1986.

Sargent M: Update on progress for the homeless mentally ill, *Hosp Community Psychiatry* 40:1015, 1989.

Selye H: *The physiology and pathology of exposure to stress,* Montreal, 1950, Acta.

Shore JH, Tatum EL, Vollmenr WM: Psychiatric reaction to disaster; the Mt. St. Helens experience, *Am J Psychiatry* 140:590, 1986.

Sierles FS and others: Posttraumatic stress disorder and concurrent psychiatric illness: a preliminary report, *Am J Psychiatry* 140:1177, 1983.

Sierles FS and others: Concurrent psychiatric illness in non-hispanic outpatients diagnosed as having posttraumatic stress disorder, *J Nerv Mental Dis* 174:171, 1986.

Solomon A, Kotler M, Mikulincer M: Combat related posttraumatic stress disorder among second-generation Holocaust survivors; preliminary findings, *Am J Psychiatry* 145:865, 1988.

Staudenmayer H, Steiner J: Post-traumatic stress syndrome (PTSS), *Escape Environ* 43:156, 1987.

Stenger CA: *American prisoners of war in WW I, WW II, Korea and Vietnam: statistical data concerning number captured, repatriated and still alive as of January 1, 1991,* Washington, DC, 1991, American Ex-Prisoners of War.

Susser E, Struening E, Conover S: Psychiatric problems in homeless men, *Arch Gen Psychiatry* 46:845, 1989.

Sutker CA, Allain AN, Motsinger PA: Minnesota Multiphasic Personality Inventory (MMPI)−derived psychopathology prototypes among former prisoners of war (POWs); replication and extension, *J Psychopathol Behav Assess* 10:19, 1988.

Sutker PB, Allain AN: MMPI profiles of veterans of WWII and Korea; former POW and combat survivor comparisons, *Psychol Rep* 68:279, 1991.

Sutker PB, Allain AN, Winstead DK: Cognitive performance in former WWII and Korean-Conflict POWs, *VA Practitioner* 4:77, 1987.

Sutker PB, Bugg F, Allain AN: Psychometric prediction of PTSD among POW survivors, *Psychol Assess* 3:105, 1991.

Sutker PB and others: Trauma induced weight loss and cognitive deficits among former prisoners of war, *J Consult Clin Psychol* 58:323, 1990a.

Sutker PB and others: Assessment of long-term psychosocial sequelae among POW survivors of the Korean conflict. *J Pers Assess* 54:170. 1990b.

Sutker PB and others: Psychopathology subtypes and symptom correlates among former prisoners of war, *J Psychopathol Behav Assess* 8:89, 1986.

Sutker PB and others: Clinical and research assessment of posttraumatic stress disorder: a conceptual overview, *J Consult Clin Psychol* 3:520, 1991a.

Sutker PB and others: Cognitive deficits and psychopathology among former prisoners of war and combat veterans of the Korean conflict, *Am J Psychiatry* 148: 67, 1991b.

Talbott J, Lamb R: Summary and recommendations. In Lamb R, editor: *The homeless mentally ill,* Washington, DC, 1984, American Psychiatric Association.

Terr LC: Chowchilla revisited: the effects of psychic trauma four years after a school-bus kidnapping, *Am J Psychiatry* 140:1543, 1983.

Tessler R, Dennis D: *A synthesis of NIMH-funded research concerning persons who are homeless and mentally ill,* Rockville, Md, 1989, National Institute of Mental Health.

Thygesen P, Hermann K, Willanger R: Concentration camp survivors in Denmark: persecution, disease, disability, compensation, *Dan Med Bull* 17:65, 1970.

U.S. Conference of Mayors: *A status report on hunger and homelessness,* Washington, DC, 1989, U.S. Conference of Mayors.

U.S. Department of Housing and Urban Development: *A report to the Secretary on the homeless and emergency shelters,* Washington, DC, 1984, The Department.

U.S. General Accounting Office: *Homeless mentally ill: problems and options in estimating numbers and trends,* Washington, DC, 1988, The Department.

Ursano RJ: The Vietnam era prisoner of war: perceptively personality and the development of psychiatric illness, *Am J Psychiatry* 138:315, 1981.

Ursano RJ: Commentary: posttraumatic stress disorder; the stressor criterion, *J Nerv Ment Dis* 175:273, 1987.

van der Kolk BA: *Psychological trauma,* Washington, DC, 1987, American Psychiatric Press.

Veterans Administration: *Caring for the older veteran,* Washington, DC, 1984, US Government Printing Office.

Wright R, Weber E: *Health and homelessness,* Washington, DC, 1987, McGraw-Hill.

Zciss RA, Dickman HR: PTSD 40 years later: incidence and person-situation correlates in former POWs, *J Clin Psychol* 45:80, 1989.

ADDITIONAL READINGS

Aldwin C: The elders life stress inventory; egocentric and nonegocentric stress. In Stephens MAP and others, editors: *Stress and coping in later life families,* New York, 1990, Hemisphere.

Aldwin C, Stokols D: The effects of environmental change on individuals and older groups: some neglected issues in stress research, *J Environ Psychol* 8:57-75, 1988.

Aldwin CM and others: Does emotionality predict stress? Findings from the normative aging study, *J Pers Soc Psychol* 56:618-624, 1989.

Barrow SM and others: *Effectiveness of programs for the mentally ill homeless: final report,* New York, 1989, New York Psychiatric Institute.

Behar D: Flashbacks and posttraumatic stress symptoms in combat veterans, *Compr Psychiatry* 28:459-466, 1987.

Belcher JR, DiBlasio FA: AIDS risk among the homeless, *J Appl Soc Sci* 15:183-191, 1991.

Bradshaw SL, Ohlde CD, Horne JB: The love of war: Vietnam and the traumatized veteran, *Bull Menninger Clin* 55:96-103, 1991.

Brown GW, Harris T: *The social origins of depression; the study of psychiatric disorder in older women,* New York, 1978, Free Press.

Card JJ: *Lives after Vietnam; the personal impact of military service,* Lexington, Mass, 1983, Lexington Books.

Card JJ: Epidemiology of PTSD in a national cohort of Vietnam veterans, *J Clin Psychol* 43:6-17, 1987.

Carver CS, Scheier MF: A control theory model of normal behavior and implications for problems in self-management. In Kendall PC, editor: *Advances in cognitive behavioral research and therapy,* San Diego, 1983, Academic Press.

Centers for Disease Control Vietnam Experience Study: Health status of Vietnam veterans: psychosocial characteristics, *JAMA* 259:2701-2707, 1988.

Coyne JC: Toward an interactional description of depression, *Psychiatry* 39:28-40, 1976.

Davidson J, Smith R, Kudler H: Validity and reliability of the DSM-III-R criteria for posttraumatic stress disorder; experience with a structured interview, *J Nerv Ment Dis* 177:336-341, 1989.

Dennis DL: Research methodologies concerning homeless persons with serious mental illness and/or substance abuse disorders (summary). proceedings of a conference sponsored by the Alcohol, Drug Abuse, and Mental Health Administration, Rockville, Md, 1987.

Denny N, Robinowitz, RN, Penk W: Conducting applied research on Vietnam combat-related post-traumatic stress disorder, *J Clin Psychol* 43:56, 1987.

Dohrenwend BP, Levai I, Shrout P: Screening scales from the psychiatric epidemiology research interview. In Weisman MM, Dunkel-Schetter C, Skokan LA, editors: Determinants of social support provision in personal relationships, *J Soc Personal Rel* 7:437, 1990.

Engdahl BE and others: Comorbidity of psychiatric disorders and personality profiles of American World War II prisoners of war, *J Nerv Ment Dis* 179:181-187, 1991.

English A: Runaway and street youth at risk for HIV infection: legal and ethical issues in access to care. *J Adolesc Health* 12:504, 1991.

Escobar JI: Commentary: posttraumatic stress disorder and the perennial stress-diathesis controversy, *J Nerv Ment Dis* 175:265-266, 1987.

Fischer V and others: *Myths and realities: a study of attitudes toward Vietnam era veterans,* Washington, DC, 1980, US Government Printing Office.

Funari DJ, Piekarski AM, Sherwood RJ: Treatment outcomes of Vietnam veterans with posttraumatic stress disorder, *Psychol Rep* 658:571-578, 1991.

Gerardi RJ, Blanchard EB, Kolb LC: Ability of Vietnam veterans to dissimulate a psycho-physiological assessment for post-traumatic stress disorder, *Behav Ther* 20:229-243, 1989.

Goldberg J and others: A twin study of the effects of the Vietnam war on posttraumatic stress disorder, *JAMA* 263:1227-1232, 1990.

Goldfinger S, Chafetz L: Developing a better service delivery system for the homeless mentally ill. In Lamb R, editor: *The homeless mentally ill,* Washington, DC, 1984, American Psychiatric Association.

Goodwin DW, Guze SB: *Psychiatric diagnosis,* ed 4, New York, 1989, Oxford University Press.

Goulart M, Madover S: An AIDS prevention program for homeless youth. *J Adolesc Health* 12:573-575, 1991.

Green BL and others: Risk factors for PTSD and other diagnoses in a general sample of Vietnam veterans, *Am J Psychiatry* 147:729-733, 1990.

Helzer JE, Ronis LN, McEvoy L: Post-traumatic stress disorder in the general population; findings from the epidemiologic catchment area survey, *N Engl J Med* 317:1630-1634, 1987.

Hendon H: "PTSD and risk of suicide": reply, *Am J Psychiatry* 149:143, 1992.

Higgins SA: Post-traumatic stress disorder and its role in the defense of Vietnam veterans, *Law Psychol Rev* 15:259-276, 1991.

Hobfill SE and others: War-related stress: addressing the stress of war and other traumatic events, *Am Psychol* 46:848-855, 1991.

Institute of Medicine: *Homelessness, health, and human needs,* Washington, DC, 1988, National Academy Press.

Keane TM, Cadell JM, Taylor KL: Mississippi scale for combat-related posttraumatic stress disorder: three studies of reliability and validity, *J Consult Clin Psychol* 56:85-90, 1988.

Keane TM, Wolfe J, Taylor KL: Post-traumatic stress disorder: evidence for diagnostic validity and methods of psychological assessment, *J Clin Psychol* 43:32-43, 1987.

Kennedy MR: Homeless and runaway youth mental health issues: no access to the system, *J Adolesc Health* 12:576-579, 1991.

Koshes RJ: Psychiatric care of the homeless mentally ill: an opportunity for military psychiatry training. *Milit Med* 156:121-126, 1991.

Kruks G: Gay and lesbian homeless street youth: special issues and concerns. *J Adolesc Health* 12:515-518, 1991.

Kulka RA: Assessment of posttraumatic stress disorder in the community: prospects and pitfalls from recent studies of Vietnam veterans. Special section: issues and methods of assessment of posttraumatic stress disorder, *Psychol Assessment* 3:547, 1991.

Levine IS: Service programs for the homeless mentally ill. In Lamb HR, editor: *The homeless and mentally ill: a taskforce report of the American Psychiatric Association,* Washington, DC, 1984, American Psychiatric Association.

Levine IS, Lezak AD, Goldman HH: Community support systems for the homeless mentally ill. In Basasuk E, editor: *New directions for mental health services,* San Francisco, 1986, Jossey-Bass.

Lezak A: *Annotated bibliography of literature on homeless women who are mentally ill and/or have alcohol abuse problems,* Rockville, Md, 1988, National Institute of Mental Health.

Lipton FR, Nutt S, Sabatini A: Housing the homeless mentally ill: a longitudinal study of a treatment approach, *Hosp Community Psychiatry* 39:40-45, 1988.

Long L: *Consumer-run self-help programs serving people who are homeless and mentally ill,* vols 1, 2, and 3, Rockville, Md, 1988, National Institute of Mental Health.

Luna GC: Street youth: adaptation and survival in the AIDS decade, *J Adolesc Health* 12:511, 1991.

Martin M: *The implications of NIMH-supported research for homeless and mentally ill racial and ethnic minority persons,* Rockville, Md, 1987, National Institute of Mental Health.

Meyers and Ross, editors: *Community surveys of psychiatric disorder,* New Brunswick, NJ, 1986, Rutgers University Press.

Miller TW, Martin W, Jay LL: Clinical issues in readaptation for Persian Gulf veterans, *Psychiatr Ann* 21:684-688, 1991.

Morrisey JP and others: Organizational barrier to serving the mentally ill homeless. In Jones BE, editor: *Treating the homeless: urban psychiatry's challenge,* Washington, DC, 1986, American Psychiatric Press.

Parson ER: The psychology of the Persian Gulf war: I. Gulf-Nam and Saddam Hussein's Nebuchadnezzar imperial complex: a political psychological analysis, *J Contemp Psychother* 21:25-52, 1991.

Parson ER: The psychology of the Persian Gulf war: II. Congressional address on the issue of veterans' acquired competence gained through national defense experience: overcoming psychological implements to community incentives. Veterans Symposium of the 20th annual Congressional Black Caucus Foundation legislative weekend. Black veterans: from national defense to community development, *J Contemp Psychother* 21:125-134, 1991.

Penk W, Robinowitz R: Post-traumatic stress disorders (PTSD) among Vietnam veterans: introduction, *J Clin Psychol* 43:3-5, 1987.

Perconte ST, Griger ML: Comparison of successful, unsuccessful, and relapsed Vietnam veterans treated for posttraumatic stress disorder, *J Nerv Ment Dis* 179:558-562, 1991.

Pollock DA: PTSD and risk of suicide, *Am J Psychiatry* 149:142-143, 1992.

Pynoos RS and others: Life threat and posttraumatic stress in school-age children, *Arch Gen Psychiatry* 44:1057-1063, 1987.

Reuler JB: Outreach health services for street youth, *J Adolesc Health* 12:561, 1991.

Ridgely S, Goldman H, Talbot J: *Chronic mentally ill young adults with substance abuse problems: a review of the literature and creation of a research agenda,* Baltimore, 1986, University of Maryland School of Medicine.

Rog DJ: *Engaging homeless persons with mental illness into treatment,* Rockville, Md, 1988, National Institute of Mental Health.

Rosenheck R, Gallup P: Involvement in an outreach and residential treatment program for homeless mentally ill veterans, *J Nerv Ment Dis* 179:750, 1991.

Royzynko V, Dondershine HE: Trauma focus group therapy for Vietnam veterans with PTSD, *Psychotherapy* 28:157-161, 1991.

Schonpflug W: Goal directed behavior as a source of stress: psychological origins and consequences of inefficiency. In Frese M, and Sabini J, editors: *The concept of action in psychology*, Hillsdale, NJ, 1985, Erlbaum.

Schram DD, Giovengo MA: Evaluation of threshold: an independent living program for homeless adolescent, *J Adolesc Health* 12:567-572, 1991.

Smart DH: Homeless youth in Seattle: planning and policy-making at the local government level, *J Adolesc Health* 12:519-527, 1991.

Snow BR and others: Post-traumatic stress disorder among American legionnaires in relation to combat experience in Vietnam: associated and contributing factors, *Environ Res* 47:175-192, 1988.

Solomon P: Services to severely mentally disabled homeless persons and to emergency food and shelter providers, *Psychosoc Rehab J* 12:3, 1988.

Sosin MR, Grossman S: The mental health system and the etiology of homelessness: a comparison study, *J Community Psychiatry* 19:337-350, 1991.

Spitzer R, Williams J, Gibbon M: *Structured clinical interview for DSM-III-R, version NP-V*, New York, 1987, New York State Psychiatric Institute, Biometrics Research Department.

Stroup NE, Morris RD: Post-traumatic stress disorder in Vietnam veterans, *DIS Newsletter* 6:5, 1989.

Toff GE, Van Tosh L, Harp H: Self-help programs serving people who are homeless and mentally ill. In: *Proceedings of the fourth Knowledge Development Meeting on issues affecting homeless mentally ill people*, Washington, DC, 1988, George Washington University, Intergovernmental Health Policy Project.

Turnbill JE and others: Who should ask? Ethical interviewing in psychiatric epidemiology studies, *Am J Orthopsychiatry* 38:228, 1988.

Turner JC, Shifren I: Community support systems: how comprehensive? In Lamb HR, editor: *New directions for mental health*, vol 2, San Francisco, 1979, Jossey-Bass.

van der Kolk B and others: Inescapable shock, neurotransmitters, and addiction to trauma: toward a psychobiology of post traumatic stress, *Biol Psychiatry* 20:314-325, 1985.

Vernex G and others: *Review of California's program for the homeless mentally ill*, Santa Monica, Calif, 1988, Rand.

Veterans' Health Care Amendments for 1983, Section 102.(a)(1), 38 U.S.C., 1983.

Welch WM, Toff GE: *Service needs of minority persons who are homeless and homeless mentally ill*, Washington, DC, 1987, George Washington University, Intergovernmental Health Policy Project.

Wexler HK, McGrath E: Family member stress reactions to military involvement separation, *Psychotherapy* 28:515-519, 1991.

Wurzbacher KV, Evans ED, Moore EJ: Effects of alternative street school on youth involved in prostitution: *J Adolesc Health* 12:549-554, 1991.

Yates GL and others: The Los Angeles system of care for runaway/homeless youth, *J Adolesc Health* 12:550-560, 1991.

Chapter 6

Situational Crises

Whenever stressful events threaten a person's sense of biological, psychological, or social integrity, some degree of disequilibrium results, along with the concurrent possibility of a crisis. Several determining factors affect the positive balance of equilibrium, and the absence of one or more could make a state of crisis more imminent.

According to Rapoport (1962), when an instinctual need or a sense of integrity is threatened, the ego usually responds characteristically with anxiety; when loss or deprivation occurs, the response is usually depression. By contrast, if the threat or loss is viewed as a challenge, there is more likely to be a mobilization of energy toward purposeful, problem-solving activities.

Circumstances that may create only a feeling of mild concern in one person may create a high level of anxiety and tension in another. Recognized factors influencing a return to a balance of equilibrium are the perception of the event, available coping mechanisms, and available situational supports. Crises may be avoided if these factors are operating at the time a stressful event is intruding into the individual's life-style.

Studies of behavior patterns that might be anticipated in response to common stressful situations have provided valuable clues to anticipatory planning for prevention as well as intervention in crisis situations. These studies include analyses of relocation through urban renewal (Brown, Burditt, and Lidell, 1965), rehabilitation of families after tornado disasters (Moore, 1958), hospitalization of children and adolescents (Vernick, 1963), crises of unwed mothers (Bernstein, 1960), separation anxiety of hospitalized children (Bowlby, 1960), and death and dying (Kübler-Ross, 1969, 1974). The results suggest that there are certain patterned phases of reactions to unique stressful situations through which select groups of people can be expected to pass before equilibrium is restored. Preventive techniques of community psychiatry focus on anticipatory intervention to prevent crises that could result from maladaptive responses as individuals attempt to return to equilibrium.

In this chapter, stressful events that could precipitate a crisis have been selected on the premise that each could affect some member of a family, regardless of its socioeconomic or sociocultural status. The case studies selected are not to be considered all-inclusive of the many situational crises with which a therapist may come in contact.

Any situation may be stressful for one person but create no stress for another person. Response is very individual, and this individuality must always be accepted, not negated. A person may encounter an event that leaves him unable to problem solve. To us, as therapists, the event may seem unimportant. It is *not* our role to judge what is or is not a crisis-precipitating event to the individual who seeks help.

It is also important to recognize that the theoretical material preceding each case study is presented as an overview, relevant to the crisis situation. Therapists already trained in crisis intervention will recognize the need for much greater depth of theoretical knowledge than is presented in this chapter. The intent is only to provide guidelines; further study of problem areas is suggested for more comprehensive knowledge.

In order to clarify the steps in crisis intervention, much extraneous case study material has been eliminated. In crisis a person may be confronted with many stressful events occurring almost simultaneously. He may have no conscious awareness of *what* occurred, let alone which event requires priority in problem solving. The studies may appear oversimplified to anyone who has struggled through the phases of defining the problem and planning appropriate intervention.

The paradigm is a means devised to keep the reader focused on the problem area and on the balancing factors that influence the presence or absence of crisis. It is doubtful that it could be successfully used as a form that could be quickly completed after the initial assessment interview; rarely are stressful events so easily defined. It is the very nature of a crisis that interrelated internal and external stresses compound the problem area and distort the causes of objective and subjective symptoms.

One responsibility essential in assuming the role of a therapist in this method of intervention is recognition of the need for knowledge of the generic development of crises.

Premature Birth—Theoretical Concepts

The birth of a premature baby is a stressful situation for any family. Even when anticipated, there is a sense of emergency both at home and in the hospital when labor begins. In the hospital, both staff and parents feel anxiety for the potential welfare of the newborn infant.

Researchers have identified the following four phases or tasks the mother must work through if she is to come out of the experience in a healthy way (Mason, 1963; Kaplan and Mason, 1965).

1. She must realize that she may lose the baby. This anticipatory grief involves a gradual withdrawal from the relationship already established with the child during pregnancy.
2. She must acknowledge failure in her maternal function to deliver a full-term baby.
3. After separation from the infant as a result of his prolonged hospital stay, she must resume her relationship with him in preparation for the infant's homecoming.
4. She must prepare herself for the job of caring for the baby through an understanding of his special needs and growth patterns.

After delivery, the infant is hurriedly taken to the premature nursery. The parents have barely had a glimpse of their new child and certainly have had no opportunity to reassure themselves about his condition. The infant is isolated from all except the medical personnel during his hospital stay, and the parents, with only limited physical contact with the child, cannot allay their anxieties. There is a realistic danger that the baby will not live or that he will not be normal. Often physicians and nurses talk about the baby in guarded terms, not wanting to give false reassurance, so that the feeling of anxiety may last for days or weeks.

The way in which the family members react to this period of stress is crucial in determining whether a crisis will develop. Studies of families who have experienced the stress of a premature birth show that some have managed very well; the mother was not apprehensive about caring for the baby, despite the special attention he required. In these families, the relationship between husband and wife was found to be good; they seemingly had adjusted to the new member of the family, and their relationship was not threatened by the increased responsibility.

Other families studied appeared to be in a state of crisis, although the premature infant was out of danger. In those cases, the relationship between the husband and wife was determined to be unstable. The baby was cared for by an overly apprehensive mother who often seemed unconcerned about important things such as the baby's weight gain, whether he was eating adequately, and the immediate prognosis.

It has been hypothesized that women who were most disturbed during the period when there was real danger to the baby dealt with this stress more effectively (Caplan, 1964). Women who showed symptoms of a crisis were those who seemingly denied the existence of any danger. They did not question the information given them or the reassurances of the treating personnel. In fact, they seemed to encourage a conspiracy of silence, avoiding any confrontations with feelings of fear, guilt, and anxiety.

Many emotions develop in parents when a new baby arrives, even when the child is full term. The mother is called on to meet additional demands on her time and may feel hostility toward the new baby. Usually, however, the strong feeling of a mother's love ensures repression of any resentment she may feel and the guilt it inspires. The usual activities of the father are not as directly interrupted, so that his resentment is usually less than that of the mother and is more often aroused by jealousy of the attention that the mother gives to the baby.

The following case study concerns a young mother of a premature baby. Clues from the initial assessment interview indicated that she was acknowledging herself to be a failure for not delivering a full-term baby. Intervention focused on relieving the immediate causes of her anxiety and depression and assisting her to adapt to subsequent phases in the characteristic responses to a premature birth.

Case Study   Premature birth

ASSESSMENT OF THE INDIVIDUAL AND THE PROBLEM

Laura and Peter G. were a young couple who had been married for 3 years. Peter, 5 years older than Laura, was the oldest of four children. Laura, a petite young woman, was an only child. They had a 2-year-old daughter and a 2-month-old son who was born prematurely.

Peter's company had transferred him to another city when Laura was 7½ months pregnant; she went into labor the day after moving into their new home 100 miles from their hometown, where both of their families lived. She delivered their son in a private hospital with excellent facilities but under the care of an obstetrician previously unknown to her as a result of their recent move. She was upset by the strangeness of the hospital, by the new physicians, and by the precarious physical condition of the son she and Peter had been hoping for. Laura did not want to discuss fears with her physician because she did not know him, or with the nurses, because they "always seemed so busy." She also thought that because she had had a baby before, she should know the answers to all the questions she had in mind.

After she and Peter brought their son home from the hospital, Laura had episodes of crying and symptoms of anxiety, including insomnia. She felt physically exhausted and increasingly fearful concerning her ability to care for her son. No matter what she did, the baby slept for only short periods and was more fretful when awake than their daughter had been. Because of the baby's small size, Peter was afraid to help with his care, so Laura was responsible for all his physical care.

Peter's mother arrived for a visit "to see how the new baby was doing." She had been critical of Laura's intention to move at the time of Peter's transfer, advising Laura to wait until after the baby's birth. Laura had now begun to think that she should have followed that advice. Her mother-in-law and she often had talks about the rearing of children. Laura had begun to have confidence in her own mothering abilities as a result of her daughter's good health and average development, but now she was doubtful again because of her apparent inability to care for her new son.

The event that precipitated the crisis was the visit of the mother-in-law, who was critical of Laura's ability to care for her new baby. "I can't understand why the baby cries so much. You must be doing something wrong. My children always slept through the night by 2 months of age and took long naps during the day," was typical of her constant comments. Peter seemed reluctant to take sides against his mother, so Laura received little support from him in dealing with these criticisms. She was finally unable to cope with her feelings of inadequacy, which were intensified by her mother-in-law's visit, and as a result became extremely upset, cried uncontrollably, and was unable to care for the baby at all. Peter's employer commented to him that he seemed upset and asked if there was anything wrong at work. Peter told him that the problem was not his job but Laura's behavior since the birth of the baby. His employer recommended that they seek help at a nearby crisis center.

The goal of intervention determined by the therapist at the crisis center was to assist both Laura and Peter in exploring their feelings about the premature birth of their son, their changed communication pattern, and the lack of support Peter was giving Laura.

INTERVENTION

During the first few weeks, Laura was able to discuss her feelings of inadequacy in the mothering role and to tell Peter of her anxieties about their son, of her fears that he would be abnormal, and of her belief that the premature birth was her fault because she had insisted on moving with Peter at the time of his transfer. Peter, in turn, could tell Laura of his feelings of guilt of not being able to help more during the move and also of the blame he placed on himself because the labor was premature. The therapist assisted them in seeing the reality of the situation. Although the move may have been a factor in the premature onset of labor, there could have been other causes.

Peter discussed his insecurities about the handling of such a small baby; Laura was then able to tell him that she felt the same way, and she feared she might be doing something wrong with this baby. The therapist gave them information about the differences in the behavior of a normal child and the care required for a premature infant. She reassured Laura that she was doing well and that in time the baby would adjust to more regular hours. She encouraged Peter to help his wife so she could get more rest; in turn, Laura helped Peter gain confidence in holding and caring for their new son.

ANTICIPATORY PLANNING

As Peter became comfortable in caring for the baby, he was encouraged to share the responsibility of caring for him in the evenings. This enabled Laura to get more physical rest. Peter's emotional support helped her to relax, and she began to sleep better.

The therapist discussed their need to continue to improve communications between them. It was stressed that they must reestablish a pattern of social activities with each other. They were assured that their new son could survive for a few hours with a competent babysitter while they were out to dinner or to play cards with other couples.

Most of the energies and concerns during the past 2 months had been concentrated on their son. It was recommended that they also devote some additional time to their 2-year-old daughter. This was a stressful time for her too! Because her mother and father could not give her their sole attention, she would be competing for time with her new brother, and feelings of sibling rivalry would emerge. She would need to feel that her position in the family was also unique and important—that is, a daughter and their firstborn. Time should be planned for her to have some activities with her parents. This would emphasize that she was "old" enough to be included in their activities.

Recent studies have strongly suggested that, if pregnancies are planned, the ideal length of time between pregnancies is 5 to 6 years. This period of time gives the parents time to adjust to the first child without taking time away from him to care for a second child. The first child is then assured that he is the "one and only child" and greatly diminishes the feelings of sibling rivalry. The first child is beginning school, and the second child is able to share the time and attention of the parents more fully (Aguilera, 1993). In this case, Laura and Peter were warned to expect some acting-out behavior and possibly some regressive behavior in their daughter's bids for "equal" attention.

During their last visit, Laura and Peter were assured that they could return to the center if they felt the need for help with a problem.

SUMMATION OF THE PARADIGM (Figure 6-1)

This case study concerned a young woman unable to cope with problems of an unexpectedly premature baby. Assessment of the stressful events precipitating the

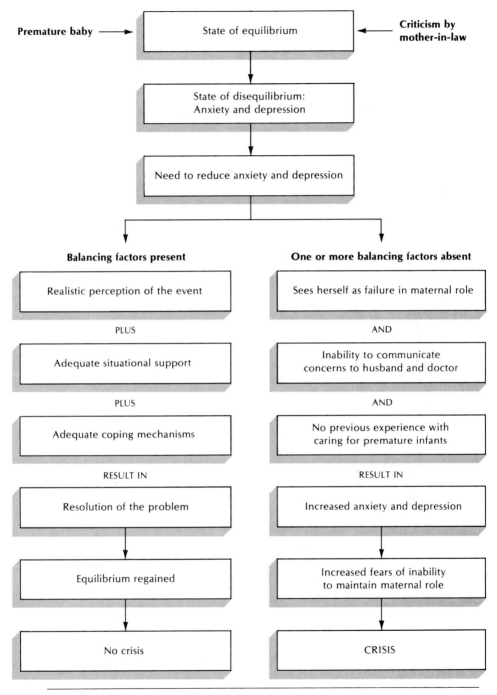

CASE STUDY: LAURA

Premature baby → State of equilibrium ← **Criticism by mother-in-law**

State of disequilibrium: Anxiety and depression

Need to reduce anxiety and depression

Balancing factors present

Realistic perception of the event

PLUS

Adequate situational support

PLUS

Adequate coping mechanisms

RESULT IN

Resolution of the problem

Equilibrium regained

No crisis

One or more balancing factors absent

Sees herself as failure in maternal role

AND

Inability to communicate concerns to husband and doctor

AND

No previous experience with caring for premature infants

RESULT IN

Increased anxiety and depression

Increased fears of inability to maintain maternal role

CRISIS

Figure 6-1

crisis indicated that Laura regarded herself as a failure for not delivering a full-term baby. This view was reinforced by the criticisms of her mother-in-law and the lack of situational support from her husband. In the assessment phase, the therapist maintained focus on the immediate area of stress that could have precipitated the crisis. After determining a possible cause-effect relationship, a goal for intervention was established. Laura was encouraged to ventilate her feelings of guilt and inadequacy in the present situation. Realistic perception of the event developed as the therapist provided information leading to an intellectual understanding of the relationship between the event and the resulting symptoms of stress. The husband was brought in as a situational support, and new as well as previously successful coping skills were used in resolving the crisis.

Child Abuse—Theoretical Concepts

According to the data available from the National Center of Child Abuse and Neglect (1992), 2,694,000 children are abused or neglected annually. In 1986 the rate was 16.3 per 1000 American children under the age of 18 years; in 1992 the total was 42—more than double. Whether this reflects an increase in the actual occurrence of child maltreatment or simply an increase in the ability of professionals to recognize countable cases is debatable. However, the research indicates that it seems reasonable to assume that, since 1980, professionals have become better attuned to the cues of maltreatment (National Committee for Prevention of Child Abuse, 1992).

The research also found that females experienced more abuse overall than did males; for every 1000 children, 13.1 females versus 8.4 males were countable as abused. The rate of female sexual abuse was nearly four times that for males; 1.1 males but 3.9 females per 1000 children were sexually abused. Research also found physical abuse to be associated with age; children 2 years of age and younger were less frequently physically abused than all other age groups, and 3-to 5-year-olds were abused less frequently than children 12 years of age and older (U.S. Department of Health and Human Services, 1991).

The following major categories of mistreatment of children were represented in these data: (1) physical abuse, (2) sexual abuse, (3) emotional abuse, (4) physical neglect, (5) emotional neglect, and (6) educational neglect. It was also found that 74% of child abuse fatalities occurred in preschool children up to the age of 5 years (U.S. Department of Health and Human Services, 1991).

Child abuse occurs in a wide variety of ways. Recent trends have moved toward greatly expanding its definition from physical abuse alone to include also emotional and sexual abuse, as well as physical and emotional neglect. In general, however, consensus is lacking among professionals for any one single definition of the terms *child abuse* or *child neglect*. Definitions vary greatly because there is much diversity in sociocultural values and practices associated with childrearing, some of which may result in physical and psychological harm to the child.

People who abuse children are not limited to any one well-defined group. They can be found among widely differing socioeconomic, racial, cultural, age, and other socially defined groups. Specific differences, however, have been identified among factors related to specific forms of abuse. For example, the physical size, strength, and power of the abuser obviously do not play as great a role in child abuse as in the abuse of adults. Obviously, few are as physically powerless as the infant or small child.

Abuse and neglect of children have been recorded throughout the centuries. It has been suggested that these are by no means new problems, but rather ones that only now are being socially recognized and legally addressed. Not until 1871 was the first child protective agency, The Society for the Prevention of Cruelty to Children, was established in New York. Nearly a century passed before all 50 states finally enacted legal mandates to report child abuse in 1968.

In 1962, Kempe originated the phrase *battered child syndrome*, which dramatically focused professional and public attention on the abusive actions by parents and other adults on select groups of children (Kempe, 1962). The phrase provided a base for the specific labeling and identification of the severest forms of child abuse, for which there is clinically verifiable evidence. Clinical signs include bruises, abrasions, lacerations, broken bones, burns, abdominal and chest injuries, and eye damage. Frequently, examination of new injuries yields clinical evidence of past injuries. Some children experience a single, violent abusive event, others a long series of violent episodes. This label was later superseded by the more comprehensive term *child abuse and neglect* (Helfer and Kempe, 1976).

The federal Child Abuse Prevention and Treatment Act was most recently reauthorized and otherwise amended by the Child Abuse, Domestic Violence, Adoption, and Family Services Act of 1992, (Public Law 102-255, 6/18/92). In it "the term *child abuse and neglect* means the physical or mental injury, sexual abuse or exploitation, negligent treatment, or maltreatment of a child by a person who is responsible for the child's welfare, under circumstances that indicate that the child's health or welfare is harmed or threatened thereby," as determined in accordance with regulations prescribed by the Secretary:

1. The term "person who is responsible for the child's welfare" includes:
   (a) any employee of a residential facility; and
   (b) any staff person providing out-of-home care;
2. The term "Secretary" means the Secretary of Health and Human Services
3. The term "sexual abuse" includes:
   (a) the employment, use, persuasion, inducement, enticement, or coercion of any child to engage in, or assist any other person to engage in, any sexually explicit conduct or simulation of such conduct, or
   (b) the rape, molestation, prostitution, or other form of sexual exploitation of children, or incest with children.
4. The term "State" means each of the several states, the District of Columbia, the Commonwealth of Puerto Rico, the Virgin Islands, Guam, American Samoa, the Commonwealth of the Northern Mariana Islands, and the Trust Territory of the Pacific Islands.
5. The term "task force" means the Inter-Agency Task Force on Child Abuse and Neglect established under section 103.
6. The term "withholding of medically indicated treatment" means the failure to respond to the infant's life-threatening conditions by providing treatment (including appropriate nutrition, hydration, and medication), which, in the treating

sician's or physicians' reasonable medical judgment, will be most likely to
effective in ameliorating or correcting all such conditions, except that the
_ does not include the failure to provide treatment (other than appropriate
nutrition, hydration, or medication) to an infant when, in the treating physician's
or physicians' reasonable medical judgment:
(a) the infant is chronically and irreversibly comatose;
(b) the provision of such treatment would
    (i) merely prolong dying;
    (ii) not be effective in ameliorating or correcting all of the infant's life-
         threatening conditions; or
    (iii) otherwise be futile in terms of the survival of the infant; or
(c) the provision of such treatment would be virtually futile in terms of the
    survival of the infant and the treatment itself under such circumstances would
    be inhumane.

Although the battered child syndrome may be among the easiest forms of child
abuse to prove legally, it has been found to be only a part of the overall problem
of abuse of children.

Incidence reports on incest and sexual exploitation of children are admittedly
incomplete and, at the most, educated estimates. Case finding is quite difficult,
most often coming to the attention of health care agencies when the child is seen
for other health care problems such as venereal disease or pregnancy. According
to Justice and Justice (1979), sexual abuse, like child abuse, most often involves
more than just the victim and the abuser. It also involves another family member
or responsible adults who allow the victimization to continue.

In general, incestuous offenders do not exhibit any overtly psychotic or deviant
behaviors (Giarretto, 1976). Generally the perpetrator is between 30 and 50 years
old, male, and, more than 75% of the time, the victim's father. Reported female
victims outnumber male victims by a wide margin. Investigations of adults who
were abused as children reveal that 20% of girls and 10% of boys had experienced
some type of sexual molestation, abuse, or exploitation (Rubinelli, 1980; Salholz
and others, 1982).

People who sexually exploit children are usually men who are emotionally dependent with feelings of inferiority and whose lives have been dominated by a
significant woman. A significantly high correlation between sexual abusers and a
history of parental abuse in childhood has also been found. The abused child
frequently knows the abuser and may become involved solely to meet nonsexual
needs for attention and affection. Children are particularly vulnerable because of
ignorance, fear of losing the caring relationship, or ambivalence, shame, guilt, and
the fear of not being believed as the "innocent" victim. All these factors contribute
to an ongoing conspiracy of silence on the part of the child.

Documentation of the psychological and sociological damage resulting from
abusive childrearing patterns has been increasing. This damage, in turn, may lead
to intergenerational patterns of abnormal parenting and increased numbers of violent
crimes perpetrated by those with histories of child abuse. Violence as the norm is
an expectation passed on from victims to the next generation (Silver, 1968; Gelles,
1972).

Other findings suggest that parents most likely to injure a small child are those who themselves were severely punished as children (Kempe and Helfer, 1972).

Three factors intrinsic to child abuse have been identified by the National Center for Child Abuse and Neglect (U.S. Department of Health and Human Services, 1991):

1. A capacity for abuse exists within the parent.
2. One child is perceived as special in some manner by the parents.
3. One or more crisis events occur before the abusive act is committed.

It is of great importance to recognize that what may appear to an observer as intentional abuse may be perceived by the victim merely as a normal way of life. Perhaps the only attention that some children can obtain from a parent or other significant person in their lives is abusive. To a child, love may be inextricably linked with violence. Unfortunately, those with whom they are closest also hold the power to punish, either physically or psychologically (Bandura, 1973). See box on p. 94 for indicators of a child's potential need for protection.

Several theories have attempted to explain why some parents abuse their children. Individually, none provides a comprehensive explanation for child abuse, yet each has contributed significantly to the overall base of information needed to explain this multidimensional problem. A broad scope of causal factors, none of which operates in isolation, is becoming increasingly evident. Each theoretical model proposes causal relationships to common problem areas. Collectively, this rapidly expanding base of knowledge supports the need for a holistic approach to intervention.

Several efforts have been made to categorize the personality traits and characteristics of child abusers in an effort to help explain their behaviors. A major problem has been that, for the most part, data for these studies have been empirical and drawn from clinical practice with identified child abusers. As such, they fail to explain why other persons with similar personality characteristics and traits and under similar circumstances do not abuse their children.

Personality or character traits that have been suggested as likely to lead to abusive behavior by parents include emotional immaturity, inability to cope with stress, chronic suspicion and hostility, and poor impulse control. Any of these could precipitate rage reactions in the parent who is confronted with frustration or undue stress. When parents with a requisite psychological profile come into confrontation with the demands of a child, an inner-directed rage reaction may be precipitated. As anger and frustration build, such parents suddenly erupt, striking out physically or psychologically at the most vulnerable person within their environment, the child (Halper, 1979; Walker-Hooper, 1981).

It is not uncommon to find the family scapegoat as the recipient of such parental acting out behavior. *Scapegoating* is an excellent example of psychological abuse. In order to survive as a unit, some families allocate the role of scapegoat to one member. Most frequently, the most vulnerable person is a child because a child is dependent and unable to retaliate against the parent's power (Vogel and Bell, 1960).

Based on the mechanisms of projection and displacement, scapegoating is often used to divert conflicts between parents. Undesirable traits or feelings are displaced or projected from the parent to the child when tensions become unbearable and parents lack the ability to discuss openly their reactions to stressful situations.

INDICATORS OF A CHILD'S POTENTIAL NEED FOR PROTECTION

Physical abuse

Physical indicators

Unexplained bruises (in various stages of healing); welts; human bite marks; bald spots; unexplained burns, especially cigarette burns or immersion burns (glovelike); unexplained fractures, lacerations, or abrasions

Behavioral indicators

Self-destructive, withdrawn, and aggressive; behavioral extremes; uncomfortable with physical contact, arrives at school early or stays late, as if afraid to be at home; chronic runaway (adolescents); complains of soreness or moves uncomfortably; wears clothing inappropriate to weather to hide body

Physical neglect

Abandonment, unattended medical needs, consistent lack of supervision, consistent hunger, inappropriate dress, poor hygiene, lice, distended stomach, emaciated, regularly displays fatigue or listlessness, falls asleep in class, steals food, begs from classmates, reports that no caretaker is at home, frequently absent or tardy, self destructive or school dropout (adolescents)

Sexual Abuse

Torn, stained, or bloody underclothing; pain or itching in genital area; difficulty walking or sitting; bruises or bleeding in external genitalia; venereal disease; frequent urinary or yeast infections; withdrawal; chronic depression; excessive seductiveness; role reversal; overly concerned for siblings; poor self-esteem, self-devaluation, and lack of confidence; peer problems; lack of involvement; massive weight change; suicide attempts (especially adolescents); hysteria; lack of emotional control; sudden school difficulties; inappropriate sex play or premature understanding of sex; threatened by physical contact or closeness; promiscuity.

Emotional Maltreatment

Speech disorders, delayed physical development, substance abuse, ulcers, asthma, severe allergies, habit disorders (sucking, rocking), antisocial, destructive, neurotic traits (sleep disorders, inhibition of play), passive and aggressive behavioral extremes, delinquent behavior (especially adolescents) or developmentally delayed.

If a child is used to maintain stable relationships between parents, that child becomes the target for blame and is scapegoated for any threats to marital stability. The scapegoat is usually seen as someone who is different or disappointing in some way (Friedrich and Boriskin, 1976).

The abusive-dynamic model constructed by Kempe and Helfer (1972) is based on the presence and interaction of multiple dynamics. Kempe postulates that there are seven dynamics that interact and affect the parent's perception of the child: mothering imprint, isolation, self-esteem, role reversal, spouse support, perception of the child, and crisis events.

Psychoanalytic theory stresses the vital importance of emotional bonding between the mother figure and the infant during the oral stage of the child's psychosocial development. This provides the child with a healthy base for the future capacity to trust and enter into positive relationships with others.

Mothering imprint is the capacity to nurture and is learned only through one's own childhood experiences. Parents whose needs were not met in a loving, nurturing manner in their infancy tend to lack the capacity for providing nurturance in the care of their children. Overwhelmed by their own unmet dependency needs, they misperceive the dependency needs of their children. Lacking childhood memories of dependency gratification, they are unable to sense their child's needs or to respond empathetically. Rather than feeling sympathy and concern when a helpless infant or child continues to fuss and cry despite their caring efforts, the parents perceive the behavior as criticism. Feelings of failure and powerlessness arise, leading to lowered self-esteem and increased frustration and anger. Unable to redirect these feelings constructively, the parents project blame for the feelings of discomfort toward the cause—the "bad child."

Sometimes an abused child may be seen as special or unique by a parent. This uniqueness may be real, such as a physical or emotional problem. It may also be imagined, or the child may be perceived as quite similar to someone disliked or feared in the parent's past memories. In either case, when such a child behaves undesirably or does not live up to the parent's needs and expectations, he creates a negative reflection on parental abilities and causes the threat of loss of self-esteem or self-control to the parent. This child becomes the "bad child," the one who needs to be corrected, to be "straightened out" (Broadhurst and others, 1992).

Thus, disciplinary actions taken by the parents are perceived as positive and corrective rather than abusive behavior. Parents who were raised by similarly abusing parents may see nothing abnormal in their abusive behaviors.

A common victim response to such abuse is to feel at fault and to feel that trying harder to be a "good child" in the future will stop further abusive episodes. This illogical response is supported by the abuser, and further blame is projected onto the victim. This vicious cycle continues until broken by circumstances that may be drastic enough to require medical-legal intervention. Examples of such could be the death of a child or injuries requiring professional care, sudden overt socially deviant behavior by the child, or a child runaway.

Role reversal is another dynamic. In this situation, the parent attributes adult powers to the child and comes to depend on the child for emotional sustenance and gratification of the parent's dependency needs. Such persons are seldom able to engage in any meaningful adult relationships or to intuit the needs of others. When this parent is confronted with the need to provide nurturance to another and is unable to meet his own emotional needs, conflict arises.

Other studies have suggested that abuse may occur when a child is perceived by one parent as winning in a competition for love and caring from the other parent. In this concept the parents are perceived as having developed a strong symbiotic relationship based on caring and love, with the advent of a child being a threat to the continuation of that relationship. Abuse is for the primary purpose of physically or psychologically eliminating the competition (Justice and Justice, 1976).

Social isolation has been identified as a contributing factor in all theoretical dels of child abuse. Persons with low self-esteem and mistrust of others are ble to develop positive interpersonal relationships or to request, accept, or use from others.

Isolation may also be a learned behavior, one which parents actively teach their children by socializing them to distance themselves from experiences that might promote learning how to establish positive social relationships. It may also be due to environmental factors such as socioeconomic deprivation, living in an isolated area, moving into a new neighborhood, or a combination of any such related factors.

People who abuse have a strong tendency to be suspicious of others, most likely because of fear of exposure. Quite frequently, such persons make a great effort to isolate their families socially and to enforce maintenance of a minimum social network. Their goal is to present the appearance of a "normally" functioning family to their community, thereby reducing chances for disclosure and outside intervention (Bohn, 1990).

Whichever the cause, social isolation has been found to reduce a person's access to situational supports and tangible resources. Without these, parents experience increased stress in childrearing and are unable to optimize their coping abilities to deal with resulting feelings of powerlessness, frustration, and anger in their parental roles.

Social explanations of child abuse and neglect stress the negative effects that the environment can have on the family. Exposure to the stresses of prolonged socioeconomic deprivation has been suggested as a major cause. According to Gil (1970, 1975), parents who are under such stress may be unable to maintain the parental mechanism of self-control and express their frustrations with their life-style through abuse of their children.

Others have suggested that a strong relationship may exist between socioeconomic stresses and *neglect*, rather than *abuse*. A major problem in analyzing these types of data is the lack of consensus concerning the definitions of *abuse* and *neglect*. Another identified problem is that lower income families are commonly overrepresented in studies of child abuse. This most likely reflects an uncontrolled bias in reporting systems. It is generally the lower-income families or those already identified as child abusers or neglecters who are most frequently referred to the public services, the major sources for these data.

The following case study involves a young divorced woman, socially isolated from her family and friends. She is the mother of two children and has physically abused her 6-year-old son. After she was seen in the emergency room with her son and daughter, it was recommended that she meet with a therapist on the hospital's crisis team.

Case Study   *Child abuse*

ASSESSMENT OF THE INDIVIDUAL AND THE PROBLEM

Alice, a 24-year-old divorced mother of two small children, was referred to the therapist by the hospital's emergency room physician. Earlier that evening, she had brought her 1-year-old daughter, Joan, to the emergency room. The little girl was bleeding profusely from a deep laceration on her forehead. Alice explained that, less than an hour before, Joan had climbed over the rails of her crib and fallen, striking her head on the edge of the crib as she fell. Alice said that she hadn't heard Joan fall because she had fallen asleep on the living room couch. They had just moved into the house 2 days ago, and she was exhausted from unpacking all day. Her 6-year-old son, Mike, had awakened her by calling loudly for her to help his sister. She had rushed to the bedroom and found Joan lying on the floor, crying loudly, and bleeding heavily from the cut on her head. Mike was vainly trying to pick her up but had only succeeded in dropping her back on the floor. When Alice arrived, he too began to cry loudly and cling to her.

Alice said that suddenly all she wanted to do was sit down and cry, too "I just wanted this all to go away—I wanted all of these problems out of my life. I have never felt so angry and helpless."

She tried to stop the bleeding. When she couldn't, she decided to take Joan to the nearby hospital. She said that she quickly told Mike to put on his bathrobe and get out to the car, but "he began to argue with me—something about getting dressed first—and then started to run out of the room. I suddenly had all I could take! I blew up and slapped him so hard that he flew across the hallway and hit the wall. I was still so angry with him that I just picked up Joan and grabbed him by the arm and dragged him along out to the car. As soon as we all got into the car, though, I began to shake all over. I was horrified at what I'd done to Mike. Sure, I've spanked him before, but I was so frightened and felt so alone right then. Right now I'm afraid to be alone with either of them again!"

After the doctor examined Joan and sutured the laceration on her head, he asked to have Mike brought into the room. An examination revealed evidence of new abrasions on the right side of his face and shoulder. Mike responded quietly to the doctor's questions about the injuries and said, "Mommy spanked me because I was a bad boy." He was no longer crying and clung tightly to his mother's hand as he spoke. There was no recent evidence of any other injuries.

In view of Alice's obvious emotional state, the doctor decided to admit the children to the hospital for overnight observation and further examination for signs of past physical injuries indicative of abuse. He strongly advised Alice to meet with a therapist on the hospital's crisis team before going home. She agreed, and a call was placed for the therapist to meet her at the hospital within an hour.

When the therapist arrived, Alice was waiting, slumped down in a chair in his office. She appeared disheveled, tearful, and physically exhausted. Her tone of voice sounded very depressed, yet defensive, as she began to speak about the incident that evening.

She said that she and the children had just moved to this city a few days ago from a small town in the northern part of the state. She was to start her new job as a receptionist in a large law firm the next week. Divorced for almost a year, she had no family or friends nearby.

When asked about her former marriage, she said that she had married when she was an 18-year-old college sophomore and that the marriage had lasted for 5 years. She added that her son Mike had been born only 5 months after the marriage. "That," she said rather cynically, "was definitely a case of 'marry in haste, repent at leisure.' We had 5 long years of trying to make a go of it. Having Joan last year was probably our last big mistake." She said that she became pregnant with Joan soon after Bob, her ex-husband, had finished his schooling and started his law practice. It was a planned pregnancy because they both believed that things in their lives would take a turn for the better as soon as Bob began to build a practice. As it turned out, his practice was slow in building, and it began to seem to her that the need for her additional income would never end. Arguments between them increased until, she said, "One day, heaven help me, I found myself agreeing with Bob when he told me that he wanted a divorce." She added that she had been given full custody of the children.

Bob had remarried less than a year ago, the day after the divorce became final, and, just 2 days before moving to this city, Alice had learned that a son had been born to Bob's new wife.

When asked about her childhood, she stated that she had been an only child and that her parents had divorced when she was 12 years old. She had remained with her mother. Her father, an attorney, soon moved to a different state and remarried about a year later. She never saw him again, but recalled him as a strict disciplinarian, someone to avoid in stressful situations because "he'd always blow up at me if I were around." He died in an auto accident when she was 15 years old. She recalled that her life with her mother after the divorce had been "rather dull and uneventful." Alice met Bob during her freshman year at college; they soon became engaged and planned to be married after Bob's graduation from law school in about 4 years. She had planned to obtain a law degree, finishing about a year after Bob.

Alice described Bob as being everything then that she thought she would ever want a man to be. She doubted that she could ever love anyone else as much and assumed that he had felt the same way about her.

After she returned to school in the fall of her second year, she discovered she was more than 4 months pregnant, too late for her to consider an abortion. She recalled that neither she nor Bob was "exactly thrilled by this news" because neither had income to support a child. They were even more concerned about their parents' reaction to the news. At the time, the only solution that seemed feasible to both of them was to get married immediately and then tell their parents that they had been secretly married the past spring.

As expected, neither family was pleased to hear about the "secret marriage" and the impending birth of a grandchild. Their general attitude was that Alice and Bob were still too young and in no financial position to support a family and continue in college. Neither set of parents was financially able to help them any more than they were at present. After much discussion, Bob finally gave in to Alice's decision that she would drop out of school and find a job to help support them both until Bob graduated. Then she would return to school and complete requirements for her degree.

She quickly obtained a part-time job as a receptionist at a law firm and worked for a few months before Mike was born. After his birth, she was asked to return full-time and had remained until just before her recent move to this city. Her new job here was similar and had been obtained through contacts made by her former employers.

As Alice described her relationships with her former husband and their children, the therapist noted that a pattern of scapegoating behavior by the parents seemed to evolve whenever she described Mike's role in the family. She frequently described

Mike as a child who had "created problems for them from the day he was born." As she recalled, she and Bob began to have their first "real" arguments about the need to place Mike in a day nursery when she returned to work. Whenever she expressed concern about leaving Mike with "strangers," Bob would get very defensive and angry with her. She remembered him once saying, "It wasn't my idea alone to get married and start raising a family so soon. You're the one who got pregnant! If you'd been careful, you could have been going to school right now. That baby's causing problems, too, not just me!"

She said that Mike never was a "cuddly" baby, often bullied the other children at nursery school, and continued to create problems for her and Bob as he grew older.

Their arguments increasingly seemed to center on Mike as he grew older. Bob constantly criticized Alice's decisions about Mike's care, yet never offered any suggestions of his own. When asked how she and Bob handled this, she responded that Bob always refused to get involved in any disciplinary problems; he always left that to her. She had never seen anything wrong with either spanking Mike or sending him to his room for a while. She added that spankings from her mother and father had never hurt her when she was young so, "whenever Mike deserved one, he got one, too."

She described her daughter, Joan, as being just the opposite of Mike, a child who was warm, loving, and very cooperative. With a sharp laugh, she added, "But Mike—heaven help me because he seems to be getting more like his father every day. He's always demanding attention and wanting to have his way about everything."

The therapist then asked her why she had decided to leave her old job and move away from her friends to this city. She responded that since the divorce the town had just seemed too small for her to avoid meetings with Bob and his new family.

After the divorce, she had encouraged Bob to keep in close contact with their children and, through them, with her. This continued even after his remarriage. She frequently found herself calling him for advice. In fact, she was surprised to find herself depending on him for advice much more than before their divorce.

Earlier this year, she had heard that Bob's new wife was pregnant. She said that her immediate reaction was concern for the children, wondering if Bob would continue to visit with them as much after his new child was born, or if he would focus all his attention on his new family and rarely visit them anymore. The more she thought about this, the more she felt an urgent need to get away from the whole situation before it even happened. As she recalled, "I suddenly felt that I couldn't stand even being in the same town with him when the new baby arrived."

She showed signs of increasing tension and anxiety as she discussed this with the therapist. Suddenly she began to pound her fists on the arms of the chair and sob loudly. "That woman! She'll get to live the sort of life with Bob that I'd always dreamed of. But me, I'm going to have to work the rest of my life and send my children off to strangers because of it. I'll never be able to get back to college and it's just not fair! I have no one anymore to help me. I'm all alone and it's Bob's fault. I hate him! I hate him! Why did he leave me to handle all these problems alone?"

PLANNING THERAPEUTIC INTERVENTION

The therapist felt that Alice had never fully accepted the divorce as final or dealt with her unrecognized feelings toward Bob. This was evidenced by her continued efforts to draw him back home through repeated requests for his advice in caring for the children and by encouraging his frequent contacts with her through the children. She was in crisis, precipitated by the news of the birth of Bob's son and the failure of her usual method of coping with her feelings toward Bob (flight from the situation). This was compounded by the stresses of moving to a new job in a new city far from her usual situational supports. She felt isolated and trapped in a situation not entirely of her own making.

Joan's sudden, unexpected injury was for Alice "the last straw." It served as a catalyst for the eruption of a rage reaction to her overwhelming feelings of frustration and anger about her current life situation. Her comment to the therapist that Mike "was getting more like his father every day" strongly suggested that her assault upon Mike was, in fact, displacement of her feelings of rage toward Bob.

The goals of intervention were to encourage Alice to explore and ventilate her unrecognized feelings about Bob and the divorce, to help her perceive the birth of Bob's new son realistically in relation to her own and her children's future, to provide her with an intellectual understanding of her psychological abuse of Mike caused by her displacement of her anger toward Bob on Mike, and to provide situational support as she learned new coping skills to deal with her new roles and responsibilities as a single parent.

INTERVENTION

Before the end of the first session, the therapist was notified that a more complete examination of Mike revealed two healed fractured ribs and a healed fracture, with no displacement, of his right shoulder. The x-ray technician told the physician that the injuries apparently had occurred at different times within the past 3 years. Alice was informed that the children would have to stay at the hospital for a few days.

Alice turned pale and began to cry. She asked the therapist, "Why? They are going to be all right, aren't they?" The therapist informed her of Mike's old injuries and asked if she knew how he had received them. She got up and began to pace the floor saying, "You don't know how difficult it is to control Mike—and Bob was never there!" The therapist asked Alice if she had beaten Mike. She looked up and replied softly, "Yes. I didn't mean to—honest—I just got so frustrated with him." It was decided that an immediate priority for her as well as for the children would be to provide her with situational support in her home as soon as possible. The purpose was to ensure protection of the children against any possible further physical abuse and to provide Alice with emotional support until she was better able to cope with the stresses of developing new social networks and adjusting to her new environment. She was given the telephone number and name of a woman who held weekly self-help support group meetings for parents who abuse their children. She was strongly encouraged to call as soon as she returned home, and she stated that she would.

The therapist explored with Alice the possibility of her having a friend or relative visit for a few weeks. Alice strongly agreed with this idea, admitting that she was fearful of being alone with the children because "I might blow up again if they made me angry. I'm just not sure how much more I can handle right now."

She decided to telephone her mother and added in a very depressed tone of voice: "It's for sure there is no point in calling Bob. He'll be much too busy with his new family to help me now." She called her mother from the therapist's office, briefly explained her need for help, and asked her to come for a few weeks. Her mother agreed immediately and promised to be there the next afternoon. Before leaving for home, Alice commented, "You know, suddenly I don't feel quite so alone. Maybe, when I get home, after I call that lady, I can just fall into bed and get some sleep for a change."

When Alice returned for her second session a week later, she appeared much more relaxed and less depressed. She said her mother had arrived just as the children came home from the hospital. "Never in my life have I been so glad to see my mother! She has been very helpful, and I never expected her to be so understanding." She had also attended one of the self-help group meetings.

Alice was particularly surprised by her mother's empathy when they discussed Alice's many problems since the divorce. Until then she hadn't realized that her mother, too, had had many of the same feelings and problems after she and Alice's father had divorced. She added that the children really enjoyed having their grandmother around and "have been behaving just like angels—I can't believe that Mike has quit bugging me all of the time."

During this session and the next two, through direct questioning and reflection, Alice began to recognize her present crisis as a reflection of her past unrealistic perception of her divorce and Bob's subsequent marriage.

Throughout her marriage, she had always seen herself as being expected to assume the role of a strong, independent decision maker so Bob could be free of family problems to devote his full attention to his law studies. She recalled that he had often commented to her and to their friends that his law degree should really have both their names on it: "I couldn't have made it through college if she hadn't taken on most of the family responsibilities and left me free to study."

When asked if she had ever discussed these feelings with Bob, she said that she had tried to at first, but he would get so angry with her and "shout and storm out of the house" that she soon learned that it was easier for her not to argue back. When asked if that made things go any better between them, she said, "Probably it didn't but at least it did help keep the peace. There were times, though, that I wanted to just scream at him and throw things. Instead, I would take it out on Mike. I'd usually get angry with Mike for some dumb thing or other."

With continued questioning and reflection, Alice gradually began to recognize how, unable to confront Bob directly with her feelings of frustration and anger, she had made Mike a scapegoat for her unhappiness. She had perceived Mike as the cause of arguments with Bob, and therefore it was Mike who she felt deserved to be punished. She seemed surprised with the realization that his behavior problems with other children possibly were his reaction to being scapegoated and abused at home. Upon further reflection, she expressed concern for its effect on his future relationships with her and with others. At the therapist's suggestion, she agreed to consider seeking a psychological evaluation and, if necessary, counseling for Mike.

She recalled that the year after Bob's graduation had been an unusually happy one for them. They had felt so optimistic about their future that they decided it would be a good time to have another child.

As things turned out, however, Bob's practice didn't do as well as anticipated, and Alice had to continue to work throughout her pregnancy. By the time Joan was born, their marriage had greatly deteriorated. They no longer seemed able to communicate anything but their anger and frustration toward each other. Bob began to spend most of his time away from home, and, when he finally suggested that they divorce, it seemed the only solution left for their problems.

When questioned directly, Alice admitted to the therapist how much she now regretted the divorce. She added that she always believed that Bob felt the same way, too. It was apparent to the therapist that Alice had still held hopes that Bob would return to her some day, despite his remarriage. His frequent visits with the children, even after his remarriage, had served to reinforce this belief in her mind. It was only when she heard that his new wife was pregnant that she began to experience some doubts and anxiety.

During the third session, through direct confrontation and reflection on her feelings about this news, she suddenly exclaimed, "Betrayed! That's how I felt when I heard the news. I felt like a betrayed wife, angry that he had done such a thing to me and our children. All of a sudden it came to me that, now, he couldn't just pack up and come back to us, even if he wanted to. Some way, I felt, I just had to get away. I just didn't want to be there to see him with a new family. If I stayed, I was sure that my life could never be peaceful again." As soon as she made that last comment, she gave a surprised laugh and said, "Did you hear what I just said? I was acting just like I did during our marriage. I was trying to keep peace by getting out of the situation—by taking a walk, or something like that. Well, I certainly took a walk, didn't I? All the way down to this city!"

She now realized that her choice of flight as a means of coping had indeed proved ineffective in that Bob's new son was born 2 days before she moved. At that time, she had regarded her overwhelming feelings of tension and anxiety as normal for anyone moving away from familiar friends and places. She had avoided any discussion of her feelings with anyone, afraid that she might have to dicuss how she felt about Bob's new baby. She behaved as though she was much too busy with packing and moving arrangements to visit with friends.

After the move she found herself isolated from any situational supports. She avoided telephoning Bob or friends, again using the excuse that she was too busy.

As her tension and anxiety increased, she soon felt too physically and emotionally exhausted to do more than feed the children their meals and try to keep them from interfering with the unpacking.

After a deep pause, she said, "You know, when I look back, I must have been like a time bomb waiting to explode. I realize now that this wasn't the first time I'd ever felt that way. Perhaps it was easier, then, to just take a walk and get away for a while. That way it was easy to avoid dealing with the real cause of my anger—Bob. It was always much easier to talk *at* Bob through Mike's problems than *to* Bob about our problems!"

ANTICIPATORY PLANNING

Providing immediate situational support while encouraging Alice to identify and ventilate her unrecognized feelings about Bob had assisted her in viewing the recent events in her life more realistically.

By the fourth week, Alice had made a good adjustment to her new job and was enjoying it very much. She had made several new friends and said that she was really enjoying time spent with her children at home. She said that she had even called Bob and congratulated him on the birth of his new son. An excellent day nursery had been found for Joan, and she had also located an after-school play group for Mike where he could be supervised until she got home from work in the evening.

As suggested by the therapist, she and Mike had visited the guidance counselor at Mike's new school and planned to meet with him regularly until Mike adjusted to the many new changes in his life. Even more important, and on her own, she had decided to attend meetings for divorced single parents, which were held regularly at a nearby YMCA, as well as continuing with the self-help group.

Reflecting back on her marriage in the final session, Alice summed it up by saying, "Maybe we'd have never married if I hadn't become pregnant. But that was never Mike's fault, and I never should have blamed him when things went wrong. It's Bob and I who are to blame. I'll never know if things might have been different if we had been able to wait longer, but I guess I always will believe that I gave up much more of my life than Bob did to keep it going as well as it did. My anger is with Bob, though. It's not with Mike. I realize now why I felt so angry and frustrated when we divorced. All that I could see was Bob being completely free to start a new life all over again. He never seemed to show any regrets about leaving me and the kids behind. I guess I'd hoped that he would feel guilty, or something, and come back to us."

After a long pause, she added, "Now I know that it wasn't Bob's new baby that upset me so much. It was because, until the very last minute, I'd prayed that Bob would come and beg me not to move away—and he never did—and that hurt the most."

Most important, Alice was able to obtain an intellectual understanding of the relationship between her pent-up feelings and her displaced rage reaction toward Mike. She told the therapist that, if nothing else, she would always remember those moments and was quite positive that it would never happen again, "even if I have to stand out in the street and scream until I feel better!"

Before termination, Alice and the therapist reviewed and assessed the adjustments that she had made and the insights that she had gained into her behavior. Alice was very optimistic about the future, both for herself and for the children. She was assured that she could always contact the therapist if she ever began to feel overwhelmed by problems again.

SUMMATION OF PARADIGM (Figure 6-2)

Alice's crisis was precipitated by the failure of her usual coping method, flight, to deal with her feelings toward Bob over the birth of his new son. This was com-

CASE STUDY: ALICE

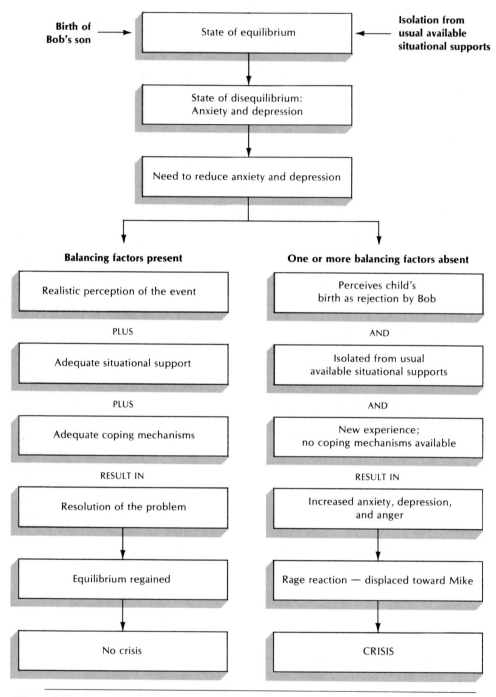

Figure 6-2

pounded by the loss of her usual available situational supports because of her move to another city. Overwhelmed by feelings of isolation, frustration, and anger, her perceptions of the event were distorted. As feelings of tension and anxiety increased to intolerable limits, Joan's injury became the last straw in a series of stressful events. Alice's feelings erupted into a rage reaction, which was displaced upon Mike. As the family scapegoat in her past relationship with Bob, he was most vulnerable to become the focus of all her negative feelings toward Bob.

A realistic perception of the event developed as Alice was assisted in identifying and ventilating her unrecognized feelings about Bob and her current life situation. She was able to obtain an intellectual understanding of the effects of her past scapegoating of Mike and his vulnerability to becoming the focus of any future rage reactions. The importance of learning alternative, adaptive methods for dealing with stress was emphasized to her.

Status and Role Change—Theoretical Concepts

Throughout life, a person is constantly in the process of joining and leaving social groups related to family, occupation, recreation, education, church, and so forth. *Status* within each of these groups is determined by the relative rights and duties that society assigns to the position. *Role* is determined by the expectations of society that a person will carry out the duties of his position. If the member's position is changed within the group, his status and role also change (Linton, 1956).

Allport (1961) cites four interrelated meanings of the term *role*. The first, *role expectation,* is what society expects of the individual. *Role conception* means how the individual perceives the effect of the role on his self-concept. He defines the role according to his perception and his needs, which are influenced by life goals, basic values, and congruency with other roles he is expected to perform. *Role acceptance,* like role conception, is a highly subjective matter. Not all roles are willingly accepted or willingly altered. The political process is one example of the kind of pressure that society can exert to force a role change. Reciprocal role changes occur for all, dependent on the winners' (and losers') new status.

Role performance depends on role expectation, conception, and acceptance. The performance of the role meets the expectations of society only to the degree that there has been mutual communication and understanding throughout the process. The greater the disagreement in any area of understanding, the greater the possibility of failure in the performance.

A person tends to perceive a role from his view of how it relates to his self-concept. The *self* might be defined as the image a person builds of himself through interpretation of what he thinks others are judging him to be. It is also derived from the reflected values that others place on him and the values that he places on himself in social roles. As new evaluations are perceived, he is obliged to reconcile these new concepts with preexisting ones. Increasing conflictual appraisals of the self result in increased tension and anxiety, leading to a state of disequilibrium. A person tries to avoid accepting a role that might threaten the security of the self-concept. Various defensive mechanisms are used to escape conflict and to ensure the integrity of self. Danger occurs when an unacceptable change in role is forced by society and cannot be avoided. For example, in the sudden death of a husband, the existing role of wife ceases to exist; the position is gone and its status with it. Without a husband, there is no wife role. Similar loss situations occur in occupations and other groups; a business closes or a position is abolished, and the need for certain roles no longer exists.

The individual's feelings of loss are in accordance with the value that he places on the role. Effects of the loss are viewed in relation to the self-image, and this involves consideration of the negative factors that might cause conflicting appraisals from others. The greater the conflict between self-concept and expectations as a result of role change, the more painful is the decision-making experience.

Changes in roles related to loss of status are particularly critical because they represent a direct threat to self-esteem and may encourage the development of a negative self-concept. If defensive coping mechanisms (such as projection or rationalization) prove ineffective in protecting the integrity of the self, anxiety and tension rise, and the balance of equilibrium is disturbed (Maloney, 1990).

The following case study illustrates a depressive reaction to a negative change in role status and loss of self-esteem. It was important in the initial interview to determine if Mr. E was suicidal before intervention was initiated. Intervention focused on clarifying the problem area and assisting him to explore and ventilate unrecognized feelings. The therapist acted as situational support until other supports could be found in his environment.

Case Study   *Status and role change*

ASSESSMENT OF THE INDIVIDUAL AND THE PROBLEM

Mr. E requested help at a crisis center on the advice of his attorney. He was in a state of severe depression and anxiety. He described his symptoms as insomnia, inability to concentrate, and feelings of hopelessness and failure. He was a well-dressed man, 47 years old, who looked older than his stated age because of tense posture; a dull, depressed facial expression; and a rather flat, low tone of voice. Married for 22 years, he had three children, a daughter 13 years old and two sons 8 and 10 years old.

His symptoms had begun about 3 weeks previously when his company closed its West Coast branch and he lost his job. His symptoms had increased in intensity during the past 2 days to the point where he remained in his room, lay in bed, and did not eat. He became frightened of his depressed thoughts and feared losing complete control of his actions.

During the initial session, he stated to the therapist that he had never been without a job before. Immediately following graduation from college 22 years before, he had started his own advertising agency in New York City. It had expanded over the years, and he had incorporated, retaining controlling interest and the position of company president. On several occasions, he had been approached by larger companies with merger proposals. About a year ago, one of the "top three" advertising companies offered him the presidency of a new West Coast branch, which he could run with full autonomy, gaining a great increase in prestige and income. All expenses were to be paid for his family's move to the West Coast.

Mr. E saw this as a chance to "make it big"—an opportunity that might never come his way again. His wife and children, however, did not share his enthusiasm. Mrs. E had always lived in New York City and objected to his giving up his business, where he was "really the boss." She liked the structured security of their life and did not want to leave it for one that she thought would be alien to her. The children sided with her, adding personal objections of their own. They had known only city life, had always gone to the same schools, and did not want to move "way out West." Despite resistance from his family, he made the decision to accept the job offer. His business friends admired his decision to take the chance and expressed full confidence in his ability to succeed. Selling out his shares in his own company to his partner, he moved west with his family within a month.

In keeping with his new economic status and the prestige of his job, he leased a large home in an exclusive residential area. He left most of the responsibility for settling his family to his wife and became immediately involved in the organization of his new business. He described her reaction to the change as being "everything negative that she told me it would be." The children disliked their schools, made few friends, and did not seem to adjust to the pace of their peer group activities. His wife could not find housekeeping help to her liking and consequently felt tied down with work in the home. She missed her friends and clubs, was unable to find shops to satisfy her, and was constantly making negative comparisons between their present life-style and their previous one. He felt that there had been a loss of communication between them. His present work was foreign to her, and he could not understand why she was having so many problems just because they had moved to a new location. Her attitude was one of constantly blaming everything that went wrong on his decision to move west and into a new job.

About a month ago, the company suddenly lost four big accounts. Although none of these losses had been a result of his management, immediate retrenchment in nationwide operations was necessary to save the company as a whole. The decision was made to close the newest branch—his branch. There was no similar position available in the remaining offices, and he was offered a lesser position and salary in the Midwest. He was given 2 months in which to close out his office and to make a decision.

Mrs. E's attitude toward these sudden events was a quick "I told you so." She blamed him for their being "stranded out here without friends and a job." He said that he was not a bit surprised by her reaction and had expected it. He had been able to tune out her constant complaints in the past months because he had been so occupied by his job, but now he was forced to join her in making plans for his family's future and in considering their tenuous economic status. He felt that he had been able to hold up pretty well under the dual pressures of closing out the business and planning for his family's future security. A week ago, his wife had found a smaller home that would easily fit into their projected budget during the interim until he decided on a new job. He had felt a sense of relief that she had calmed down and was "working *with* me for a change."

Two days ago, however, their present landlord had sent an attorney, threatening a lawsuit if Mr. E broke the lease on their present home. His wife became hysterical, blaming him for signing such a lease and calling him a self-centered failure who had ruined his family's lives. "Suddenly I felt as though the bottom had fallen out of my world. I felt frozen and couldn't think what to do next, where to go, and who to ask for help. My family, my employees, everyone was blaming me for this mess! Maybe it *was* all my fault."

Until now, Mr. E had always experienced a series of successes in his business and home life. Minor setbacks were usually anticipated and overcome with little need for him to seek outside guidance from others. Now, for the first time, he felt helpless to cope with a stressful situation alone. The threat of having to fulfill the lease on a house he could no longer afford not only destroyed his plans for his family but also broke off what little support he had been receiving from his wife. His feelings of guilt and hopelessness were reinforced by the reality of the threatened lawsuit and the loss of situational support.

PLANNING THERAPEUTIC INTERVENTION

Because of his total involvement in his new work, Mr. E had withdrawn from his previous business and family supports. The sudden loss of his job threatened him with role change and loss of status for which he had no previous coping experiences. Perceiving himself as a self-made success in the past, he now perceived himself as a self-made failure, both in business and in his parent and husband roles.

When asked by the therapist about his successful coping methods in the past, he said that he had always had recourse to discussions with his business friends. He now felt ashamed to contact them, "to let them know I've failed." He had always felt free to discuss home problems with his wife, and they usually had resolved them together. Now he seemed no longer able to communicate at home with his wife. When questioned if he was planning to kill himself, he said, "No, I could never take *that* way out. That never entered my mind." After determining that there was no immediate threat of suicide, the therapist initiated intervention.

One goal of intervention was to assist Mr. E in exploring unrecognized feelings about his change in role and status. His loss of situational supports and lack of available coping mechanisms for dealing with the present stressful situation were recognized as areas in need of attention.

INTERVENTION

In the next 4 weeks, through direct questioning, he began to see the present crisis as a reflection of his past business and family roles. Mr. E had perceived himself as being a strong, independent, self-made man in the past, feeling secure in his roles as boss, husband, and father. He now felt shame at having to depend on others for help in these roles. Coping experiences and skills learned in the past were proving to be inadequate in dealing with the sudden, unexpected, novel changes in his social orbit. The loss of situational support from his wife had added to his already high level of tension and anxiety, which resulted in the failure of what coping skills he had been using with marginal success and in precipitation of the crisis.

After the fourth session Mr. E's depression and feelings of hopelessness had diminished. His perception of the total situation had become more realistic, and he realized that the closing of the branch office was not the result of any failure on his part. It was, in fact, the same decision that he thought he would have made, had he been in charge of the overall operation. He further recognized what great importance he had placed on the possibility that this job would have been his "last chance to make it big." His available coping skills had not lessened in value but had, in fact, been increased by the experience of the situation.

By the fifth week, Mr. E had made significant changes in his situation, both in business and in his family life. He had been able to explore his attitudes about always feeling the need to be the boss and a sense of shame in being dependent on others for support in decision making. He was now able to perceive the stressful events realistically and to cope with his anxieties.

He met with his former landlord and resolved the impending lawsuit, breaking the lease with amicable agreement on both sides. His family had already decided to move into a smaller home, and his wife and children were actively involved with the planning. He had contacted business friends in the East and accepted one of several offers for a lesser position. He would return East alone, his family choosing to follow later when he had reestablished himself. His wife and children made this choice rather than repeat the sudden move into an unsettled situation as they had a year ago.

He felt pride that his friends had competed for his services rather than giving him the "I told you so" that he had been dreading.

ANTICIPATORY PLANNING

Before termination, Mr. E and the therapist reviewed the adjustments and the tremendous progress Mr. E had made in such a short period of time. It was emphasized that it had taken a great deal of strength for him to resolve such an ego-shattering experience. He was also complimented on his ability to recognize the factors he could change, those he would be unable to change, and his new status in life.

He viewed the experience as having been very disturbing at the time but believed he had gained a great deal of insight from it. He thought that he would be able to cope more realistically if a similar situation occurred in the future. He was quite pleased with his ability to extricate himself from a seemingly impossible situation. In discussing his plans for the future, he stated that he no longer believed he had lost his chance for future advancement. He was realistic about past happenings and the possiblity that such a crisis could occur again. He was relieved about his family's rapid adjustment to the lesser status of his new position. They were happy to be returning to family and friends on the East Coast. He expressed optimism about again rising to a high position in business, concluding, "I wonder if I could ever really settle for less."

SUMMATION OF THE PARADIGM (Figure 6-3)

Mr. E's crisis was precipitated by a sudden change in role status (loss of his job) and threatened economic, social, and personal losses. Assessment of the crisis situation determined that he was depressed but not suicidal. Because he was overwhelmed by a sense of failure in both business and family roles, his perceptions of the events were distorted. Having no previous experience with personal failure

CASE STUDY: MR. E

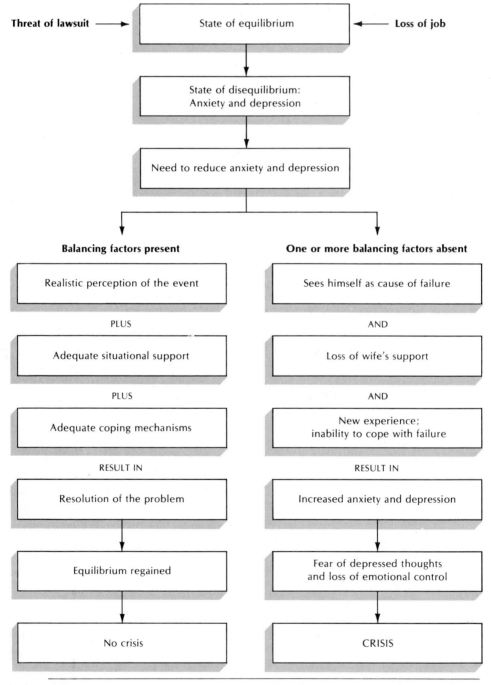

Figure 6-3

of this scope, he was unable to cope with his feelings of guilt and depression. His wife's actions reinforced his low self-esteem, and she withdrew as situational support.

Realistic perception of the event developed as the therapist assisted him in exploring and ventilating unrecognized feelings; he was able to gain insight into relationships between his symptoms of depression and the stressful events. Mrs. E resumed her role of situational support as his new coping skills were successfully implemented in resolving the crisis.

Abortion—Theoretical Concepts

Abortion and arguments about abortion have been a common feature of the American scene for at least the last century and a half (Mohr, 1978). For most of its history, the discussion about abortion in the United States was conducted by professionals, usually male physicians. As a result, until very recently, the abortion debate most resembled the disputes over the bioethical issues; it was quiet, collegial, and restrained. None of these adjectives begins to describe the emotional and volatile abortion debate today. On the contrary, over the last few decades the subject has galvanized and polarized Americans in the same way moral issues such as abolition and temperance once did (Luker, 1984).

The reason for this transformation is complex. Physicians, who had successfully controlled the right to make all decisions about legal abortions since the nineteenth century, began to disagree among themselves. Technical advances in obstetrics meant that only a *minority* of abortions after 1940 were undertaken to preserve the physical life of the pregnant woman. Once abortion could no longer be presented as a case of trading the life developing in the womb against that of a pregnant woman, physicians were forced to confront the underlying dilemma. Is the embryo or fetus a person or only a *potential* person? Both positions have long philosophical traditions, and both have existed side by side over the long history of abortion in America (Luker, 1984; Huser, 1942; Griseg, 1970).

The debate taking place today, unlike earlier rounds, largely involves two very different groups of women. These women are differentiated not only by their beliefs about abortion but by the circumstances of their lives as well. The life circumstances and beliefs of the activists on both sides of the issue serve to reinforce one another in such a way that the activists have little room and few incentives for dialogue (Luker, 1984).

The abortion debate is now controlled by women on both the *prochoice* and *prolife* sides; it is a grass-roots movement. Given the historical patterns of power in American society and the history of earlier rounds of the abortion debate, however, it is not surprising that the top of the leadership structure still contains many male activists (Luker, 1984).

These male activists tend to be holdovers from the early phases of the debate when the major disputants were male physicians, lawyers, and theologians. Because practitioners of those professions often have similar social and demographic profiles, it is not surprising that the male activists have a great deal in common with one another, even though they are on opposite sides of this issue (Luker, 1984).

When women activists are considered, a very different story emerges. Women who are engaged in the abortion debate are separated from one another by income, education, family size, and occupation, as well as by their different opinions about abortion. The abortion debate grows out of two very different social worlds that support very different aspirations and beliefs (Granberg, 1981).

The typical *prochoice* activist is a 44-year-old married woman whose father was a college graduate. She married at age 22 or older, has one or two children, and has some graduate or professional training after her baccalaureate. She is married to a professional man, is herself employed, and has a family income of more than $50,000 a year. She attends church rarely, if at all; religion is not particularly important to her (Degler, 1980).

The average *prolife* activist is also a 44-year-old married woman. She married at age 17 or older and has three or more children. Her father graduated from high school, and she probably has not gone on to college herself. She is not employed and is married to the owner of a small business or a lower-income white-collar worker; her family income is less than $30,000 a year. Her religion is one of the most important aspects of her life; she attends church at least once a week. She is probably Catholic, but she may be a convert to Catholicism. A number of public opinion polls have shown that Catholics and evangelical Protestants are beginning to approve of abortion in proportions close to those of non-Catholics and nonevangelicals (Granberg and Granberg, 1980).

Prolife activists see the world as divided into two spheres—public life and private life—and believe that each sex has an appropriate, natural, and satisfying place in his or her own sphere. In this view, everyone loses when traditional roles are lost. Men lose the nurturing that women offer, the nurturing that gently encourages them to give up their potentially destructive and aggressive urges. Women lose the protection and cherishing that men offer. Children lose full-time loving by at least one parent, as well as clear models for their own futures (Luker, 1984).

Prochoice activists reject this notion of separate spheres. They believe that men and women are fundamentally equal, by which they mean substantially similar, at least as in terms of rights and responsibilities. As a result, they see women's reproductive and family roles not as a natural niche but as a potential barrier to full equality. They believe that as long as society is organized to maintain motherhood as an involuntary activity, women can be relegated to a potentially low-status, unrewarded role at any time (Luker, 1984).

The two sides are diametrically opposed not only on the issue of abortion but also on what abortion means. For prochoice women to achieve their goals, they *must* argue that motherhood is not a primary, inevitable, or natural role for women. For prolife women to achieve their goals, they *must* argue that it is. The debate about abortion rests on the question of whether women's fertility is to be socially recognized as an asset or as a burden. In a world where men and women have traditionally had different roles to play and where male roles have traditionally been the more socially prestigious and financially rewarding, abortion has become a symbol distinguishing those who wish to maintain this ancient division of labor and those who wish to challenge it (Luker, 1984).

For these reasons, it is likely that the abortion debate will remain heated, passionate, and bitter. It is likely to be with us for some time. It is entirely possible the candidates' stance on the abortion issue was a strong factor in the election for president in 1992. President Clinton was vocally prochoice and former President Bush was just as verbally prolife. With the country in a deep recession, the strong support for prochoice could have tipped the scales in President Clinton's favor.

In 1992, there were 1.2 million adolescent pregnancies. Approximately 612,000 (51%) of these pregnant teenagers had their babies. Only a small number of them, approximately 4%, gave their infants up for adoption (Department of Health and Human Services, 1992). Multiple studies have reported on the results of teenage pregnancies. The babies tend to be low-birth-weight infants, and their mortality rate is nearly double that of first babies born to older women (McCormick, Shapiro, and Starfield, 1984). The adolescent mother faces a greater risk than her nonpregnant female peers of becoming a school dropout, experiencing unemployment and poverty, needing welfare, and having marital problems, with higher separation and divorce rates. The adolescent mother is also likely to have more unwanted, out-of-wedlock children spaced closer together than her peers. The costs to society for obstetric and pediatric care and for welfare assistance are astronomical. Teenage pregnancies in 1985 cost taxpayers at least $16.6 billion (Deibel, 1986). Teenagers who chose abortion presented an insignificant ($460,000) expense to taxpayers in contrast to those adolescents who carried to term and kept their babies.

It is common for adolescents to have ambivalent feelings about sexual activity, contraception, and possible pregnancy. Cultural, economic, political, social, religious, familial, and moral values have a role in the development of these conflictual feelings. In addition, the use of contraception is also influenced by knowledge, availability, effectiveness, financial costs, acceptance of the birth control method, and belief in its safety (Nakashima, 1986).

Teenagers have consistently waited until later in their pregnancies to seek termination by abortion. Reasons for delay include ignorance of the symptoms of pregnancy, denial, ambivalence, fear, lack of information and funds, inaccessibility of abortion services, and concern about parental reactions. Consequently, adolescents are twice as likely as older women to undergo abortion procedures after 12 weeks' gestation (Zakus and Wilday, 1987).

An unplanned and/or unwanted pregnancy creates a crisis in a life of any woman, and symptoms of anxiety, depression, and disorganization are common. There is no painless way to deal with this problem. Crisis intervention is the counseling method of choice in treating these situations (David, 1972). The ultimate goal is to restore, maintain, and enhance the patient's current and future level of functioning.

Counseling concerning an unwanted pregnancy may involve several different stages that frequently overlap. Successful resolution at an early stage may prevent later problems. The first level of intervention occurs during the decision-making process. If abortion is chosen, the second stage is to work through the loss of the potential child and to deal with facing a painful surgical procedure. Counseling also includes alleviating guilt, increasing responsibility for contraception, and preventing future problems in the areas of sexuality and parenthood. The third level of intervention is focused on emotional problems following the abortion.

The following case study concerns a 16-year-old girl who was 8 weeks pregnant. Intervention focused on helping her make a decision regarding her pregnancy.

Case Study   *Abortion*

ASSESSMENT OF THE INDIVIDUAL AND THE PROBLEM

Cindy came to a crisis center at the suggestion of her best friend, Katie. Cindy and Katie both attended a private school and would be graduating in 6 months. Cindy was attractive and looked younger than her 16 years. On her chart, she had stated that she "was having problems at home." She had asked for a "female therapist," and fortunately one was available.

The therapist went to the reception room and asked Cindy to come to her office. Cindy asked if Katie could come with her (obviously for moral support). The therapist replied, "Of course."

Cindy was pale and appeared anxious. Katie was very calm, cool, and collected. The therapist said to Cindy, "You stated that you are having problems at home. Could you be more specific, Cindy?" Cindy looked at Katie, and Katie said, "It's all right, Cindy, tell her everything. I've been to this center before. You can trust her."

Cindy looked at the therapist and said, "I don't have family problems—*yet*—but I will if they find out." She was asked, "Find out what?" She hesitated and then said, "I'm pregnant—2 months pregnant!"

The therapist asked, "What about the father—do you plan to marry him?" Cindy looked shocked and answered, "Good heavens, no! I don't love him! I want to graduate and go to the university." The therapist then asked, "What do you plan to do about the baby?" Cindy replied, crying, "I don't know. I don't want a baby. I'm too young and I have other plans for my life—but I'm afraid to have an abortion!" The therapist answered, "Cindy, you don't have to make a decision today—you should take some time to think about what you really want to do."

Katie spoke up and said, "I had an abortion last year at a clinic. It didn't hurt that much. I just had some cramping. My family didn't even know. I could go with you." The therapist said, "Katie, that was you and your life; this has to be Cindy's decision." She added, "Cindy, you could have the baby and keep it, give it up for adoption, or have an abortion. But you don't have to decide immediately. Think about all the options open to you." Cindy asked, "How much time do I have—*if* I decide to have an abortion?" The therapist replied, "Before the twelfth week, if possible. That gives you 4 weeks to decide." Cindy seemed relieved and answered, "I'll decide by then."

"What do you plan to major in at the university?" asked the therapist. Cindy smiled and replied, "I want to be an attorney—I always have—my mother is an attorney and she's great! I want to be just like her."

"You admire your mother very much. Do you also feel close to her?" asked the therapist. Cindy replied, "Yes, very close. My dad has his own business and travels a lot, so Mother and I are very close."

The therapist asked Cindy, "Have you considered telling your mother about being pregnant?" "Yes," answered Cindy, "but I know she would be very disappointed in me. You see, we had a long discussion about birth control—we discussed everything! I was so stupid I forgot to take my pills."

"Your mother sounds very open and broad-minded," said the therapist. "You apparently trust her. She may be disappointed but she would still love you and want to help you, wouldn't she?" asked the therapist. Cindy hesitated and then replied, "Yes, I think she would."

The therapist said, "I'm certain she would, and she could help you make a decision that will be very important to your future."

Cindy smiled and said, "You're right. I know she loves me and I know she would want to help. I'll go home and talk to her."

The therapist smiled and said, "Great! Let's make an appointment for next week. Bring your mother if she would like to come. I would like to meet her."

PLANNING THERAPEUTIC INTERVENTION

Cindy looked and acted immature and was unable to problem-solve. She was confused and ambivalent over her unplanned and unwanted pregnancy. The only element she was certain of was that she did not want to get married. She had some plans for her future, to become an attorney like her mother. The therapist believed that Cindy's mother would be invaluable in assisting her to make a very difficult decision. It was obvious that Cindy was very close to her mother and that her logic as an attorney would be greatly respected. Her mother could be a strong situational support. Katie was a peer and was apparently exercising some pressure on Cindy to have an abortion. Cindy was uncertain. Therefore, the therapist viewed Katie as a possible negative influence.

INTERVENTION

The intervention focused on Cindy's strong relationship with her family rather than on peer pressure from Katie.

In the next 4 weeks, Cindy and her mother (Helen) and father (David) came to the therapy sessions with Cindy. They were supportive and nonjudgmental when discussing Cindy's pregnancy. They agreed that regardless of Cindy's decision they would stand by her and give her any help she needed.

Cindy vacillated between having the baby and giving it up for adoption and having an abortion. The therapist, Helen, and David would present the pros and cons of each decision. No verbal or nonverbal cues were ever given to persuade Cindy toward either choice.

At the fifth session, the family entered the therapist's office and Helen said, "Cindy has decided what she wants to do about her pregnancy." Cindy said, "I really have been thinking about the present *and* the future. More than anything, I want to go to the university and then enter law school and become an attorney. I am scheduled for an abortion tomorrow and Mother is going with me. I made a very stupid mistake, but I won't let it ruin my life. I feel very lucky to have such a great Mom and Dad." Helen and David hugged Cindy with tears in their eyes. It was obvious they were pleased that she had made her own decision.

The therapist stated, "Cindy, I am happy that you were able to make your own decision. How do you feel about having an abortion?" Cindy replied, "Mom gave me tons of things to read on prolife and prochoice. We discussed both issues thoroughly. I made the mistake and now I will have to live with my decision. I will *never* again use abortion as a method of birth control—that, I know! But I do believe in prochoice."

The therapist wished her good luck, and they made an appointment for the next session.

ANTICIPATORY PLANNING

The last session was spent with Cindy alone. She discussed the abortion and her feelings. She admitted that she felt "nervous and a little afraid" and glad that her mother had been with her. She denied any feelings of guilt but admitted that she might have some later. The rest of the session was spent discussing her need to use her contraception ("pills") regularly—not "hit and miss." The therapist also discussed sexually transmitted diseases with her, specifically AIDS, because she had been sexually active. Cindy said that she and her parents had talked about this in depth.

She said that she planned to "abstain from sex until I am ready to get married. I want a career first and I plan to make *that* my top priority." Cindy was reassured that she could return for help with any future crisis, should the need arise.

SUMMATION OF THE PARADIGM (Figure 6-4)

Cindy felt that her future plans to be an attorney were impossible because of her unplanned and unwanted pregnancy. She was afraid to tell her parents, fearing their disappointment and possible rejection. Because she lacked any previous coping experience with being pregnant, her anxiety and depression increased to an intolerable level; Cindy was in a state of crisis.

Intervention was focused on having Cindy's family become involved in helping her to look at her options, to provide situational support, and to help her problem-solve about her available options.

Rape—Theoretical Concepts

The word *rape* arouses almost as much fear as the word *murder*. In a sense, it kills both the rapist and his victim. The rapist dies emotionally because he can no longer express or feel tenderness or love, and his victim suffers severe emotional trauma.

Women have nightmares about being sexually assaulted; they anguish over what to do. Either they can resist, hoping to fend off the rapist, or they can obey his commands, hoping he will leave without seriously injuring or killing them. Unfortunately in 1993, the multitude of sexually transmitted diseases only compounds their fears: the reality of being raped is exacerbated knowing that they may have contracted AIDS, herpes, venereal warts, chlamydia, or another sexually transmitted disease (STD).

The 1990s are also chacterized by a phenomenon that has occurred for a long time but is now receiving a great deal of attention—date rape. In all probability,

CASE STUDY: CINDY

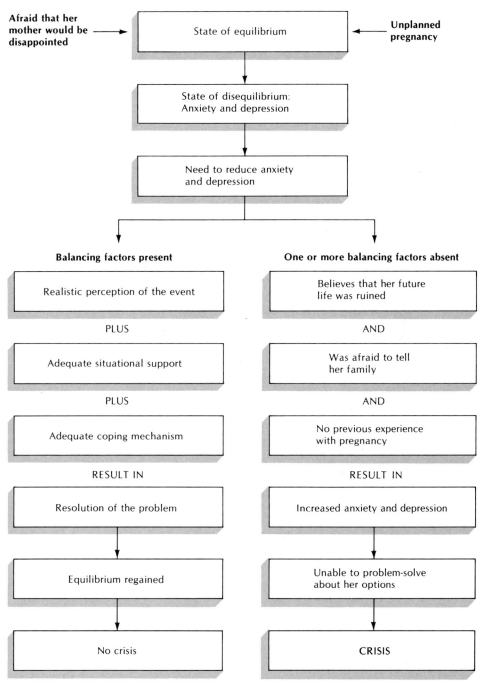

Afraid that her mother would be disappointed → State of equilibrium ← Unplanned pregnancy

State of disequilibrium: Anxiety and depression

Need to reduce anxiety and depression

Balancing factors present

Realistic perception of the event

PLUS

Adequate situational support

PLUS

Adequate coping mechanism

RESULT IN

Resolution of the problem

Equilibrium regained

No crisis

One or more balancing factors absent

Believes that her future life was ruined

AND

Was afraid to tell her family

AND

No previous experience with pregnancy

RESULT IN

Increased anxiety and depression

Unable to problem-solve about her options

CRISIS

Figure 6-4

the increased recognition and publicity are due to the feminist movement. Women are more aware of their rights and are acting upon them. Too long have they been the silent majority.

Rape is defined in numerous ways, usually including terms such as *forcible carnal knowledge* (McDonald, 1971), *unlawful carnal knowledge* (Amir, 1971), and *against the will* or *without the consent* (McDonald, 1971) of the victim. For this purpose, *rape* is defined as forcible carnal knowledge of a woman without consent and against her will.

Rape, although an overtly sexual act, is properly considered an act of violence with sex utilized as the weapon (Burgess and Holmstrom, 1974). Viewing the victim of rape as a victim of violence might assist in a more objective and non-judgmental approach to the victim. The victim of any other type of physical violence is never treated with the same type of emotional, superstitious approach that the victim of rape must endure.

The victim of rape is the victim of medical and cultural myths. The medical myth insists that a healthy adult woman cannot be forcibly raped with full penetration of the vagina unless she actively cooperates (Amir, 1971). The medical myth does not seem to consider emotional reactions, such as fear and panic, or logic reactions, such as submissiveness, to ensure life. Neither does the use of weapons, fists, or threats by the offender seem to have a role in the medical myth. The medical myth must spring from the cultural myth that "whatever a man does to a woman she provokes" (McDonald, 1971). The low esteem that society in general holds for women is reflected in both the medical and the cultural myths.

Sociological studies reflect that the most typical female victim is between 15 and 24 years of age, of the same race as the offender, and of the lower socioeconomic group of the society. The initial contact for the rape or the rape itself occurs in the approximate neighborhood of the offender and the victim (Amir, 1971).

The victim's emotional reactions to rape have been classified into phases. McDonald (1971) classifies the emotional reactions of victims into phase I, acute reaction; phase II, outward adjustment; and phase III, integration and resolution. Burgess and Holmstrom (1974) classify the rape trauma syndrome into the acute phase (disorganization) and the long-term process (reorganization).

McDonald's "acute reaction" and Burgess and Holmstrom's "acute phase" are very similar. The victim is seen in a disorganized, emotionally active state, weeping, distraught, and unable to think clearly, or, conversely, as emotionally contained with only occasional signs of emotional pressure, such as inappropriate smiling and increased motor activity.

McDonald's "outward adjustment phase" is described as a period when the victim goes through a denial of the emotional impact of the rape. She goes back to work, restores her social life, rejects any attempts at assisting her, and in general attempts to carry on as though nothing had happened.

Burgess and Holmstrom's long-term process of reorganization seem to contain elements of McDonald's phase II and phase III. The emphasis in both studies is on the necessity of emotional confrontation with the experience, changes in life space because of the trauma, the resultant dreams, and deterioration of sexual relationships.

The treatment of the rape victim is not well studied or documented. McDonald emphasizes traditional short-term psychotherapy, whereas Holmstrom and Burgess (1975) emphasize the crisis intervention model. Perhaps McDonald's finding of depression in the third phase and Burgess and Holmstrom's lack of emphasis on depression are the result of the different modes of treatment utilized. Crisis intervention seems to be an ideal model for use with rape victims. Rape is a sudden, overwhelming experience for which the usual coping mechanisms probably are inadequate. The victim needs an opportunity for emotional catharsis, reality testing for self-blame, active support on a short-term basis, and someone who will assist in identifying the situational supports available. Crisis intervention seems to be well defined to reach this group of people.

Crisis intervention is also increasingly available in the area where rape victims are initially brought to the attention of the health care system—the emergency room. Prompt referral and active intervention in the emergency room may well prevent deterioration of the victim's emotional status (Burgess and Holmstrom, 1973).

The crisis precipitated by rape seems to be approachable by the generic type of crisis intervention. There are recognized patterns of behavior, a characteristic course of behavior results, and specific interventions seem to be effective with the majority of the victims. The exceptions to the generic approach are those victims with compounded reactions because of a history of physical, psychological, or social problems. In those instances, the usual physician, therapist, or agency probably should handle the case.

To be a genuine victim in our society means that one must have people available who can accept and acknowledge that something extremely disruptive has occurred in one's life. In other words, the victim's claim to having been victimized needs to receive confirmation from others.

There are three basic types of rape. The first type is rape involving persons who know one another, for example, neighbors, separated husbands and wives, former friends or current friends (date rape), fathers and daughters, and prostitutes and dissatisfied clients. The second type of rape is gang rape, in which two or more men, usually young men, rape one woman; these encounters follow different patterns. It is the third type, the stranger-to-stranger rape, that women fear most, and it is this type of rape that follows an identifiable pattern.

In stranger-to-stranger rape, first a potential rapist looks for a woman who is vulnerable to attack. Rapists differ in defining who is vulnerable. Some look for victims who are handicapped or who cannot react appropriately or swiftly to the threat of rape. Such a man might prey on retarded girls, old women, sleeping women, or women who are intoxicated.

Other rapists look for environments that are easily entered and relatively safe. They make certain that the victim is alone and that they will not be interrupted. This type often commits his crime in a rundown section of town where many women live alone.

Rapists often select their victims long before they approach them, and they usually are very consistent in how they do it; they repeat the same pattern over and over again. Rapists seem to have a sixth sense for identifying women who live alone, and they are especially good at finding streets, laundromats, or theater rest rooms that are isolated but that draw unsuspecting victims.

Housing that is easy to enter and the isolation of the victim are two obvious factors that make women particularly vulnerable to rape, but women who are usually friendly and who like to help others are also courting danger. Teachers, nurses, volunteers, and other women who have learned to serve others, to be charitable, and to give of themselves are especially vulnerable to sexual exploitation.

A woman's first act of resistance should be to refuse to help—or be helped by—strange men. It is not wise to stop on a street to give a man a light or to explain street directions. It may be rude but it is much safer to state firmly, while continuing to walk, "I don't have a match" or "I don't know." Do not smile and say, "I'm sorry but....."

Women should refuse to let a stranger in their apartments or homes to make an emergency phone call or for any other reason. These may be ploys, and there are hundreds of clinical case histories and police reports to validate this method of entry for the purpose of rape.

After finding a vulnerable target, the rapist proceeds, in essence, to ask his victim, "Can you be intimidated?" If she can, he then threatens her life. For example, a rapist may approach a victim on the street and ask her for a light. If she provides it, he may ask her an intimate question. If she reacts submissively or fearfully, he knows he has intimidated her and that she likely will submit to his demands.

This testing phase is crucial for the rapist. If he guesses incorrectly about whether a woman can be intimidated, he will lose the opportunity to rape her, and if he is incorrect about the victim's situation, he may be caught, convicted, and sentenced to a penitentiary. The rapist tests his victim's responses to threats for intimidations such as "Don't scream!" "Don't shout!" or "Take your clothes off!"

The safest stance for a woman alone either on the street or in her home is to be aloof and unfriendly. This is her first line of resistance to rape.

When a rapist attacks a woman without warning, that is, climbs into her bedroom while she is asleep, or pulls her into a dark alley, she must decide whether to use direct methods of resistance or to submit.

In the third or "threat" stage of rape, we find the rapist telling his victim what he wants from her and what he will do to her if she refuses to cooperate. Most important, he tells her what reward she will receive if she submits. Typically, he says he will kill her if she does not cooperate and that he will not hurt her if she does. If the victim is terrified, immobilized, or hysterical, the rapist may reassure her. He will repeatedly promise her that nothing will happen to her if she does as he tells her. He may express concern for her health or future relationships with her husband or boyfriend.

The final stage of rape is the sexual transaction itself. Vaginal intercourse occurs in less than half of rape victims; anal or oral intercourse is common. In this stage we see the rapists's fantasy life in full blossom. Here he imprints his unique personality on the crime. Some rapists create a false identity and describe a non-existent person to the victim; others reveal their split personalities by telling the victim, "It isn't really me doing this" or "I can't help it."

Most rapists fall into two categories. One type includes those who are usually victims of what analysts call ego splits. They are married, young, employed, and living a life that you could not describe as typical of a person who is mentally ill. However, their family life is disturbed; they cannot relate successfully to their wives or parents, and as youngsters they had problems with an older sister, cousin, or aunt.

After the crime, these men deny their behavior. Typically, they say, "I don't remember," "It wasn't me," or "I felt like I was watching a movie." If they do not harm their victims, these rapists often get a suspended sentence or are sent to reformatories where they can get work releases and return to their communities in a matter of months. The courts generally give them a second chance on the condition that they receive psychotherapy. Most rapists fall into the first category.

The other type of rapist is a predator. Often he is a man who goes into a place to rob it. In the course of the crime, he enters a bedroom where he finds a lone woman sleeping. On the spur of the moment, he decides to rape her. These men are out to exploit or manipulate others, and sometimes they do it through rape.

The rapist who requires his victim to pretend to respond sexually has often failed to please his wife or lover. On a deeper level, he may be trying to maintain his shaky defenses about his own sexual inadequacy.

Most rapists have narcissistic and self-centered relationships with women. They have only a minute awareness of their partner's social needs or of the social situation itself.

A rapist also writes his diagnostic signature in the sign-off, or termination, stage of rape. A rapist who assumes the victim will report the crime terminates the rape by trying to confuse the woman. He may say, "Don't move until you count to 100." Then he will go into another room and wait to see if she moves. A minute later, he will reenter the room and, if the victim has moved, berate her for failing to follow his directions. He may do this several times. Other offenders act guilty or apologetic when they leave. They plead for the victim not to call the police. Still others threaten future harm if she calls for help.

Unfortunately, most rapists can neither admit nor express the fact that they are a menace to society. Even convicted rapists who are serving long prison terms deny their culpability; they tenaciously insist that women encourage and enjoy sexual assault. These men tell others that they are the greatest lovers in the world.

The case study that follows concerns a legal secretary who was raped. She went to work after first going home to shower and change her clothes. She was obviously in a state of shock and disbelief.

Case Study   *Rape*

ASSESSMENT OF THE INDIVIDUAL AND THE PROBLEM

Ann, an attractive 26-year-old legal secretary, was brought to the crisis center by her employer. That morning on her way to work, she had been raped. After being raped, she returned to her apartment, showered, changed her clothes, and calmly went to work.

At approximately 11:30 A.M. she matter-of-factly announced to her employer that she had been raped and told him the details. He was shocked and horrified. He asked her to go to the hospital for treatment and to notify the police. She stated very unemotionally that she was "fine" and had only numerous superficial cuts on her breasts and abdomen and would continue working. By midafternoon, she appeared to her employer to be in a state of shock and was acting disoriented and confused. He drove her to the crisis center where she was seen immediately as an emergency by a female therapist who had expertise in working with rape victims.

The therapist offered Ann a cup of coffee, and she accepted. While they were drinking their coffee, the therapist quietly asked Ann to tell her what had happened. Ann began to sob. The therapist handed her some tissues, put her arms around her shoulders, held her close, and told her that she understood how she was feeling. Gradually Ann calmed down and stopped crying. She then said, "I feel so filthy. I feel I should have resisted more. I am so confused." She was reassured that these feelings were normal and was asked to tell what happened.

Ann stated that she always got up early and took the bus to work because it was very convenient, and she arrived before anyone else was in the office. She liked to get her desk in order for the day and make the coffee so that she could serve coffee to the attorney she worked for when he arrived. She smiled slightly and said, "He isn't fit to talk to until he has finished his second cup of coffee in the morning. He commutes in from a suburb, and he has to battle the traffic for at least an hour or an hour and a half." The therapist smiled and asked her to continue. She took a deep breath and stated that this morning she had gotten up as usual and ridden the bus to work. As she was walking from the bus stop to her office building, approximately three blocks, a man walked toward her. He was tall, attractive, and well dressed. When he approached her, he smiled and said, "Can you tell me where Fifth Street is?" She returned his smile and said, "You are going the wrong way. It's the next street up" (pointing in the direction she was walking). He said, "Thank you" and, turning around, fell into step with her and started talking about the weather—"what a beautiful morning"—and other small talk. They had walked approximately 100 yards when he suddenly pulled out a knife, shoved her against a car, put the knife to her throat, and said, "Don't scream or I'll kill you. Get in the car." Ann began to tremble and tears rolled down her cheeks. The therapist said, "How frightening! What did you do?" Ann said, "I was so shocked and terrified, I thought he *would* kill me. So when he opened the car door, I got in."

Ann continued to tell what had happened. He made her slide over to the driver's seat, keeping the knife firmly at her waist, ordered her to start the car, and told her where to drive (an isolated area near the river). He then made her get in the back seat and undress. He started caressing her and talking obscenities to her, telling her how he was going to make love to her "like no other man could." Ann said that she began to cry and plead with him, but it only seemed to make him angry. He began making small cuts on her breasts and abdomen and kept saying he would kill her if she did not "cooperate." Ann said that he acted "spaced out" and had a glazed look in his eyes, as if he were not really raping her *personally*—just somebody.

Ann stated that after he raped her, he seemed to "come to" and started to cry, saying, "I'm so sorry. I didn't mean to hurt you. Please forgive me, I just can't help it. Please don't tell anyone." Ann got dressed, and he helped her into the front seat and kept asking her if she was all right and generally expressing concern for her well-being. He asked if he could drive her someplace, and Ann asked him to drop her off approximately four blocks from her apartment, telling him she was going to a girlfriend's to "clean up." He dropped her off and again begged her not to tell anyone and to please forgive him. Ann said that when she was certain he had driven away, she walked to her apartment in a daze. All she could think about was taking a shower to "get clean again" and to change her clothes completely to try to erase her feelings of degradation. She stated that she thought she should go to work "to keep her mind off it." Only later in the afternoon as she "relived" the events in her mind did she begin to feel terribly guilty over not "resisting" or "fighting back" when he first pulled the knife. She said (with a tone of great remorse), "I didn't even scream!"

PLANNING THERAPEUTIC INTERVENTION

The therapist felt that Ann should go to the hospital immediately for treatment of her numerous cuts and determination of the presence of spermatozoa in the vagina, and then report the incident to the police. After this was done, she should return to the center to meet with the therapist and continue her mental catharsis. The therapist explained to Ann that someone from the rape hot line would go with her to the hospital and remain with her constantly there and while she gave her report to the police. She was assured that the therapist would contact the hospital to arrange that Ann be examined by a female physician and that she would be interrogated by a female police officer. Ann agreed to go, and a member of the rape team was called to be with her and then to return her to the center.

INTERVENTION

When Ann returned, she was pale and trembling but apparently in control of her emotions. Again she was offered coffee, which she accepted, and she and the therapist discussed how things had gone at the hospital and with the police interrogation. Ann stated it was definitely *not* pleasant, but that it was not as bad as she had thought it would be. She added, "Thank God I didn't take a douche!"

The therapist asked Ann if she had a friend or family member that she would like to contact and possibly have spend the night with her because she was still very frightened by her experience. Ann turned even paler and explained, "Oh, my God—Charles!" She was asked, "Who is Charles?" She replied, hesitantly, "My fiancé." The therapist asked Ann if she could call Charles and tell him what happened. Ann began to cry and said, "I am so ashamed. He will probably hate me. He probably will never want to touch me again. What have I done?" She was comforted by the therapist and told that *she* had done nothing wrong. She continued to cry and berate herself. The therapist gave her a mild sedative and asked her to lie down and rest. Twenty minutes later, Ann asked the therapist if she would call Charles and tell him what had happened, but she said that she did not want to see him until she knew how he felt about her being raped. The therapist agreed and asked for Charles's telephone number.

The call was placed to Charles, and a brief explanation was given by the therapist about Ann being raped and that she was not severely injured but psychologically very traumatized. Charles responded with concern and anger and asked if he could see Ann. He was told to come to the center and to ask for the therapist.

Charles arrived and was extremely upset and angry. The therapist took him to her office and explained fully what had happened to Ann and what had been done for her. He started to cry and to curse, stating, "My God, poor Ann" and "I'll find that dirty bastard and kill him!" The therapist allowed him to ventilate his feelings of pity and anger, and he began to calm down. When he seemed calmer, he was asked, "Does this change your feelings for Ann?" He appeared startled and said, "No, I love her. We are getting married!" He was told that Ann was afraid he would not love her anymore, and so forth. He replied, "It wasn't her fault. Of course, I still love her!"

It was explained that after being raped women usually felt "guilty," "unclean," and very fearful of intimacy with another man, even though they loved them very much. The therapist added that Ann needed his strength, love, and constant reassurance that nothing had changed between them. He listened and said, "I'll do anything I can to help her forget this."

The therapist asked if he sometimes stayed overnight at Ann's apartment, and he answered, "Yes, often." He was asked if he would spend the night with her (if she agreed) and hold her (if she would let him), touch her, reaffirm his love for her, and speak about their coming marriage but not attempt sexual intercourse unless she asked him; he agreed and asked to see Ann. The therapist asked for a few minutes alone with Ann first.

Ann was lying on the couch staring at the ceiling when the therapist entered. She turned her head and looked fearfully at the door. The therapist smiled, sat down by Ann, held her hand, and said, "I like your Charles. He is a fine young man. He will probably break down that door if I don't let him in to see you!" Ann said, "What did he say?" The therapist told her that he had stated he loved her very much and that he would do anything to help her forget, that it was not her fault, and that he would like to "kill the bastard who hurt you."

Ann said hesitantly, "Are you sure?" The therapist replied firmly, "Positive! Now comb your hair and put some makeup on, so I can let him in!" Ann smiled weakly and complied.

Charles entered the office, took Ann in his arms, and held her gently, stroking her hair and face, saying "I'm so sorry, my love. Let me take care of you. Everything is going to be all right. I love you. You are the most precious thing in my life." Ann cried softly on his shoulder.

The therapist said, "Why don't you two go home and get some rest, and I'll see you both next week." Ann and Charles agreed and left with their arms around each other and Ann's head on his shoulder.

(*Note*: The therapist had listened to Ann's account of the rape and modus operandi with increasing feelings of helplessness and anger because in the past 3 months she had worked with two other rape victims who had described the same details but with one major difference: the first victim had only one minute cut on her throat, which she received when he pushed her against the car; the second had several small superficial cuts on her breasts; and now the third victim, Ann, had numerous cuts on her breasts and abdomen. The rapist was obviously becoming increasingly violent with each rape.)

ANTICIPATORY PLANNING

The next sessions were spent in collateral therapy with Ann and Charles. The focus was on ventilation of their feelings and helping Ann begin to express anger toward her rapist. By the end of six sessions, they had resumed their normal sexual activities and had advanced their wedding date 3 months. Charles felt he was really living at Ann's apartment because he wanted to be with her as much as possible; therefore, they agreed to get married sooner than they had planned.

SUMMATION OF THE PARADIGM (Figure 6-5)

Because rape is so emotionally traumatic, Ann was treated as an emergency situation by the therapist. The sooner intervention begins with a rape victim, the less psychological damage occurs.

Most women are totally unprepared for rape; therefore, it is a new traumatic experience to cope with, and previous defense mechanisms are usually ineffective to resolve the crisis.

Ann greatly feared total rejection by her fiancé (a very real and common occurrence). This is why the therapist saw both Ann and Charles in collateral sessions; thus both would have a chance to explore and ventilate their feelings together.

The event, rape, was perceived by Ann as being her fault because she did not resist immediately and did not scream. Again, these feelings are common in women who have been raped. Usually everything occurs rapidly, and the ever-present fear of being killed or seriously injured tends to immobilize the victim.

ADDENDUM

Four months later, a patient was referred to the center because he was on probation for rape, and he became the same therapist's patient. When questioned about how and why, as he described his modus operandi, the therapist *knew* he was the one who had raped Ann and the two other victims. After the rapist discussed his feelings—guilt, shame, and helplessness in controlling his actions—the therapist asked about his background and family. This new patient, Phillip, described his childhood as one deprived of affection. His mother had left his father, and Phillip had been reared by an aunt who was very cold, undemonstrative, and—to him—uncaring and rigid.

When questioned about his present living circumstances, he stated that he was married (happily) and had three small children. When asked why he felt the need to rape, he stated, "I don't know." He began to cry and said, "Please help me. I can't help myself."

When the therapist asked if his wife knew that he was on probation for rape, he said, very hesitantly; "No, but I *know* she thinks something is wrong with me." The therapist told Phillip that she had worked with three of his victims, and she felt that he was becoming increasingly more violent, as evidenced by the increasing use of the knife and the sight of blood to stimulate him.

Phillip stared intently at the therapist and said with amazement in his voice, "My God, don't you hate me? I hate myself." The therapist was able to admit that her bias was toward his victims but that she felt he needed help because she was afraid

CASE STUDY: ANN

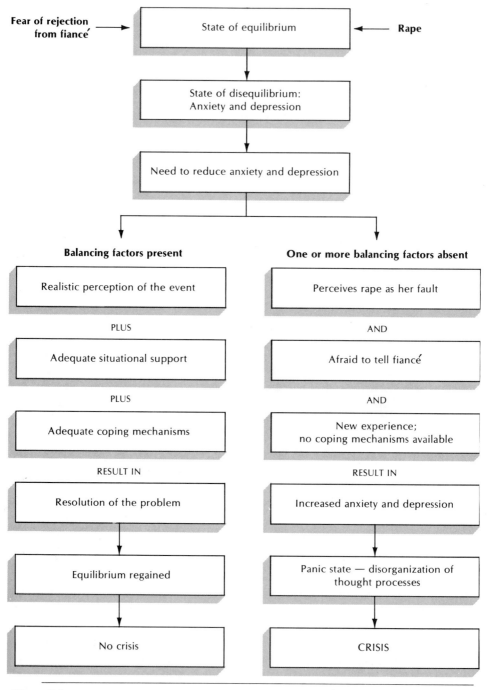

Fear of rejection from fiancé → State of equilibrium ← Rape

State of disequilibrium: Anxiety and depression

Need to reduce anxiety and depression

Balancing factors present

Realistic perception of the event

PLUS

Adequate situational support

PLUS

Adequate coping mechanisms

RESULT IN

Resolution of the problem

Equilibrium regained

No crisis

One or more balancing factors absent

Perceives rape as her fault

AND

Afraid to tell fiancé

AND

New experience; no coping mechanisms available

RESULT IN

Increased anxiety and depression

Panic state — disorganization of thought processes

CRISIS

Figure 6-5

he might kill his next victim. He admitted that he did not know whether he *would* or *would not* kill someone.

The therapist then asked him how his wife and children would feel if they found out he was a potential murderer. He shuddered and said, "Help me! I don't know what to do!" The therapist stated that he should tell his wife about being on probation and about the rapes, and then the therapist would do all she could to get him help. He agreed and called his wife and asked her to come to the center.

His wife arrived, and Phillip, with the therapist present, told her what he had done, and the possibility of what he could do in the future. She began to cry and said, "I've *known* something was wrong, but I didn't know what." She turned to the therapist and asked, "What can we do?" The therapist was very candid and stated that Phillip should be at a well-known maximum security prison where he could receive consistent, intensive psychiatric therapy in order to protect the reputation of their family and to protect the community.

They agreed with this decision. The therapist then called the judge and told him the facts. He agreed that maximum security was needed and said he would send a car to transport Phillip to the facility.

It must be noted that *rarely* does a therapist work with rape victims and then with their offender. It was extremely difficult to remain "cool, calm, and collected" while Phillip related his modus operandi; however, he too was a "victim" who needed help, and help he did receive.

Physical Illness—Theoretical Concepts

Diseases are known to have their places as well as their times (see Chapter 8 on AIDS). Primitive societies have been characterized by health problems related to recurrent famines, and urban societies by epidemics of infectious disease. Modern industrial societies are characterized by a new set of diseases: obesity, arteriosclerosis, hypertension, diabetes, and widespread symptoms of anxiety. Arising from these are two of the three greatest disablers of our own place and time: coronary heart disease and stroke. In recent years, increasing concern has focused not only on the etiology and epidemiology of cardiac disease but on factors affecting the process of recovery.

The unexpected recognition that one has heart disease is usually a crisis event for an individual. The disease could also be a chronic condition, persisting throughout life and precipitating a series of crises both for the patient and for his family.

The conceptualization of the recovery process in heart disease as a response to crisis provides strategic advantages in approaching the problem. It leads to focusing on the kinds of adaptive and maladaptive mechanisms that patients employ in coping with this illness, on the stages of recovery, and on the resources that patients use and require at each stage. Viewing response to coronary heart disease as a problem that can be approached through crisis intervention permits the use of concepts and formulations inherent in crisis theory.

In a discussion of the rehabilitation of patients with cardiac disease, a report by the World Health Organization in 1990 distinguished between phases of the recovery process in terms of time and coping tasks. The first phase is categorized as one in which the patient spends approximately 2 weeks in bed, with minimal physical activity. In the next phase, the patient spends approximately 6 weeks at home with a variety of sedentary activities. In the third phase, which lasts from 2 to 3 months, the patient makes a gradual reentry into the occupational world.

Lee and Bryner (1961) conceptualize phases according to the kinds of care the physician must provide for the patient at each point of the process. They specify (1) evaluation of the patient and his environment, (2) management of the patient, and (3) reestablishment of the patient in his community.

In other formulations of recovery phases, emphasis is on the kinds of therapeutic or rehabilitative relationships that predominate at each point. Hellerstein and Goldstone (1954) describe the first, or acute, phase as one in which the relationship between the physician and patient is of the utmost importance. The convalescent phase then follows, with the relationship between the patient and family and friends becoming primary. During the recovery, or third, phase the employer or vocational counselor becomes the vital participant in the rehabilitation of the patient with cardiac disease.

Phases have also been viewed in terms of the emotional adaptation of the patient. Kubie (1955) suggests that the first phase is marked by initial shock and the second by appreciation of the full extent of the disability. In the third, there is "recovery from the lure of hospital care"; in the fourth and final phase, there is "a facing of independent, unsupported, competitive life."

Among the most obvious and critical determinants of the outcome of the recovery process are the severity of heart damage, the degree of impairment, and the physiological resources of the patient. Whereas cardiac damage has much to do with setting limits on performance and affecting levels of adjustment, studies of physiological factors alone contribute only partially to understanding the recovery process. Research on the importance of the premorbid personality of the patient as a determinant of adjustment to illness suggests that it is a second important factor in the recovery process.

Other important factors bearing on the recovery process include the various psychological mechanisms that the patient uses in handling illness. If the recovery process is viewed as a response to a crisis situation, then the individual mechanisms used by patients appear particularly important in the resolution of the crisis. The significance of emotional response to disease has often been underlined in discussing the elements that determine recovery. McIver (1960) states, "The way in which a crisis is handled emotionally may significantly influence the eventual outcome of a case in terms of the extent of recovery and the degree of rehabilitation achieved." Reiser (1951) emphasizes that it is essential to deal with the anxieties associated with the diagnosis and symptoms of heart disease if the therapy of cardiac disease is to attain its optimal effect.

A common view is that during the acute phase of any serious illness the patient's emotional state is characterized by fear because the illness threatens his total integrity as well as his sense of personal adequacy and worth to others.

Compared with other serious illnesses, heart disease has several unique features. Associated as it is with sudden death, it is viewed by the patient and family as an immediate and severe threat to life. Hollender (1958) has written that even in the most stable patients the onset of heart disease is associated with an onslaught of anxiety. During the first days of illness, the patient with heart disease must assume a passive role, and some believe that this role tends to compound anxiety. Physical restriction usually increases feelings of helplessness, vulnerability, and depression. The patient is then handicapped in utilizing defense mechanisms that should ultimately help him to adjust to an altered status.

Although coping responses vary widely, there appears to be a core of relatively uniform responses of adjustment. For example, depression and regression have often been reported as the initial reaction to the illness. Some patients display aggression and hostility, placing the blame for the illness on external factors. Some deal with the threat to life by denial of the illness.

It has been suggested that certain coping responses are appropriate at one stage of recovery but are inappropriate at another. When patients at the same stage of recovery are compared, similar responses may function in different ways: constructively for some patients but hindering recovery for others. There is disagreement at present about the role denial plays in recovery. Some regard denial, which may lead to noncooperation with the physician, as a response of self-destruction. Others consider that denial arises from a belief in the integrity of the self and the invulnerability of the body and regard it as constructive and associated with the maintenance of health.

Because each patient reacts as an individual in this life-threatening situation, the therapist, in all probability, sees a variety of coping responses being utilized. It is not the therapist's role to change the patient's pattern of coping but to understand that his reaction to illness is part of the patient's defense.

King (1962) has stated: "Man's basis for action in health and disease is a composite of many things. One crucial variable is the way that he sees or perceives the situation . . . and all of the social ramifications that accompany it." These perceptions are conditioned by socialization in a sociocultural context. How the patient responds to the disease is influenced by what he has learned. The content of the learning is in turn determined by the norms and values of the society in which he lives. The meaning of the disease, attitude toward medical practitioners, willingness to comply with medical advice, and the patient's mangement of his life after a heart attack are all influenced by the attitudes and beliefs that he has learned.

Pertinent to the recovery process is the conceptualization of the "sick role," which Parson (1951) describes as a social role, with its own culturally defined rights and obligations. Although a person may be physiologically ill, he is not recognized as legitimately ill unless his illness fulfills the criteria or standards set by the society. Once defined as legitimately able to be in the "sick role," he is expected to meet certain expectations of others. The person is expected, for example, to make an effort toward becoming well and to seek help. In turn, he has the right to expect certain kinds of behavior from others toward him, including a willingness to permit him to relinquish his normal social role responsibilities.

Willingness to accept the sick role may mean that a patient with heart disease is likely to follow the regimen of his physician and to care for himself in ways that maximize his recovery. At the same time, reluctance to accept the sick role may also influence the recovery process favorably. Such a patient may be anxious to avoid being defined as sick. Like the willing patient, he too may follow the therapeutic regimen in order to shorten the period of incapacity. However, reluctance to view himself as sick may lead a patient to comply minimally with medical advice and to attempt full activity before he is physically able to do so.

In essence, social and cultural standards and expectations may have a strong influence on the kinds of action a patient with cardiac disease may take concerning his own health status.

The following case study illustrates how a businessman responded to a sudden heart attack with inappropriate and excessive denial.

Case Study   *Physical illness*

Mr. Z, age 43, was chairing a board meeting of his large, successful manufacturing corporation when he developed shortness of breath, dizziness, and a crushing, viselike pain in his chest. The paramedics were called, and he was taken to the medical center. Subsequently, he was admitted to the coronary care unit with a diagnosis of impending myocardial infarction.

Mr. Z was married, with three children: Steve, age 14; Sean, age 12; and Liza, age 8. He was president and the majority stockholder of a large manufacturing corporation. He had no previous history of cardiovascular problems, although his father had died at age 38 of a massive coronary occlusion. His oldest brother had died at the age of 42 from the same condition, and his other brother, still living, was a semi-invalid after suffering two heart attacks at the ages of 44 and 47.

Mr. Z was tall, slim, suntanned, and very athletic. He swam daily, jogged every morning for 30 minutes, played golf regularly, and was an avid sailor who participated in every yacht regatta, usually winning. He was very health conscious, had annual physical checkups, watched his diet, and quit smoking to avoid possible damage to his heart, determined to avoid dying young or becoming an invalid like his brothers.

When he was admitted to the coronary care unit, Mr. Z was conscious. Although in a great deal of pain, he seemed determined to control his own fate. While in the coronary care unit he was an exceedingly difficult patient, a trial to the nursing staff and his physician. He constantly watched and listened to everything going on around him and demanded complete explanations about any procedure, equipment, or medication he received. He would sleep in brief naps, and only when he was totally exhausted. Despite his obvious tension and anxiety, his condition stabilized. The damage to his heart was considered minimal, and his prognosis was good. As the pain diminished, he began asking when he could go home and when he could go back to work. He was impatient to be moved to a private room so that he could conduct some of his business by telephone.

Mr. Z denied having any anxiety or concerns about his condition, although his behavior in the unit contradicted his denial. Recognizing that Mr. Z was coping inappropriately with the stress of illness, his physician requested as consultant a therapist whose expertise was crisis intervention to work with Mr. Z to help him through the crisis period.

The therapist agreed to work with Mr. Z for 1 hour a week for 6 weeks. Their first session was scheduled the second day of his stay in the coronary care unit.

ASSESSMENT OF THE INDIVIDUAL AND THE PROBLEM

The therapist reviewed Mr. Z's chart and talked with his physician before the first session in order to gain an accurate assessment of Mr. Z's physical condition and to gain some knowledge of factors (socioeconomic status, marital status, family history, and so on) to assist in assessing his biopsychosocial needs.

In the first session, the therapist observed Mr. Z's overt and covert signs of anxiety and depression and determined, through discussion with him, his perception of what hospitalization meant to him, his usual patterns of coping with stress, and available situational supports. Through direct questions and reflective verbal feedback, she was able to elicit the reasons for his behavior and reactions to his illness and to his confinement in the coronary care unit.

Observing his suntanned, youthful appearance and the general physical condition of a very active and persistent athlete, the therapist questioned him about his lifestyle before his hospitalization. Mr. Z was quite adamant about his "minor" condition and the possibility of curtailed activity. He stated that he was very aware of his family's tendency toward cardiac conditions, but added, "I have always taken excellent care of myself to avoid the possibility of becoming a cardiac cripple like my brother." Apparently he was not too concerned about the prospect of dying; in fact, he might prefer it to the overwhelming prospect of being a useless, dependent invalid.

He expressed concern about the length of time he might have to spend in the hospital. When questioned about his concern, he stated: "I *have* to be in good shape by the second of December [approximately 3½ months]: I've entered the big yacht race, and I plan to win again!"

When he was asked how his wife and children were reacting to his illness and hospitalization, Mr. Z's facial expression and general body tension relaxed noticeably. He smiled and said, "My wife, Sue, is simply unbelievable; she takes everything in stride. She is always cool, calm, and collected. She even met with the board of directors and told them to delay any major decisions until I return—but that any minor decisions she could handle!"

The therapist asked if she could meet his wife. Mr. Z replied that his wife would be in to see him soon and suggested she stay and meet her.

After meeting with them briefly, the therapist asked Mrs. Z to stop by her office before leaving.

Session with Mrs. Z. Mrs. Z arrived at the office and sank gratefully into a chair, losing the bright, cheerful, and optimistic manner she had maintained while with her husband. Observing her concerned expression and slumped posture, the therapist inquired, "You are very concerned about your husband, aren't you?" Mrs. Z readily admitted that she was concerned but did not want her husband to know. When asked what specifically concerned her, she replied: "Jim's inability to accept any type of forced inactivity and his refusal to accept the possibility that he might have to change his hectic life-style. He can't *bear* the thought of being ill or being dependent on anyone or anything!"

The therapist explained that it is difficult for many patients to accept a passive, dependent role while ill and that it takes time for them to adjust to a changed lifestyle. She then explained to Mrs. Z that the physician had arranged for Mr. Z to have therapy sessions for the next 6 weeks to help him through his crisis. Mrs. Z seemed relieved that someone else recognized the problems confronting her husband and would help him as he worked through his feelings about his illness and unwanted but inevitable changes in life-style.

The therapist suggested that Mrs. Z might also need some support, as she too had to adjust to Mr. Z's illness. They agreed to meet for an hour each week so they could work together toward a resolution of the crisis. A convenient time was arranged each week when Mrs. Z came to visit her husband.

PLANNING THERAPEUTIC INTERVENTION

Mr. Z's denial of the possibility that he might die like his father and oldest brother or that he might become an invalid, "useless and dependent," like his other brother was considered of prime importance. It was felt that the first goal of intervention was to assist Mr. Z to ventilate his feelings about his illness and hospitalization. A second goal was to assist him to perceive the event realistically. A third goal was to give support to Mrs. Z and assist her in coping with the stress induced by her husband's hospitalization.

INTERVENTION

It was believed that Mr. Z's high anxiety level would interfere with his ability to express his feelings about his illness and his hospitalization. In an attempt to reduce his anxiety, the therapist made two recommendations to his physician, which were accepted. The first recommendation was that Mr. Z be moved out of the coronary care unit to a private room as soon as possible. The environmental surroundings in the coronary care unit, with its overwhelming and complex equipment, strange sounds, and constant activities of the staff, apparently increased Mr. Z's anxiety. Because of the stressful situation, he was not getting sufficient rest. After his move to a private room later that afternoon, he began to relax noticeably, became much less demanding of the staff, and began sleeping and eating better.

The second recommendation was that he be permitted to use the telephone for 30 minutes three times a day. Thus, he was able to conduct some of his business from his bed. This apparently made him feel less dependent, and the increased mental activity relieved some of his anxiety about becoming a "helpless" invalid.

In the next sessions, Mr. Z began to discuss—hesitantly as first, and then more freely—his feelings about his illness and his reaction to hospitalization. He discussed his father's sudden death when he was in his teens and how lost he would have felt if his older brother had not stepped in and taken over. All three brothers were very close, and the death of the oldest one, while Mr. Z was in college, reactivated the grief he had felt for his father. He was just beginning to accept his oldest brother's death when, a year later, his other brother had a severe heart attack and was unable to continue in the family business. As Mr. Z saw it, his brother was a "helpless" invalid. Mr. Z, the youngest son, then became president of the corporation and controlled the majority of the stocks.

He stated that while he certainly didn't *want* to die, he was less afraid of dying than he was of becoming useless, helpless, and a burden to his family.

Through discussion and verbal feedback, it was possible to get Mr. Z to view his illness and the changes it would make in his life in a realistic perspective. No, he was *not* an invalid. Yes, he *would* be able to work and live a normal life. No, he would not have to give up sailing, just have someone else do most of the crewing. Yes, he would be able to resume his activities but would continue them at a more leisurely pace: instead of scheduling fifteen things to do in a day, schedule seven, and so forth. Gradually, he became more accepting as he began to realize that the mild myocardial infarction was a warning he should heed and that with proper care and some diminishing of his usual hectic pace he could continue to live a productive and useful life.

The therapist continued to meet with Mrs. Z to give her support and began anticipatory planning for her husband's convalescence at home. She discussed with her Mr. Z's strong need to feel independent and in control of all situations and encouraged her to continue to let her husband make decisions for the family. She assured Mrs. Z that he would be able to continue a relatively normal life and that she did not need to protect and "coddle" him, something he would greatly resent! When asked how their children were reacting to their father's hospitalization, Mrs. Z replied, "At first they were terribly concerned and silent; now they are beginning to ask, 'When is he coming home, and what can we do?'" It was obvious that Mr. Z had strong situational support in his family!

Mr. Z's recovery progressed fairly smoothly, and he began to ambulate and take care of his basic needs. Although more accepting of his need for some assistance, he still became upset and impatient if the staff attempted to assist him in routine care.

Mr. Z was discharged after his second week, with instructions for his convalescence at home. The therapist continued to meet with Mr. and Mrs. Z at their home during the rest of the sessions to assist the family toward stabilization as Mr. Z adjusted to his new regimen of reduced activity and to provide anticipatory planning for their future.

ANTICIPATORY PLANNING

By the end of the fifth week, with the strong support of his family and the therapist, Mr. Z was able to view his illness and his feelings about curtailing some of his hectic activities in a more accepting and realistic manner. His family still consulted him for advice and opinions about family decisions. This made him feel he was still an active, participating member of the family.

He was able to conduct a large part of his business from his home by having board meetings there and by holding periodic telephone conversations to his office. His secretary came to his home 3 days a week to take dictation and to secure his signature when needed on documents. He ordered two modems and had them connected to his home and office computers. He also telefaxed materials and orders to his office employees. Thus, he still remained in control of his business life, which contributed greatly to his self-esteem.

The children and Mrs. Z were encouraged to continue in their usual daily activities so that Mr. Z would not feel that his being at home was disrupting to their lives. It also helped Mrs. Z to cope with her feelings and her desire to protect her husband from stress. Gradually, she was able to realize that he was capable of coping with some stress and that he was not as fragile as she had believed him to be.

Before termination, the therapist and Mr. Z reviewed the adjustments he had made and the insights he had gained into his own behavior. He was intellectually able to understand his reasons for his denial and dependence-independence conflicts.

He was very optimistic about his future and believed that he could adjust to a reduced-activity schedule. He still, rather wistfully, was hoping his physician would approve his entering the yacht race.

He was realistic about his physical condition and the possibility that a coronary attack could occur again, stating, "At least now I've learned to relax and roll with the punches."

Mrs. Z and the children felt they would be able to cope with the occasional bouts of frustration and temper flare-ups of Mr. Z. They were now aware of how difficult it was for him to make the many adjustments necessary to his new way of life.

SUMMATION OF THE PARADIGM (Figure 6-6)

Mr. Z's fear of becoming a "cardiac cripple" like his brother distorted his perception of the event. He was unable to relax and be dependent in the coronary care unit. His anxiety and tension made him unable to accept the fact that he had had a myocardial infarction. His family and his colleagues—his usual situational supports—were unable to be with him because of hospital rules and his restricted activity. He used denial excessively because he was unable to accept the fact that he might have to change his life-style. Because this was his first hospitalization and the first time he had to be in a dependent role, his anxiety increased considerably.

ADDENDUM

Several months later, the physician informed the therapist that he had permitted Mr. Z to enter the yacht race as a passenger, not as crew, and that his yacht had finished third.

Alzheimer's—Theoretical Concepts

The term *organic brain syndrome* (OBS) is used to describe symptoms of emotional, perceptual, and cognitive dysfunction arising from disturbances in previously unimpaired brain structure and mental functioning. These symptoms may be caused by physical or chemical insult to the brain, overload or deprivation of sensory input, overwhelming stress and anxiety, or degenerative disease of the brain caused by factors as yet generally unknown (Mace and Rabins, 1981; Seltzer and Frazier, 1978; Heller and Kornfeld, 1975).

Organic brain syndrome is one of the most prevalent causes for abnormalities in judgment, intellectual functioning, and behavior. It is usually classified in two major categories, acute and chronic. The generally accepted distinguishing factor between them is reversibility of symptoms as a result of appropriate medical intervention (Lipowski, 1980). When symptoms are reversible, the diagnosis is "acute organic brain syndrome"; when irreversible, the disorder is termed "chronic organic brain syndrome."

When no particular pathological process can be identified directly as the cause of chronic, or irreversible, brain syndrome, the condition is considered to be primary

CASE STUDY: MR. Z

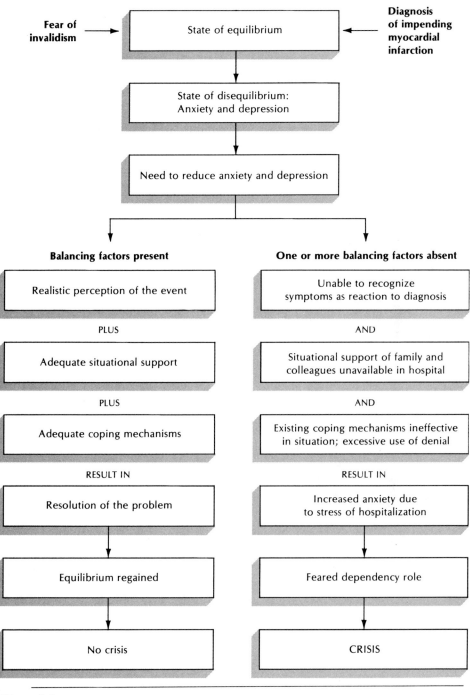

Figure 6-6

and classified according to age of onset. A diagnosis of "primary degenerative dementia, presenile" indicates that the condition occurred before the sixth decade in life, and one of "primary degenerative dementia, senile" indicates that it occurred after that age. However, according to Seltzer and Frazier (1978), this has always been somewhat of an arbitrary designation.

Of those conditions for which no primary, underlying cause can be identified, Alzheimer's disease appears to be the most frequent. Definitive diagnosis still depends on the presence or absence of specific abnormalities within the structure of the brain tissue. At present, no specific treatment is available, even if a diagnosis is confirmed (Mace and Rabins, 1981; Reisberg, 1981).

Alzheimer's is a progressive, degenerative disease that attacks the brain and impairs judgment with mental functioning. Its victims generally experience confusion and personality and behavior changes, and ultimately they require full-time supervision or custodial care. From onset of symptoms, the life span of an Alzheimer's victim can range from 3 to more than 20 years (Alzheimer's Disease and Related Disorder Association [ADRDA], 1991).

It is estimated that approximately 4 million Americans are afflicted with Alzheimer's. It is the fourth leading cause of death among adults, with more than 100,000 lives lost annually (ADRDA, 1991).

Unless a cure or means of prevention are found for Alzheimer's, an estimated 12 to 14 million Americans will be affected by the year 2000.

Approximately 10% of the population over 65 years of age is afflicted with Alzheimer's. The percentage rises to 47.2% in those over the age of 85, which is the *fastest*-growing segment of the U.S. population. This is significant because the nation's entire aged population is increasing rapidly, and it is estimated that by the year 2050, the United States will have 67.5 million people over the age 65, compared with 25.5 million today. It is truly the "graying of America!"

More than 50% of all nursing home patients are victims of Alzheimer's Disease or a related disorder. The annual cost of nursing home care ranges between $24,000 and $36,000.

Financing for care for Alzheimer's disease, including costs of diagnosis, treatment, nursing home care, informal care, and lost wages, is estimated to be more than $80 billion each year. The federal government covers $4.4 billion and the states another $4.1 billion. Much of the remaining costs are borne by patients and their families.

Congress appropriated $138 million for Alzheimer's disease research in fiscal year 1990. This figure represents a 12% increase over 1989 levels, but still amounts to just over $35 per patient. In addition, neither Medicare nor most private health insurance programs pay for the long-term health care required by Alzheimer's patients. Approximately 90% of the cost is borne by victims and their families (ADRDA, 1991).

The initial symptoms of Alzheimer's are insidious and often imperceptible as organic changes start to occur in the brain and a decline in many areas of intellectual and physical abilities begins. Initially, no objective or subjective symptoms are reported. As the disease progresses, the earliest noticeable symptoms are generally related to memory impairment. Whereas motor activities are not affected at this time, subjective awareness of memory loss begins to interfere more and more with the person's daily living activities. It is a rare person among us who has not occasionally misplaced needed items, forgotten familiar addresses and telephone numbers, and even forgotten the names of close friends. If these lapses do not happen too often, the usual response can be momentary embarrassment or irritation. We blame it on being tired or under stress or on just having too much on our minds to remember, but there is always a sense of self-confidence that the memory will return.

For the Alzheimer's patient, however, such forgetfulness begins to become chronic, something that cannot be shrugged off so easily as only temporary. As subjective awareness and concerns over memory loss increase, self-confidence in an ability to recall lost memories diminishes. For many, written checklists and notes of things to do become a way of life. Eventually, however, these no longer suffice as memory supports as they, too, become lost and forgotten.

As memory loss increases, signs of early confusional behavior begin. A person easily becomes lost in unfamiliar places and needs to depend increasingly on others for help in finding his way when away from home or other familiar locations. Changes to new environments create much anxiety, particularly when combined with stressful events such as an illness requiring hospitalization. The person's forgetfulness begins to be noticed by others and can no longer be seen simply as temporary or "normal" behavior. At the same time, recent memory loss becomes much more subjectively noted. Ability to concentrate decreases, and the use of denial as a defense mechanism increases.

From this stage in intellectual decline, identifiable overt symptoms of Alzheimer's begin, and regression continues into a late confusional stage. The person can still handle his own immediate physical needs, yet motor skills gradually decrease. Language becomes affected, and it becomes increasingly difficult for the person to find the right words. The ability to concentrate diminishes greatly, and the ability to handle finances, cooking, and other daily decision-making activities suffers accordingly. The individual becomes more withdrawn and anxious. Frustration and anger increase as the use of denial becomes less effective. No longer can he deny to himself or to others that something is wrong with him.

Inevitably, whether slowly or rapidly, regression continues into a period of early dementia. At this stage, such persons can survive no longer without assistance from others. Now there is time disorientation and frequently forgetfulness of familiar family names. Although the person is still capable of handling the basic functions of daily living (such as feeding himself, bowel and bladder control, and bathing), caretaking needs increase greatly as intellectual and motor skills continue to decline. For many, this is a period of rapid decline as the disease progresses toward the stage of middle dementia.

By this time, there are symptoms of hallucinatory types of perceptions, which are responded to with fear, agitation, and even violence. Familiar faces may be recognized, but name recall is nearly nil. Variable awareness of recent events and past memories may be sketchy and incomplete.

As motor skills decrease, bowel and bladder incontinence begins. Constant attendance becomes necessary for all activities of daily living. Caretaking activities may exceed the abilities of family and friends; institutionalization may be the only family recourse. In the final, late dementia stage of Alzheimer's, the person becomes increasingly vegetative and requires total care. Speech decreases to one or two words, all intellectual skills disappear, and motor skills decline until full assistance is needed to eat, drink, and even turn in bed. Eventually, there is coma and finally death.

Alzheimer's disease usually leads to death within 7 to 10 years. However, some deaths may occur within as little as 3 to 4 years, and others may not occur for 15 years (Mace and Rabins, 1981).

A diagnosis of Alzheimer's for a family member means that the whole family, as well as the patient, must learn to live with the condition. Alzheimer's is insidious in its onset; a misdiagnosis of early symptoms can create added stress for everyone concerned. Too often the early symptoms of memory loss, depression, passive dependency, and emotional lability are misunderstood or passed off as transient reactions to situational stress.

As the disease progresses, a person with Alzheimer's becomes impaired in his ability to control the appropriate expression of his own emotions and comprehend the effect of his behavior on others. He is emotionally labile, overreacts, and often appears insensitive to others' feelings. Emotional changes often appear as exaggerations of previously established behavioral characteristics. For example, the passive and withdrawn person may become even more dependent, suspicious, and depressed; the characteristically independent, aggressive person may appear demanding, hysterical, and even manic in behavior.

As organic changes in the brain occur, dependency on others increases. This may not be too disturbing for one whose past personality characteristics were those of passive dependency. However, for one whose personality characteristics emphasized independent, aggressive behaviors, feelings of frustration and anger increase as dependency needs increase. This can lead to what has been termed *catastrophic reaction,* which is best described as an emotional overreaction, one that is obviously out of proportion to an anxiety-provoking situation. It occurs as intellectual impairment increases and emotional control decreases. This is a fairly common response as the affected individual is increasingly confronted with failure in achieving what formerly were, to that person, simple tasks. Often believing that the individuals concerned have full control over their behavioral changes, family and friends may respond inappropriately in turn. Such a reaction may only serve to increase stress and, consequently, the severity of the symptoms exhibited. Family members almost invariably need to cope at some time with feelings of fear, anger, guilt, shame, and isolation, as well as persistent feelings of grief and mourning. These feelings may arise intermittently and in varying degrees, dependent on each member's past experiences, values, personal resources, and current life situation.

Any unusual problems arising with the patient may, in fact, be a symptom of family dysfunction. It would not be unusual for family members, no longer able to relate to each other openly and directly, to relate through problems as they arise in the patient. It is as though there is a need for the patient to have problems in order for family members to continue to relate. This, of course, only serves to reinforce the patient's problematic behaviors.

Once the diagnosis of Alzheimer's has been confirmed and denial of the illness diminishes, each family member begins to face the reality of its consequences for himself as well as for the patient. Each member strongly feels a need to find a satisfactory reason or meaning for the occurrence of the illness. Until one is found—real or imagined—feelings of helplessness, powerlessness, and insecurity exist. It is realistic for family members to be anxious, confused, and fearful and to feel alone with the situation. It is not at all unusual for them to be completely uninformed when a diagnostic label like this is attached to one of their members. Their only source of knowledge could be one of hearsay misinformation. There may also be misperception of correct information provided them at the time of the diagnosis.

One natural outcome is feelings of anger and aggression, which can mobilize members toward constructive actions, thereby reducing feelings of helplessness and powerlessness. Another outcome may be outwardly destructive behavior, which leads to increased feelings of helplessness and anger, compounded by feelings of guilt. Depression and discouragement are the most common feelings for close relatives or friends of those with chronic, irreversible diseases. Anger and frustration leading to rage reactions or internalized toward feelings of suicide are not uncommon during the progressive course of the illness.

As a family develops, highly structured roles, functions, and expectations are established for each member. None is created in isolation, and all are reciprocal. A change in any one member almost inevitably results in changes throughout the structure of family roles. Equilibrium within the family system depends largely on all members' continuing acceptance and performance of their unique roles, responsibilities, and expectations.

Family members are faced with the need to identify the meaning of the functional loss of one of their members and what it will mean to each member as family roles are redefined and functions redistributed. Until these are dealt with, conflict and chaos are inevitable. The family system becomes less cohesive and could eventually break up or disintegrate. Any one role change, subtle or otherwise, almost invariably leads to change in those of other members. Welcome or unwelcome, planned or unplanned, a role change can affect each member's usual ways of thinking, feeling, and behaving. Feelings in particular strongly affect perceptions and the thinking processes.

Not everyone who becomes aware that a family member has an irreversible illness responds the same way. The degree to which an individual reacts is, in great part, determined by how much he perceives the illness interfering in his daily life.

If a parent is affected and children are involved in the caretaking process, role reversal becomes an inevitable problem with which they must deal. This occurs as responsibilities and control—from the more abstract, intellectual, decision-making responsibilities to, eventually, basic physical functions—gradually must be taken from the affected person. This is particularly difficult for many to accept because of the relatively early age at which Alzheimer's occurs and the insidious nature of its onset and progress. It would not be unusual to find strong feelings of ambivalence, anger, and reluctance to accept the loss of the child role and the reversal of dependency roles with the parent. These feelings are compounded by the fact that the parent may physically appear quite well and capable of self-care until the later stages of the illness. To accept the reversal in roles is also to acknowledge anticipation of an ultimate desertion by death.

Family members experience many conflicting and unique feelings as the disease progresses. Emotions may run the gamut from hopeful optimism to hopeless despair. All these emotions are as highly complex and variable as is each member's perception of the situation and its effect on his own life.

There may be feelings of frustration and anger as caregivers' patience wears thin and the caregiving chores continue to increase. It is not uncommon at all to observe the attitude switch from "What did *he* ever do to deserve this?" to "What did *I* ever do to deserve this?"

It is not uncommon to read in your local newspaper of the murder/suicide of an older couple. The autopsy more often than not reveals that the individual who was killed suffered from Alzheimer's disease, and the individual who committed suicide was the family's caretaker, that is, the husband or wife. The caretaker apparently feels physically and psychologically unable to "take care" anymore.

Denial is not an uncommon initial response when a person is overwhelmed with a stressful situation. However, for those who do not cope through use of denial, the grief process may begin in anticipation of the loss. The more a person is emotionally invested in the loved one, the more threatened that person may feel in anticipation of the loss.

The four phases of grief and mourning are a response to any situation involving loss, not just the death of a loved one. Families of patients with Alzheimer's are faced with prolonged periods of grief and mourning. This greatly differs from an overwhelming feeling of grief that gradually lessens as time passes after a loved one's death. Grief and mourning for death is sanctioned by our society, but overt, prolonged grief and mourning for a chronically ill person, particularly one who looks physically well, is rarely accepted as connected with death. More often, such mourning may be perceived as self-pity or weakness.

When the stresses of caring for the affected person become so great that a family or personal crisis is precipitated, professional counseling may be required to avert maladaptive problem-solving behavior. The case study that follows depicts a crisis that was precipitated by a daughter who could not cope with caring for her mother, who had Alzheimer's.

Case Study   *Alzheimer's*

ASSESSMENT OF THE INDIVIDUAL AND THE PROBLEM

Frank was referred to a community crisis clinic by his family physician because of his increasing symptoms of tension, anxiety, and depression. When he arrived, he appeared quite tense with visible hand tremors. The receptionist contacted a therapist, and Frank was directed to the therapist's office.

When asked by the therapist why he had come to the clinic that day, Frank replied in a very depressed tone of voice, "My whole world is collapsing around me. My wife, Molly, is sick, but I've been able to handle it—until now. My daughter has always been such a help, but now she is walking out on us. I just can't handle much more; I can't do it alone."

He became increasingly agitated as he spoke, his voice rising in anger. After a long pause, he seemed to regain his composure. In response to direct questioning by the therapist, he slowly described the problem that had led up to this visit to the clinic for help.

Frank said that he and his wife, Molly, who were both 56 years old, had been married for 20 years. They had one daughter, Kim, who was 17 years old and had just graduated from high school. He described his family life as "good, no more problems than most people," until about a year ago when Molly had had to quit her job. She had worked for the same person all of their married life. When that person had retired a year ago, Molly was reassigned to a new office in the same company. Within a few days, she had begun to complain that her new boss was very disorganized and seemed to go out of his way to find fault with her work. She said that she had even been accused of such ridiculous things as misplacing records and forgetting to tell him of his appointments. She had started going to work earlier and staying later in an effort to "get the boss organized," but he continued to criticize and complain about her work. Frank said that Molly became increasingly irritable, preoccupied, and forgetful at home during that time. It seemed as though she were scapegoating him and Kim for all her problems at work.

Finally, she came home one day and told him that she had been given the option of resigning or being demoted. With Frank's encouragement, she decided to resign and take a few week's vacation before looking for another job. Frank had hoped that, with time and some rest, she would "pull herself together, and eventually become her cheerful, organized self again." This, however, was not to be the case.

As the weeks passed, Molly seemed to become even more disorganized and forgetful. She never again spoke of looking for a new job. She argued increasingly, accusing him and Kim of misplacing her personal items, losing telephone messages, and so on. Bills were left forgotten and unpaid in her desk until Frank learned to watch for them in the mail.

Neither he nor Kim seemed able to reason with her any longer about these incidents. Any references to her forgetfulness were met with denial and angry responses. Finally, they learned to cope as best they could with her erratic, irresponsible behaviors. Over time, they gradually took over many of her household responsibilities.

Molly first displayed overt signs of confusion, disorientation, and memory loss about 6 months before Frank came to the clinic, when she was hospitalized for elective surgery. Nurses had found her late at night wandering down the halls in her bare feet, "looking for my bedroom." When the nurses suggested that she had lost her way, she became verbally abusive to them for saying that to her. Before dawn, she was found fully dressed and sitting on a chair in the hallway. When questioned, she replied that she was "waiting for Frank to drive me to work." Further questioning revealed that she was disoriented as to place, could not recall the day of the week or her physician's name, and had forgotten why she had come to the hospital.

Following this episode, further tests and examinations were completed, and a diagnosis of Alzheimer's disease was made. Findings suggested that Molly had progressed into the early confusional stage.

When asked how he and Molly responded to this news, Frank said that their initial feelings were quite mixed. "We were glad to finally find a physical reason for her behavior changes but were shocked and really couldn't believe that there was no known cure for it. It made me really angry that this could happen to any of us."

When it was strongly suggested that Frank contact a local Alzheimer's support group for ongoing support and information about Molly's care at home, Frank saw no immediate need to do so. To him, Molly appeared quite healthy. As he perceived it, all that he and Kim would need was "a little more patience with Molly when she forgot things or lost her temper." Over time, they had learned to help her avoid stressful situations, even though it sometimes made life more stressful for them. Gradually, however, the relationship between him and Kim distanced as he spent increasing amounts of time away from home at his job.

At first, Kim never complained about having to spend more time at home with her mother. Neighbors and friends visited often, and she could still leave Molly alone for brief periods. As Molly's memory loss increased, however, Molly's frustration tolerance decreased. Her unprovoked irritability became much more frequent; soon, visitors rarely came to see them.

At the same time, Kim found herself having to assume an increasing number of the household roles and responsibilities formerly held by her mother. Any attempts to bring in a housekeeper or a companion for her mother were met with overt antagonism from Molly.

Two evenings ago, Frank had come home late and was confronted by a tearful, angry Kim. She told him that she "couldn't take it anymore" and was going to move out if he didn't find someone else to take care of her mother. He said that her outburst really took him by surprise. When he asked her the cause of this sudden change in attitude, she angrily responded, "Sudden? There is nothing sudden about this! For weeks I've been telling you how I feel, but you never listen to me anymore. You're always too busy at work, and when you come home you seem to ignore just how much mother has changed. She's become like a spoiled, demanding little child. I feel more like a live-in babysitter than like her daughter. I have no life of my own anymore—and you don't seem to care what happens to me!" The conversation was abruptly ended by Kim leaving the house and slamming the door behind her. She called her father about an hour later to say that she was going to spend the night at a friend's house. She added that she still had a lot to think over but would be home the next morning.

Frank said that he never slept that night, his mind in a turmoil of thinking about what Kim had said. He felt shocked and overwhelmed with strongly ambivalent feelings toward Molly, who slept quietly upstairs in their bedroom. He said that he "suddenly faced reality—and hated it." He felt completely alone and trapped, with no way out of the whole situation. As he described it, "By morning I had the shakes, couldn't concentrate on anything, and felt like hell."

When Kim came back the next morning, neither mentioned what had been said the night before. He left for his office as quickly as he could.

For the next several hours, he drove his car randomly about the city, thinking about what had been happening to his life for the past year. It was only then, he said, that he finally faced the reality that he had lost forever the Molly that he had loved and married. Now he was in danger of losing Kim, too. He suddenly felt so overwhelmed with grief that he pulled the car to the side of the street and parked. He felt so sick and trembled so severely that he was afraid to drive. As soon as he felt able, he drove directly to his physician's office, where he was seen immediately. It was from there that he had been referred to the clinic.

PLANNING THERAPEUTIC INTERVENTION

The therapist's assessment was that, until his confrontation with Kim, Frank had successfully used denial to cope with Molly's illness. This evaluation was supported by his avoidance of opportunities to obtain more information about Alzheimer's from one of the local support groups.

As Molly's symptoms became more overt, he avoided having to "do something about it" by extending his time at work. When Kim had tried to communicate her need for help and understanding, he effectively managed to tune her out. As a result, he was not consciously lying when he said that he was shocked at the "sudden change in Kim's attitude."

Frank's crisis was precipitated by the threatened loss of his daughter and compounded by unresolved feelings of grief and mourning for the anticipated loss of his wife.

The goals of intervention were to assist Frank to identify and ventilate his unrecognized feelings about his wife, to help him obtain appropriate situational support for himself and Kim as he dealt with plans for Molly's future care, and to help him obtain an intellectual understanding of role reversal as it was affecting Kim's relationship with her mother.

INTERVENTION

During the first session, it was determined that Frank was not suicidal. When asked to describe himself as he "usually was," he said that he was a person who prided himself on being able to maintain control over his life. He believed that, to be successful, a person should be able to set goals and, with good planning, achieve them.

Reflecting further on his feelings about Molly, he admitted to the therapist that, deep down, he had always believed that Molly could have controlled her behavior if she really wanted to do so. He had felt that her failure to do so was, in some way, a personal rejection of him. No longer able to communicate with her about his feelings, he had used denial and avoidance to cope.

As Molly's condition deteriorated, he had felt more angry and frustrated with her and used his work to justify the increasing amount of time spent away from home.

With further discussion and reflection about Molly's behavioral changes, it became very apparent that Frank had little factual information about Alzheimer's disease. His anxiety had been so high when he was first informed by the doctors that he remembered hearing little other than that her memory loss would continue to get worse and that there was no cure.

As Molly's increasing episodes of unprovoked anger increased, their few remaining friends had gradually begun to avoid contact with her. Recalling this now with the therapist, he acknowledged that, in fact, this had been a relief for him.

He no longer had to worry about what she might do or say to their friends if she became upset.

What he had failed to realize, though, was the added stress that this had placed on Kim. Upon further questioning and reflection, he said, "Could it be that I didn't listen to Kim because I didn't want to know? I didn't want to hear how bad things had really become?" He paused, and then said softly, "The Molly that I loved so much left me long ago. I miss her so much and wish that she could come back, even for a little while. There's so much I want to say to her. While I stay away from home, I can make believe that she's still there, waiting for me. Going home hurts so very much."

It was suggested that he now contact the local Alzheimer's support group to learn about alternative ways available to him for Molly's care at home. He was made to realize that, unless he began to face the reality of Molly's illness and the situation at his home, he might well lose Kim, too.

When questioned further about his confrontation with Kim the evening before, he seemed unable to understand why Kim felt so angry about her mother. Further discussion focused on the way Kim's roles and responsibilities in the family had changed during the past few months. As he slowly identified these changes for the therapist, he began to obtain an intellectual understanding of parent-child role reversal and its effect on the child, particularly on one as young as Kim.

Gradually, he began to recognize Kim's confrontation for what it was: a cry for his understanding of what was happening to her. She was overwhelmed by her inability to meet the ever-increasing dependency needs of her mother without some help from him. Unable to communicate her own dependency needs to either him or her mother, she saw escape from the entire situation as her only solution.

It was suggested to Frank that one of his first priorities was to find someone else to assume major responsibility for Molly's care and supervision. Until this happened, he could expect further confrontations with Kim and should not be surprised if Kim carried out her threat to leave home.

As an interim measure, Frank decided to take a few weeks of long overdue vacation time and stay home to help out until he could find someone to provide full-time help with Molly's care.

During the second session, Frank appeared much more optimistic as he described his past week at home. He said that he and Kim had talked together "for hours" the evening after his first session at the clinic. He reflected that it had been difficult at first for both of them to face the other with their feelings. "But," he added, "it was such a relief when we did. Until then, neither of us had realized just how far apart we had become and how much we needed to stick together to work things out."

During the past week, Frank also had contacted the local Alzheimer's support group. By prearrangement, two members visited his home to meet with him, Kim, and Molly. He recalled his surprise at how easily Molly had appeared to accept the "strangers'" visit and the apparent ease with which they included her in the conversation. As a result of the visit, appropriate resources were identified for assistance in Molly's care. After several interviews with applicants for a housekeeper's position and with Molly's agreement, they finally hired a woman who seemed best able to cope with Molly's needs. The woman had moved in 2 days before this session and, he reported, "Molly hasn't scared her off yet." However, he would continue to remain at home for another week to help Molly adjust to any new changes in her daily activities.

Frank and Kim also had attended a meeting of the local Alzheimer's group. It surprised them both to find several other young people of Kim's age present. When asked to describe his feelings about the meeting, he said that both he and Kim had gone to the meeting "not expecting much, maybe coffee, cake, and sympathy, but that's all." Instead, they found a group of people who, he said, seemed to know exactly what his family had been going through. He learned that many of his experiences were not unique, but common to all of them. "For the first time," he said, "I was able to get some answers that were useful to us. Maybe no one could tell us *why* she got this disease, but this group of people could give me some good suggestions of how to help all of us deal with it." Most important for both him and Kim, as they left the meeting, was their feeling of no longer being alone with their problems and that now a support group was available to them as problems arose.

ANTICIPATORY PLANNING

Before the end of the session, the therapist and Frank reviewed and assessed the adjustment that he had made and his insights into his own feelings about Molly and the effects of her illness on his future. They also discussed his understanding of the effect that the process of role reversal with her mother was having on Kim. It was strongly suggested that he encourage Kim's continued attendance at the Alzheimer's group meetings. The purpose was to provide her with ongoing peer support as she dealt with her changing relationship with her mother.

He was commended for taking direct action during the past week and obtaining appropriate resources to help him with his ongoing situation at home. Such action strongly suggested that he no longer was coping solely through denial and avoidance but was making a conscious effort to perceive the situation realistically.

Frank was encouraged to continue to be more direct in his communications with Kim and to let her know that he was recognizing that she had needs, too. Before termination, he was reassured that he could return for help with any future crises, should the need arise.

SUMMATION OF THE PARADIGM (Figure 6-7)

Frank had used denial and avoidance as methods for coping with his feelings toward Molly's illness and eventual death. Kim saw his behavior as a rejection of her efforts to communicate to him the realities of her mother's deteriorating condition and its effect on her own unmet dependency needs. Failing to recognize the extent to which the process of role reversal with her mother had affected Kim's life, Frank perceived her threat to leave home as yet another rejection and threatened loss of someone close to him. Lacking any previous coping experience with his new role demands, his anxiety and depression increased to an intolerable level; Frank was in a state of crisis.

Intervention focused on helping him to identify and understand his unrecognized feelings toward Molly, to obtain an intellectual understanding of the effects of role

CASE STUDY: FRANK

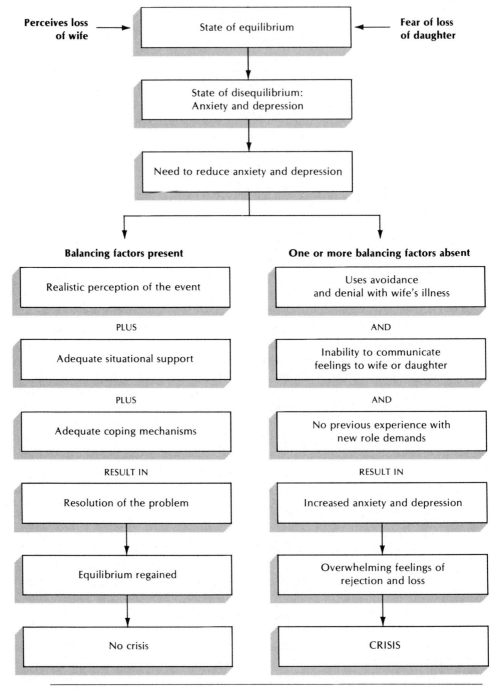

Perceives loss of wife →	State of equilibrium ← **Fear of loss of daughter**

State of disequilibrium:
Anxiety and depression

Need to reduce anxiety and depression

Balancing factors present	**One or more balancing factors absent**
Realistic perception of the event	Uses avoidance and denial with wife's illness
PLUS	AND
Adequate situational support	Inability to communicate feelings to wife or daughter
PLUS	AND
Adequate coping mechanisms	No previous experience with new role demands
RESULT IN	RESULT IN
Resolution of the problem	Increased anxiety and depression
Equilibrium regained	Overwhelming feelings of rejection and loss
No crisis	CRISIS

Figure 6-7

reversal on Kim, and to obtain appropriate situational support for the family because they, individually and as a unit, would undoubtedly be confronted with more stress-provoking situations in the progress of Molly's illness.

Elder Abuse—Theoretical Concepts

If the 1960s were devoted to child abuse and the 1970s to spouse abuse, then the 1980s and 1990s have certainly been the decades devoted to elder abuse. From the latter part of the 1970s to the present, researchers, academicians, professionals in applied settings, and policymakers at all levels of government have given increasing attention to elder abuse (Kosberg, 1988).

The multitude of empirical investigations of the incidences, causes, effectiveness of interventions, and consequences of elder abuse have been paralleled by the number of critical assessments of these research efforts (Hudson, 1986; Johnson, 1986; O'Rourke, 1981; Pedrick-Cornell and Gelles, 1982; Yin, 1985).

In addition to the empirical research on elder abuse has been the attention given to the problem by social, legal, and health care professionals. Academicians, community-based professionals, and the general public have been working closely with one another to address elder abuse. Efforts at the community level have focused on communitywide education, detection, mechanisms, and coordination of resources (Caro, 1966; Douglas and Hickey, 1983; Hooyman, 1983; Sager, 1986).

Assessment protocols have been developed that concentrate on physical and behavioral symptoms of elder abuse. These protocols are focused on identifying abuse but were developed with the assumption that problems can be identified after abuse has occurred. Protective services and mandatory reporting of elder abuse resulted in the identification of potential problems (Faulkner, 1982; Salend and others, 1984). Despite these measures, elder abuse is an invisible problem. In *Elder Abuse: The Hidden Problem* (U.S. Congress, House Select Committee on Aging, 1980), it was estimated that one of every three cases of child abuse is reported, but only one of every six cases of elder abuse is reported. Several explanations for the invisibility of elder abuse reflect factors that affect both research and applied efforts.

The family is sacrosanct, and interference with family life by outsiders is not tolerated, even when professionals believe they are justified in intervening when there are family dysfunctions. Family members may engage in a conspiracy of silence and reject attempts by outsiders to explore or intervene in their lives.

The American Medical Association (AMA) has issued its first guidelines on elder abuse, urging physicians and other health care professionals to be more alert to signs of mistreatment or neglect of older patients by their families or caregivers (Formica, 1992). The 42-page guidelines, part of a new AMA campaign against family violence, come amid growing national concern about a long-hidden problem in which as many as 2 million elderly Americans are believed to be victims of abuse or neglect (Formica, 1992).

Russell (1992) has stated that the identifying signs of possible mistreatment are the following:

Physical abuse: Violence that may result in pain or injury. Signs include unexplained injuries or inconsistent explanations involving bruises, welts, cuts, fractures, burns, or other problems.

Physical neglect: Failure of the caregiver to provide necessary services, such as adequate nutrition or physical aids like eyeglasses, hearing aids, or false teeth. Signs include dehydration, malnutrition, ulcers, poor hygiene, and lack of compliance with medical regimens.

Psychological abuse: Conduct that causes mental anguish, like verbal harassment, threats of punishment, or isolation. Signs include extreme withdrawal, depression or agitation, infantile behavior, and ambivalent feelings toward caregivers.

Psychological neglect: The failure to provide social stimulation, as when a dependent older person is left alone for long periods of time or is ignored or given the silent treatment. Signs include withdrawal, depression, agitation, and infantile regressive behavior.

Financial abuse or neglect: Misuse of the older person's income or resources or failure to use available funds and resources as necessary to the health and well being of the older adult. Signs include substandard care in the home despite adequate financial resources, confusion by patient about his financial situation, and sudden transfers of funds.

Violations of personal rights: Ignoring older persons' rights and capability to make their own decisions, especially about such private matters as health care or living arrangements. Signs include reports by the patients or observations of interactions with the caregiver.

Burns (1992) states that the nonprofit Elder Abuse Prevention Program in Denver lists five indications of signs of financial abuse. The five indications are listed in the box at right.

Because abuse occurs within the confines of a private dwelling, it is hidden from outside scrutiny. Unlike the circumstances of children, whose abuse can be detected outside the home, there are no requirements such as school attendance and required health checkups for the elderly. They do not need to leave their homes and risk being seen by nonfamily members.

The elderly are reluctant to report abuse by relatives. Lau and Kosberg (1979) found that one third of the elderly who were judged to have been abused denied any problem. It is not difficult to understand the reasons the elderly do not report abuse. They may believe that the problem is a family affair. They may fear reprisals by the abuser or may be embarrassed or ashamed of the behavior of the abuser. The elderly may be reluctant to initiate legal or criminal action against a relative for fear that the solution will be worse than the problem itself—institutionalization. They may believe that they are being paid back for their earlier abusive behavior toward others, such as a child or spouse.

The invisibility of elder abuse can result from the failure of professionals to detect or report the problem, even in states having mandatory reporting legislation. Although empirical verification is lacking, the reluctance on the part of professionals to report child abuse may also be a characteristic of the professional responses to mandatory reporting laws for elder abuse. It is suspected that not all professionals in states with mandatory reporting legislation are aware of their responsibility (O'Brien, 1986).

For these reasons, elder abuse often remains invisible. Community efforts, protective services, and mandatory reporting legislation affect only a fraction of the

---

INDICATIONS OF FINANCIAL ABUSE

1. Unusual activity in bank accounts, such as withdrawals from automated teller machines when the person cannot walk or get to the bank.
2. A power of attorney given when the person is unable to comprehend the financial situation and, in reality is unable to give valid power of attorney.
3. Numerous unpaid bills, especially overdue rent, when someone is supposed to be paying the bills.
4. Recent acquaintances expressing gushy, undying affection for a wealthy older person.
5. A friend or housekeeper trying to isolate the older adult from friends or family.

---

abused elderly and only after the abusive behavior has occurred. Accordingly, it is important to place frail and vulnerable elderly persons in the care of appropriate family members or other persons.

Family membership does not prevent people from engaging in abusive behavior; in fact, family members have been found to be the major perpetrators of elder abuse. The instinctive and uncritical use of family members as caregivers of vulnerable, elderly persons should not continue. A systematic assessment of the capacity of potential or present family caregivers to provide nonabusive care is needed (Kosberg, 1988).

The predominant image of elder abuse, which has been derived from earlier studies and reinforced by the popular media, is that abuse is primarily committed against the elderly by their children. The stereotype is that of a mentally and physically dependent elder who moves in with and becomes a difficult burden to a resentful daughter or son. The son or daughter, in response to frustration, lashes out or withholds certain necessities of life. Pillemer and Finkelhor (1988) found that 58% of elder abuse was committed by the victim's spouse; 24% of the abusers were the victim's children. Among elders who lived with their spouses alone, the rate of abuse was 41 per 1000. Among those who lived with their children alone, the rate was 44 per 1000. The percentage difference is because many more elderly live with their spouses than with their children. Actually, spouses do not seem inherently more violent toward their partners than children toward their parents, but spouses are more likely to be present in an elderly person's household and thus their opportunities for abusive behavior are greater.

Elder abuse has been the most recent and most neglected form of family violence to vie for public attention. Those who have sought to gain this attention have cast the problem in its most compelling light. The image of one elderly person hitting or neglecting another does not convey the same pathos as an elderly person being abused by an adult child.

Although ample evidence of variables associated with elder abuse exists, inappropriate placements continue to result in problems for vulnerable, elderly persons. Most community programs and state legislation focus on the problem of elder abuse after it has occurred and necessitate the detection and reporting of abuse. Yet the problem is essentially invisible, and greater attention should be given to assessing the potential caregivers of impaired older persons. Assessment should include attention to high-risk indicators for the aged person, caregiver, and family system, along with the perceptions of family members. Such assessments will not eliminate the problem, but public education, professional awareness, detection protocols, alternatives for and support of family care, and social legislation may contribute to a comprehensive effort in preventing this form of abuse (AMA, 1992).

Collaboration between researchers, legislators, practitioners, professionals, and the general public needs to continue. Those working with the elderly should remember that no group of elderly persons is immune to the possibility of abusive behavior.

Elder abuse will continue as long as ageism and violence exist. The following characteristics appear to make the elderly especially vulnerable to elder abuse:

1. *Female.* Simply because there are more older women than there are older men, more of the abused elderly are women. Older women also are less likely to resist abusive behavior and are more vulnerable to sexual molestation.
2. *Advanced age.* The older the person, the higher the risk of abusive behavior. Advanced age is also associated with physical and mental impairments and an inability to resist adversities.
3. *Dependency.* Older persons who depend on others for their care are more vulnerable. Economic dependency can result in hostility by a caregiver and lead to abuse.
4. *Internalizing blame.* Older persons engaged in self-blame may be especially vulnerable to elder abuse through self-deprecating behavior. They may fail to acknowledge the abuse as the fault of the abuser.
5. *Excessive loyalty.* An older person who has a strong sense of loyalty to an abusive caregiver will probably not seek to report the problem.
6. *Past abuse.* Older persons who have been subjected to abusive behavior by a family member in the past are candidates for similar treatment when they display increasing impairments and dependency.
7. *Isolation.* An older person isolated from others may be especially vulnerable to abusive behavior because of the lack of detection and intervention by neighbors, friends, other relatives, or service providers.

People who provide services to the elderly need to be educated about the problem of spouse abuse. If their image of elder abuse is limited to the current stereotype of elderly persons mistreated by their adult children, they are not likely to properly identify situations where the aged are being abused by their spouses.

The elderly themselves need to be educated about spouse abuse. They grew up in an era when spouse abuse was tolerated more and when information on the subject was not available. Elderly victims may be vulnerable to spouse abuse because they believe it to be acceptable. They need to be encouraged not to accept it and to see it as a serious problem. Education can reduce the feelings of embarrassment and shame at being a victim and make it easier to take actions to stop the abuse.

Services need to be provided that are tailored to the problem of spouse abuse among the elderly. Nursing homes, which are used as a solution to elder abuse in a substantial number of cases, are often inappropriate because they are designed for persons much less capable of taking care of themselves. Shelters for battered women may be better solutions, but many of these shelters are not suited to the needs of the older woman. Furthermore, the presence of young women and children may intimidate older women from seeking assistance. It would be more appropriate to establish safe apartments in congregate housing units where abused elders can take refuge. The types of self-help groups that have been effective with younger abused wives should be offered to groups of abused elderly women. Perhap they can help the elderly stop the abuse, escape from it, or get other kinds of assistance (Pillemer and Finkelhor, 1988).

The following case study concerns the abuse of a 72-year-old woman, Hattie, by her 76-year-old husband, Max.

Case Study   *Elder abuse*

ASSESSMENT OF THE INDIVIDUAL AND THE PROBLEM

A young boy visiting friends in the neighborhood where Hattie and Max lived accidentally threw his ball into their backyard. He climbed the fence to get his ball and heard Hattie crying for help. The boy looked in the window and saw that Hattie had bruises on her face, a black eye, and blood pouring from her nose. He ran to the house he was visiting and reported what he had observed; the neighbors then called the police and paramedics.

The paramedics took Hattie to a local hospital. She was seen in the emergency room immediately. The physician discovered that she had a broken nose, a concussion, and a compound fracture of the right forearm, in addition to multiple facial bruises and a black eye. She was emaciated and confused, and when she was asked what had happened, she said, "I must have fallen." When asked if she was married, Hattie said, "Yes. Max went to the market."

The police had left a note on the door saying that Hattie had been taken to the local hospital. After about an hour, Max showed up at the hospital and was met by the police. He was very angry and wanted to know where his wife was and what she was doing at the hospital. It was apparent to the police that he had been drinking. They asked him where he had been and he said, "I went to the market; I was out of beer." He was told of Hattie's injuries and asked if he had beaten her. He responded, "Hell, no! All I did was give her a shove. She didn't have dinner ready on time—she never does!" They told him that his wife would have to be hospitalized and that they were taking him into custody until his wife could tell them how she had been injured.

Hattie was hospitalized and most of her injuries were treated; her arm would require surgery. The physician requested a consultation with members of the hospital's Elder Assessment Team (EAT). The team consists of nurses, social workers, physicians, psychologists, and an ethics specialist. He met briefly with representatives of the EAT and told them of Hattie's injuries and his belief that her husband, Max, had beaten her. Ellen, a nurse, and James, a psychologist, would interview Hattie. Bill, a social worker, and Alan, the ethics specialist, agreed to interview Max at the city jail the next day.

Ellen and James went to Hattie's room. She was drowsy from the pain medication but did not appear confused. They introduced themselves and explained that they were members of the EAT. They asked Hattie if she felt like talking. She hesitated with tears in her eyes and said, "Yes, I do. Max is a good man and he really doesn't mean to hurt me. I just can't seem to please him. It really is my fault, I know he likes his dinner at 6 P.M. every night—not 5 minutes early or 5 minutes late. It's my fault, it always is. Can we talk tomorrow? I'm getting sleepy. Can we call our daughter, Angela, tomorrow?" Ellen and James agreed to meet with Hattie the following day and to help her call her daughter.

PLANNING THERAPEUTIC INTERVENTION

The first priority was to get help for Hattie. The second priority was to find out from Hattie and Max how long he had been abusing her. The third priority was to talk with their daughter, Angela, to determine if she was aware of the abuse and what she could do to help her mother and father.

INTERVENTION

The morning following Hattie's admission, the EAT members met to discuss the information received from their interviews with Hattie and Max.

Bill and Alan, who had visited Max at the jail, told the team what they had learned from Max. Max said that he had retired late (at age 70) and that he had been an engineer—"a damn good one." He and Hattie had been married for 52 years and had one daughter, Angela, age 49. Angela was divorced and lived in another state approximately 2500 miles away. Max said that they rarely saw her because she was a "big-shot career woman." Hattie had worked as a "dumb cashier" until they had married. He had made her quit. "I made *good* money—no wife of mine was going to work." When asked what Hattie did all day when he was working, he said, "What a wife is *supposed* to do, take care of the house. You know, clean, cook, wash and iron clothes, mow and water the lawn. She had enough to keep her busy!" He was then asked what Hattie and he did after he retired. He looked confused and said, "What do you mean? Nothing *changed.* She took care of the house and I watched television." When asked if they ever went out with friends or traveled, he responded, "What for? I don't need to waste my money on things like *that,* and believe me, I have enough to take care of *me* for as long as I live. I've never been sick a day in my life."

Bill and Alan admitted that they were very frustrated with Max. When Alan asked Max, "Why did you hit Hattie?" Max answered angrily, "She asked for it! Always with her nose stuck in a book or knitting. She knows I always want my dinner on the table at 6:00 sharp! She hadn't even started dinner and it was 5:45!"

Alan asked, "Do you beat her often when your dinner is late?" Max replied, "I don't call it beating, I just knock her around a bit." Bill said, "We *do* call it beating. Do you know the extent of her injuries?" Max looked a little guilty and said, "Well, I probably had one or two beers too many." Bill replied, "How many beers do you usually have during the day?" "Maybe a six-pack," said Max, "sometimes more." "You always have at least six beers a day and sometimes more?" asked Alan. "Yeah," replied Max. "So what? I buy it!"

Bill and Alan told the EAT members that they strongly believed that Max was a chronic abuser. They asked Ellen and James what they had learned about Hattie. Ellen said that after talking with Hattie, they had met with the radiologist. He

CASE STUDY: HATTIE

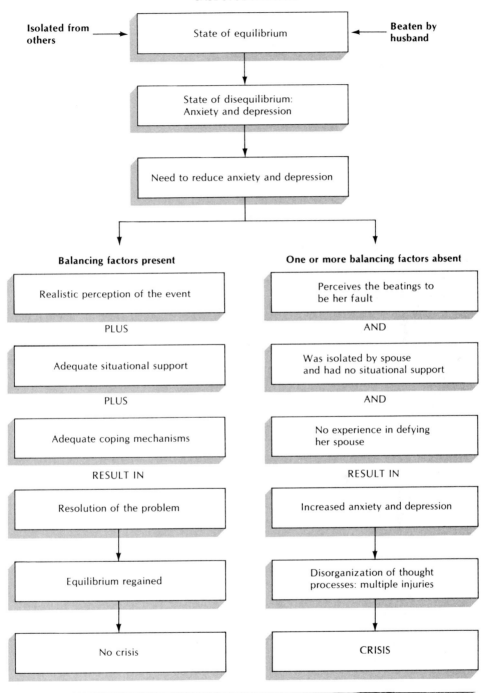

Figure 6-8

showed them the x-rays he had taken. They disclosed previous multiple fractures of her ribs, fingers, toes, and the bones in her face. They also agreed that Hattie had been abused over many years by Max.

James had called Angela and told her of Hattie's injuries. Her response was, "I'm amazed he didn't kill her. He has always slapped or knocked her around for as long as I can remember. I left home as soon as I could. He hit me one time when I was 13. I told him I would kill him if he ever touched me again. Mom just never had the guts to stand up to him. I have begged her to leave him and move here, but she wouldn't leave him. I'll fly out there this weekend and *make* her come back with me."

The team agreed that they would do everything they could to persuade Hattie to leave Max and live with or near her daughter.

ANTICIPATORY PLANNING

The orthopedic surgeon was asked to treat Hattie's arm as soon as possible. He agreed. Hattie came through the surgery quite well and was getting stronger every day. She was eating and sleeping well. Angela arrived and talked with her mother at length. Hattie agreed to return with her but stated she didn't want to live with her. Angela told her mother that there was an excellent retirement home close to where she lived. Hattie agreed to try it but was worried that Max wouldn't agree to pay for her leaving him and moving away. Angela told her mother, "He'll pay or I'll see that he never gets out of jail. I've already talked with an attorney here, and you will get half of everything Dad has, *and* more!" Hattie said, "Well, in that case, I won't worry. I just didn't want to be a burden to you. You work so hard." Hattie asked when they could leave. She was reassured by Angela and the EAT members that she could leave the next day. Hattie and Angela were both very pleased.

SUMMATION OF THE PARADIGM (Figure 6-8)

Hattie has been abused repeatedly by her spouse, Max. She always believed the beatings to be her fault. Max kept her isolated, and she was not permitted to have friends. Their only daughter lived out of state. Hattie had never stood up to her husband or defied him. After a severe beating, she was hospitalized and her husband put in jail. Her daughter came and took her back with her to live in a nearby retirement home.

Chronic Psychiatric Patient—Theoretical Concepts

Crisis intervention has gained recognition as a viable therapy modality to assist individuals through acute traumatic life situations. As large psychiatric facilities are beginning to shorten the length of hospitalization—slowly or rapidly according to the individual state laws—the chronic psychiatric patient is returning to his community where continuity of care must be maintained. The questions to be asked and answered are: (1) Does crisis intervention work successfully with chronic psychiatric patients? (2) If not, what other methods must be used to keep this patient functioning in his community?

With a chronic psychiatric patient, as with any patient, the crucial factors in resolving his crisis are identification of the precipitating event, the symptoms the patient is exhibiting, his perception of the event, his available situational supports, and his usual coping mechanisms.

Situational supports are those persons in the environment whom the therapist can find to lend support to the individual. A patient may be living with his family or friends; are they concerned enough—and do they care enough—to give him help? The patient's situational supports can serve as "assistants" to the therapist and the patient. They are with him daily and are encouraged to have frequent communication with the therapist. Situational supports are usually included in some part of the therapy sessions. This provides them with the knowledge and information they need to help the *identified* patient.

If the patient is living in a board-and-care facility, the therapist must determine if any of its members are concerned and willing to work with the therapist to help the individual through the stressful period. This involves visiting the facility and conducting collateral or group therapy with the patient and other members to get and keep them involved in helping to resolve the crisis.

Occasionally, the patient has *no* situational supports. He may be a social isolate; he may have no family and may have acquaintances but no real friends with whom he can talk about his problems. Usually an individual such as this has many difficulties in interpersonal relationships at work and school and socially. It is then the therapist's role to provide situational support while the patient is in therapy.

In the 1980s and early 1990s, inpatient and outpatient psychiatric facilities underwent a tremendous change because of the economic depression and the lack of foresight of those in charge of the mental health of the United States. This is not to say that all of the homeless are mentally ill, either acutely or chronically. One might recognize the fact that many are the "walking mental ill." They have no place to live, their families do not want them, and they are unable to find a job in a society that literally has no jobs that they could do, given their fragile mental state.

Experience has verified that crisis intervention can be an effective therapy modality with chronic psychiatric patients. If a psychiatric patient with a history of repeated hospitalizations returns to the community and his family, his reentry creates many stresses. Although much has been accomplished to remove the stigma of mental illness, people are still wary and hypervigilant when they learn that a "former mental patient" has returned to the community.

In his absence, the family and community have, consciously or unconsciously, eliminated him from their usual life patterns and activities. They then have to readjust to his presence and include him in activities and decision making. If for any reason he does not conform to their expectations, they want him removed so that they can continue their lives without the possibility of disruptive behavior.

The first area to explore is determining who is in crisis: the patient or his family. In many cases, the family is overreacting because of its anxiety and is seeking some means of getting the *identified* patient back into the hospital. The patient is usually brought to the center by a family member because his original maladaptive symptoms have begun to reemerge. Questioning the patient or his family about the medication he received from the hospital and determining if he is taking it as prescribed are essential. If the patient is unable to communicate with the therapist about what has happened or what has changed in his life, the family is questioned about what might have precipitated his return to his former psychotic behavior.

A cause-and-effect relationship usually exists between a change, or anticipated change, in the routine patterns of life-style or family constellation and the beginnings of abnormal overt behavior in the identified patient. Often families forget or ignore telling a former psychiatric patient when they are contemplating a change because "he wouldn't understand." Such changes could include moving or changing jobs. This is perceived by the patient as exclusion or rejection by the family and creates stress that he is unable to cope with; he thus retreats to his previous psychotic behavior. Such cases are frequent and can be dealt with through the theoretical framework of crisis intervention methodology.

Rubinstein (1972) stated that family-focused crisis intervention usually brings about the resolution of the patient's crisis without resorting to hospitalization. In a later article in 1974, he advocated family crisis intervention as a viable alternative to rehospitalization. Here, the emphasis is placed on the period immediately after the patient's release from the hospital. He suggested that conjoint family therapy begin in the hospital before the patient's release and then continue in an outpatient clinic after his release. This approach has also served to develop the concept that a family can and should share responsibility for the patient's treatment.

In Decker and Stubblebine's 1972 study, two groups of young adults were followed for 2½ years after their first psychiatric hospitalization. The first group was immediately hospitalized and received traditional modes of treatment, and the second group was hospitalized after the institution of a crisis intervention program. The results of the study indicated that crisis intervention reduced long-term hospital dependency without producing alternate forms of psychological or social dependency and also reduced the number of rehospitalizations.

The following brief case study illustrates how a therapist can work with a chronic psychiatric patient in a community mental health center using the crisis model.

Case Study *Chronic psychiatric patient*

ASSESSMENT OF THE INDIVIDUAL AND THE PROBLEM

Jim, a man in his late 30's, was brought to a crisis center by his sister because, as she stated, "He was beginning to act crazy again." Jim had had many prior hospitalizations, paranoid schizophrenia. The only thing Jim would say was, "I *don't* want to go back to the hospital." He was told that our role was to help him stay out of the hospital if we possibly could. A medical consultation was arranged to determine if he needed to have his medication increased or possibly changed.

Information was then obtained from his sister to determine what had happened (the precipitating event) when his symptoms had started and, specifically, what she meant by his "acting crazy again." His sister stated that he was "talking to the television set, muttering things that made no sense, staring into space, prowling around the apartment at night" and that "this behavior started about 3 days ago." When questioned about anything that was different in their lives before the start of his disruptive behavior, she denied any change. When asked about any changes that were contemplated in the near future, she replied that she was planning to be married in 2 months but that Jim did not know about it because she had not told him yet. When asked why she had not told him, she reluctantly answered that she wanted to wait until all the arrangements had been made. She was asked if there was any way Jim could have found out about her plans. She remembered that she had discussed them on the telephone with a girlfriend the week before.

She was asked what her plans for Jim were after she married. She said that her boyfriend had agreed, rather reluctantly, to let Jim live with them.

Because her boyfriend was reluctant about having Jim live with them, other alternatives were explored. She said that they had cousins living in a nearby suburb but that she did not know if they would want Jim to live with them.

PLANNING THE INTERVENTION

It was suggested that Jim's sister call her cousins, tell them of her plans to get married and her concerns about Jim, and in general find out their feelings about his living with them. The call was placed, and she told them her plans and concerns. Fortunately, their response was a positive one. They had recently bought a fairly large apartment building and were having difficulty getting reliable help to take care of the yardwork and minor repairs. They felt that Jim would be able to manage this, and they would let him live in a small apartment above the garage.

INTERVENTION

Jim was asked to come back into the office so that his sister could tell him of her plans to marry and the arrangements she had made for him with their cousins. He listened but had difficulty comprehending the information. He just kept saying, "I *don't* want to go back to the hospital."

He was asked if he had heard his sister talking about her wedding plans. He admitted that he had and that he knew her boyfriend would not want him around: "They would probably put me back in the hospital." As the session ended, he still had not internalized the information he had heard. He was asked to continue in therapy for 5 more weeks and to take his medication as prescribed. He agreed to do so.

By the end of the sixth week, he had visited his cousins, seen the apartment where he would be living, and had discussed his new "job." His disruptive behavior had ceased, and he was again functioning at his precrisis level.

ANTICIPATORY PLANNING

Because Jim had had many previous hospitalizations and did not want to be re-hospitalized, time was spent in discussing how this could be avoided in the future. He was given the name, address, and telephone number of a crisis center in his new community and told to visit there when he moved. He was assured that the center could supervise his medication and be available if he needed someone to talk to if he felt he again needed help.

SUMMATION OF PARADIGM (Figure 6-9)

Jim's sister neglected to tell him about her impending marriage, which he perceived as rejection. Because of his numerous hospitalizations, he feared that his sister would have him rehospitalized "to get rid of him." He was unable to verbalize his

CASE STUDY: JIM

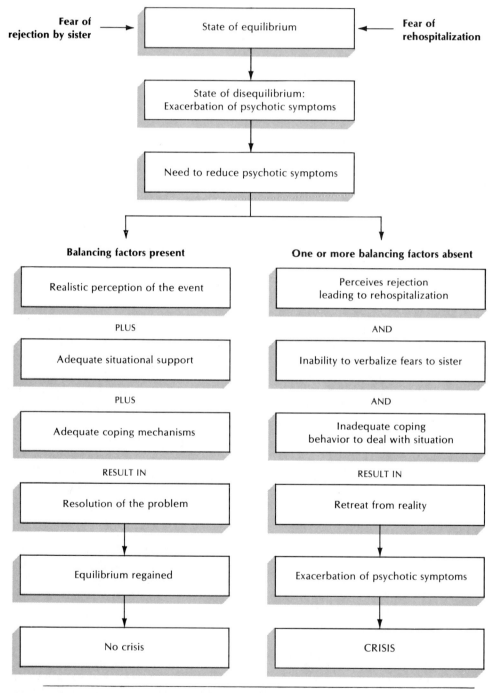

Figure 6-9

fears, retreated from reality, and experienced an exacerbation of his psychotic symptoms.

The therapist adhered to the crisis model by focusing the therapy sessions on the patient's immediate problems, *not* on his chronic psychopathology.

Battered Wife—Theoretical Concepts

Throughout history, women have been subjected to the whims and brutality of their husbands. In the United States, the statistics reflect no sudden epidemic of domestic violence, only a recent effort to collect often inexact figures that are startling even when allowances are made for error. Nearly 7.5 million wives are abused by their husbands in any given year; some 3600 to 5900 women are beaten to death annually. The police spend one third of their time responding to domestic violence calls. Battery is the single major cause of injury to women, more significant than automobile accidents, rapes, or muggings.

In the United States, wife beating is no longer widely accepted as an inevitable and private matter. This change in attitude, although far from complete, has come about in the past 15 to 20 years as part of the transformation of ideas about the roles and rights of women in society. Legal structures and social service networks, prompted by grass-roots women's organizations, have begun to redefine spouse abuse as a violation of the victim's civil rights and a criminal act of assault subject to the same punishments as other acts of violence (O'Reilly, 1983).

Marital abuse has been called "the silent crime." Bringing it out into the open by talking about it is the first step toward a solution. For most people, however, including the victim and the abuser, the almost reflexlike response to the subject is to deny its existence (Smolowe and Purvis, 1992).

Battering involves a pattern of escalating abuse in a situation from which the victim believes she cannot escape. Because they are usually physically stronger than their wives, men are less likely to be battered. Often a battered women has grown up with violence and accepts it as a pitiful form of caring, or at least as something inevitable in a relationship. She may believe that the world is a dangerous place and that she needs a protector, even a man who beats her. Ashamed, terrified that any resistance will provoke greater violence, isolated from her family and friends, often without any means of support other than her husband, many a battered woman sinks into despairing submission from which the only escape is eventual widowhood, her own murder (or her husband's), or suicide.

Doctors, social workers, and psychiatrists have frequently been less helpful than the police. Straus (1981), in a study of family violence, concluded that the medical profession and social agencies are an essential part of the battered syndrome. They often treat the women like they are "crazy"; physicians fail to note signs of abuse, label battered women psychotic or hypochondriacal, prescribe tranquilizers, and tell them to go home. They make battered women doubt their own sanity by sending them to a family therapist for psychotherapy.

What kind of man would hit a woman—not only hit her, but blacken her eyes, break the bones in her face, beat her breasts, kick her abdomen, and menace her with a gun? There is a very good chance that he was beaten as a child. Perhaps because of his early trauma, he is often emotionally stunted. An interesting analogy exists between a male batterer and a 2- or 3-year-old child; their tantrums are very similar. Like a narcissistic child, the batterer bites when throwing a tantrum.

The wife beater probably drinks, but he does not beat because he drinks; rather, he drinks to beat. Unemployment does not cause battering, but hard times make it worse. The typical spouse beater is unable to cope with the traditional notion of masculinity, or the male role, which requires men to be stoic. It requires men not to need intimacy, to be in control, to be the "big wheel," and when there is a problem to "give 'em hell." The difficulty is that nine of ten men fail at that list, at least in their own judgment. The batterer is often afflicted with extreme insecurity. The man's wife is the emotional glue that holds him together, and, as a consequence, he is desperately afraid of losing her. The husband is trying to make her be closer to him by controlling her physically, but he does not realize that he is driving her away (O'Reilly, 1983).

Batterers can be very calculating in how they deal with their wives and with the authorities once they are caught. They are frequently charming to a fault. They can play therapy off against the court system and not have to be responsible.

The first self-help group for abusive men was formed in Boston in 1977. There are now about 85 such groups. Very few men go to such centers on their own. Either their partner has left or is threatening to, or they are attending under court order. By and large, they do not believe they have done anything wrong, sometimes insisting they are not batterers at all. Those who own up to being violent frequently believe their partners are at fault.

Historically, batterers have fallen between the cracks and were considered neither crazy nor criminal, at least by the standards of the day. A man beats up his wife because he can. He usually does not beat up his boss or male acquaintances; the consequences—loss of job, a charge of criminal assault, immediate physical retaliation—are simply too great. Now, the consequences are rising for violence against one's wife. Shelters for abused women have created a safety net for wives who previously would have been afraid to take their husbands to court. Newspapers, judges, hospitals, neighbors, and even a growing number of once exasperated police officers are beginning to understand the dimensions of the problem. More important, states and municipalities are enacting laws that give women a realistic chance of getting protection and redress through the courts.

Ten years ago, there were no real, specific laws providing remedies for women. If a woman wanted protection using the courts, she would have to get it as part of a domestic relations proceeding, that is, separation or divorce.

At that time, police could not make an arrest without actually witnessing violence or seeing compelling physical evidence of abuse. Nowadays, such requirements are being eased (Appleton, 1980).

The tightening of laws against wife beating has resulted in higher conviction rates. Still, only a fraction of abusive husbands are even reported to the authorities, much less arrested and convicted. For the glib, angry men who pummel their wives, a brush with the law sometimes has a sobering effect. In general, arrests work because they show the man that such behavior is inappropriate. They also show the woman that somebody will help her.

The crackdown represents an important shift in how the nation views the battered wife. No longer does a woman have to go it alone in a legal system that is stacked against her; no longer does she have to deny the suggestion, either stated or implied, that she got what she deserved. Now the courts and the community are swinging to her side, and the bullying husband is beginning to pay the price.

The following case study of a battered wife illustrates how women who have been repeatedly beaten by their husbands assume, although incorrectly, that they "deserve it." The crisis represented below was precipitated when a young woman was hospitalized with serious injuries.

Case Study   *Battered wife*

ASSESSMENT OF THE INDIVIDUAL AND THE PROBLEM

Suzan, a 39-year-old housewife and mother of two daughters (Karen, age 15, and Leslie, age 12), was admitted to a large metropolitan hospital. Her husband, Ron, age 43, drove her to the emergency room and stated that she had "fallen down the stairs at home." When asked by the resident the name of their family physician, Ron casually shrugged his shoulders and said, "We don't have one." The resident asked permission to call in an internist and an orthopedic specialist because he believed that Suzan was badly injured.

The resident ordered x-rays for Suzan "from head to toe" and then contacted an internist and orthopedist and told them he suspected a possible case of wife beating. Both physicians stated they would be at the hospital within 30 minutes to see the x-rays and Suzan. Suzan went through the series of x-rays and was admitted to the hospital.

The internist, Dr. W, and the orthopedist, Dr. V, looked at the x-rays with a sense of shock and disbelief. Suzan's current injuries included two black eyes, two fractures in the pelvic girdle, and two fractured ribs. The x-rays also revealed past injuries: four fractured ribs, fractures of the left wrist and left arm in two places, and fractures of the right ankle.

The two physicians went to Suzan's room, introduced themselves, and asked Suzan if they could sit down. Suzan's blackened eyes were almost swollen shut, but both physicians could see the fear in her eyes as she looked past them to see if her husband was with them. Dr. W ordered no visitors for Suzan, including family, unless they had the permission of one of the doctors. Suzan appeared to relax slightly.

During the taking of her medical history, Suzan stated that she had no previous injuries. Dr. W then casually asked Suzan how she had sustained her present injuries. Suzan responded quickly, "I tripped and fell down the stairs at home."

Dr. V told her about her current injuries, stating that they were quite extensive for a fall down a flight of stairs. Dr. V then told Suzan that she would have to stay in the hospital from 4 to 6 weeks for the fractures in her pelvic girdle to heal. Suzan gasped and repeated, "Four to six weeks! What about my daughters? They need me!" Dr. V asked, "Don't you have family that could stay with them?" Suzan replied, "My mother would love to come out and take care of them, but Ron doesn't get along with her."

The doctors explained the extent of Suzan's injuries to Ron, and then Dr. W told him that Suzan's mother would be called to take care of their daughters. Dr. W called Suzan's mother, who, when told of her daughter's injuries, commented that Ron had probably beaten her again. Her mother made arrangements to be at the hospital the next morning.

Dr. W then faced Suzan with her mother's accusation that Ron had beaten her in the past; Suzan denied this. After discussing the case, Dr. W and Dr. V decided to call in a psychotherapist with experience in dealing with battered wives.

PLANNING THERAPEUTIC INTERVENTION

The clinical psychologist called in to assist believed that he would have to work with Suzan's mother and her two daughters to break through Suzan's denial. The first step would be to confront Suzan with the x-rays that clearly showed the previous injuries and to demand an explanation. He would use Suzan's mother's statement that Ron had "beaten her many times before" as leverage against Suzan's denial. He would plan to see the daughters alone to see if they would admit that their father had abused their mother in the past as well as in the most recent "accident." The second step would be to get Suzan to realize that other women had been battered by their spouses and that it was not her fault that she had been beaten. She had to be made to view the events in a realistic manner. The third step was to get situational support for Suzan and have her talk with other wives who had been battered and hear how they had coped with their situations. The fourth step would be to tell Suzan about the facilities that were available for battered wives and the therapeutic groups her husband could attend with other men who had battered their wives.

INTERVENTION

The next morning, Suzan was introduced to the psychotherapist and told that one of his areas of expertise was working with battered wives. The therapist showed Suzan all her old fractures on the x-rays. He asked her when and how she had received them and told Suzan that he would ask her mother and her daughters if she did not answer. Then, the therapist sat back in his chair and waited in silence as Suzan began to cry. As Suzan continued to cry, occasionally he handed her more tissues but said nothing. Finally Suzan asked, "Aren't you going to say something?" The therapist replied, "No. It's time for you to answer my questions." (Because most individuals have difficulty coping with silence, it can be a very effective technique in psychotherapy—if the therapist can handle it.)

Suzan finally commented that none of the other doctors had ever asked her any questions, and the therapist asked her to start at the beginning. Suzan began by saying, "I know Ron loves me and I love him. You'll see, I'll probably receive a dozen yellow roses today with a card asking me to forgive him. And I will, I always do. I probably deserve to be beaten. I am not a good wife or mother."

Suzan continued, "It really is my fault. Ron didn't want to get married, but I got careless and ended up pregnant. Ron wanted me to have an abortion, but I refused. I just couldn't. I'm Catholic but Ron isn't, so we got married. Karen was born 7½ months after we were married. I loved him so much, and I really believed that he loved me." She said he was a good husband and a very good father. "I had no experience in taking care of a house, husband, or a baby. I didn't even know how to cook—thank heavens, someone gave me a good cookbook when we got married. I still can't iron his shirts to suit him. I have truly been a failure. You see, I was an only child and my mother and father spoiled me rotten. I never had to do anything around the house."

The first time Ron had hit her was after they had been married about 1½ years because she had burned the dinner. She said she had been taking care of Karen, who had a fever, and completely forgot the roast in the oven. When Ron came home, she was rocking Karen trying to get her to sleep. He walked into Karen's room and said very coldly, "Put the baby in her crib and come with me." Suzan put Karen down, and Ron grabbed her by the arm and pulled her into the kitchen He had taken the roast out of the oven. It was burned to a crisp, and the kitchen was filled with smoke. Ron said, "Do you think money grows on trees?" and he slapped her. Then he just kept hitting her. She said, "I begged him not to, but he just kept punching me. Finally, he stopped, probably because he was tired, but that is when I received my first black eye. So, you see, I did deserve it. It was my fault." The therapist told Suzan she did *not* deserve that beating and asked if the beatings continued. Suzan said that she "just couldn't seem to please him. He didn't like the way I ironed his shirts—that's when he broke my ribs. If I didn't season the food to his liking, another beating. Almost anything I did wrong ended up with his beating me. That's why we have never had just one doctor, he would take me to a different one or to a different emergency room every time."

The therapist asked Suzan if Ron drank much. She said that he usually had a couple of beers, maybe more occasionally. The therapist asked her if she could remember if he usually had been drinking when he beat her. She replied, "Yes, yes, I remember; every time he beat me he had been drinking. He wasn't drunk, you understand. Even last night he had been drinking!" She asked, "Do you think his drinking makes him beat me?" The therapist answered, "Not really. Although he drinks to beat you, he doesn't beat you because he drinks."

The therapist asked about Ron's family. Suzan said that she really did not know them, and Ron wasn't very close to them. His father was apparently a violent man who had beat his three sons and his wife. She continued, saying that Ron's father was an alcoholic and that his mother had died 5 years ago. The therapist told Suzan that because Ron's father had beaten him and his mother he considered this acceptable behavior between a husband and wife.

The therapist explained to Suzan that shelters had been established for battered women and their children and that therapy groups had been formed for men who battered their wives. The therapist then asked if he could have a woman who lived in one of the facilities come and talk to her. Suzan said that she would like very much to talk to someone who had been through what she had been through. The therapist told Suzan he would arrange it as soon as possible. He reminded her that she was safe in the hospital, but she must seriously think about whether she wanted to return home to more beatings or go with her daughters to one of the facilities.

As Suzan had predicted, Ron sent her roses and asked for her forgiveness. At the same time the flowers came, Suzan's mother arrived at the hospital, and the therapist left so that Suzan and her mother could talk. When he returned, they had decided that Suzan would divorce Ron and she and her daughters would move to Chicago and live with Suzan's parents. Suzan called Ron to come to the hospital so she could tell him of her decisions.

When Ron arrived, Suzan very quickly told him that she wanted a divorce and that she and the girls would be moving. At first, Ron was shocked and briefly tried to change her mind. He became angry with Suzan's mother, who he assumed was responsible for Suzan's unexpected actions. At this point, the therapist ushered Ron from the room and offered to talk with him later about his problems concerning his beating Suzan. Ron said he would call in a few days and then left the hospital.

ANTICIPATORY PLANNING

Ron never called, but the therapist continued to see Suzan every few days until she was discharged in the fifth week. She fairly blossomed under the loving care of her mother. She filed for divorce, with no protest from Ron. Her daughters were delighted at the thought of moving to Chicago to live with their grandparents. They admitted they were terrified of their father and had been afraid of saying anything to anyone. They said he had moved out of the house because he could not stand being around their grandmother.

SUMMATION OF THE PARADIGM (Figure 6-10)

Suzan had been made to feel totally inadequate as a wife and mother. She had led a very sheltered life until her marriage and had no experience in keeping a home or caring for children. She felt that she deserved the beatings by her husband, and she was too embarrassed and ashamed to let anyone know that she was a battered wife. She had an unrealistic perception of the event. Her only situational supports were her family, who lived in another state. She had no adequate coping mechanisms. Her injuries from the last beating were so extensive that she was unable to deny her fear of her husband and thus entered a state of crisis.

Divorce—Theoretical Concepts

In Western society, divorce has become a common rather than a rare occurrence. According to the National Center for Health Statistics (July 29, 1988), the number of divorces in the United States fell less than 1% between 1986 and 1987; there were 1,159,000 divorces in 1986 and 1,157,000 in 1987. The divorce rate for 1987, 4.8 per 1000 population, was the same as that for 1986. Throughout the 1960s and 1970s, the divorce rate rose fairly steadily, reaching a peak of 5.3 in 1979 and 1981. The divorce rate stabilized between 1982 and 1985, fluctuating between 4.9 and 5.0. The 1986 and 1987 rates of 4.8 are the lowest until 1991. In 1991, the divorce rate stabilized at 4.7 per 1000 population.

There may be several reasons for this stabilization. Let us not forget that the sexual revolution is *over*. Now, society is not out for a night of fun sex, with "no involvement." We are now confronted with "safe sex." We do not want to be exposed to or possibly get a sexually transmitted disease from a casual affair (see Chapter 8 on AIDS). Much has been written and hypothesized about the causes and effects of divorce on individuals and family members. Because divorce rates

CASE STUDY: SUZAN

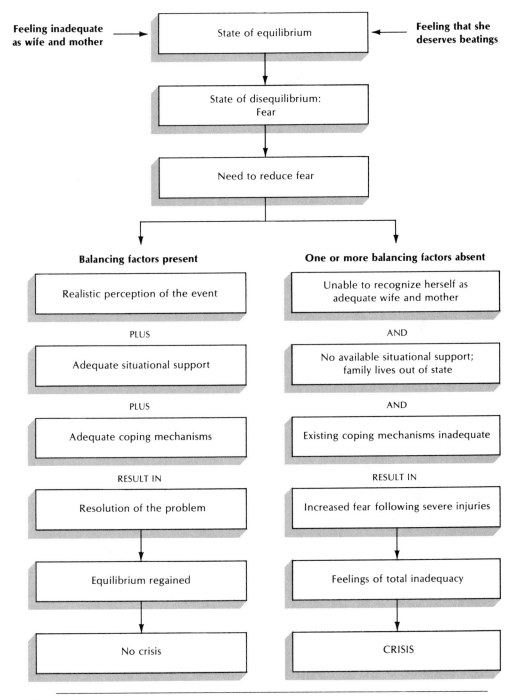

Figure 6-10

are high and many marriages are centers of friction and unhappiness, something must be lacking in the preparation for marriage. No event in life of equal importance is viewed with so little realism, and marriage seems to come about with little or no preparation.

Marriage and its demands on individuals can be stressful, and failure to sustain a marriage can precipitate a crisis. Rapoport (1963) delineates three subphases of marriage when stress is the most common: the engagement, honeymoon, and early marriage. Engaged couples confront major tasks on two levels: intrapersonal and interpersonal. The intrapersonal task implies a review of readiness for marriage on a conscious, preconscious, or unconscious level of psychological maturity. This readiness is affected by the individual needs of the person and by the perceived subcultural norms. The interpersonal tasks are concerned with developing an in-terpersonal adjustment or accommodation that will be satisfactory in the marital relationship. The engagement period involves a process of separation from previous life patterns and of commitment of the couple to one another. The honeymoon period is a time for establishing a basic sense of harmony. The early marriage phase (the first 3 months) involves establishing a system of authority, decision-making patterns, and patterns of sexual relationships.

It is evident that individuals do not always accomplish these necessary tasks in the first few months of marriage. For some, it may easily extend into the first few years of marriage. Additional stress factors may occur in this period to create even greater disequilibrium.

The largest proportion of divorces occurs in the early years of marriage among childless couples. The peak period for divorce is in the second year of marriage, after which the rate drops rapidly. A number of factors, other than those previously mentioned, are precipitating causes of divorce. Among these are urban background, early marriage (15 to 19 years of age), short courtship, short engagement, mixed racial or religious marriages, disapproval of friends and relatives, dissimilar back-grounds, and unhappy parental marriages (McDaniel and Landau-Stanton, 1991).

Today, there is greater acceptance of the possibility of divorce; because of this acceptance, divorced persons have lost some of the feelings of failure and guilt that were formerly associated with it. The divorce rate may reflect new values placed on marriage. Marriage is no longer accepted as an endurance race that is doggedly maintained "for the sake of the children." The current demands are for a "good marriage," one that meets the needs of the individuals involved. Even from the point of view of the children, who seemingly pay the highest price for marital failure, divorce in certain circumstances may create fewer psychological problems, provided the children are not used as pawns by the separating parents.

The rate of remarriage after divorce is quite high; if both parties have been divorced two or more times, the ratio climbs even higher. Greene (1968) assumes that divorce is a repetitive phenomenon. It is apparent that an unresolved neurotic pattern, carried over from one marriage to another, would tend to reinforce the individual's failure pattern in the subsequent marriage.

This case study (Morley, Messick, and Aguilera, 1967) concerns a young woman, 23 years of age, who sought help from a crisis center on the advice of her attorney because of an impending divorce. Neither Margie nor her husband had attained the psychological maturity or "readiness" necessary to enter marriage. Margie's impulsive marriages after brief courtships indicated her unrealistic expectations and attitudes toward marriage.

Clues given in the assessment phase indicated that she believed herself a failure as a woman. These guilt feelings and lack of her usual situational supports precipitated a crisis. Intervention was planned to assist her to cope with her feelings of failure and guilt and to view her divorce in more realistic terms.

Case Study *Divorce*

ASSESSMENT OF THE INDIVIDUAL AND THE PROBLEM

Margie, an extremely attractive young woman in the process of divorce from her third husband, was referred to a crisis center for help because of severe depression and anxiety. Manifested by insomnia, lack of appetite, tremulousness, inability to concentrate, and frequent crying spells. These symptoms had begun 3 weeks earlier when she was notified of the date of the divorce proceedings. She had lost her job because she was unable to control her crying spells and had subsequently developed bursitis in her shoulder, which further limited her ability to work. Her symptoms had intensified so much in the past 3 days that she felt she was losing complete control over her emotions and needed help.

During the initial session, Margie stated that she did not want a divorce and that she still loved her husband, even though he did not love her. When questioned about the increased intensity of symptoms that had begun 3 days ago, she stated that at that time she had been informed by her attorney that the only way she could receive alimony would be to countersue for divorce.

In Margie's previous two divorces she had remained a passive participant; her husbands had sued her for divorce. She had accepted this and had not contested. Now, for the first time, because of her inability to work, she was forced to become an active participant in a divorce she did not want. She stated frequently that "something must be wrong with me if I can't hold a husband" and later commented, "I don't feel this is a good marriage—but I hate to fail again." This ambivalence and her expressed guilt feelings were believed to be part of the crisis-precipitating event, as was the necessity of being forced to take an active part in a divorce she did not want.

As a result of the assessment, the therapist thought that, although Margie was depressed and expressed feelings of worthlessness, she was not suicidal and did not constitute a threat to others.

PLANNING THERAPEUTIC INTERVENTION

Margie had almost totally withdrawn from her social and family contacts. Her mother came occasionally to give her money for rent and bring her food. Beyond this social contact, she remained isolated in the apartment she had previously shared with her husband and was weeping at intervals, staring at her husband's picture, and unable to decide whether to contest the divorce.

Because she had not been forced into active decision making in her previous divorces, she had no coping experiences in this specific situation. When questioned about her previous methods of coping with stress, she stated that usually she had no problems because she remained involved in her work and its many social contacts, usually bowling and going to bars with friends. Her present inability to work eliminated these sources of social support and distractions from the problem, and her previous successful coping mechanisms could not be used.

The goal of intervention was established by the therapist to assist Margie to recognize and cope with her feelings of ambivalence and guilt. Unrecognized feelings about her marriage and the impending divorce were also to be explored.

INTERVENTION

In the next 3 weeks, through direct questioning and reflection of verbal and nonverbal clues to Margie, it became possible for her to view the present crisis and its effect on her in relationship to her previous marriages and divorces.

Margie wanted desperately to marry in order to become a housewife and mother. Her usual social contacts and previous patterns of meeting men (bowling alleys and bars) and her impulsive marriages (Las Vegas, three times) and reasons for marriage ("I thought I could help him—he needed me") were not meeting this need. The men she had met and married, and who later divorced her, were men who did not want to settle down with a wife and children. Instead, they wanted a fun-loving, attractive companion to show off to their friends. Margie always hoped that they would change after marriage. However, they remained unchanged and divorced Margie when she persistently suggested "starting a family." With each marriage and subsequent divorce, her guilt feelings about her ability to be a good wife magnified. Because Margie could not use her previous coping mechanisms, the third divorce precipitated a crisis.

By the close of the third session, Margie's depression and symptoms had lessened as she recognized the possibility that the failure of her marriages may not have been because of her "inability to be a good wife" but in the disparity between what she wanted and expected from a marriage and what the men she had married wanted and expected.

ANTICIPATORY PLANNING

Exploration with Margie about her usual modes of social contact and her impulsive marriages (usually after only 3 or 4 weeks of courtship) assisted her in viewing her current divorce in more realistic terms. This was an important phase in anticipatory planning.

By the fourth week, Margie had made significant changes in her patterns of living. She moved from the apartment she had previously shared with her husband to a small house near her mother. She also signed the papers to contest the divorce and found a new job.

Margie was granted the divorce and was apparently able to view her past experience as a traumatic but valuable learning experience.

During the discussion and review of her future plans, Margie was cautious but realistic. She was enjoying her new job and new friends, going to movies and

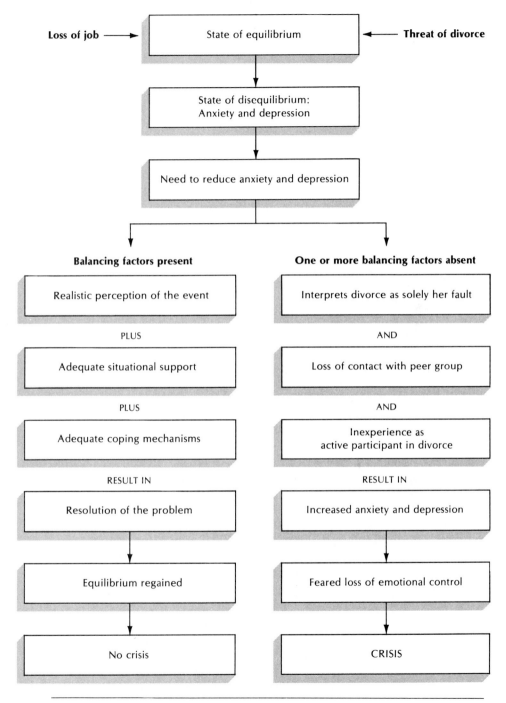

CASE STUDY: MARGIE

Loss of job ⟶ State of equilibrium ⟵ Threat of divorce

State of disequilibrium:
Anxiety and depression

Need to reduce anxiety and depression

Balancing factors present

Realistic perception of the event

PLUS

Adequate situational support

PLUS

Adequate coping mechanisms

RESULT IN

Resolution of the problem

Equilibrium regained

No crisis

One or more balancing factors absent

Interprets divorce as solely her fault

AND

Loss of contact with peer group

AND

Inexperience as
active participant in divorce

RESULT IN

Increased anxiety and depression

Feared loss of emotional control

CRISIS

Figure 6-11

occasionally dinner with girlfriends. She stated that she was not accepting dates from men yet, "although I've been asked," and that if she married again, "it would not be in Las Vegas!"

Before termination, Margie and the therapist reviewed and assessed the adjustments she had made in coping with the crisis, the insight she had gained into her own feelings, and her needs regarding future plans.

At termination Margie, was reassured that she could obtain assistance in any future crisis that might occur.

SUMMATION OF THE PARADIGM (Figure 6-11)

Margie's inability to cope with a third divorce was precipitated by the lack of her usual situational supports, that is, her involvement and social contacts at work. This was also the first time Margie was forced into the role of an active participant in the divorce process, and she had no previous coping skills. Her inability to work as a result of illness further isolated her from her usual contacts; she became introspective about her previous divorces and saw herself as a failure as a woman. As her doubts increased, her feelings of guilt and failure magnified until she feared complete loss of emotional control.

The intervention was focused on encouraging Margie to bring her feelings of failure and guilt into the open. By direct questioning and reflecting the information back to Margie, it became possible for her to view her current divorce and its effect on her in more realistic terms. She was given support by the therapist as she began to explore what she wanted and expected from marriage in the future.

Substance Abuse: Cocaine—Theoretical Concepts

Cocaine is a vegetable alkaloid derived from leaves of the coca plant. It is often referred to as coke, C, snow, happy dust, and white girl. Cocaine has become the all-American drug. No longer is it a sinful secret of the moneyed elite or an exclusive glitter of decadence in raffish society circles. In the recent past, the price of cocaine ($3000 per ounce of unadulterated material) was so high that it served as a deterrent to frequent use for most people. Today, the costs have decreased and the suppliers remain abundant. In the United States, recent flooding of the marketplace with crack (ready-made free-base in $10 or $20 packages) has resulted in an upsurge of new consumers (Jeri, 1984). There are more than 120 street expressions for cocaine free-base, including crack, rock, white tornado, white cloud, and super white.

Superficially, cocaine appears to be a beguiling and relatively risk-free drug— so its devotees innocently claim. Yet, cocaine can be a very dangerous drug. The euphoric lift, that is the feeling of being confident and on top of things that comes from a few brief "snorts," is often followed by a letdown. Regular use can induce depression, edginess, and weight loss. As usage increases, so does the danger of paranoia, hallucinations, and a total physical collapse. Usage does tend to increase.

Cocaine, like opium, heroin, and morphine, is classified as a narcotic. Opium, heroin, and morphine are "downers," which quiet the body and dull the senses; cocaine is an "upper"—a stimulant, similar to amphetamines. It increases the heartbeat, raises the blood pressure and body temperature, and curbs the appetite.

Unlike such downers as heroin and Quaaludes, cocaine is physically and psychologically addictive. It can damage the liver, cause malnutrition, and increase the risk of heart attacks. Coming down from a high may cause such deep gloom that the only remedy is more cocaine. Bigger doses often follow, and soon the urge may become a total obsession. This pattern can lead to a psychological dependence, the effects of which are not all that different from physical addiction. There is growing clinical evidence that when cocaine is taken in the most potent and dangerous forms—injected in solution or chemically converted and smoked in a process called free-basing—it becomes addictive.

Crack is not a new drug, but it does represent a new strategy in the sale and marketing of street cocaine. Crack is ready-made free-base cocaine sold in the form of tiny pellets or "rocks," which can be smoked with no further chemical processing. The significance of this shift in cocaine vending patterns stems from the fact that it makes the practice of smoking cocaine free-base more readily accessible to potential users (Washton and Gold, 1987).

A cocaine high is an intensely vivid, sensation-enhancing experience; there is no evidence, as claimed, that it is an aphrodisiac. Indeed, there is evidence that the sustained use of cocaine can cause sexual dysfunction and impotence. Even casual sniffing can lead to more potent and potentially damaging ways of using cocaine and other drugs. Many cocaine users take sedative pills such as Quaaludes to calm them down after the high and to take the edge off their yearning for more cocaine. A few smoke marijuana for the same purpose or mix their cocaine with heroin in a process called speedballing or boy-girl, which produces a tug-of-war wherein the exhilaration of cocaine is undercut by the heroin.

A few middle-class users who dabble with heroin in conjunction with cocaine smoke it rather than inject it; they believe this prevents addiction. This belief is false; heroin, however used, is a fiercely addictive drug. Treatment centers are receiving an influx of well-dressed, well-to-do men and women who have gravely underestimated heroin's effects. One of cocaine's biggest dangers is that it diverts people from normal pursuits; it can entrap and redirect a person's activities into an almost exclusive preoccupation with the drug.

New drugs and ways to get high appear at various times. Some remain for a length of time due to being "new" and their effect on the individual using them. Two "soft" drugs have been introduced in the 1990s. One is "blond hash," which produces a "giddy high"; the second is "dark hash," which is used for a serious "zonking."

A 1993 new illegal drug is "ice." Ice originated in the Philippines; from there it traveled to Hawaii, and from Hawaii to the mainland. It has at least three times the potency of speed, and has caused many deaths.

A second 1993 new drug is "cat," a powder that is easily produced from household chemicals such as battery acids and aerosols. Snorted like coke, it is relatively inexpensive to make ($25), and the "high" from cat can last 3 days! This, too, has resulted in many deaths.

A method being used to get high in 1993 is called "autoerection ejaculation." This is done in a shower. The shower massage tubing is placed around the individual's neck. He then hangs himself until he is almost unconscious, and he has a tremendous ejaculation. Unfortunately, he may be too unconscious to release the tubing and dies of hanging.

In Somalia, six or seven men gather every afternoon to gossip and to chew qut (sometimes spelled *khat* or *kat*) until they are in a narcotic euphoria. Qut is a pale green plant, when chewed it provides the user brief moments of a feeling of well-being.

Qut is a way of life and no small contributor to the anarchy that turned Somalia into a wasteland of brutality and starvation. The drug is cultivated in neighboring Kenya. Qut is a boom to dealers. It costs pennies to produce and abundant amounts of qut are flown into Somalia on charter planes costing $8000 a flight. There is no evidence that U.S. troops are bringing home any of Somalia's qut. One American civilian official said it might happen in the future because the drug now is finding a market in the United States (Freed, 1992).

Despite the influx of new uppers and downers, little likelihood exists that the cocaine blizzard will soon abate. A drug habit born of a desire to escape the bad news in life is not likely to be discouraged by bad news about the drug itself. Americans will continue to succumb to the powder's crystalline dazzle. Few are yet aware or willing to concede that, at the very least, taking cocaine is dangerous to their psychological health (Demarest, 1981).

Today's drug was yesterday's drug as well; we are now experiencing the third or fourth cocaine epidemic. Historically, it dates back 5000 years. Its real claims to fame occurred in the nineteenth century. Angelo Mariani, a Corsican chemist, may have come the closest to "turning the world on" by inventing an elixir with coca and alcohol. Numerous medical giants including Freud, Koller, Corning, Halsted, Crile, and Cushing praised the merits of the "discovery of the age"; cocaine's benefit to mankind would be incalculable. Its opponents labeled it the third scourge of mankind (after alcohol and morphine). The *New York Times* stated that it wrecks its victim more swiftly and surely than opium. CocaCola went "clean," replacing coca with caffeine. In the Harrison Tax Act (1914), cocaine was classified as a narcotic, and since then debate has continued about its abuse and addictive potential.

In the United States between 1975 and 1980, the number of individuals seeking treatment for cocaine abuse increased fivefold, the number of emergency room admissions fourfold, and the number of deaths fourfold. At least 1 million Americans are now profoundly dependent on cocaine, a new corps more numerous than heroin addicts. About 10% of high school seniors are regular users. Cocaine has become a $25 billion business, ranking it in sales among the top 10 U.S. companies. No longer is it the recreational drug of the affluent; 20% of blue-collar workers engage in frequent cocaine misuse. Men users outnumber women by a 2:1 ratio, with current profile remaining that of a white, college-educated man in his 30s with an annual income of $25,000. Recent bumper crops in South America, will unfortunately, alter the supply-demand ratio to lower the price and augment the already massively escalating epidemic.

A survey conducted by the National Institute on Drug Abuse (1982) revealed that 22 million Americans had used cocaine at least once. A 1985 survey revealed that 17% of American high school seniors had tried cocaine. The rising population of cocaine users has been accompanied by a similar increase in the number of heavy abusers who have had to seek medical treatment because of cocaine-related difficulties. The number of medical emergencies resulting from cocaine use increased by 900% between 1976 and 1985, while cocaine-related deaths increased by over 1100%. Cocaine has become a widely prevalent drug that is being used by all levels of our society, by men and women, adolescents and adults, rich and poor (Weiss and Mirin, 1987).

Cocaine is readily absorbed from all mucous membranes, although concomitant local vasoconstriction limits its rate of absorption. Despite this fact, absorption may easily exceed the rate of detoxification and excretion, leading to high toxicity. Cocaine undergoes rapid biotransformation in the body. Its two main metabolites, ecgonine and benzoylecgonine, are excreted in the urine in amounts equivalent to one fourth to one half the original dose within 24 to 36 hours. Depending on urine acidity, 10% to 20% of cocaine is excreted unchanged. To avoid detection, addicts attempt to enhance excretion by consuming large volumes of cranberry juice or ingesting megadoses of vitamin C. Physicians treat in attempt to increase excretion by giving the patient intravenous ammonium chloride. After 100 mg of intravenous cocaine has been taken, a plasma peak occurs at 5 minutes; the distributional half-life is 20 to 40 minutes. The most popular routes for abuse purposes are intranasal (snorting), intravenous (running), and free-basing inhalation (smoking) (Hankes, 1984).

Cocaine is a beguiling drug that does not result in hangovers, lung cancer, or holes in the arm. Instead, a user takes a snort, and for the next 20 to 30 minutes there is an increase in drive, sparkle, and energy without a feeling of being drugged. Reported subjective effects include mood elevation to the point of euphoria, decrease in hunger, increases in energy and sociability, indifference to pain, and significant decrease in fatigue. Users experience a feeling of great muscular strength and increased mental capacity, leading to an overestimation of their capabilities. The powerful experience of the cocaine high can lead the user into a pattern of regular and escalating use. The most commonly reported side effects of regular use include anxiety, dysphoria, suspiciousness, disruption in eating and sleeping habits, weight loss, fatigue, irritability, concentration difficulties, and perceptual problems. Increasing use may lead to hyperexcitability, marked agitation, paranoia, hypertension, and tachycardia. As the individual becomes more and more "strung out," alcohol, sedatives, or other narcotics are often taken to combat the overstimulation.

Paranoid psychoses are manifested by a variety of symptoms such as visual distortion and hallucinations (geometric patterns—"snow lights"), tactile hallucinations (sensation of insects on, in, or under the skin—cocaine "bugs"), delusions (being chased by the police—"bull horrors"), and violent behavior. Cocaine interacts with the catecholamine neurotransmitters, norepinephrine, and dopamine, and alters normal interneuronal communication. It augments the effects of these catecholamines, probably by blocking (or prolonging) reuptake at the synaptic junction, leaving an excess of these neurotransmitters to restimulate receptors. Dopamine is a precursor of norepinephrine and is found in the corpus striatum— part of the network governing motor functions—and in that portion of the hypothalamus regulating thirst and hunger. Norepinephrine is the prime neurotransmitter of the ascending reticular activating system (RAS), regulating mechanisms of external attention and arousal. It acts as a vital transmitter as well in the hypothalamus, which regulates body temperature, sleep, and sexual arousal and, in general, mediates emotional depression. It also mediates neural activation in the median forebrain bundle of the hypothalamus, which is believed to serve as an individual's "pleasure center."

When we look at a drug taken, but not prescribed, for a mood or behavioral change, we consider the following: first, the potential for overdose; second, the potential for acute toxicity; third, physical derangements; fourth, its effects on mental status; and fifth, behavioral modification. That is, how much does it incapacitate a person or hinder his ability to function in an environment that was not a preexisting problem? Acute consequences include hyperpyrexia; hypertension with possible cerebrovascular accident, arrhythmia, or myocardial infarct; accidents because of impaired judgment and timing; and the dangers that lurk around some less than desirable purchase zones. Seizures are common and often progress to status epilepticus. Chronic complications depend on purity, route of administration, frequency of use, and sterility. All too often, users confuse cleanliness with sterility.

One of the frequent chronic medical complications is not strictly medical but dental. Cocaine is a powerful local anesthetic, and users often neglect their teeth because they are not aware of any discomfort or pain. They are often found to have missing fillings, cavities, loose teeth, impaction with inflammation, and even periodontal abscesses. A detailed oral examination is mandatory (Woods and Downs, 1973).

Malnutrition is common because food intake is ignored. Most patients are thin (rarely are they obese), and some are emaciated; 73% have at least one major vitamin deficiency, usually pyridoxine followed by thiamine and ascorbic acid. Intranasal users develop rhinorrhea, nasal septal necrosis and perforation, hoarseness, aspiration pneumonia, and frontal sinusitis. Routine chest and frontal sinus x-ray examinations are suggested. Free-basing often results in burns from explosion of the volatile ether used in preparation of the base. Chronic users who prefer to smoke cocaine should be evaluated for pulmonary function. Intravenous users are subject to infections of the skin, lung, heart valves, brain, and eye by multiple unusual bacteria and fungi. Some 86% of intravenous coke users have antibody evidence of prior exposure to hepatitis B. Talc and silicone adulterants produce granuloma formation in the lungs, liver, brain, and eye. Cocaine is metabolized by the liver and excreted by the kidney; any preexisting dysfunction exacerbates most conditions previously discussed.

Patients often "tank up" just before admission, that is, use very large doses in anticipation of cold turkey withdrawal. This increases the toxicity potential, and some centers are reluctant to admit patients on weekends and nights unless medical supervision is available. The lethal dose of cocaine is about 1.2 gm, but severe toxicity has occurred with an average dose of 20 mg. Tolerance and route of administration play an important role in the lethal dose. Sudden death from cocaine is so sudden that the only medical person to see the patient is often the coroner. Death occurs from status epilepticus, respiratory paralysis, myocardial infarction or irritability, and rarely, anaphylaxis. It does not appear that antiepileptic medications reduce or block cocaine-related seizures. The combined chronic lack of sleep and throat anesthesia may interact to cause a deep "crash" (sleep), which is accompanied by airway obstruction (suffocation) induced by a flaccid jaw or failure to remove secretions (drowning). The number of deaths resulting from the combined use of cocaine with other drugs has also rapidly increased but not as rapidly as the number of cocaine-related homicide victims. Death can and does occur in people who drink and use cocaine. The cocaine keeps the person awake enough to continue drinking and try to drive home; the cocaine wears off before the alcohol, and the high blood alcohol level oversedates, causing a fatal accident. Often only the blood alcohol level is analyzed, which falsely attributes the death to alcohol alone. Concomitant use of narcotics in an attempt to boost the cocaine high or to self-medicate its side effects often results in disaster. Another factor involved in cocaine-related deaths is cocaine-related suicides. These dependent individuals feel hopeless and helpless. Suicide may be seen as the only solution to deteriorating health and personal, domestic, or financial situations. However, fear of disability or disease from various sources does not deter use because most users discount these medical reports or doubt that any disability or disease will happen to them (Hankes, 1984).

The life-style generally accepted as normal involves major efforts to obtain and enjoy food, water, shelter, friendship, and a sexual partner. Researchers assume that a major function of the brain's reinforcement centers is to make it possible for the individual to strive to achieve these goals despite the fact that their availability is limited. Cocaine's main danger is its bypassing of the normal reinforcement process. It reprograms or reprioritizes the person so that getting cocaine is supreme and all normal drives are subverted. People and their cocaine problems can be classified on the basis of access. Pharmacists and doctors who have tried cocaine or who have access to pharmaceutical cocaine have a special kind of problem. People who have a lot of disposable income (such as athletes and entertainers) have the different problem of unlimited access; they can easily end up addicted. Cocaine is a drug of disposable income: What you have the drug will soon dispose of (Zinberg and Robertson, 1972).

Many physicians and users debate whether cocaine is addicting, the underlying premise being that if it is not addicting, it is not dangerous. The definition of *addiction* encompasses three concepts: compulsive use, loss of control when using the drug, and continued use despite adverse consequences. Using this definition, cocaine is obviously very, very addicting. It lends itself to reinforcement. Toxic manifestations do not even curtail use. Taking cocaine stimulates taking cocaine. Drug-craving and drug-seeking behavior are notable with cocaine, clearly indicating a high level of psychological dependence. This effect, coupled with cocaine's property to reinforce its own abuse, leads to disaster. Regular users, especially high dose snorters, free-basers, and injectors, generally want to maintain the elation. Cocaine's price and pharmacology do not lend themselves to a self-regulated maintenance program. Users may "base" continuously for days or inject intravenously every 10 minutes. For some, the anxiety, suspiciousness, and hypervigilance become overwhelming. Even as the user comes down and recalls the paranoid experience, he generally starts up again with the notion that this time he will stop short of insanity. Success-oriented people who rarely use drugs may discover cocaine and in less than 2 or 3 years find themselves hopelessly involved in illicit activities or facing incarceration. Consistent use can result in a severe depressive reaction, which may be the result of depleted norepinephrine stores. This may lead to another temporary "cure," perpetuating the habit. Others with mild depression self-medicate with cocaine. They quickly learn that they are nothing and that the drug is everything. Any subsequent success is misattributed to the drug, and these abusers come to believe that normal functioning without the drug is nearly impossible (Garwin and Kepler, 1984).

TREATMENT OF ACUTE COCAINE REACTION

Medical intervention must be without hesitation and directed to support of cardio-vascular and respiratory functions. A source of positive pressure ventilation, sup-plemental oxygen, proper endotracheal equipment, suction, a stretcher that allows the Trendelenburg position, intravenous infusion lines, continuous ECG monitor, and proper medications are needed. All drugs should be titrated to clinical need. For signs of advancing central nervous system stimulation, 2.5 to 5 mg diazepam may be given intravenously and repeated as many as four times at 5-minute intervals. If impending disaster is perceived, the fast-acting barbiturate thiopental, 50 to 100 mg, along with the depolarizing muscle relaxant, succinylcholine, 40 to 100 mg, may be given for immediate control of the airway and ablation of convulsive movement. Should tachycardia, hypertension, or ventricular ectopy appear, 1 mg propranolol by intravenous bolus may be given. This may be repeated six times at 1-minute intervals. Titration to a diastolic pressure of about 90 and an apical/radial pulse around or less than 100 is recommended. Lidocaine may be employed to suppress ventricular ectopy in a dosage of 50 to 100 mg intravenous bolus; intra-venous lines should be kept open in order to administer 2 to 4 mg lidocaine per minute, as needed. Core temperature should be monitored with a cooling blanket, fans, and cold sponging available. Metabolic acidosis should be treated with bi-carbonate. When drugs are being administered, the dangerously high levels of catecholamines must be remembered. Central nervous system and cardiovascular events must be scrupulously watched.

TREATMENT OF CHRONIC COCAINE TOXICITY

A common clinical phenomenon is the admission of a patient 3 to 14 days into a binge who exhibits signs of late stage I (premonitory to the collapse of stages II and III). These individuals show hyperkinetic behavior, tachycardia, hypertension, tachypnea, dyspnea, tics, jerks, tremors, stereotypical movements, distorted per-ception, and, possibly, violent protective behavior, which is delusional. Such pa-tients are at prime risk for cardiac arrhythmia, cerebrovascular accident, and high-output congestive heart failure. Such cases of adrenergic or dopaminergic storm have responded dramatically to the lytic effects of propanolol. Again, careful mon-itoring is mandatory. Propanolol is given either in slow intravenous increments of 1 mg at 1-minute intervals up to a total of 6 mg or orally in a dosage of 40 to 80 mg at 4- to 6-hour intervals for a period of up to 1 week with a pulse of 90 or less the goal. The patient is given sips of 5% glucose solution or perhaps cranberry juice, which is rich in benzoic acid. Urine is acidified with IV ammonium chloride at 75 mg per kg four times daily, with a maximum dose of 6 g per day. Diazepam should be administered at bedtime. Using the IV method, the hyperkinetic state will be reversed within 3 to 5 minutes, and following oral medication, it will be reversed within 20 to 40 minutes. The use of phenothiazines and haloperidol have been specifically avoided because of their propensity to lower the seizure threshold. The tricyclic antidepressants are avoided because of the danger of the appearance of true life-threatening arrhythmias in an already sensitized patient.

WITHDRAWAL

The actual existence of physiological dependency and a related cocaine abstinence syndrome is widely debated, yet a relatively consistent withdrawal syndrome is observed following cessation of chronic use. It consists of irritability, alternating anxiety and depression, boredom, perceptual problems, inability to concentrate, hypersomnia, fatigue, and intense drug craving. Medical detoxification should be accomplished in an inpatient, medically supervised setting. Premature departures against medical advice occur most frequently at 24 and 96 hours. These are the times when drug craving is most intense, paranoid ideation increases, and intolerance to rigid treatment unit regulations surfaces. The science of "ART" should be employed: "A" is acceptance as a caring, understanding intermediary, which is essential; "R" is reduction of stimuli, because rest and reassurance diminish most disruptive behavior; "T" is "Talkdown," a technique with sincere concern and gentle manipulation will abort hostile actions. Initial restrictions should include no pass, phone, or visitor privileges. After 2 days, daytime naps are not allowed. (The night personnel then often need extra staffing to handle the increased hallway traffic.) L-tryptophan, 2 g before meals three times daily, and 4 gm at bedtime with a carbohydrate snack is an effective aid to sleep. Tyrosine is being studied as an adjunctive measure. Vigorous structured physical activity also plays an important role. Diazepam appears to be the ideal sedative for the over-"amped" cocaine user. Oral dosage of 10 to 20 mg every 6 to 8 hours is quite effective.

POSTDETOXIFICATION

Does cocaine addiction require a specific therapeutic program? This is an unsettled question. More often than not, the traditional 28-day inpatient alcoholism program is the only available resource. Administrators of such programs frequently do not want to handle cocaine abusers because they believe cocaine abuse is a completely different problem. Although it is true that it is overly simplistic to lump all addictions under the umbrella of "chemical dependency," the striking similarities between cocaine addiction and alcoholism merit treating both in similar fashion. These considerations as well as the existence of any polydrug abuse should be noted when structuring and tailoring a treatment plan specifically for cocaine addiction. In the meantime, traditional inpatient alcoholism programs appear to have the most to offer the cocaine addict. Didactic education, individual and group counseling, cognitive restructuring based on reality therapy, family therapy, and ongoing participation in posttreatment self-help groups are essential ingredients of an effective treatment program.

Cocaine addiction is viewed by "addictionologists" as a primary disease of multifactorial etiology. The addiction is not merely a symptom of underlying psychopathology. This is a critical distinction. For therapy to be successful, treatment must focus on the toxic consequences of cocaine. The goal must be a cocaine-free recovery. To accomplish this, the treatment team helps the patient find positive and constructive alternatives to deal with the drug hunger, emphasizing that any attempt to return to the drug is a relapse. Once an addictive disease is established, the person cannot return to any recreational use; total abstinence is required (Laurie, 1971).

The case study that follows depicts the tragic circumstances that occurred when a young physician abused cocaine.

Case Study   *Substance abuse*

ASSESSMENT OF THE INDIVIDUAL AND THE PROBLEM

Late one Thursday afternoon, Steve D, an open-heart surgeon, called his friend, a psychotherapist. He was quite concerned that no one hear their conversation; he wanted to talk to his friend but not at the hospital where other staff members might see him. They made arrangements for him to meet with the therapist at her home early that evening. The therapist recalled that Steve had a very distinguished background: his father, grandfather, and great-grandfather had been highly respected physicians; and Steve was a Phi Beta Kappa from a well-known and distinguished eastern school, had graduated magna cum laude, had married an intelligent and attractive woman, had three lovely children, had finished at the top of his class, and had done his residency with a famous cardiologist-surgeon. Everyone, including peers, nursing staff, and patients, respected and liked him. In other words, he had everything going for him.

When Steve arrived at his friend's home, she immediately noticed that he was tense and trembling. Then he lit a cigarette, which she had never seen him do before; he had always disapproved of smoking. He seemed hesitant about telling the therapist what was wrong. She reminded him that she could not help him if she did not know what the problem was, and he obviously had a problem.

Steve began by telling her that he had been indefinitely suspended from the hospital staff. His explanation started with his internship, when the hours were long and the physical and emotional demands were constant. He had started using cocaine then, "not every day or night, just when I was so tired I didn't think I could keep my eyes open from fatigue and complete exhaustion."

The therapist was shocked and saddened by his confession, but she made no outward sign of her feelings and told him to continue his story. The residency had been difficult; Steve had felt that nothing he did pleased the surgeon. However, when the residency was completed, the surgeon wrote a "glowing report," which stated that Steve had a "brilliant career" ahead of him and that he had been the surgeon's most outstanding resident. Steve told the therapist he had used cocaine while he was a resident, maybe a little more than when he was an intern, but not every day.

The therapist asked how he was using it and he replied, "I was just snorting it—then." She asked about the present, and he said, "Now I'm smoking it—free-basing—and injecting it." He also said that he was not combining heroin with it when he injected it because he was "not that crazy." He had been free-basing for about 2½ years and injecting for a little over a year.

She asked Steve who found out about his cocaine use and when. He started pacing up and down and asked for a drink. Since he had admitted to smoking some coke right before coming to see her, the therapist refused his request. She became very firm with him and offered him a choice of answering her questions right then or leaving. After only a moment's hesitation, Steve started talking. He had scheduled a triple bypass on a patient for the previous Monday morning. He explained that he never injected himself for 3 days before surgery, but he did free-base. He made it a point to be scrubbed early, before anyone else was around, and gowned so no one could see his arms (with tracks from injecting the cocaine). He said everything was going well in surgery on this particular morning until he accidentally cut his finger with a scalpel. He added that he had been a little shaky that morning for some reason (probably because of his heavy use of cocaine). One of his partners took his place to continue the surgery, and he went out to rescrub. Unfortunately, Dr. A, the chief of staff, was in the scrub room when Steve entered. Steve stripped his gloves and gown off and started to rescrub at a basin as far from Dr. A as possible. Dr. A asked him why he was rescrubbing, and Steve explained that he had cut his finger. Dr. A asked to see his finger. Steve quickly held up his hand and said it was nothing. However, the other doctor apparently saw the tracks on Steve's arm and quietly but firmly asked him to hold out both his arms. Steve did as he was asked, and Dr. A looked at his arms and told him to stay where he was. Dr. A then called for a resident to replace Steve in surgery and told Steve to cancel all his appointments for the rest of the week and wait for Dr. A in his office. Dr. A arrived at his office and asked Steve what he had been shooting up on, how long, and why. After Steve related his story, Dr. A told him he had no excuse; they were all dealing with human lives and could not afford to make even one mistake. Dr. A called an emergency staff meeting of the ethics committee for an hour later. He made it clear that he was doing nothing to help Steve, who was to "try to explain" his behavior to the committee members.

Steve stopped talking at this point and had to be prodded into continuing. He said the committee meeting was "horrible," that the persons attending "stared at me as if they had never seen me before." All they had asked him was how much he was using and where he got his supply (by writing prescriptions for nonexistent patients). They informed him that he would have to enter a substance abuse facility and stay there until he was determined "clean" by the discharge clinic staff. He was automatically suspended from hospital privileges immediately. If he did not report to a facility by the end of the week, they would notify the Board of Medical Quality Assurance, and his license to practice medicine would be revoked.

The therapist asked him if he was going to do as the committee had told him by the next day. He replied, "I don't know. That's why I had to talk to you. Can't you work with me and get me over the need to use coke?" She answered firmly, "Absolutely not, it can't be done!" She explained that the amount he used, the methods, and the length of time all made outpatient psychotherapy inappropriate and dangerous. She told him he could die trying to get "clean" himself.

At that point, Steve said, "It would be better if I were dead." His friend pointed out to him that he would be leaving his wife and children a terrible legacy. She told him that he could continue to be a surgeon, but that it would not be easy. She then asked if he had discussed the matter with his wife, Jennifer, and he said no.

The therapist sent Steve home to talk to his wife and told him to bring her back with him that night. While he was gone, she would make some plans for him. He agreed to do as she said.

PLANNING THERAPEUTIC INTERVENTION

The first step would be to talk with Steve and Jennifer together to determine if his wife would stand by the decision that he enter a substance abuse facility. The next step would be to contact the best facility the therapist knew to see if a private room was available for Steve. She also needed to know if he could be admitted that night. The facility under consideration was approximately 125 miles away. The therapist did not think Steve would willingly accept a facility in the city.

INTERVENTION

The psychotherapist called the substance abuse facility and related her story to the director, Mr. B, a friend of hers. Mr. B informed her that he had a room and suggested that Steve might want to use an assumed name while there. He agreed that Steve and Jennifer should come that night; he would make the train reservations and meet them at the station.

Steve returned to the therapist's home with his wife. Jennifer was shaken by what her husband had told her, but she said they were very willing to do anything that the therapist suggested to help her husband. The therapist told them to make arrangements immediately to go to the facility that night. She told Steve that she would talk to the chief of staff and inform him of Steve's decision. Before leaving, Jennifer requested therapy after she returned from the facility; she did not understand how her husband could have become involved in using cocaine.

After they left, the therapist called Dr. A and told him what had happened that evening. He asked her what she felt the chances were for Steve to come out of his addiction really clean, with no desire to go back on cocaine. She responded that if he could get through the first week, he might make it. The length of time he had been using it and the methods he used made a more optimistic response impossible. However, the therapist felt they had done all they could for him.

During the night, the therapist received a call from the director of the facility. He informed her that Steve had died on the train; he had apparently "tanked up" and died in his sleep. Jennifer had been admitted to the hospital in a state of shock.

ANTICIPATORY PLANNING

Because nothing could be done for Steve, anticipatory planning would involve helping his wife and children through the grief and mourning process. They would have to rebuild their lives without him.

CASE STUDY: STEVE

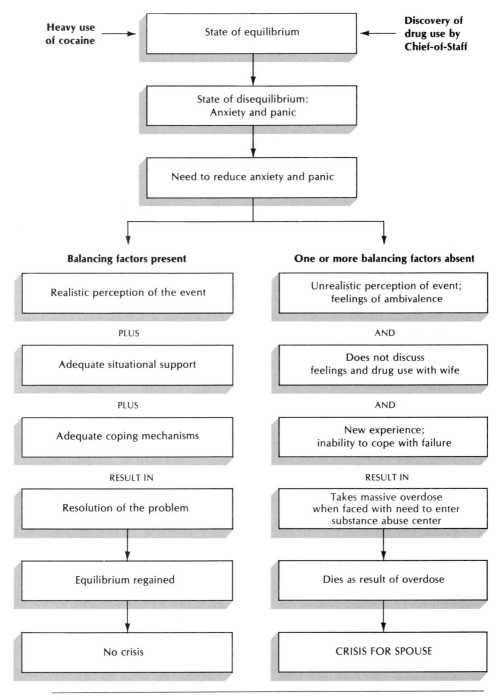

Figure 6-12

SUMMATION OF THE PARADIGM (Figure 6-12)

Steve was accustomed to success, to being "the best at everything he tried." His use of cocaine, which became heavy and dangerous, was discovered by his chief of staff. Suddenly he was faced with entering a substance abuse facility or having his license revoked. He agreed to enter a facility but was ambivalent because of his heavy use. He did not use his available situational support, his wife. He took a massive overdose and died on the way to the facility. This left his wife in a state of crisis.

Suicide—Theoretical Concepts

According to the National Center for Health Statistics (1990-1991), suicide ranks eighth as a cause of death in the United States; 13.6 persons per every 100,000 population commit suicide. Statistics for various age groups are as follows: 15 to 24 years, 11.9; 25 to 34 years, 14.4; 35 to 44 years, 14.4; 45 to 54 years, 14.6; 55 to 64 years, 14; 65 to 74 years, 19.9; 75 to 84 years, 29.2; 85 years and over, 27.6. The age range with the greatest number of suicides is 75 to 85 years.

At large general hospital emergency rooms, a night rarely goes by without at least one admission for attempted suicide.

The most common form of attempted suicide is the ingestion of a sedative or hypnotic drug. Suicide attempts by other methods, such as hanging, wrist cutting or other body mutilation, gas inhalation, gunshot wounds, and jumping from high places, are less frequent (Carter and Brooks, 1990).

In addition to actual suicide attempts, other persons are referred or brought to hospitals or mental health centers because they have threatened suicide or because they have demonstrated some form of self-destructive behavior, such as running into highway traffic or threatening to jump from a bridge or freeway overpass. Regardless of how the suicidal behavior is manifested, the basic question remains, "Why suicide?" There is no single answer to this question. The complex motivations, weaknesses, and strengths that determine all types of human behavior also apply to suicide. Consequently, there are many roads that individuals may take in reaching a decision to commit suicide. Usually the process is long, and often it is complicated by other physical and emotional symptoms of distress. Despite the multiplicity of causes and patterns, suicidal behavior can usually be related to three primary motivations: loss of communication, ambivalence about life and death, and the effects of the suicidal behavior on significant others (Simonds and others, 1991).

COMMUNICATION

Suicidal reactions are usually associated with feelings of hopelessness and helplessness and are often related to the separation or loss of a significant or valued relationship. Suicidal behavior can best be understood as an expression of intense feelings when other forms of expression have failed. The expression of feelings can range from sad cries for help to desperate statements of despair. A suicidal person is driven to this act because he feels unable to cope with a problem and believes that others are not responding to his need. The suicidal behavior becomes expressed verbally or by actions. Either directly or indirectly, the communication is frequently aimed at a specific person—the significant other. Recognizing the intent of the disguised message and understanding its real content becomes a problem for the recipient when the message is indirectly communicated.

AMBIVALENCE

Only a small number of people who threaten or attempt suicide actually succeed. The general explanation for an incomplete or partially effective suicidal act is that the individual is filled with contradictory feelings about living and dying. This state is termed *ambivalence*. Ambivalence is a universal human trait. We all have it at times, and it is not a weakness. Everyone feels ambivalence over decisions at some point in choosing a career, a spouse, or a place to live. The choice of a place and time to die is no exception. In making the decision of whether to live or die, one would expect to find even more than the normal amount of ambivalence. This psychological characteristic accounts for the sometimes puzzling fact that a person takes a lethal or near-lethal action and then counterbalances it with some provision for rescue. The very fact that every person is divided within himself over decisions provides the chance for successful intervention with a suicidal patient. By making use of the patient's wish to live, his "cry for help," suicide may be averted. The myth that "if a person talks about suicide, he won't do it" is actually that—a myth. Every statement or ideation of the wish to die should be taken seriously and explored with the individual.

EFFECTS ON OTHERS

Suicidal behavior can be further understood in terms of its effect on those receiving the communication. A suicidal attempt may arouse feelings of sympathy, anxiety, anger, or hostility on the part of the individual's family or friends and therefore serve to manipulate relationships. The therapist may also experience similar feelings unless he can anticipate and counteract these reactions. The therapist must resist the desire to be omnipotent. No one is truly omnipotent, just as no one can solve all the problems and meet all the demands of every patient. This is especially true when dealing with intensely dependent patients who often attribute tremendous powers to the potential rescuer. Many suicidal situations arouse feelings of anxiety and self-doubt in the therapist about his own ability to handle them. Although a moderate level of anxiety is appropriate, too much may seriously hamper the effort to help, especially if it is transmitted to the patient, who is depending on someone to help him solve his problems. Already feeling helpless and lost, the suicidal person who perceives excessive anxiety in a therapist may lose hope of being helped and bluntly state so. As in any form of intervention, the therapist develops confidence in his ability with training and experience.

SUICIDAL POTENTIAL

Before considering the factors that influence the probability of suicide, the therapist should consider his own attitudes toward suicide and death because they definitely affect how he will function with patients. Death is a process that is a part of life and living. From the moment one is born, movement toward death begins. Unfortunately, Western cultures have surrounded death with many powerful taboos. The feelings that these taboos can arouse may very well interfere in the therapist's interactions with his patients. He must be sensitive to his own thoughts about death and suicide, and, regardless of personal attitudes, he must avoid any moralistic judgments about what has happened. The professional point of view must be that death is to be prevented, if possible. A therapist is often placed in the position of actually debating life-and-death questions with upset people. Although he must recognize the existence and merits of other viewpoints, his role is to represent life and to assist distressed, helpless people.

From the first conversation with a suicidal individual, a therapist immediately assumes some responsibility for preventing the suicide. In working out some plan for prevention, the therapist must first determine the individual's suicidal potential, that is, the degree of probability that the person will try to kill himself in the immediate or near future. In some individuals, the suicidal potential is minimal, whereas in others it is immediate and great. The therapist must decide the degree of risk for each patient (Kaye and Soreff, 1991).

The prediction of suicide is by no means an exact science. Even the most experienced therapist can be misled in assessing a problem. However, certain criteria allow suicidal potential to be evaluated with some assurance. Assessment of suicidal potential depends on obtaining detailed information about the patient in each of the following categories.

Age and sex. Statistics indicate that women *attempt* suicide more often than men but that men *commit* suicide more often than women. Currently, this trend is changing as women are beginning to feel the same stresses in their changing social roles that men feel. They are also beginning to use more lethal methods in their suicide attempts. It is also known that the rate for completed suicide rises with increasing age. Consequently, an older man presents the greatest threat of actual suicide and a young woman the least. Within this framework, age and sex offer a general, although by no means clear-cut, basis for evaluating suicidal potential. One must remember that young women and young men do kill themselves, even when their original aim is to manipulate other people. Each case requires individual appraisal.

Suicidal plan. How an individual plans to take his life is one of the most significant criteria in assessing suicidal potential. The therapist must consider the following three elements:

1. Is it a relatively lethal method? An individual who intends to commit suicide with a gun, by jumping from a tall building or bridge, or by hanging is a far greater risk than someone who plans to take pills or cut his wrists. Because the person who plans either of the latter two methods is amenable to treatment or resuscitation, these methods are less lethal than the irrevocable consequences of putting a gun to one's head.

2. Does the individual have the means available? It must be determined if the method of suicide the individual has considered is in fact available to him. A threat to use a gun, if the person has one, is obviously more serious than the same threat without a gun.

3. Is the suicide plan specific? Can the individual say exactly when he plans to do it (for example, after the children are asleep)? If he has spent time thinking

out details and specific preparations for his death, his suicidal risk is greatly increased. Changing a will, writing notes, collecting pills, buying a gun, and setting a time and place for suicide suggest a high risk. When a patient's plan is obviously confused or unrealistic, one should consider the possibility of an underlying psychiatric problem. A psychotic person with the idea of suicide is a particularly high risk because he may make a bizarre attempt based on his distorted thoughts. The therapist should always find out if the patient has a past history of any emotional disorder and whether he has ever been hospitalized or received other mental health care.

Stress. The therapist needs to find out about any stressful event that may have precipitated the suicidal behavior. The most common precipitating stresses are losses: the death of a loved one; divorce or separation; loss of a job, money, prestige, or status; loss of health through illness, surgery, or accident; and loss of esteem or prestige because of possible prosecution or criminal involvement. Not all stresses are the result of bereavement. Sometimes increased anxiety and tension are a result of success, such as a promotion with increased responsibilities. Always investigate any sudden change in the individual's life situation.

Learning to evaluate stress from the individual's point of view rather than from society's point of view is necessary. What may be minimal stress for the therapist could be perceived by the patient as severe stress. The relationship between stress and symptoms is useful in evaluating prognosis.

Symptoms. The most common and most important suicidal symptoms relate to depression. Typical symptoms of severe depression include loss of appetite, weight loss, inability to sleep, loss of interest, social withdrawal, apathy and despondency, severe feelings of hopelessness and helplessness, and a general attitude of physical and emotional exhaustion. Other persons may exhibit agitation through such symptoms as tension, anxiety, guilt, shame, poor impulse control, or feelings of rage, anger, hostility, or revenge. Alcoholics and all other substance abusers tend to be high suicidal risks. The patient who is both agitated and depressed is particularly at high risk. Unable to tolerate the pressure of his feelings, the individual in a state of agitated depression shows marked tension, fearfulness, restlessness, and pressure of speech. He eventually reaches a point where he must act in some direction to relieve his feelings. Often he chooses suicide.

Suicidal symptoms may also occur with psychotic states. The patient may have delusions, hallucinations, distorted sensory impressions, loss of contact with reality, disorientation, or highly unusual ideas and experiences. As a baseline for assessing psychotic behavior, the therapist should use his own sense of what is real and appropriate.

Resources. The patient's environmental resources are often crucial in helping the therapist decide how to manage the immediate problem. Who are his situational supports? The therapist must find out who can be used to support him through this traumatic time: family, relatives, close friends, employers, physicians, or clergy. To whom does he feel close? If the patient is already under the care of a therapist, the new therapist should try to contact him.

The choice of various resources is sometimes affected by the fact that the patient and the family may try to keep the suicidal situation a secret, even to the point of denying its existence. As a general rule, this attempt at secrecy and denial must be counteracted by dealing with the suicidal situation openly and frankly. It is usually better, for both the therapist and the patient, if the responsibility for a suicidal patient is shared by as many people as possible. This combined effort provides the patient with a feeling that he lacks: that others are interested in him, care for him, and are ready to help him.

When there are no apparent sources of help or support, the therapist may be the person's only situational support, his one link to survival. This is also true if available resources have been exhausted or family and friends have turned away from the individual. In most cases, however, people will respond to the situation and provide help and support if given the opportunity.

Life-style.   How has the person functioned in the past under stress? First, has his style of life been stable or unstable? Second, is the suicidal behavior acute or chronic? The stable individual describes a consistent work record, sound marital and family relationship, and no history of previous suicidal behavior. The unstable individual may have had severe character disorders, borderline psychotic behavior, and repeated difficulties with major situations, such as interpersonal relationships or employment.

A suicidal person responding to acute stress, such as the death or loss of someone he loves, bad news, or loss of a job, presents a special concern. The risk of early suicide among this group is high; however, the opportunity for successful therapeutic intervention is greater. If the suicidal danger can be averted for a relatively short period of time, individuals tend to emerge without great danger of recurrence.

By contrast, individuals with a history of repeated attempts at self-destruction may be helped through one emergency, but the suicidal danger can be expected to return at a later date. In general, if an individual has made serious attempts in the past, his current suicidal situation should be considered more dangerous. Although individuals with chronic suicidal behavior benefit temporarily from intervention, the emphasis should fall more on continuity of care and the maintenance of relationships.

Acute suicidal behavior may be found in either a stable or an unstable personality; however, chronic suicidal behavior occurs only in an unstable person. In dealing with a stable person in a suicidal situation, the therapist should be highly responsive and active. With an unstable person, the therapist needs to be slower and more thoughtful, reminding the patient that he has withstood similar stresses in the past. The main goals are to help him through this period and assist him in reconstituting an interpersonal relationship with a stable person or resource.

Communication.   The communication aspects of suicidal behavior have great importance in the evaluation and assessment process. The most important question is whether communication still exists between the suicidal individual and his significant others. When communication with the suicidal patient is completely severed, it indicates that he has lost hope of any possibility of rescue.

The form of communication may be either verbal or nonverbal, and its content may be direct or indirect. The suicidal person who communicates nonverbally and indirectly makes it difficult for the recipient of the communication to recognize or understand the suicidal intent of these communications. Also, this type of communication in itself implies a lack of clarity in the interchange between the suicidal person and others. At the same time, it raises a danger that the individual may act out suicidal impulses. The primary goal is to open up and clarify communication among everyone involved in the situation.

The patient's communications may be directed toward one or more significant persons within his environment. He may express hostility, accuse or blame others, or demand openly or subtly that others change their behavior and feelings. His communication may express feelings of guilt, inadequacy, and worthlessness or indicate strong anxiety and tension.

Significant Other.   When the communication is directed to a specific person, the reaction of the recipient becomes an important factor in evaluating suicidal danger. One must decide if the significant other can be an important resource for rescue, if he is best regarded as unhelpful, or if he might even be injurious to the patient.

The unhelpful significant other either rejects the patient or denies the suicidal behavior itself by withdrawing, both psychologically and physically, from continued communication. Sometimes this other person resents the patient's increased demands, insistence on gratification of dependency needs, or the demands to change his own behavior. In other situations, the significant other may act helpless, indecisive, or ambivalent, indicating that he does not know what the next step is and has given up. A reaction of hopelessness gives the suicidal individual a feeling that aid is not available from a previously dependable source. This can increase the patient's own hopelessness.

By contrast, a helpful reaction from the significant other is one in which the other person recognizes the communication, is aware of the problem, and seeks help for the individual. This indicates to the patient that his communications are being heard and that someone is doing something to provide help (Yu-Chin and Arcuni, 1990).

In the following case study, Carol attempted suicide because of lack of communication with a significant other. She anticipated a rejection because of a similar past experience.

Case Study   *Suicide*

ASSESSMENT OF THE INDIVIDUAL AND THE PROBLEM

Carol was referred to a crisis center for help by a physician in the emergency room of a nearby small suburban hospital. The night before, she had attempted suicide by severely slashing her left wrist repeatedly with a large kitchen knife, and she had severed a tendon as a result.

When she was first seen by the therapist at the center, her left wrist and arm were heavily bandaged. She appeared tense, disheveled, very pale, and tremulous. She described her symptoms as insomnia, poor appetite, recent inability to concentrate, and overwhelming feelings of hopelessness and helplessness. Carol, a 30-year-old single woman, lived alone. She had come to a large midwestern city about 4 years ago, immediately after graduating from an eastern university with a master's degree in business administration. Within a few weeks she had obtained a management trainee position with a large manufacturing distribution company. In the next 3 years, she advanced rapidly to her current position as manager of the main branch office. She stated that her co-workers considered her highly qualified for the position. She denied any on-the-job problems other than "the usual things that anyone in my position has to expect to deal with on a day-to-day basis." As a result of her rapid rise in the company, however, she had not allowed herself much leisure time to develop any close social relationships with either sex.

About a year ago, Carol met John, a 40-year-old widower who had a position similar to hers with another company. His office was on the same floor as hers. Within a few weeks, they were spending almost all their leisure time together, although still maintaining separate apartments.

Carol's symptoms began about 2 weeks ago, when John was offered a promotion to a new job in his company, which he accepted before mentioning it to her. It meant that he would be transferred to another office about 30 miles away in the suburbs. She stated that she did feel upset "for just a few minutes" after he told her of his decision; "I guess that was just because he hadn't even mentioned anything about it to me first."

They went out that evening for dinner and dancing to celebrate the occasion. Before dinner was over, John had to bring her home because she "suddenly became dizzy, nauseated, and chilled" with what she described as "all of the worst symptoms of stomach flu."

Carol remained at home in bed for the next 3 days, not allowing John to visit her because she felt she was contagious. After she returned to work, she continued to feel very lethargic, had difficulty concentrating, could not regain her appetite, "and felt quite depressed and tearful for no reason at all."

Convincing herself that she had not yet fully recovered from the "flu," she canceled several dates with John so that she could get more rest. She described him as being very understanding about this, even encouraging her to try to get some time off from work to take a short trip by herself and really rest and relax.

During this same time, John had begun to spend increasing amounts of time at his new office. Their coffee break meetings at work became very infrequent. Within the next week, he expected to be moved completely. The night before Carol came to the crisis center, she had come home from work expecting to meet John for dinner; instead, she found a note under her door written by her neighbor. It said that John had telephoned him earlier and left word for her that he had "suddenly been called out of town—wasn't sure when he would be back, but would get in touch with her later."

She told the therapist, "Suddenly I felt empty . . . that everything was over between us. It was just too much for me to handle. He was never going to see me again and was too damned chicken to tell me to my face! I went numb all over—I just wanted to die." She paused a few minutes, head down and sobbing, then took a deep breath and went on, "I really don't remember doing it, but the next thing I was aware of was the telephone ringing. When I reached out to answer it, I realized I had a butcher knife in my right hand and my left wrist was cut and bleeding terribly! I dropped the knife on the floor and grabbed the phone. It was

John calling me from the airport to tell me why he had to go out of town so suddenly—his father was critically ill."

Through the sobs she told him what she had done to herself. He told her to take a kitchen towel and wrap it tightly around her wrist. After she had done that, he told her to unlock the front door and wait there, that he would get help to her.

He immediately called the neighbors, who went to her apartment and found her with blood soaked towels around her wrist and sitting on the floor beside the door. They took her to the hospital, and John continued on his trip. After being treated in the emergency room, Carol went home to spend the night with her neighbors. They drove her to the crisis center the next morning.

During her initial session, Carol told the therapist that she had no close relatives. Her father and mother had died within a few months of each other during her last year in college. Soon after, she had fallen in love with another graduate student, and at his suggestion they had moved into an apartment together. She had believed that they would marry as soon as they had both graduated and had jobs.

Just before graduation, however, her boyfriend had come home and informed her that he had accepted a postdoctoral fellowship in France and would be leaving within the month. They went out for dinner "to celebrate" that night because, she said, "I couldn't help but be happy for him—it was quite an honor—I just couldn't tell him how hurt I felt."

The next morning after he had left for classes, she stated that she "suddenly realized I would never see him again after graduation—that he had never intended to marry me—and I was helpless to do anything about it." She took some masking tape and sealed the kitchen window shut, closed the door and put towels along the bottom, and turned on all of the stove gas jets.

About an hour later, a neighbor smelled the gas fumes and called the fire department. The firemen broke into the apartment, found her lying unconscious on the floor, and rushed her to the hospital. She was in a coma for 2 days and remained in the hospital for a week. Her boyfriend came only once to see her. When she returned to the apartment, she found that he had moved out, leaving her a note saying that he had gone home to see his family before leaving for France. He never contacted her again. A month later Carol moved to the Midwest.

For the first few months after meeting John, Carol was very ambivalent about her feelings toward him. She frequently felt very anxious and fearful that she was "setting myself up for another rejection." Even when John proposed marriage, she found herself unable to consider it seriously and told him that they should wait a while longer "to be sure that they both wanted it." Continuing, she stated, "Until about 2 days ago I had never felt so secure in my life. I'd begun to seriously consider proposing to him! Then, suddenly, the bottom began to fall out of everything."

When John accepted the new job without telling her first, Carol saw this as the beginning of another rejection by someone highly significant in her life. As her anxiety increased, she withdrew from communication with John "because of her flu." John's well-intentioned agreement to cancel several dates so that she could get more rest further cut off her opportunities to communicate her feelings to him. His suggestion that she take a trip alone compounded her already strong fear of imminent rejection by him.

Finding the neighbor's note under the door was, for her, "the last straw," final proof that he was leaving her, "just like my boyfriend did in college."

Unable to cope with overwhelming feelings of loss and anger toward herself for "letting it happen to me again," she impulsively attempted suicide.

PLANNING THERAPEUTIC INTERVENTION

Carol's two suicide attempts, except for the method used, were quite similar. Both were precipitated by the threat of the loss of someone highly significant in her life; both were impulsive, maladaptive attempts to cope with intense feelings of depression, hopelessness, and helplessness; and both demonstrated an inability to communicate her feelings in stressful situations. When asked by the therapist how she coped with anxiety in the past, Carol said that she would keep herself so busy at work that she did not have much time to worry about personal problems. This had been her method of coping with anxiety at school, too, until her first suicide attempt. Because she had been too ill to work full-time the past 2 weeks, her previous successful coping mechanisms could not be effectively used.

The goal of intervention was to help Carol gain an intellectual understanding of the relationship between her crisis and her inability to communicate her intense feelings of depression and anxiety caused by the threat of losing John.

INTERVENTION

Before the end of the first session, the therapist's assessment was that Carol was no longer acutely suicidal. However, because of her continuing feelings of depression, a medical consultation was arranged and an antidepressant prescribed. A verbal contract was agreed on; Carol was to call the therapist if she felt suicidal again. Carol agreed to the suggestion that she have a friend move into her apartment to help her out until her arm was less painful. Before leaving, she assured the therapist that she would call him immediately if she again began to feel overwhelmed by anxiety before her next appointment.

When Carol returned for her next session, she was markedly less depressed. She told the therapist that John had called her soon after she came home from the center the week before. Although he had expressed great concern for her, she had been unable to tell him exactly why she had attempted suicide. "I just couldn't tell him that I thought he had left me for good. He'd think that I was trying to blame him. After all, I've been telling him for months that we both should keep our independence!" However, she said she felt much more reassured of his love for her. John expected to be back in about 2 more weeks.

During this and the next few sessions, the therapist explored with Carol why she found it difficult to communicate her feelings to someone so significant in her life. Carol was reluctant at first to admit that this was a problem that could have contributed to her recent crisis. She saw herself as someone who was completely self-sufficient and denied any dependency needs on John. As a child, she had been expected to control her emotions, to appear "ladylike" and composed at all times. Efforts on her part to communicate her feelings as she passed through the normal maturational crises of childhood and adolescence were met with rejecting behavior from those most significant in her life—her parents. Slowly, she began to gain

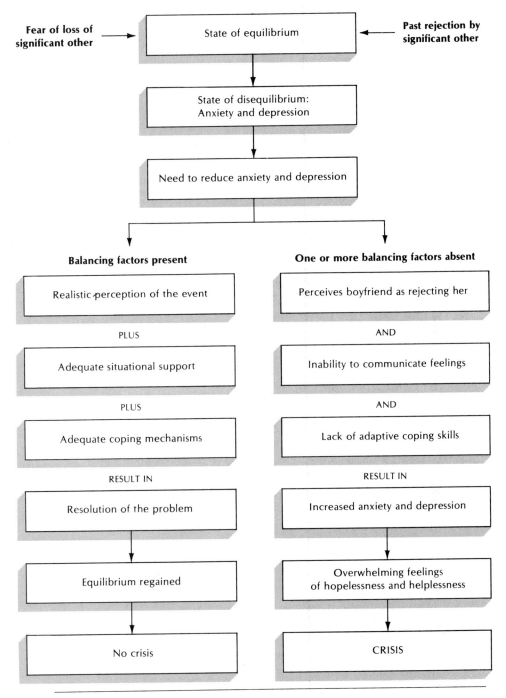

CASE STUDY: CAROL

Fear of loss of significant other → State of equilibrium ← Past rejection by significant other

State of disequilibrium: Anxiety and depression

Need to reduce anxiety and depression

Balancing factors present

Realistic perception of the event

PLUS

Adequate situational support

PLUS

Adequate coping mechanisms

RESULT IN

Resolution of the problem

Equilibrium regained

No crisis

One or more balancing factors absent

Perceives boyfriend as rejecting her

AND

Inability to communicate feelings

AND

Lack of adaptive coping skills

RESULT IN

Increased anxiety and depression

Overwhelming feelings of hopelessness and helplessness

CRISIS

Figure 6-13

insight into the ways in which she had learned maladaptive methods to cope with stress, such as withdrawing from contact with others whenever she felt threatened by a stressful situation; by somatizing her anxiety rather than admitting it was more than she could handle. By the end of the third session, she reported that she had been able to communicate her feelings to John more openly and honestly than she had ever done in the past. She appeared to be surprised and pleased that John had responded so positively to her. When asked what she would have done if he had not responded this way, she paused thoughtfully, then answered, "It was a risk I had to take. I just had to find out for sure if I could handle it this time." She added that, although she had been very anxious while talking to him, she at no time felt as though she could not go on living if things had turned out differently.

By the end of the fourth session, John had returned to the city, and Carol had returned to her job full time. She no longer felt depressed, and her wrist was slowly regaining its functioning. They were seeing each other frequently despite the distance between their offices, and Carol now said that she felt much more comfortable talking things out with him.

ANTICIPATORY PLANNING

Because Carol had attempted suicide once before under much the same crisis-precipitating stressful situation, she continued in therapy for the full 6 weeks. The purpose was to ensure that she could depend on situational support from the therapist while adjusting to the fact that she would no longer be seeing John every day. She was encouraged to telephone the therapist at any time she began to feel a recurrence of her earlier symptoms and felt unable to communicate these feelings to John.

Because she now seemed to have a better understanding of the relationship between her suicide attempts and the precipitating events, she said that she felt more secure in being able to cope with stressful situations in a more positive manner.

SUMMATION OF PARADIGM (Figure 6-13)

Carol's distorted perception of rejection by John was compounded by her previous experience in losing someone highly significant in her life. Unable to directly communicate her feelings to John, her anxiety and depression increased. Lacking adequate coping mechanisms and situational support, she became overwhelmed with feelings of hopelessness and helplessness. Anticipating another rejection, Carol, entering a state of crisis, impulsively attempted suicide. Intervention was focused on getting her to understand why she was unable to communicate and cope with her intense feelings of inadequacy in interpersonal relations.

Death and the Grief Process—Adult Theoretical Concepts

Death is a certainty. This universal phenomenon is ominous because it is inescapable. Because every human being will at some time experience death, it seems that death is most significant. Much is unknown of the process of death, and human beings are noted for their fear of the unknown. It might be said that this is a basic fear, and throughout the ages human beings have sought self-preservation. Advances in medical science and allied areas support this contention.

The critical question is not the sham dichotomy of life and death but the way in which each person relates to the knowledge that death is certain. This fear may be the prototype of human anxiety. Throughout history, death has posed an external mystery that is the core of religious and philosophical systems of thought. Anxiety relates to the fact that each person is powerless; he may postpone death, may lessen its physical pain, may rationalize it away or deny its very existence, but there is no escape from it, and so the fight for self-preservation is inevitably lost.

The attitudes of the persons involved in the situation are basic to the process of dying. Concepts, philosophies, and attitudes about death evolve from centuries of conflicting ideas and thought. Traditionally, the attitude of a society toward death has been a function of its religious beliefs. Religion denies the finality of death and affirms the continuation of the human personality either in its psychophysical totality or as a soul. The medical and social sciences, by challenging these traditional beliefs, have indirectly caused alienation and a serious mental health problem.

Family reaction to the death of a member develops in stages varying in time. The death of a loved one must produce an active expression of feeling in the normal course of events. Omission of such a reaction is to be considered as much a variation from the normal as is an excess in time and intensity. Unmanifested grief will be expressed in some way or another; each new loss can cause grief for the current loss as well as reactivate the grieving process of previous episodes.

Lindemann (1944) states that following loss there are three phases of mourning.

PHASE I: SHOCK AND DISBELIEF

There is a focus on the original object with symptoms of somatic distress occurring in waves, lasting from 20 minutes to an hour at a time, a feeling of tightness in the throat, choking with shortness of breath, need for sighing, an empty feeling in the abdomen, and lack of muscular power. There is commonly a slight sense of unreality, a feeling of increased emotional distance from other people, and an intense preoccupation with the image of the deceased.

There is a strong preoccupation with feelings of guilt. Accusing himself of negligence and exaggerating minor omissions, the bereaved searches the time before death for evidence of failure to do right by the lost one.

PHASE II: DEVELOPING AWARENESS.

Disorganization of personality occurs in this phase, accompanied by pain and despair because of the persistent and insatiable nature of yearning for the lost object. There is weeping and a feeling of helplessness and possible identification with the deceased.

PHASE III: RESOLVING THE LOSS.

Resolution of the loss completes the work of mourning. A reorganization takes place with emancipation from the image of the lost object, and new object relationships are formed.

Engel (1964) states that the clearest evidence that mourning or grieving is successfully completed is the ability to remember completely and realistically the pleasures *and* disappointments of the lost relationship. In this phase, one must also consider pathological mourning, in which there is an inability to express overtly these urges to recover the lost object. When all reactions are repressed, they influence behavior in a strange and distorted way; for example, a schizophrenic person's reaction to the death of a significant individual may be laughter. There may be a delayed reaction or an excessive reaction, or the grief reaction may take the form of an agitated depression with accompanying tension, agitation, insomnia, feelings of worthlessness, bitter self-accusation, and obvious need for punishment. Individuals reacting in this way may be dangerously suicidal.

Proper management of grief reactions may prevent prolonged and serious alterations in an individual's social adjustment. The essential task is that of sharing and understanding the individual's grief work. Comfort alone does not provide adequate assistance. He has to accept the pain of the bereavement. He has to review his relationships with the deceased, and express his sorrow and sense of loss. He must accept the destruction of a part of his personality before he can organize it afresh toward a new object or goal. Although they are unwelcome, such phases are a necessary part of life (Lindemann, 1944).

The following case study concerns a retired widower who is threatened by a second loss before completing "grief work" from the recent death of his wife. Initial assessment of the crisis situation provided clues in the determination that he was probably in the last phase of mourning and became overwhelmed by the threat of losing his son. The goal of intervention was to assist Mr. P in reentering his social world and in gaining an intellectual understanding of the grief process as it related to his symptoms.

Case Study   *Death and the grief process (adult)*

ASSESSMENT OF THE INDIVIDUAL AND THE PROBLEM

Mr. P, 67 years old and recently widowed, came to a crisis center for help on the advice of his family physician because of severe depression and anxiety. He described his symptoms as loss of appetite, inability to concentrate, rest-Lessness, insomnia, and loss of energy. These symptoms had been first manifested a month earlier, following the death of his wife. He thought that they had been subsiding, but they suddenly increased to an intolerable level and he feared loss of emotional control. He denied any suicidal ideas, stating, "I don't want to die, it's just that I've lost all interest in life and no longer care what happens to me."

During the initial visit, Mr. P was at first unable to determine any specific event that might have caused the sudden and acute rise in his symptoms. His wife's death was not unexpected, and he had felt "well prepared" for a future life without her. He viewed himself as realistic in his attitudes and planning before she died and as having experienced a "normal amount of grief" afterward.

After a mandatory retirement when he was 65 years old, he had devoted most of his time to helping care for his wife, a semi-invalid with severe coronary disease. "I think I was really glad when I retired, because I'd had so little time for myself in those last few years, working all day and then going home and trying to catch up with things I had to do there." Having little time for social activities with his business friends, he had felt little sense of their loss when he left his job.

He had one son, married and living nearby. The son and his wife had had close relationships with Mr. and Mrs. P, helping them out with their household activities and with the care of Mrs. P. Mr. P had made tentative plans to move into an apartment after his wife's death, feeling fully able to care for his own needs. However, just after his wife's death, his son and daughter-in-law brought up the idea of their moving into his home with him. It was a large home, much larger than their rented one, and they would pay him monthly amounts toward eventually buying it from him. He said that he was quite pleased with the idea, preferring to remain in his home but unable to justify to himself any reason for staying there alone. They had moved in 2 weeks ago, and he had felt an immediate lessening in his grief reaction to his wife's death.

A week ago, his son had received an unexpected offer of a better job in another state. Mr. P related that he felt very proud of the offer to his son and strongly urged him to accept it. The decision had to be made within the month. Because he had previously begun plans to live alone, he had not felt too concerned for himself if his son and daughter-in-law did decide to leave.

PLANNING THERAPEUTIC INTERVENTION

Mr. P had few social contacts because of his total involvement with the care of his wife during the past few years. His son and daughter-in-law had been providing situational support before and during his period of mourning, and this support was now in jeopardy. He had unrecognized ambivalence with regard to the job offer made to his son. Although intellectualizing plans to move into an apartment by himself, he lacked skills that would be necessary to repeople his social world. The anxiety generated by his unresolved grief and his ambivalence about his personal future was then compounded by the unexpected threat of a new loss.

When asked how he had coped with stress in the past, he said that he had always been able to keep busy caring for his wife and the housework. He had also been able to talk things over with his son. He now felt unable to talk to his son about his present feelings "for fear he might think he'd have to give up the job offer and stay here with me."

The goal of intervention was to help Mr. P gain an intellectual understanding of his crisis in order to recognize the relationship between the threatened loss of his son and his present severe discomfort. His unrecognized ambivalence between his needs for independence as opposed to dependency would be explored.

INTERVENTION

During the next 2 weeks, it became possible for him to see the present crisis and its accompanying symptoms in relation to his reactions to the loss of his wife and the threatened loss of his son.

During Mrs. P's illness he had narrowed his own life-style to conform to hers. In failing to acknowledge his lack of the interpersonal skills necessary to maintain a social life of his own, he justified his action as "what would be expected of any husband in a similar situation." Mrs. P had been the dominant member of the marriage. Even when bedridden, she had guided the decision making that he thought was independent on his part. The additional support and assistance by his son and daughter-in-law only served to increase his dependency on others for decision making.

At times during the past few years, he had thoughts of "all the things we could have done if I'd retired when my wife had not been so ill." He had deflected these thoughts into overt sympathy for her rather than for himself and what he was missing. As her death became imminent and inevitable, his wife began to make plans with him for his future. She told him to sell the home and to move into an apartment, even selecting which furniture he should keep and which he should give away. When she died, he was finally faced with the reality of his inability to cope with the changes. Crisis at this time was circumvented by the offer of his son to move into his home. He was able to continue in much the same life pattern that had previously existed for him, with the son and daughter-in-law assuming the leadership role. With their strong situational support, the work of grief had not become over-whelming.

The sudden threat of their loss had precipitated the crisis. Unrecognized feelings of inadequacy and dependency had come into painful focus. He feared both the physical loss of his son and the loss of his son's love if the job were turned down "because he'd think I couldn't take care of myself if he left me here alone."

By the third session, through discussion and clarification with the therapist, Mr. P was able to recognize his ambivalent feelings and relate them to his own needs for dependency. He saw the disparity between his concept of what he thought others expected of him and what he could actually achieve alone. His acceptance of this enabled him to reestablish meaningful communication with his son and to gain his support in making more realistic plans.

ANTICIPATORY PLANNING

Mr. P's exploration of his feelings related to his loss and subsequent grief helped him to gain an intellectual understanding of the process of working through the period of mourning. His recognition of his symptoms as part of the process helped to reduce his anxiety and enabled him to perceive the reality of the situation and to utilize his existing coping skills. Realization was gained that he himself was withdrawing from available situational support because of his concept that his role was to be "an independent person." He was able to accept the fact that this might not be true and, as a result, he felt better about communicating his fears to his son and enlisting his assistance in planning.

By the third week, his son had made the decision to accept the position and move out of the state in another month. Through joint efforts they located an apartment-hotel for Mr. P, where he would have the independence to "come and go as I'd always planned for in my retirement." Because the hotel preferred its guests to be in the retirement-age group, there were programs established for the guests' interest and social needs.

Mr. P moved into the hotel 3 weeks before his son left town. The period of transition was facilitated with minimal rise in his anxiety. There was a gradual removal of his son's situational support, which was being replaced by the support

CASE STUDY: MR. P

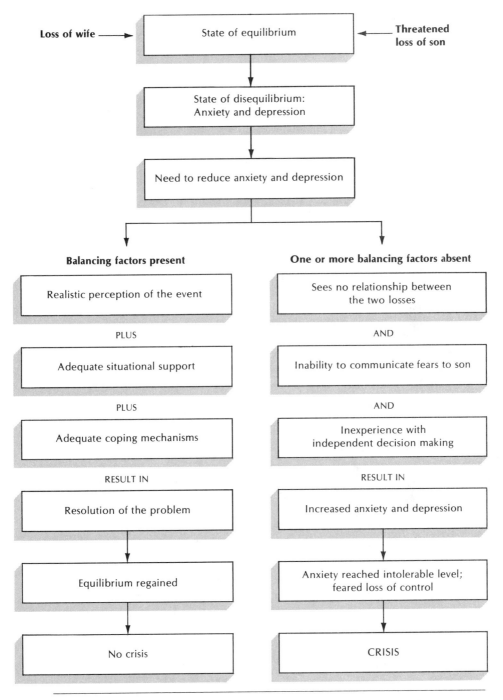

Figure 6-14

gained in new social contacts. Although he felt grief when his son and daughter-in-law left town, Mr P could recognize and relate his symptoms to the event and so was able to cope with them.

In discussion and review of his future plans, Mr. P was optimistic about his ability to live independently within the framework of his new environment. He was slowly entering new activities and making new friends, although he admitted "being a bit rusty about how to do it."

Before termination of therapy, Mr. P and the therapist reviewed the adjustments that he had made, as well as his new insights into his own feelings. He thought that the crisis situation, although being very painful to him at the time, had provided him with a "good idea of how to face up to things in the future." His future plans were also reviewed, and he was reassured by the therapist that he could always return for future help, should the occasion arise.

SUMMATION OF THE PARADIGM (Figure 6-14)

Mr. P had failed to recognize any relationship between his feelings of increased anxiety and the death of his wife. His inexperience with independent decision making made him inadequate to cope with the stressful event alone. Intervention with strong situational support by his son and daughter-in-law assisted him to begin to work through the grief process and averted a crisis.

The unexpected threat of his son and daughter-in-law's departure and his inability to communicate his fears resulted in their loss to him as situational supports. These factors were compounded by uncompleted grief work and a failure to see any connection between his recurrence of severe anxiety and his reaction to a second loss.

In the assessment phase, the therapist kept the focus on the areas of stress to determine the adequacy of his past coping skills with bereavement. Intervention was directed toward assisting him to explore and ventilate his feelings of dependency. Anticipatory planning was directed toward providing him with situational supports when his son moved from town.

Death and the Grief Process (Child)—Theoretical Concepts

Because death occurs regardless of age, the death of a child is one occurrence that brings unbearable pain to all concerned. If it is accidental or by a disease process, our questions of why are especially poignant. What has an innocent young child done to deserve such a short life span? The question of why haunts us with the death of a young adult, but with the death of a young child, we become angry and want to flail at a supreme being for the injustice of the loss of a child (Aguilera, 1993). We are unable to conceive the grief and pain of a parent who has lost a child, unless we too have lost a child to death. The death of a child sinks deep into our subconscious; we never forget. We compare the lost child with others we may have. It is not that we love them less or more. The lost child, whom we had for such a short time, becomes an enigma. What would he have been like:

I think he had my eyes. His personality was more like his father, I think. I'll never know if he would he have been happy...or smart...or athletic. He had such a happy laugh but he was always getting into things; he was definitely not passive. As he grew up, would he have been in trouble in school or drugs or in jail? No! Of course, not; he was my son. Why can't I grieve? Why do I think of him constantly? It has been 6 months. I have shut everyone out of my life, except my memories of him, especially the last memories before he was killed by that car. Why? He was only 2½ years old; he forgot and ran into the street to get his ball.

I can't blame the woman who hit him and killed him. It was not her fault; it was Jason's or was it mine? Of my four children, he was going to be the best...the most successful...the happiest. Why can't I grieve for him as I did when my mother died 3 years ago? Why is this so different? Why do I feel so dead inside? Men just don't understand. I carried Jason in my body for 9 months. No, I am wrong, Jim is hurting just as much as I am, he is just stronger. He just holds me at night and tells me to cry, but I can't, not anymore. Why can't I forget the pain; why doesn't it go away? Will I ever forget his laugh, the mischief in his eyes?

Grief wears many faces. There is not one book or one article that would tell you all about death and dying and grief and mourning. Unfortunately, there is also no one book or one article that can teach you how to deal with someone in the process of grief and mourning (Birenbaum and Robinson, 1991).

The Vulnerable Child Syndrome

The vulnerable child syndrome is quite common, but unless one is knowledgeable of how it is manifested, it is usually ignored.

When a child is in a serious accident or has a life-threatening illness but recovers completely (no residual effects), his parents then treat him "differently" than they treat his siblings. When discussing this child (the "vulnerable" one) the parents, nine times out of ten, state that "we almost lost him" or "he almost died." They then go into a graphic description of how "they almost lost him." The child can be in his 40s or 50s but he is always the "vulnerable child." His parents, siblings, and even some of his teachers treat him as if he is "special." He is excused from certain duties and responsibilities because "we are so lucky to have him."

The vulnerable child can respond to being treated differently and "special" in two ways. He may accept his special treatment and take advantage of being "different." He may become whining and passive and expect to be catered to by his parents and his peers. In essence, he begins to enjoy the attention he gets from being treated differently. He may begin to show signs of hypochondria. He reinforces the feelings and attitudes of his vulnerability with his parents and peers.

The second way a vulnerable child can respond to his parent's concept that he is special or different is with anger and honesty. He can confront them with the reality of the present situation. He can refuse to accept the role of the vulnerable child. He can refuse different or special treatment from his siblings and his peers. If a choice can be accepted by parents, then it is obvious that the second method is the most psychologically healthy. This is the choice that mental health specialists should work toward (Aguilera, 1993).

The Grief and Mourning Process

PHASE I: SHOCK AND DISBELIEF

With the sudden death of a child, the state of shock and disbelief is usually prolonged. Family members have very strong feelings of guilt and express feelings of "if only": I should have been there. It is my fault. Why didn't I. . . ? There may be feelings of blame and intense anger at the parent who was with the child, which only increases that person's feelings of guilt and negligence. The bereaved response is one of feeling that everything is in slow motion. They may use denial in their state of disbelief. Nothing around them seems to be real: some state that they are "only dreaming" and that this just can not be happening.

PHASE II: DEVELOPING AWARENESS

The bereaved becomes disorganized in thoughts and feelings. The increasing awareness of their loss brings intense pain and despair. Weeping can be prolonged, or they may retreat from others. They may isolate themselves in the child's room, touching his clothes and favorite toys. They may refuse to eat or to sleep. They may pace the floor, again asking the unanswerable question of why.

PHASE III: RESOLVING THE LOSS

With the death of a child, there may be no evidence of resolution of the loss. As stated earlier, the bereaved will never forget the child that they lost. They will always remember the important dates of his birth (e.g., "he would be 10 or 11 next week") or how old he was when he first walked. It may lead to a closer relationship between the parents as they work through their grief, or one parent may blame the other parent so strongly that the marriage is in serious jeopardy. A wedge of blame may precipitate a divorce.

Mental health specialists should work with the family to help them resolve their loss in a positive manner. They should contact Compassionate Friends, a support group of those who have also lost a child, to understand how they are feeling and help them cope with their loss in a positive manner.

The following case study concerns the sudden death of a 2½-year-old boy, Jason, and his family's response to the grief process.

Case Study   *Death and the grief process (child)*

ASSESSMENT OF THE INDIVIDUAL AND THE PROBLEM

Mr. Anders came to a crisis center on the advice of his pastor. He was married, and he and his wife, Peggy, had three children. Nine months ago, their 2½-year-old son, Jason, had run out into the street in front of their house to get his ball. Jason was hit by a car and killed instantaneously. Mr. Anders was working on his car in the driveway and watching Jason while his wife and the other two children had gone to the market. The therapist read his chart and then went to the reception room to meet him and take him to her office. She called his name, he stood up, and the therapist introduced herself and asked him to come to her office. Mr. Anders asked the therapist to call him Dean, and she agreed.

In her office she asked him to have a seat. Dean was 46 years old, approximately 6 feet tall, and obviously in great distress. The therapist told him that she had read what he had written in his chart and asked how she could help.

Dean ran his fingers through his hair, looked at the therapist, and said, "I don't know. I only hope you can." He took an envelope out of his pocket, handed it to her, and said, "Please read that and tell me what to do." The therapist read what he had handed her, divorce papers. She asked him when he had received the papers and he answered, "This morning in my office at work. I don't *want* a divorce, and I don't believe Peggy does either. She blames me for Jason's death." He continued, "Since Jason was killed she has completely shut me out of her life. He was the baby and I know she felt very close to him. We had talked with Jason time and time again about never going into the street for any reason. I do blame myself. I was working on my car, but I could hear him laughing and talking and he had never gone into the street before."

The therapist asked Dean how Peggy was "shutting him out." Dean answered, "In every way. She only talks to me if it is necessary. She won't let me touch her, or make love to her; She just goes stiff." The therapist asked how she was treating the other children. Dean replied, "Like she isn't really there. She cooks for them, washes their clothes, the usual things, but she doesn't talk to them either. All day she stays in Jason's room." The therapist asked how the children were responding to Jason's death and their mother's behavior. Dean said, "At first they cried a lot and talked about him, but they are hurt and confused by their mother's behavior." The therapist asked if she could call Peggy and get her to come to the crisis center. Dean said that she could and only hoped she could get her to come in.

PLANNING THERAPEUTIC INTERVENTION

The therapist would try to get Peggy to come to the center. She was apparently in pathological mourning. If she would not come to the center, she would contact Compassionate Friends and get their help.

INTERVENTION

The therapist contacted Mrs. Anders and told her that her husband, Dean, was very concerned about her. She asked if she would come to the crisis center and meet with the therapist. Mrs. Anders refused. She said that she did not want to come to the center. The therapist asked if Mrs. Anders would see someone who had also lost a child and knew how she must be feeling. Mrs. Anders hesitated and then said, "Have them call me and then I'll decide if I want to see anyone." The therapist told her that she would be contacted by someone from Compassionate Friends.

The therapist called Compassionate Friends and talked with them about Mr. and Mrs. Anders. She requested that if at all possible they should send a married couple in their 40s with other children to talk to Peggy Anders. She told them everything she knew about the family. They agreed to call her and get an appointment to go to their house to meet with Mr. and Mrs. Anders.

Over the next 3 weeks, Compassionate Friends met with Mr. and Mrs. Anders and made a great deal of progress. Dean came to his appointments and told the therapist everything that was happening. Peggy was listening to the couple, who

CASE STUDY: MR. AND MRS. ANDERS

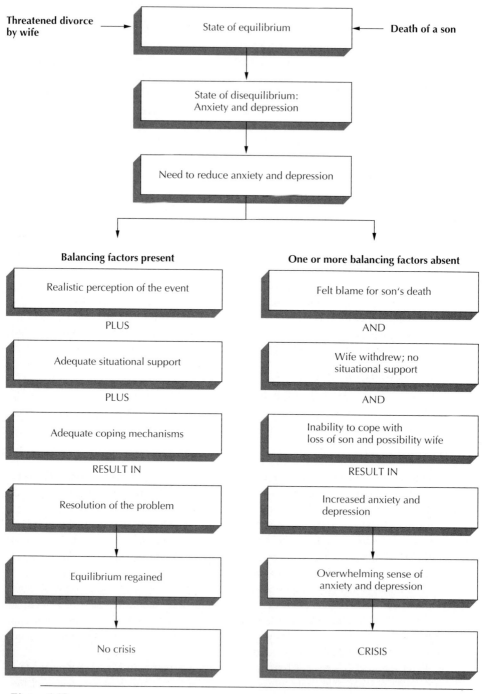

Figure 6-15

came over for coffee and to talk. By the fourth week, Peggy had agreed to come to the Compassionate Friends meeting and was much more like herself.

ANTICIPATORY PLANNING

The therapist discussed with Dean the importance of remaining in contact with Compassionate Friends and working with them as Peggy continued to improve.

Before termination of therapy, the therapist and Dean reviewed the progress both he and Peggy had made. He was reassured by the therapist he could always return to the center in the future if he felt the need.

SUMMATION OF THE PARADIGM (Figure 6-15)

Mr. Anders was unable to deal with his son's death and the threatened divorce by his wife.

He blamed himself for the death of this son. He had no situational support when his wife withdrew from him and threatened divorce. He had no coping skills to cope with two losses.

Mr. and Mrs. Anders were put in touch with Compassionate Friends to help them understand their response to the loss of their son.

REFERENCES

Aguilera DC: The vulnerable child syndrome, *Am J Orthopsychiatry* (in press).
Allport GW: *Pattern and growth in personality,* New York, 1961, Rinehart & Winston.
American Medical Association: *Panel to curb elderly abuse,* New York, 1992, American Medical Association.
Amir M: *Patterns in forcible rape,* Chicago, 1971, University of Chicago Press.
Appleton W: The battered woman syndrome, *Ann Emerg Med* 9:84, 1980.
Bandura A: *Aggression: a social learning analysis,* Englewood Cliffs, NJ, 1973, Prentice Hall.
Bernstein R: Are we still stereotyping the unmarried mother? *Soc Work Health Care* 5:22, 1960.
Birenbaum LK, Robinson MA: Family relationships in two types of terminal care, *Soc Sci Med* 32:95, 1991.
Bohn D: Domestic violence and pregnancy implications for practice, *J Nurse Midwifery* 35:86, 1990.
Bowlby J: Separation anxiety, *Int J Psychoanal* 41:89, 1960.
Broadhurst DD and others: Early childhood programs and the prevention and the treatment of child abuse and neglect, *The Users Manual Service,* Washington, DC, 1992, US Department of Health and Human Services.
Brown HF, Burditt VB, Lidell WW: The crisis of relocation. In Parad HJ, editor: *Crisis intervention,* New York, 1965, Family Service Association of America.
Burgess AW, Holmstrom LL: The rape victim in the emergency ward, *Am J Nurs* 73:1741, 1973.
Burgess AW, Holmstrom LL: Rape trauma syndrome, *Am J Psychiatry* 131:982, 1974.
Burns J: Elderly abuse, signs of trouble, *Los Angeles Times,* Dec 11, 1992.
Caplan G: *Principles of preventive psychiatry,* New York, 1964, Basic Books.
Caro FG: Relieving informal care giver burden through organized services. In Pillemer KA and Wolf RS, editors: *Elder abuse: conflict in the family,* Dover, Mass, 1986, Auburn House.

Carter BF, Brooks A: Suicide postvention: crisis or opportunity, *School Counselor* 37:378, 1990.

David H: Abortion in the psychological perspective, *Am J Orthopsychiatry* 42:61, 1972.

Decker JB, Stubblebine JM: Crisis intervention and prevention of psychiatric disability: a follow-up study, *Am J Psychiatry* 129:725, 1972.

Degler C: *At odds: women and the family in America from the revolution to the present,* New York, 1980, Oxford University Press.

Deibel M: Teen pregnancy cost U.S. $16 billion in 1985, *Rocky Mountain News,* Feb 19, 1986.

Demarest M: Cocaine: middle class high, *Time,* July 6, 1981.

Douglas RL, Hickey T: Domestic neglect and abuse of the elderly: research findings and a systems perspective for service delivery planning. In Kosberg J, editor: *Abuse and maltreatment of the elderly: causes and interventions,* Littleton, Mass, 1983, John Wright–PSG.

Drake VK: Battered women: a health case problem in disguise, *Image* 14:40, 1982.

Engel GL: Grief and grieving, *Am J Nurs* 64:93, 1964.

Faulkner LR: Mandating the reporting of suspected cases of elder abuse: an inappropriate, ineffective and ageist response to the abuse of older adults, *Fam Law Quart* 16:69, 1982.

Formica PE: AMA hopes to curb abuse of the elderly, *Washington Post,* Dec 3, 1992.

Freed K, Chewing the fat, with a side of gut, *Los Angeles Times,* Dec 26, 1992.

Friedrich WN, Boriskin JA: The role of the child in abuse: a review of the literature, *Am J Orthopsychiatry* 46:580, 1976.

Garwin F, Kepler H: Cocaine abuse treatment, *Arch Gen Psychiatry* 41:903, 1984.

Gelles RJ: *The violent home,* Beverly Hills, Calif, 1972, Sage.

Giarretto H: Humanistic treatment of father-daughter incest. In Helfer RE and Kempe CH, editors: *Child abuse and neglect: the family and the community,* Cambridge, Mass, 1976, Ballinger.

Gil DC: *Violence against children,* Cambridge, Mass, 1970, Harvard University Press.

Gil DC: Unravelling child abuse, *Am J Orthopsychiatry* 45:352, 1975.

Glass AT: Observations upon the epidemiology of mental illness in troops during warfare. *In Symposium on Preventive and Social Psychiatry Sponsored by Walter Reed Army Institute of Research, Walter Reed Medical Center, and National Research Council,* Washington, DC, April 15-17, 1957, US Government Printing Office.

Granberg D: The abortion activists, *Fam Plann Perspect* 13:138, 1981.

Granberg D, Granberg BW: Abortion attitudes, 1965-1980: trends and determinants, *Fam Plann Perspect* 12:250, 1980.

Greene BL: Sequential marriage: repetition or change. In Rosenbaum S and Alger I, editors: *The marriage relationship,* New York, 1968, Basic Books.

Griseg G: *Abortion, the myths, the realities, and the arguments,* New York, 1970, Corpus Books.

Halper M: *Helping maltreated children: school and community involvement,* St Louis, 1979, Mosby–Year Book.

Hankes L: Cocaine: today's drug, *J Fla Med Assoc* 71:235, 1984.

Helfer RD, Kempe CH, editors: *Child abuse and neglect: the family and the community,* Cambridge, Mass, 1976, Ballinger.

Heller S, Kornfeld D: Delerium and related problems. In Reiser M, editor: *America's handbook of psychiatry,* vol 4, New York, 1975, Basic Books.

Hellerstein H, Goldstone E: Rehabilitation of patients with heart disease, *Postgrad Med* 15:265, 1954.

Hollender MH: *The psychology of medical practice,* Philadelphia, 1958, WB Saunders Co.

Holmstrom LL, Burgess AW: Assessing trauma in the rape victim, *Am J Nurs* 75:1288, 1975.

Hooyman NR: Elder abuse and neglect: community intervention. In Kosberg J, editor: *Abuse and maltreatment of the elderly: causes and interventions,* Littleton, Mass, 1983, John Wright–PSG.

Hudson MF: Elder mistreatment: current research. In Pilemer KA and Wolf RS, editors: *Elder abuse: conflict in the family,* Dover, Mass, 1986, Auburn House.

Huser R: *The crime of abortion in canon law,* Washington, DC, 1942, Catholic University of America Press.

Jeri FR: Coca paste smoking in some Latin American countries: a severe and unabated form of addiction, *Bull Narc* 36:15, 1984.

Johnson T: Critical issues in the definition of elder mistreatment. In Pilemer KA and Wolf RS, editors: *Elder abuse: conflict in the family,* Dover, Mass, 1986, Auburn House.

Justice B, Justice R: *The abusing family,* New York, 1976, Human Sciences Press.

Justice B, Justice R: *The broken taboo,* New York, 1979, Human Sciences Press.

Kaplan DM, Mason EA: Maternal reactions to premature birth viewed as an acute emotional disorder. In Parad HJ, editor: *Crisis intervention,* New York, 1965, Family Service Association of America.

Kaye NS, Soreff SM: The psychiatrist's role, responses, and responsibilities when a patient commits suicide, *Am J Psychiatry* 148:6, 1991.

Kempe CH: The battered child syndrome, *JAMA* 181:17, 1962.

Kempe CH, Helfer R: *Helping the battered child and his family,* Philadelphia, 1972, JB Lippincott Co.

King SH: *Perceptions of illness and medical practice,* New York, 1962, Russell Sage Foundation.

Kosberg J: Preventing elder abuse: identification of high risk factors prior to placement discussions, *Gerontologist* 28:43, 1988.

Kubie LS. Cited by Kaufman JG, Becker MD: Rehabilitation of the patient with myocardial infarction, Geriatrics 10:355, 1955.

Kübler-Ross E: *On death and dying,* New York, 1969, Macmillan.

Kübler-Ross E: *Questions and answers on death and dying,* New York, 1974, Collier Books.

Lau EE, Kosberg JI: Abuse of the elderly by informal care providers, *Age Ageing,* Sept-Oct, 10, 1979.

Laurie P: *Drugs: medical, psychological and social facts,* ed 2, Middlesex, England, 1971, Pelican, C Nicholls & Co.

Lee PR, Bryner S: Introduction to a symposium on rehabilitation in cardiovascular disease, *Am J Cardiol* 7:315, 1961.

Lillard J and McFann CL: A marital crisis: for better or worse, *Hospice J* 6:96, 1990.

Lindemann E: Symptomatology and management of acute grief, *Am J Psychiatry* 101:141, 1944.

Linton R: *Culture and mental disorders,* Springfield, Ill, 1956, Charles C Thomas.

Lipowski J: A new look at organic brain syndrome, *Am J Psychiatry* 137:674, 1980.

Luker K: The war between the women, Fam Plann Perspect 16:105, 1984.

Mace NL, Rabins PV: *The 36-hour day,* Baltimore, 1981, Johns Hopkins University Press.

Maloney JJ: Control theory psychology and crisis intervention counseling, *J Reality Ther* 9:50-52, 1990.

Mason EA: Method of predicting crisis outcome for mothers of premature babies, *Public Health Rep* 78:1031, 1963.

McCormick MG, Shapiro F, Starfield B: High risk young mothers: infant mortality and morbidity in 4 year areas in the U.S., 1973-1978, *Am J Public Health,* 74:18, 1984.

McDaniel SH, Landau-Stanton J: Family of origin work and family therapy skills training, *Fam Process* 30:459, 1991.

McDonald JM: *Rape: offenders and their victims,* Springfield, Ill, 1971, Charles C Thomas.

McIver J: Psychiatric aspects of cardiovascular diseases in industry. In Warshaw LJ, editor: *The heart in industry,* New York, 1960, Harper & Row.

Mohr J: *Abortion in America: the origins and evolution of national policy,* New York, 1978, Oxford University Press.

Moore HE: *Tornadoes over Texas: a study of Waco and San Angelo in disaster,* Austin, 1958, University of Texas Press.

Morley WE, Messick JM, Aguilera DC: Crisis: paradigms of intervention, *J Psychiatr Nurs* 5:540, 1967.

Nakashima I: *Adolescent pregnancy.* In Kelly V, editor: *Practice of pediatrics,* Philadelphia, 1986, Harper & Row.

National Committee for Prevention of Child Abuse: (Interior Report), p. 4, Apr 1992.

National Institute on Drug Abuse: *National survey on drug abuse,* Rockville, Md, 1982, National Clearing House for Drug Abuse Information.

O'Brien J: *Elder abuse: barriers to identification and intervention.* Paper presented at the meeting of the Gerontological Society of America, Chicago, Ill, Nov 1986.

O'Reilly J: Battered wives, *Time,* p 23, Sept 5, 1983.

O'Rourke M: *Elder abuse: the state of the art,* Cambridge, Mass, 1981, National Conference on Abuse of Older Persons.

Parson F: *The social system,* New York, 1951, Free Press.

Q 4:221, 1991.

Pedrick-Cornell C, Gelles RJ: Elder abuse: the status of current knowledge, *Fam Relat* 31:457, 1982.

Pillemer K, Finkelhor D: The prevalence of elder abuse: a random sample survey, *Gerontologist* 28:51, 1988.

Rapoport L: The state of crisis: some theoretical considerations, *Soc Serv Rev* 36:211, 1962.

Rapoport R: Normal crises, family structure, and mental health, *Fam Process* 2:68, 1963.

Rehabilitation of patients with cardiovascular diseases, *WHO Tech Rep Ser* 1990.

Reisberg B: *A guide to Alzheimer's disease,* New York, 1981, Free Press.

Reiser MF: Emotional aspects of cardiac disease, *Am J Psychiatry* 107:781, 1951.

Rubenstein D: Rehospitalization versus family crisis intervention, *Am J Psychiatry* 129:715, 1972.

Rubenstein D: Family crisis intervention as an alternative to rehospitalization, *Curr Psychiatric Ther* 14:191, 1974.

Rubinelli J: Incest: it's time we faced reality, *J Psychiatr Nurs* 18:17, 1980.

Russell C: The identifying signs of possible mistreatment, *Los Angeles Times,* Dec 3, 1992.

Sager A: Mobilizing adequate home care resources: a mutual aid response to stress within the family. In Pillemer KA and Wolf RS, editors: *Elder abuse: conflict in the family,* Dover, Mass, 1986, Auburn House.

Salend E and others: Elder abuse reporting: limitations of statutes, *Gerontologist* 24:61, 1984.

Salholz E and others: Beware of child molesters, *Newsweek,* p 45, Aug 9, 1982.

Seltzer B, Frazier S: Organic mental disorders. In Nicholi A, editor: *The Harvard guide to modern psychiatry,* Cambridge, Mass, 1978, Harvard University Press.

Silver LB: Psychological aspects of the battered child and his parents, *J Child Hosp Clin Proc* 24:355, 1968.

Simonds JF, McMahon T, Armstrong D: Young suicide attempters compared with a control group: psychological, affective, and attitudinal variables, *Suicide Life Threat Behav* 21:124, 1991.

Smolowe J, Purvis A: What the doctors do: Domestic violence, *Time* Jun 29, 1992.

Straus M: *Behind closed doors: violence in the American family,* Garden City, NY, 1981, Anchor Books.

U.S. Congress, House Select Committee on Aging: *Elder abuse: the hidden problem,* Washington, DC, 1980, United States Government Printing Office.

U.S. Department of Health and Human Services: Bethesda, Md, 1992, The Department.

U.S. Department of Health and Human Services, National Center for Health Statistics: *Monthly vital statistics report,* 36, July 29, 1988, DHHS Publ No (PHS) 88-1120, Hyattsville, Md, 1988, Public Health Service.

U.S. Department of Health and Human Services, National Center for Health Statistics, 1990-1991, *Vital Statistics Report,* vol 40, no 13, September 30, 1992, Hyattsville, Md, Public Health Service.

U.S. Department of Health and Human Services: *Executive summary: national study of the incidence and severity of child abuse and neglect,* DHHS Publ No (OHDS) 81-30329, Washington, DC, 1991, U.S. Government Printing Office.

U.S. Department of Health and Human Services: *Study of national incidence and prevalence of child abuse and neglect,* DHHS Publ No (OHDS) 105-85-1702, Hyattsville, Md, 1992, U.S. Government Printing Office.

Vernick J: The use of the life span interview on a medical ward, *Soc Casework* 44:465, 1963.

Vogel EF, Bell NW: The emotionally disturbed child as a family scapegoat, *J Psychoanal* 47:21, 1960.

Walker-Hooper A: Domestic violence: assessing the problem. In Warner CG, editor: *Conflict intervention in social and domestic violence,* Bowie, Md, 1981, Brady.

Washton AM, Gold MS, editors: *Cocaine: a clinician's handbook,* New York, 1987, Guilford.

Weiss RD, Mirin SM: *Cocaine,* 1987, American Psychiatric Press.

Woods JH, Downs DA: The psychopharmacology of cocaine. In *Drug use in America: problem in perspective,* vol 1, Washington, DC, 1973, National Commission on Marijuana and Drug Abuse.

Yin P: *Victimization and the aged,* Springfield, Ill, 1985, Charles C Thomas.

Yu-Chin R, Arcuni OJ: Short term hospitalization for suicidal patients within a crisis intervention service, *Gen Hosp Psychiatry* 12:153, 1990.

Zakus G, Wilday S: Adolescent abortion option, *Soc Work Health Care* 12:77, 1987.

Zinberg NE, Roberston JA: *Drugs and the public,* New York, 1972, Simon & Schuster.

ADDITIONAL READINGS

Adams JF, Piercy FP, Jurich JA: Effects of solution focused therapy's "formula first session task" on compliance and outcome in family *therapy, J Marital Family Ther* 17:277-290, 1991.

Bright LK: Videodisc development for human service professions: potentials and risks for production by university faculty, *Comput Human Serv* 7:247,1990.

Brown VB: The problem of substance abuse, *New Directions Student Serv* 49:35-44, 1990.

Carter BF, Brooks A: Suicide postvention: crisis or opportunity? *School Counselor* 37:378-390, 1990.

Charles G, Matheson J: Suicide prevention and intervention with young people in foster care in Canada, *Child Welfare* 70, 1991.

Corporate Alternatives, Inc: *Values survey and focus groups,* Springfield, IL, 1991, Department of Children and Family Services.

Cox JW, Stoltenberg CD: Evaluation of a treatment program for battered wives, *J Family Violence* 6:395-413, 1991.

Daro D, McCurdy K: *Current trends in child abuse reporting and fatalities: the results of the 1990 annual fifty state survey,* Chicago, 1991, NCPCA.

Dawson NJ: Need satisfaction in terminal care settings, *Soc Sci Med* 32:83-87, 1991.

Douglas H: Assessing violent couples, *Families Society* 72:525-535, 1991.

Duffy M, Iscoe I: Crisis theory and management: the case of the older person, *J Ment Health Counsel* 12:303-313, 1990.

Flowers JV, Booraem CO: Focusing on emotion in group therapy: what clients, what problems, and what for, *Psychol Rep* 69:369-370, 1991.

Gilligan C: Women's psychological development: implications for psychotherapy. *Women Ther* 11:5-31, 1991.

Haskett ME and others: Factors associated with successful entry into therapy in child sexual abuse cases, *Child Abuse Negl* 15:467-476, 1991.

Jones E, Ackatz L: *Availability of substance abuse treatment programs for pregnant women: results from three national surveys,* Chicago, 1992, NCPCA.

Jones E and others: *Substance abuse treatment programs for pregnant and parenting women: a program guide,* Chicago, 1992, NCPCA.

Kaplan S: *Child fatality legislation: sample legislation and commentary,* Chicago, 1991, American Bar Association.

Leenaars AA: Suicide notes and their implications for intervention, *Crisis* 12:1-20, 1991.

Maloney JJ: Control theory psychology and crisis intervention counseling, *J Real Ther* 9:50-52, 1990.

Maltsberger JT: Consultation in a suicidal impasse, *Int J Psychoanal Psychother* 10:131, 1984-85.

Marchetti J: Role change, stress . . . and you! Moving up from clinical nurse to management, *Nurs Success Today* 2:30, 1985.

Martin CA, Warfield MC, Braen GR: Psychotherapy of rape, *Curr Psychiatr Ther* 23:65, 1986.

Martin PY, DiNitto DM: The rape exam: beyond the hospital emergency room, *Women Health* 12:5, 1987.

Marwick C: Presidential commission recommends campaign against drug abuse to help combat AIDS, *JAMA* 259:2195, 1988.

Mason JK: The right to die, *Singapore Med J* 28:379, 1987.

Matlaw JR, Mayer JB: Elder abuse: ethical and practical dilemmas for social work, *Health Soc Work* 11:85, 1986.

McCarthy BW: A cognitive-behavioral approach to understanding and treating sexual trauma, *J Sex Marital Ther* 12:322, 1986.

McCracken LM: Cognitive behavioral treatment of rheumatoid arthritis: a preliminary review of efficacy and methodology, *Ann Behav Med* 13:57-65, 1991,

Meyer CB, Taylor SE: Adjustment to rape, *J Pers Soc Psychol* 50:1226, 1986.

Mezey G, King M: Male victims of sexual assault, *Med Sci Law* 27:122, 1987.

Mezey GC: Rape—victiminological and psychiatric aspects, *Br J Hosp Med* 33:152, 1985.

Miller DB, Gulle N, McCue F: The realities of respite for families, clients, and sponsors, *Gerontologist* 26:467, 1986.

Miller HL and others: An analysis of the effects of suicide prevention facilities on suicide rates in the United States, *Am J Public Health* 74:340, 1984.

Miller J, Hirst S: Aged maltreatment: a definition dilemma, *AARN News Lett* 43:1, 1987.

Miller TW, Veltkamp LJ: Disputed child custody: strategies and issues in mediation, *Bull Am Acad Psychiatry Law* 15:45, 1987.

Milner JS, Gold RG: Screening spouse abusers for child abuse potential, *J Clin Psychol* 42:169, 1986.

Mittleman RE, Mittleman HS, Wetli CV: What child abuse really looks like, *Am J Nurs* 87:1185A, 1987.

Moore J: Rape: the double victim, *Nurs Times* 81:24, 1985.

Morris RG, Baddeley AD: Primary and working memory functioning in Alzheimer-type dementia, *J Clin Exp Neuropsychol* 10:279, 1988.

Mullen PE and others: Impact of sexual and physical abuse on women's mental health, *Lancet* 1:841, 1988.

Muram D: Rape, incest, trauma: the molested child, *Clin Obstet Gynecol* 30:754, 1987.

Nash KL: It's still a baby! *Midwives Chron* 100:123, 1987.

Nelson FL: Evaluation of a youth suicide prevention school program, *Adolescence* 22:813, 1987.

Newald J: Plans under way for Alzheimer's Center in Illinois, *Hospitals* 60:92, 1986.

Newberger CM, Melnicoe LH, Newberger EH: The American family in crisis: implications for children, *Curr Probl Pediatr* 16:669, 1986.

Newcomb MD, Bentler PM: Impact of adolescent drug use and social support on problems of young adults: a longitudinal study, *J Abnorm Psychol* 97:64, 1988.

Ney PG, Herron JL: Childhood crises—who to tell? *N Z Med J* 98:283, 1985.

Ney PG, Johnston ID, Herron JL: Social and legal ramifications of a child crisis line, *Child Abuse Negl* 9:47, 1985.

O'Brien JG: Elder abuse and the physician, *Mich Med* 85:618, 1986.

O'Connor A: Female sex offenders, *Br J Psychiatry* 150:615, 1987.

O'Malley TA and others: Categories of family-mediated abuse and neglect of elderly persons, *J Am Geriatr Soc* 32:362, 1984.

Oppenheimer K: The impact of daily stressors on women's adjustment to marital separation, *J Fam Pract* 24:507, 1987.

Orbach I: The "insolvable problem" as a determinant in the dynamics of suicidal behavior in children, *Am J Psychother* 40:511, 1986.

Parker G: Professional and non-professional intervention for highly anxious primiparous mothers, *Br J Psychiatry* 146:287, 1985.

Pary R, Lippmann S, Tobias CR: A preventative approach to the suicidal patient, *J Fam Pract* 26:185, 1988.

Patwell TC: Familial abuse of the elderly: a look at caregiver potential and prevention, *Home Healthcare Nurse* 4:10, 1986.

Payne JS, Downs S, Newman K: Helping the abused women, *Nursing* 16:52, 1986.

Peck DL: Social-psychological correlates of adolescent and youthful suicide, *Adolescence* 22:863, 1987.

Peck ML, Berkovitz IH: Youth suicide: the role of school consultation, *Adolesc Psychiatry* 14:511, 1987.

Phillips LR: Abuse and neglect of the frail elderly at home: an exploration of theoretical relationships, *J Adv Nurs* 8:379, 1983.

Phillips LR, Rempusheski VF: Caring for the frail elderly at home: toward a theoretical explanation of the dynamics of poor quality family caregiving, *ANS* 8:62, 1986.

Pianta RC, Egeland B, Hyatt A: Maternal relationship history as an indicator of developmental risk, *Am J Orthopsychiatry* 56:385, 1986.

Piesse B: Nurse and the law: the importance of confidentiality, *Aust Nurses J* 16:48, 1987.

Pillemer K, Finkelhor D: The prevalence of elder abuse: a random sample survey, *Gerontologist* 28:51, 1988.

Pluckhan ML: Alzheimer's disease—helping the patient's family, *Nursing* 16:63, 1986.

Polk GC and Brown BE: Family violence: development of a master's level specialty track in family abuse, *J Psychosoc Nurs Ment Health Serv* 26:34, 1988.

Pollick MF: Abuse of the elderly: a review, *Holist Nurs Pract* 1:43, 1987.

Powills S: Elder abuse: what role do hospitals play? *Hospitals* 62:84, 1986.

Rabins PV: Establishing Alzheimer's disease units in nursing homes: pros and cons, *Hosp Community Psychiatry* 37:120, 1986.

Rabins PV: Science and medicine in the spotlight: Alzheimer's disease as an example, *Perspect Biol Med* 31:161, 1988.

Rangell L: The decision to terminate one's life: psychoanalytic thoughts on suicide, *Suicide Life Threat Behav* 18:28, 1988.

Ranieri WF and others: Relationships of depression, hopelessness, and dysfunctional attitudes to suicide ideation in psychiatric patients, *Psychol Rep* 61:967, 1987.

Raskind SM: Suicide by burning: emotional needs of the suicidal adolescent on the burn unit, *Issues Compr Pediatr Nurs* 9:369, 1986.

Reeder TM, Hohmann M: Alzheimer's disease: using direct drug infusion to the central nervous system, *AORN J* 44:222, 1986.

Rhodes AM: Identifying and reporting child abuse, *MCN* 12:399, 1987.

Rhodes AM: The nurse's legal obligations for reporting child abuse, *MCN* 12:313, 1987.

Richter JM: Support: resource during crisis of mate loss, *J Gerontol Nurs* 13:18, 1987.

Roberts BL, Algase DL: Victims of Alzheimer's disease and the environment, *Nurs Clin North Am* 23:83, 1988.

Rose DS: "Worse than death": psychodynamics of rape victims and the need for psychotherapy, *Am J Psychiatry* 143:817, 1986.

Rose K and Saunders DG: Nurses' and physicians' attitudes about women abuse: the effects of gender and professional role, *Health Care Women Int* 7:427, 1986.

Rosswurm MA: Relocation and the elderly, *J Gerontol Nurs* 9:632, 1983.

Rothberg JM and others: Suicide in United States Army personnel, 1983-1984, *Milit Med* 153:61, 1988.

Rowden R: Do we call this care? *Nurs Times* 83:22, 1987.

Rowles H: Alzheimer's disease: "We don't know the half!" *Geriatr Nur (London)* 6:24, 1986.

Ryback RF, Bassuk EL: Homeless battered women and their shelter network, *New Dir Ment Health Serv* 3:55-61, 1986.

Rynearson EK: Psychotherapy of pathologic grief: revisions and limitations, *Psychiatr Clin North Am* 10:487, 1987.

Sadoff RL: Sexual violence, *Bull NY Acad Med* 62:466, 1986.

Saltzman LE, Levenson A, Smith JC: Suicides among persons 15-24 years of age, 1970-1984, *MMWR CDC Surveill Summ* 37:61, 1988.

Saunders E, Awad GA, White G: Male adolescent sexual offenders: the offender and the offense, *Can J Psychiatry* 31:542, 1986.

Sayger TV, Szykula SA, Laylander JA: Adolescent-focused family counseling: a comparison of behavioral and strategic approaches, *J Fam Psychotherapy* 2:57-80, 1991.

Schuerger JM, Reigle N: Personality and biographic data that characterize men who abuse their wives, *J Clin Psychol* 44:75, 1988.

Schwartz RS: The double life of a psychiatrist: role changes between hospital and office, *Psychiatry* 50:83, 1987.

Schwartzberg AZ: The adolescent in the remarriage family, *Adolesc Psychiatry* 14:259, 1987.

Scott JP and others: The role of coping behaviors for primary caregivers of Alzheimer's patients, *Tex Med* 83:48, 1987.

Scott RL, Tetreault LA: Attitudes of rapists and other violent offenders toward women, *J Soc Psychol* 127:375, 1987.

Segal S, Fletcher M, Meekison WG: Survey of bereaved parents, *Can Med Assoc J* 134:38, 1986.

Seligman PJ and others: Sexual assault of women at work, *Am J Ind Med* 12:445, 1987.

Selkirk D: Family violence: opportunity for change, *Axone* 9:3, 1987.

Seltzer B and others: The short-term effects of in-hospital respite on the patient with Alzheimer's disease, *Gerontologist* 28:121, 1988.

Shearer SL, Herbert CA: Long-term effects of unresolved sexual trauma, *Am Fam Physician* 36:169, 1987.

Sheehan M, Oppenheimer E, Taylor C: Why drug users sought help from one London drug clinic, *Br J Addict* 81:765, 1986.

Shelowitz PA: Drug use, misuse, and abuse among the elderly, *Med Law* 6:235, 1987.

Sherman KO: The battered woman, *Dimens Crit Care Nurs* 2:30, 1983.

Shore JH, Tatum EL, Vollmer WM: Psychiatric reactions to disaster: the Mount St Helens experience, *Am J Psychiatry* 143:590, 1986.

Shrover JL, Hutton JT, Anderson GM: The Alzheimer patient: interior design considerations, *Tex Med* 83:54, 1987.

Shutty MS, Sheras P: Brief strategic psychotherapy with chronic pain patients: Reframing and problem resolution, *Psychotherapy* 28:636, 1991.

Silver HM: Alzheimer's disease: ethical and legal decisions, *Med Law* 6:537, 1987.

Smith JC, Mercy JA, Conn JM: Marital status and the risk of suicide, *Am J Public Health* 78:78, 1988.

Snyder CA and others: "Crack smoke" is a respirable aerosol of cocaine base, *Pharmacol Biochem Behav* 29:93, 1988.

Sorenson SB and others: The prevalence of adult sexual assault: the Los Angeles Epidemiologic Catchment Area Project, *Am J Epidemiol* 126:1154, 1987.

Soule DJ, Bennett JM: Elder abuse in South Dakota, Part 1: the who, how and why of abuse, *S D J Med* 40:7, 1987.

Soule DJ, Bennett JM: Elder abuse in South Dakota, Part 2: what can we do about it?, *S D J Med* 40:5, 1987.

Speight N: Case conferences for child abuse, *Arch Dis Child* 62:1063, 1987.

Squyres BN: Alzheimer's disease and exercise, *Tex Med* 83:51, 1987.

Stearn M: Social and psychological aspects of pregnancy, *Nursing (Lond)* 3:17, 1986.

Stewart BD and others: The aftermath of rape: profiles of immediate and delayed treatment seekers, *J Nerv Ment Dis* 175:90, 1987.

Stewart-Dedmon M: Strain and strategy, *Nurs Times* 84:38, 1988.

Stark E, Flitcraft AH: Women and children at risk: a feminist perspective on child abuse, *Int J Health Serv* 18:97, 1988.

Stonddard FJ, Cahners SS: Suicide attempted by self-immolation during adolescence. II. Psychiatric treatment and outcome, *Adolesc Psychiatry* 12:266, 1985.

Straus MA: Domestic violence and homicide antecedents, *Bull N Y Acad Med* 62:446, 1986.

Subramanian K: Reducing child abuse through respite center intervention, *Child Welfare* 64:501, 1985.

Swartz J: Abuse of elderly subject of Toronto conference, *Can Med Assoc J* 138:261, 1988.

Tavani-Petrone C: Psychiatric emergencies, *Prim Care* 13:157, 1986.

Tejedor MC and others: Suicidal behavior in schizophrenia, *Crisis* 8:151, 1987.

Tekavcic-Grad O, Zavasnik A: Comparison between counselor's and caller's expectations and their realization on the telephone crisis line, *Crisis* 8:162, 1987.

Thobaben M: Another view of Alzheimer's disease, *Home Healthcare Nurse* 5:52, 1987.

Thobaben M: Abuse: the shameful secret of elder care, *RN* 51:85, 1988.

Thornton JE, Davies HD, Tinklenberg JR: Alzheimer's disease syndrome, *J Psychosoc Nurs Ment Health Serv* 24:16, 1986.

Tibbits-Kleber AL, Howell RJ, Kleber DJ: Joint custody: a comprehensive review, *Bull Am Acad Psychiatry Law* 15:27, 1987.

Tilden VP, Shepherd P: Battered women: the shadow side of families, *Holist Nurs Pract* 1:25, 1987.

Tolle SW and others: Communication between physicians and surviving spouses following patient deaths, *J Gen Intern Med* 1:309, 1986.

Trad PV, Pfeffer CR: Treatment of an abused preadolescent and the role of parental self-reporting, *Am J Psychother* 42:124, 1988.

Trillins JS, Greenblatt L, Shephard C: Elder abuse and utilization of support services for elderly patients (clinical conference), *J Fam Pract* 24:581, 1987.

Tyson JR: Suffer the little children, *AARN News Lett* 44:24, 1988.

Urakami K, Adachi Y, Takahashi K: A community-based study of parental age in Alzheimer-type dementia in western Japan, *Arch Neurol* 45:375, 1988 (letter).

Valente S: The suicidal teenager, *Nursing* 15:47, 1985.

Vanderschaeghe L: Child abuse and community mental health practice, *Can J Psychiatr Nurs* 27:13, 1986.

Van Dongen CJ: The legacy of suicide, *J Psychosoc Nurs Ment Health Serv* 26:8, 1988.

Veltkamp LJ, Miller TW: Family mediation: clinical strategies in mediating child custody, *Fam Med* 18:301, 1986.

Ventrua WP: Cocaine use: your choice now—no choice later, *Imprint* 35:28, 1988.

Vogel R, Wolfersdorf M: Staff response to the suicide of psychiatric inpatients, *Crisis* 8:178, 1987.

Vousden V: Child abuse: behind closed doors, *Nurs Times* 83:24, 1987.

Wallerstein JS: Children of divorce: report of a ten-year follow-up of early latency-age children, *Am J Orthopsychiatry* 57:199, 1987.

Waugaman WR: Surgery and the patient with Alzheimer's disease, *Geriatr Nurs (New York)* 9:227, 1988.

White FZ, Myers JL: Teen suicide, *IMJ* 74:174, 1988.

Wilber CG: Some thoughts on suicide. Is it logical? *Am J Forensic Med Pathol* 8:302, 1987.

Wilkinson S: Hidden loss, *Nurs Times* 83:30, 1987.

Willette RE: Drug testing programs, *Natl Inst Drug Abuse Res Monogr Ser* 73:5, 1986.

Williams L: Alzheimer's: the need for caring, *J Gerontol Nurs* 12:20, 1986.

Winogrond IR and others: The relationship of caregiver burden and morale to Alzheimer's disease patient function in a therapeutic setting, *Gerontologist* 27:336, 1987.

Wolf RS: Elder abuse: ten years later, *J Am Geriatr Soc* 36:758, 1988.

Wolfe DA and others: Child witnesses to violence between parents: critical issues in behavioral and social adjustment, *J Abnorm Child Psychol* 14:95, 1986.

Wolfe DS: Child abuse prevention and intervention, *Pediatr Ann* 13:766, 1984.

Wolfersdorf M and others: Delusional depression and suicide, *Acta Psychiatr Scand* 76:359, 1987.

Wolf-Klein GP, Silverstone FA: A hot-line emergency service for the ambulatory frail elderly, *Gerontologist* 27:437, 1987.

Woolsey SF: A medical school course in coping with death: an opportunity to consider some basic health care issues, *J Behav Pediatr* 6:91, 1985.

Yarmey AD: Verbal, visual, and voice identification of a rape suspect under different levels of illumination, *J Appl Psychol* 71:363, 1986.

Young I: I just didn't want him, *Nurs Times* 84:32, 1988.

Young SH, Muir-Nash J, Ninos M: Managing nocturnal wandering behavior, *J Gerontol Nurs* 14:6, 1988.

Zarmansky A: Cruelty in an old people's home, *Lancet* 1:62, 1988 (letter).

Chapter 7

Maturational Crises

A person's life-style is continually subject to change by the ongoing processes of maturational development, shifting situations within the environment, or a combination of both. Potential crisis areas occur during the periods of great social, physical, and psychological change experienced by all human beings in the normal growth process. These changes could occur during concomitant biological and social role transitions such as birth, puberty, young adulthood, marriage, illness or death of a family member, the climacteric, and old age. Maturational crises have been described as normal processes of growth and development. They usually evolve over an extended period of time, such as the transition into adolescence, and they frequently require that the individual make many characterological changes. There may be an awareness of increased feelings of disequilibrium, but intellectual understanding of any correlation with normal developmental change may be inadequate.

The hazardous situations that occur in daily life may serve to compound normal maturational crises. When a person requests help at these times, it is necessary to determine what part of the presenting symptomatology is the result of transitional maturational stages and what, in turn, is the result of a stressful event in his current social orbit.

The theoretical concepts used in this chapter are derived primarily from Erikson's (1950, 1959, 1963, 1992) psychosocial maturational tasks (trust, autonomy, initiation, industry, identity, intimacy, generativity, and integrity); Piaget's (1963, 1989) ontogenetic development of intellectual abilities (sensorimotor, birth to 2 years; preoperational thought, 2 to 7 years; concrete operations, 7 to 11 years; and formal operations, 11 to 14 years); and Cameron's (1963) personality development, which is based on a synthesis of theories of general psychology and dynamic psychopathology.

For the sake of clarity, the maturational crises discussed here are presented in the more generally familiar phases: infancy and early childhood, preschool, prepuberty, adolescence, young adulthood, adulthood, late adulthood, and old age.

The case studies and paradigms presented here illustrate some common maturational crises. It must be emphasized that seldom are hazardous events and maturational crises this clearly defined.

Infancy and Early Childhood—Theoretical Concepts

The *epigenetic principle* is Erikson's term (1963, 1992) for the process that guides development through the life cycle (Stantrock, 1989). The epigenetic principle states that anything that grows has a blueprint, each having a special time of ascendancy, until all of the parts have arisen to form a functioning whole. Erikson developed a theory that emphasizes eight psychosocial stages of development: trust versus mistrust, autonomy versus shame and doubt, initiative versus guilt, industry versus inferiority, identity versus identity confusion, intimacy versus isolation, generativity versus stagnation, and integrity versus despair. Strengths of the psychoanalytic theories are an emphasis on the past, the developmental course of personality, mental representation of the environment, unconscious mind, and emphasis on conflict. Weaknesses are the difficulty in testing main concepts, lack of an empirical data base and overreliance on past reports, too much emphasis on sexuality and the unconscious mind, and a negative view of human nature.

The first year of life is one of almost total helplessness and dependency. The infant must learn to trust the maternal figure and become able to allow her out of his sight without fear or rage. He must also be able to develop confidence in the sameness and continuity of his environment and to internalize it through his developing tactile, auditory, olfactory, and visual senses. Deprivation in any one or a combination of these senses could lead to maladaptive response patterns affecting his biopsychosocial development.

During this stage, the symbiotic relationship that develops between the infant and the maternal figure forms a foundation for the behavioral patterns of later personality development. This relationship goes beyond the symbiosis of mutual dependency for biological survival; in the psychosocial development of the infant, it implies that the mother is willing and ready to assume responsibility for the infant, who in turn accepts her care passively without reciprocating. During infancy, the mouth is the primary organ of gratification and exploration; feeding becomes an important aspect of meeting needs. This is controlled by someone else, usually the mother, and her consistency in meeting her infant's needs for oral gratification is the beginning of his development of trust in his environment.

As a result of the varied experiences that he and his mother share, the infant develops confidence that his needs will be met. Through her own dependability, the mother structures these situations so that there is a basis for a mutual sense of confidence. For example, if the infant is fed regularly at times when he has come to expect a feeding, his sense of trust is encouraged. Should the feedings become sporadic, however, he will become uncertain and anxious about his environment, and a sense of mistrust will begin to appear. His resulting fretful, anxious behavior may inspire further inadequate mothering. Another essential component of the healthy symbiotic relationship is the comfort brought by the mother; if discomfort is inflicted, any continued trust can be destroyed.

Environmental consistency and stimulation are important for cognitive and effective growth. The infant usually becomes aware of his mother as a person by 9 months of age; however, absence of *mothering* can provoke symptoms of insecurity at 4 weeks, such as crying and rocking, withdrawal, depression, and even death.

Piaget's (1963, 1989) theory and concrete operational thought are described as made up of *operations*, mental actions that allow the child to do *mentally* what was done before *physically*. Concrete operations are also mental actions that are reversible. The concrete operational child shows *conservation* and *classification skills*. The concrete operational child needs clearly available perceptual supports to reason; later in development, thought becomes more abstract.

Piaget's ideas have been applied extensively to children's education. Emphasis is on *communication* and the belief that the child has many ideas about the world, that the child is *always* learning and unlearning, and that the child is by nature a knowing creature. Piaget was a genius at observing children, and he developed fascinating insights about children's cognition; he showed us some important things to look for in development and mapped out some general cognitive changes in development. Criticisms of Piaget's ideas focus on the belief that the stages are not as unitary as he thought, that small changes in procedures affect the child's cognition, that children can sometimes be trained to think at higher stages, and that some cognitive skills appear earlier than Piaget thought, while others are more protracted than he thought. Children's long-term memory improves during middle and late childhood. Control processes and strategies such as *rehearsal, organization,* and *imagery* are among the important influences that are responsible for improved long-term memory. Children's knowledge also influences their memory.

This is the segment of acquired knowledge that involves cognitive matters, especially the way the human mind works. Many developmentalists believe that metacognitive knowledge is beneficial in school learning.

This is the process of taking stock of what one is currently doing, what will be done next, and how effectively the mental activity is unfolding. The source of much cognitive monitoring in children is other people. Instructional programs in reading comprehension, writing, and math have been designed to foster children's cognitive monitoring of these activities. Reciprocal teaching is an instructional procedure used to develop children's cognitive monitoring.

A schema is a cognitive structure, a network of associations that organizes and guides an individual's perceptions. Schemas influence the way children process information. A script is schema for an event. Among the positive effects of computers on children's development are those involving a computer as a personal tutor (computer-assisted instruction), and as a multipurpose tool, as well as the motivational and social aspects of computers. Among the potential negative effects of computers are those involving regimentation and dehumanization of the classroom, unwarranted "shaping" of the curriculum, and the generalization and limitations of computer-based teaching.

Piaget (1963, 1989) describes the infant's development of intelligent behavior in this stage as *sensorimotor*. During the first year, the reflex patterns he was born with are repeated and strengthened with practice. As a newborn, the infant is capable of grasping, sucking, auditory and visual pursuit, and other stereotyped behavior patterns. These can be activated by nonspecific stimuli in the environment; after being activated a number of times, the response becomes spontaneous without further external stimulation. For example, at birth the infant is able to suck at the breast; continued practice improves his coordination and facility until this ability becomes well adapted to the goal of taking nourishment.

These primary reflex actions become coordinated into new actions. For example, the hand accidentally comes in contact with the mouth and initiates sucking movements that may lead to more coordinated actions and to thumbsucking as an established form of behavior. Later actions become oriented toward objects in the environment that stimulate seeing and hearing, and intentional behavior emerges as the infant seeks to repeat these actions. He learns to begin meaningful actions in sequence and to explore new objects within reach, thus developing goal-oriented activity. In this way, physical activity patterns develop into mental activity patterns of response.

By the end of the first year, the stage of purposeful behavior is reached, and exploration of further boundaries of the environment is begun. Motor actions have gradually become internalized as thought patterns. During this period, the trend is toward a higher level of sensory experiences and related mental activities. By the end of the second year, there is a functional understanding of play, imitation, causality, objects, space, and time. By the age of 2 years, a child can truly imitate such behavior as eating, sleeping, washing himself, and walking.

If the child does not develop the beginnings of trust, in later life there may be a sense of chronic mistrust, dependency, depressive trends, withdrawal, and shallow interpersonal relationships.

During the second year, the child begins a struggle for autonomy. He shifts from dependency on others toward independent actions of his own. As his musculature matures, it is necessary for him to develop coordination skills such as holding on and letting go. Because these are highly opposing patterns, conflict may occur; one example is the conflict arising over bowel and bladder control. A power struggle may develop between the child and his parents because elimination is completely under his control, and approval or disapproval becomes a strong influence because of his parents' attitudes toward eliminative habits. The child is expected to abandon his needs for self-gratification and substitute ones that meet the demands of his parents, representing the later demands of society. Cognitive development in this stage includes the first symbolic substitutions, words and gross speech. The child begins to manipulate objects and will look for hidden items. He recognizes differences between *I, me,* and *mine,* and *you* and *yours.* He also begins to manipulate others by words such as *no,* and the origins of concrete literal thinking are developed; this is the period of *preoperational thought* that continues to the age of 7 years (Piaget, 1963, 1989). One of its characteristics is egocentrism, in which the child is unable to take the viewpoint of another person; at the end of this period, egocentrism is replaced by social interaction. The child has now formed concepts in primitive images, thing to thing. He cannot cope intellectually with problems concerning time, causality, space, or other abstract concepts, although he understands what each is by itself in concrete situations. His perceptions dominate his judgments, and he operates on what can be seen directly.

The psychosocial task during this stage is to develop self-esteem through limited self-control. The achievement of bowel and bladder control within the prescribed cultural expectations allows also for self-control without loss of self-esteem. This is an important time for establishing a ratio between love and hate, cooperation and willfulness, and freedom of self-expression and its suppression. Failure during this stage is manifested in childhood by feelings of shame and doubt, fear of exposure, and ritualized activity; in later adulthood, the failure to achieve autonomy is seen in the individual who is a compulsive character with an irrational need for conformity and a concomitant irrational need for approval.

Preschool—Theoretical Concepts

Erikson (1950, 1959, 1963, 1992) believes that in the preschool stage the child has the task of developing *initiative*. He will discover what kind of person he is going to be, he learns to move around freely and has an unlimited radius of goals, his language skills broaden, and he asks many questions. His skill in using words is not matched by his skill in understanding them, and he is thus faced with the dangers of misinterpretation and misunderstanding. Language and locomotion allow him to expand his imagination over such a broad spectrum that he can easily frighten himself with dreams and thoughts.

The prerequisites for masculine and feminine initiative are developed. Infantile sexual curiosity and preoccupation with sexual matters arise. Oedipal wishes can occur as a result of increased imagination, and terrifying fantasies and a sense of guilt over these fantasies may develop.

Initiative becomes governed by a firmly established conscience. The child feels shame not only when he is found out but also when he fears being found out; guilt is felt for thoughts as well as deeds, and in this stage anxiety is controlled by play, by fantasy, and by pride in the attainment of new skills.

The child is ready to learn quickly and to share and to work with others toward a given goal; he begins to identify with people other than his parents and to develop a feeling of equality of worth with others despite differences in functions and age.

At 4½ to 5 years, the shift from infantile to juvenile body build is rapid, and the beginning of hand-eye coordination, as well as an intellectual growth spurt, occurs. The social base of gender role is firmly laid down by the end of the fifth year. If this stage is successfully accomplished, the child develops the fantasy of "I who can become"; if the child is excessively guilt-ridden, his fantasy is "I who shouldn't dream of it." The desired self-concept at the end of this stage is "I have the worth to try even if I am small."

Failure or trauma at this time leads to confusion of psychosexual role, rigidity and guilt in interpersonal relations, and loss of initiative in the exploration of new skills.

Prepuberty—Theoretical Concepts

Prepuberty years are characterized as the learning stage; that is, "I am what I learn" (Erikson, 1959, 1992). The child wants to be shown how to do things both alone and with others; he develops a sense of industry in which he becomes dissatisfied if he does not have a feeling of being useful or a sense of his ability to make things and make them well, even perfectly. He now learns to win recognition by *producing things*. He feels pleasure when his attention and diligence produce a completed work.

Slow but steady growth occurs as maturation of the central nervous system continues. In terms of psychosexual development, pressure is reduced in the exploration of sensuality and the gender role while other skills are developed and exploited.

The cognitive phase of development includes the mastery of skills in manipulating objects and the concepts of his culture. Thinking enters the period of *concrete operations* (Piaget, 1963, 1989), and the ability to solve concrete problems with this ability increases, so that toward the end of this period the child is able to abstract problems. The solution of real problems is accomplished with mental operations that the child was previously unable to perform. By puberty, the child exhibits simple deductive reasoning ability and has learned the rules and basic technology of his culture, thus reinforcing his sense of belonging in his environment.

Self-esteem is derived from the sense of adequacy and the beginning of "best" friendships and sharing with peers. This also marks the beginning of friendships and loves outside the family, as he begins to learn the complexities, pleasures, and difficulties of adjusting himself and his drives, aggressive and erotic, to those of his peers. By learning and adjusting, he begins to take his place as a member of their group and social life. In making this adjustment, he seeks the company of his own sex and forms groups and secret societies. The gangs and groups, especially the boys, fight each other in games, baseball, and cops and robbers, working off much hostility and aggression in a socially approved manner (Homonoff, 1991).

Feelings of inadequacy and inferiority may begin if the child does not develop a sense of adequacy. Family life may not have prepared him for school, or the school itself may fail to help him develop the necessary skills for competency. As a result, he may feel that he will never be good at anything he attempts.

In general, children are better able to cope with stress when normal familial supports are available. Any real or imagined threat of separation from a nuclear family member could drastically reduce a child's abilities to cope with new or changing psychosocial demands. Children are particularly vulnerable to such crisis-precipitating situations as the loss of a parent through death. Equally as stressful are recurring partial losses of a parent from the child's usual environment. Examples of the latter are repeated episodes of parental hospitalization or frequent, extended absences from home by one or both parents (Cassell, 1991).

An increasingly common source of emotional distress for children of this age group is the entry or reentry of the "homemaker" parent into the work field. This major change in the parenting role demands reciprocal changes in the child's role. For some children, externally imposed demands to assume increased independence and responsibility for self may be more than the child is maturationally able to cope with. Not yet able to assume the level of expected independence, the child may actually perceive this action as a form of rejection by the parent.

A common symbol of this role change is the home "latchkey" that is bestowed upon the child, much like a rite of passage and with the accompaniment of new social rules and regulations. In general, such rules and regulations focus on protection of the child and the home, with the child given implicit or explicit responsibility for ensuring that neither is violated in the parent's absence.

The following case study is about Billy B, an 8-year-old boy for whom the latchkey symbolized only rejection.

Case Study   *Prepuberty*

ASSESSMENT OF THE INDIVIDUAL AND THE PROBLEM

Billy B, 8 years old, was referred with his mother to the school counseling psychologist by his homeroom teacher. For the past few weeks, she reported, Billy had changed from his usual cheerful, outgoing, alert behavior to moodiness and apparent preoccupation. He was falling behind in his schoolwork, and twice during the past week he had failed to return to his classes after the lunch hour. The first time that he had done this, the school had contacted his mother at her place of work. She told them that Billy had already telephoned her from home. He told her that his stomach was upset, so he had decided to go home and call her from there. She was planning to go directly home when the call came from the school.

Yesterday, the counselor was told, Billy again failed to return to his classes after the lunch hour. This time he did not call his mother and he did not go home. After being notified by the school, his mother had telephoned home. She thought that Billy would be there, as before. Failing to get any answer, she went directly home from work to begin looking for him around the neighborhood. About an hour later, while making his routine security rounds, the apartment house custodian heard muffled sounds coming from a basement stairway and went to investigate. He found Billy crouched on the top steps, his head on his knees and sobbing. He was taken immediately to his mother. When questioned, he denied having been threatened by anyone or being injured, and he showed no signs of physical abuse. He refused to say why he had left school early again, or why he had not gone directly home.

Mrs. B immediately called the school and told them that Billy had been located and was safe. She was asked, and agreed, to come to school the next day with Billy to meet with his homeroom teacher. At her request, during the meeting the following day a referral was made for Billy and her to meet with the counseling psychologist.

Billy was seen initially without his mother present. He was average in height and weight, appeared physically healthy, although pale, and spoke hesitantly. He sat slouched in his chair, his eyes downcast, and appeared rather depressed. When asked why he had left school without permission twice that week, he muttered, "I don't know what everyone is so excited about. I can take care of myself—ask my mother—I can go home alone because I have the house key and can get in when my mother isn't home."

He stated that he had always liked school, got A's and B's, particularly enjoyed gym and outdoor sports, such as soccer and football. Until a week ago, he had attended an afterschool boys' sport group with many of his friends. This, however, had been suddenly canceled when the group director had resigned and moved to another city. He also said that his parents had been divorced when he was "a little kid" (4 years old) and that he now lived with his mother. He had frequently visited with his father, who lived nearby, until about 4 months ago. At that time his father had remarried and, a month later, his father's company had transferred him out of state.

After seeing Billy alone, the counselor talked to Mrs. B to verify and clarify this information and to assess her feelings about his problems and her ability to cope with them.

Mrs. B was a tall, attractive, well-dressed woman who gave the impression that she was deeply concerned about the recent changes in Billy's behavior. She stated that Billy, an only child, had always been considered "well adjusted," got along well with his friends, and, until recently, could always be depended on to keep up with his schoolwork. She went on to say that she and the boy's father had been particularly concerned about what effect their divorce might have on him. They had met regularly with a family therapist during that period to help Billy through their separation and eventual divorce.

Mrs. B had met her husband in college and they had married right after graduation. He was an electronics engineer and she had majored in business administration. During the 3 years before Billy was born, she had advanced to a well-paying position as administrative assistant to the director of a large advertising company. When she learned that she was pregnant, she arranged to take a 6-month leave of absence after his birth. However, as she described it to the counselor, Billy was not a healthy baby and seemed to have one medical problem after another for more than 2 years. She described Billy's father as very possessive and domineering whenever it came to any decisions about Billy's care. "In fact," she said, "when the time came that I felt that I could safely leave Billy with a sitter and go back to work, it became clear to me that our marriage was in for a lot of rocky days. " After many days of arguing and eventual compromise, it was agreed that she would return to work on a part-time basis and this only if they were both satisfied that the babysitter was giving Billy the best of care.

Furthermore, the father completely refused the idea of a day nursery, insisting that they get a sitter to come to their home, stating, "It's his home as much as it is ours, and he is entitled to be here—not in some stranger's house where I can't check up on things whenever I want."

By the time Billy was 3 years old, his mother reported, both parents realized that he was being emotionally "Ping-Ponged" between them and that her returning to work, even for a day, would always be a point of conflict with her husband. He had grown up in a very patriarchal family, with his mother never daring even to dream of any other role than that of "Kinder, Kirche, und Kuche." It was difficult for him to consider any other role for his wife, now that they had a family.

By contrast, Billy's mother had grown up in a family that encouraged equal rights for women. Her mother was a practicing attorney while rearing four children, and her father had managed a produce company. She just could not understand why she and her husband were having so many conflicts with only *one* child. By the time Billy was 4 years old, they had separated, and they were eventually divorced when he was 5. The final decree provided Mr. B with ample visitation rights, and they shared equally the responsibility for child support funds.

Until 4 months ago, Billy's mother had been able to manage on part-time work and was able to be home each day when he returned from school. However, earlier this year Mr. B had remarried and, when he transferred out of state 4 months ago, he was more than 6 months delinquent in payments for his share of child support. Being, as she put it, "a very realistic person," Mrs. B decided that she could no longer depend on Billy's father for regular payments in the future. Three months ago she went to her boss and asked if she could be reassigned to full-time work on an ongoing basis as soon as possible. She stated that Billy had never expressed any particularly negative feelings about his father remarrying and moving away, only that he would miss seeing him as often as he had in the past. She had taken particular care in planning with Billy for her return to full-time work. She knew, for example, that she would not be able to be home before he got back from school at the end of the day, so they planned for him to join an afterschool supervised sport group. This was one that would pick him up at the school and return him to his home by suppertime each day. "By that time," she said, "I would be home and he wouldn't come home to an empty apartment." This, she felt, also took care of her worry about his playing unsupervised in the neighborhood without her there to "keep an eye on things."

Three weeks ago Mrs. B had started her full-time work. She had always managed to get home before Billy returned from the sports group. It seemed to her that there would be no major changes for either of them to adjust to. One week ago, however, the director of the sports group suddenly resigned without notice. A replacement had not yet been found, and the group had been temporarily canceled. As the only interim choice that she could think of, Mrs. B decided to give Billy his own key to the apartment.

Worried about all of the real and imagined things that might happen to him before she got home, she accompanied the key with many admonishments about coming directly home from school, checking in with the apartment manager when he got there, and being sure to keep the door locked until she got home. She said that Billy did not seem to object to this at all. In fact, he had purchased a key chain to hook on his belt just like the one the building manager wore.

When the school called her the first time Billy cut classes and went home, she had counseled him to remain at school the next time he felt ill, and she would pick him up there. She had told him that he must "never go home alone again without first telling her or someone at the school. I don't like the idea of your being alone and sick. You know I would worry about you." She had also reminded him that they had planned this together and that they both had certain responsibilities to each other in working out this new living schedule. "Neither of us had much choice in this, you know," she told the counselor. "I'm making the best of things that I know how, and Billy is just going to have to cooperate. I just don't know why he is acting this way now."

PLANNING THERAPEUTIC INTERVENTION

The sudden, rapid changes in Billy's life during the past few months had forced him into assuming a degree of independence and self-responsibility beyond his maturational level of skills. Not yet accepting the loss of his father and perceiving it as a rejection of himself, he was forced into full dependence on his mother for any sense of security and all decision making. The timely entrance into the afterschool sports group had provided him with opportunities to express his feeling of anger and hostility about the situation through the competitive, aggressive sports activities with his peers. Unfortunately, the group was canceled about the same time his mother started her new job, and he lost his normal outlet for expressing such feelings. Not only did he lose the situational support of his peers when he most needed it, but also he had the further situational loss of his mother from her familiar roles. He could no longer depend on her being at home when he might need her during the day. His anxiety increased, as he perceived this to be another sign of rejection from a parent figure. Billy had no coping mechanisms in his repertoire with which to handle these feelings of added anxiety and depression. At the particular time when he needed to use his usually successful coping behaviors, the opportunity was not available because of the demand by his mother that he "come home directly after school. You can't play in the neighborhood after school with your friends."

It was believed that Mrs. B needed assistance in gaining a realistic, intellectual understanding of the situation as it related to Billy's current behaviors. Increasingly anxious about the added responsibility that had been placed on her during the past few months, she was possibly projecting her own feelings of insecurity into over-protective behaviors toward Billy; that is, "it is Billy, not *I*, who should not be out alone and unprotected. Something terrible might happen to *him* when there is no longer a strong, dependable person nearby to help keep an eye on things."

Billy would need to explore his perceptions and feelings about the psychosocial losses of both parents from the usual family roles that they had occupied in his life. He needed to be helped to express his feelings constructively and to make a positive adaptation to the new role demands made of him.

INTERVENTION

During the first session, the counselor focused on identifying with Mrs. B the many critical changes that had occurred in Billy's life during the past few months and their impact on his level of maturational skill development. The goal was to provide her with insight into how Billy might be perceiving such events at his level of comprehension and concrete thinking. Although he was old enough to be fully aware of the events happening, he was still too young to deal with them abstractly. For example, when his father had remarried and then moved away soon after, Billy most likely had perceived these actions as signs of complete rejection by his father and blamed himself in some way. In his mind, he may have wondered, "Why else would my father marry someone else and then move away, abandoning both me and my mother?"

It was also suggested to Mrs. B that her comments at the time (such as "If I don't go back to full-time work, we won't have a roof over our heads or food to eat") were probably taken quite literally by Billy. So, also, was her later admonishment to him always to come straight home from school, implying that he was one more source of problems for her.

In the next two sessions, through the use of direct questioning and reflection of verbal and nonverbal clues with Mrs. B, it became possible for her to express her own feelings about the recent chain of events in her life and to begin to relate them to Billy's behavioral changes. It was suggested that she try to find some alternative supervised peer group activities for Billy after school. The purpose was to reinstate, for him, the opportunity for some normal, acceptable outlets for the angry, hostile feelings that he must still be having from the recent losses in his life.

The counselor met with Billy at the beginning of each session to discuss with him how he was doing in school classes and what things he was doing to occupy his time after school before his mother got home from work. Billy's feelings of rejection and insecurity were dealt with during this time.

The remaining time was spent with Mrs. B. She was encouraged to continue to provide Billy with as much independence as feasible, yet not expect him to assume any more than he could comfortably cope with at this time. The importance of providing Billy with every opportunity to learn new social skills and to develop strong feelings of competency and self-adequacy was emphasized. The fact that closing off his access to usual afterschool activities with his peers would greatly limit his chances for new learning experiences was discussed. It might also precipitate his return to the same maladaptive coping behaviors that he had been demonstrating during the past few weeks.

Mrs. B was not able to locate another supervised activity group for her son to attend after school. However, she did make arrangements with a retired gentleman who lived in the same apartment house to keep an eye on Billy and to be a contact for him when he came home and played in the neighborhood with his friends after school.

ANTICIPATORY PLANNING

An important focus of anticipatory planning was to review with Mrs. B the maturational changes that she could expect to see developing in Billy over the next few years. The need for her to continue to allow him normal opportunities for growth and development was stressed. The fact that Billy was now a member of a single-parent family should not create any particular peer group problems, because this situation was increasingly common among children his age. However, potential stressful situations were identified and discussed in terms of how she might approach coping with them as they arose, both for herself and in her dealings with Billy.

Billy was encouraged to be more direct in questions to his mother and in letting her know when he felt confused or angry about things that were happening to him. He understood that he could stop in and talk to the counselor whenever the need arose, but that he would also be expected to keep in close touch with his mother about his feelings in the future.

SUMMATION OF THE PARADIGM (Figure 7-1)

Billy had perceived his father's remarriage and move out of state as a rejection of himself. Unable to express his feelings to his mother, he coped by acting out his anger and hostility in competitive, aggressive sports activities with his peers. Despite Mrs. B's assumptions to the contrary, planning with Billy for her return to full-time work had served to reactivate his fears of another rejection. No longer having his sports activities available to him as before, his anxiety increased. Lacking any other available coping skills, he became overwhelmed.

CASE STUDY: BILLY

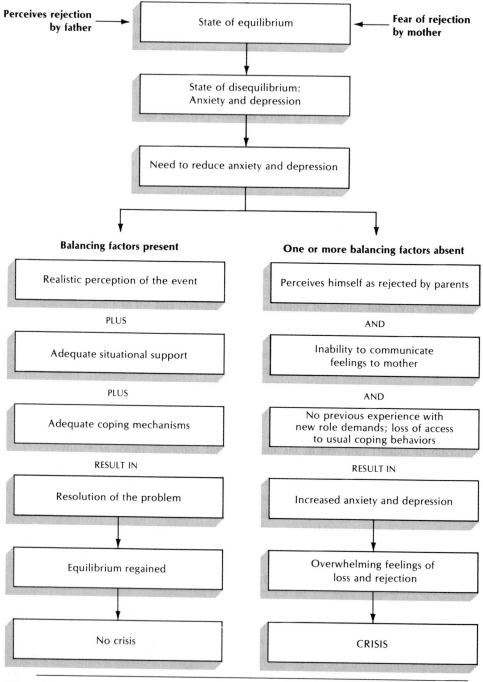

Figure 7-1

Intervention focused on helping Billy explore his feelings of loss and rejection. Time was spent with his mother, helping her understand his level of maturational skills and the need to better recognize when her demands or expectations might exceed his abilities to meet them.

Adolescence—Theoretical Concepts

The adolescent has a strong need to find and confirm his identity. Rapid body growth equals that of early childhood, but it is compounded by the addition of physical-genital maturity. Faced with the physiological revolution within himself, the adolescent is also concerned with consolidating his social roles. He is preoccupied with the difference between what he appears to be in the eyes of others and what he believes himself to be. In searching for a new sense of continuity, some adolescents must refight crises left unresolved in previous years (Adler and Clark, 1991).

Changes that occur while secondary sex characteristics emerge make the adolescent self-conscious and uncomfortable with himself and with his friends. Body image changes, and the adolescent constantly seeks validation that these physiological changes are "normal" because he feels different and is dissatisfied with how he thinks he looks. If sudden spurts of growth occur, he concludes he will be too tall; conversely, if growth does not occur as expected, he thinks he will be too short, or too thin, or too fat. In this period of fluctuation, half-child and half-adult, the adolescent reacts with childish rebellion one day and with adult maturity the next (Lau, 1991).

The adolescent is as unpredictable to himself as he is to parents and other adults. On the one hand, he seeks freedom and rebels against authority; on the other, he does not trust his own sense of emerging maturity and covertly seeks guidelines from adults. In his struggle for an identity, he turns to his peers and adopts their mode of dress, mannerisms, vocabulary, and code of behavior, often to the distress of adult society. The adolescent desperately needs to belong, to feel accepted, loved, and wanted.

This is the age for cliques and gangs. The in-group can be extremely clannish and intolerant of those who do not belong. Banding together against the adult world, its members seek to internalize their identity, but because of different and often rebellious behavior they are frequently incorrectly labeled as delinquent.

Having achieved a sense of security and acceptance from peers, the adolescent begins to seek heterosexual involvement. This occurs first at group-oriented social events, such as dances, parties, and football games. As comfort and confidence increase, the adolescent progresses to more meaningful and deeper emotional involvements in one-to-one heterosexual relationships. Because of conflict between sexual drives, desires, and the established norms of society, this stage can be extremely stressful, and again the adolescent is faced with indecision and confusion (Rose-Gold, 1991).

Occupational identity also becomes a concern at this time. There are continual queries by parents and school authorities about career plans for the future. Uncertainties are compounded when a definite choice cannot be made because of an inability to identify fully with the adult world of work. Having only observed or participated in fragments of work situations, the adolescent finds it difficult to commit himself to the reality of full-time employment and its inherent responsibilities. It is easier and more realistic to state what is *not* wanted rather than what is wanted as a career (Baack, 1991).

Piaget (1963, 1989) refers to the cognitive development at this stage as *formal operations,* the period in which the capacity for abstract thinking and complex deductive reasoning becomes possible. At this time, the goal is "independence," and in midadolescence acceptance of the idea that it is possible to love and at the same time to be angry with someone is one problem that should be solved. If this stage is successfully negotiated, the individual develops a capacity for self-responsibility; failure may lead to a sense of inadequacy in controlling and competing.

Because of the number and wide variety of stimuli and rapid changes to which he is exposed, the adolescent is in a hazardous situation. A crisis situation may be compounded by the normal amount of flux characteristic of adolescent development (Cameron, 1963; Erikson, 1950, 1959, 1963, 1989; Piaget, 1963, 1992; Zachry, 1940).

The following case study illustrates some of the conflicts that adolescents face while trying to find their identity, strive for independence, and win acceptance from their peer group. It also points out the need for understanding and patience on the part of parents as their adolescents grow up.

Case Study   *Adolescence*

ASSESSMENT OF THE INDIVIDUAL AND THE PROBLEM

Mary V, a 14-year-old high school sophomore, was referred to a crisis center with her parents by a school nurse. During the past few weeks, she had shown signs of increased anxiety, cried easily, and had lost interest in school activities. That morning, for no apparent reason, she had suddenly left the classroom in tears. The teacher followed and found her crouched in a nearby utility closet, crying uncontrollably. Mary seemed unable to give a reason for her loss of control and was very anxious. When her mother came in response to a call from the school nurse, they agreed to follow her advice and seek family therapy.

During the first session, the therapist saw Mary and her parents together in order to assess their interaction and communication patterns and to determine Mary's problems.

Mrs. V was quiet and left most of the conversation up to her husband and Mary. When she attempted to add anything to what was being said, she was quickly silenced by Mr. V's hard, cold stare or by Mary exclaiming in an exasperated tone, "Oh, Mother!" Mr. V spoke in a controlled, stilted manner, saying that he had no idea what was wrong with Mary, and Mrs. V responded hesitantly that it must be something at school.

Mary was particularly well developed for her age, a fact that was apparent despite the rather shapeless dress she was wearing. She might have been very attractive if she had paid more attention to her posture and general appearance.

When questioned, Mary said that she had not been sleeping well for weeks, had no appetite, and could not concentrate on her schoolwork. She did not know why she felt this way, and her uncontrolled outburst of tears frightened and embarrassed her. She was also afraid of what she might do next, adding that her crying that morning was probably because she had not slept well for the past two nights. At first, she tried to brush this off as final exam jitters.

She evaded answering repeated questions about sudden changes in her life in the past few days. When the therapist asked if she would be comfortable talking alone, without her parents, she gave her father a quick glance and replied that she would. Mr. and Mrs. V were asked if they objected to Mary talking to the therapist alone. Both agreed that it might be a good idea and went to the waiting room.

For a time, Mary continued to respond evasively. It was obvious that she had strongly mixed feelings about how to relate to the male therapist. Should it be "woman to man" or "child to adult"? Throughout this and the following sessions, she alternated between her child and adult roles. The therapist recognized the role ambivalence of adolescence and adjusted his role relationship, using whichever was most effective in focusing on the problem areas and making Mary more comfortable.

Mary eventually relaxed and began to talk freely about her relationship with her family, her activities at school, and some of the feelings that were troubling her. She said that she had two older brothers. The younger of the two, Kirk, was 16 years old and a senior in high school. She felt closer to him because "he understands and I can talk to him." Mary said that she had had "as good a childhood" as the rest of her friends. However, she did think that her father kept a closer eye on her activities than did the parents of most of her friends. He still called her his "baby" and "my little girl" and lately had begun to place more restrictions than usual on her friendships and activities.

She admitted that during the past year she had gone through a sudden spurt of body growth and development. She was keenly aware of these differences in her appearance and sensed the changing attitudes of her father and her friends. She felt her father was worried about her growing "up and out so fast." He was the one who insisted that she wear the almost shapeless dresses. She said she knew "it wasn't really because I outgrow things so fast right now—he thinks I look too sexy for my age!"

About 3 weeks ago, she had been invited to the junior-senior prom by a friend of her brother Kirk. She liked the boy and wanted to go but was not sure Kirk would approve because he would be at the prom too. Another problem was getting her parents' permission to buy the necessary formal. She had looked at dresses and knew exactly the one she wanted but knew her father would not let her have it.

Mary was asked if she felt able to tell her parents these things that were bothering her if the therapist were present to give her support. She thought that she could if he would "sort of prepare them first" and explain how important it was for her to go dressed like the rest of her girlfriends. He suggested that Mary discuss the situation with Kirk to see how he felt about her going to the prom with his friend, and she agreed to do this before the next session. The therapist assured her that he would spend the first part of the next session with her parents to discuss and explore their feelings about the prom.

PLANNING THERAPEUTIC INTERVENTION

It was thought that Mary needed support to assist her in convincing her parents that she be allowed to grow up. Mr. and Mrs. V needed to gain an intellectual understanding of some of the problems that adolescent girls face as they search for an identity, seek independence, and feel the need to be like their peers. Mrs. V would have to be encouraged to give support and guidance to Mary and help to resist Mr. V's attempts to keep Mary as the baby of the family.

INTERVENTION

At the next session the therapist went to the waiting room to get Mr. and Mrs. V and saw that Mary had brought her brother Kirk with her. She asked if he could come in with them at the last half of the session when the family would be together. The therapist agreed, realizing that Mary had brought additional support and that apparently Kirk had approved of her going to the prom.

The first part of the session was spent discussing with the parents the general problems of most adolescents, as well as the reasons behind their often erratic and unusual behavior. Both parents seemed willing to accept this new knowledge, although Mr. V said that he had not noticed any of this with the boys. Mrs. V said, "No, but you treated them differently. You were glad they were becoming men." The therapist supported Mrs. V and said that this was one of Mary's specific problems. He then repeated to the parents what Mary had said about the things that were bothering her. Both parents seemed slightly embarrassed, and Mr. V's voice and manner became quite angry as he tried to explain why he wanted to "protect" Mary. "She's so young, so innocent—someone may take advantage of her," and so on.

Discussion then focused on Mary's anxiety and the tension she was feeling because her father had made her feel different from her friends. Compromise between Mr. and Mrs. V and Mary was explored when Mary and Kirk joined their parents in the last half of the session. Mary was more verbal with Kirk present to support her, and Kirk told his father, "You are too old-fashioned. Mary's a good kid; you don't have to worry about her. You make her dress like a 10-year-old," and so on. Mr. V was silent for a while and then said, "You may be right, Kirk, I don't know." He then asked him, "Do you think I should let her go to the prom?" Kirk answered, "Yes, Dad, I'll be there; she can even double with me and my date." Her father agreed, adding that Mrs. V should go with her to pick out a "fairly decent dress." Mary began to cry, and Mr. V in great consternation asked, "What's wrong now?" She replied, "Daddy, I'm so happy. Don't you know women cry when they are happy too?"

ANTICIPATORY PLANNING

The next few sessions were spent in supporting the family members in their changing attitudes toward each other. Anticipatory planning was directed toward establishing open communication between the parents and Mary to avoid another buildup of tensions and misunderstandings. Mary was encouraged to use Kirk as a situational support in the future, because he and his father were not in conflict.

CASE STUDY: MARY

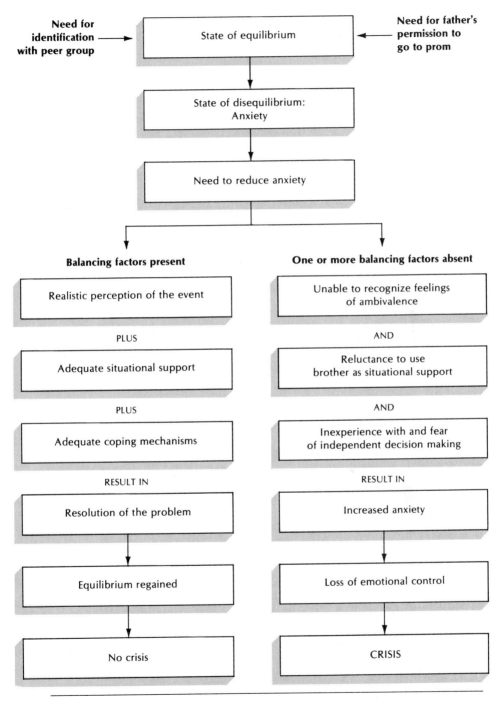

Figure 7-2

The family was told they could return for help with future crises if necessary and were assured that they had accomplished a great deal toward mutual understanding.

SUMMATION OF THE PARADIGM (Figure 7-2)

Mary suffered acute symptoms of anxiety because she had to ask her father for permission to go to a dance. She wanted to be a member of her peer group but felt uncomfortable because she was not allowed to dress as they did. She wanted independence but was inexperienced and afraid to make a decision that would oppose her father. Because the situation involved possible conflict with her brother, she did not feel comfortable talking with him about her problem.

Intervention was based on exploring areas of difficulty with the family and assisting them to recognize, understand, and support Mary's adolescent behavior, her bid for independence, and her need to become a member of her peer group.

Young Adulthood—Theoretical Concepts

Young adulthood is the time in which childhood and youth come to an end and adulthood begins. It involves studying for a specific career or seeking employment, as well as sociability with either sex. According to Cameron (1963), socioeconomic developments make it difficult to determine the transition from adolescence to adulthood. Originally, it was determined by the young adult maintaining an independent job, having the capacity for marrying, and forming a new family unit. The young unemployed tend to live at home with their families in a dependent relationship that has some of the characteristics of adolescence and some of the independence of adulthood. The young adult can no longer look forward confidently to gainful employment; without technical or professional education, he may have to be satisfied with unskilled temporary jobs. The more time he spends in technological or professional training, the longer he remains financially dependent on his family, and changes and uncertainties in modern socioeconomic situations may extend the period of dependence into the middle or late 20s. If the preceding stages of maturation have been successfully negotiated, the young adult will have confidence in himself and his ability for decision making and, as a result, will be able to establish and maintain a real intimacy with others. Adult society demands that young adults not deviate from the established norm: They are expected to remain in school if studying for a career or be consistent and productive in a job while maintaining an active social life.

There is an exploration and exploitation or denial of cultural and familial heritage, as well as a clarification of self-identity and the social role. The psychosexual task is one of differentiating self from family without complete withdrawal from the family. Cognitive development should be at the level of deductive and inductive logic, with expansion and exploration of cognitive capacities and the beginning of creativity.

Unsuccessful transition at this stage or lack of inner resources may lead to confusion when decisions are made regarding future goals. There is an inability to establish a true and mutual psychological intimacy with another person; there is also a tendency toward self-isolation and the maintenance of only highly stereotyped and formal interpersonal relationships, characterized by a lack of spontaneity, warmth, and honest exchange of emotional involvement.

In the next case study, a young adult is faced with the problem of making a choice between conforming to society's norms for choosing a vocation and marriage or remaining self-absorbed in his own immature interests.

Case Study   *Young adulthood*

ASSESSMENT OF THE INDIVIDUAL AND THE PROBLEM

Bob M, 18 years old, came for help at a crisis center and stated he was "feeling bad." When the therapist asked him to be more specific, he said he was not sleeping, was nervous, and things seemed unreal to him. When asked who referred him to the center, he replied a friend who had been there when he had been in trouble.

Bob was small in stature, slim, with a shaggy black beard; he was neatly dressed in Levis, sport shirt, and cowboy boots. During the initial session, Bob appeared overtly nervous and depressed. He sometimes spoke in short, rapid bursts, usually after a period of silence, but more often he spoke in a slow, hesitant manner. He would neither establish nor maintain eye contact with the therapist, and continually looked down at the floor.

When asked about events occurring before the onset of his symptoms, Bob said that "during the past 10 days so many things have happened it's difficult to remember what happened first." He began to recite events. After working on his car for 6 months, "it blew up" the first time he drove it. This was also the first time he had been able to drive in 6 months because his driver's license had been revoked for speeding. This precipitated a quarrel with his girlfriend, Lauri, because he had promised to take her out when his driver's license was reinstated and his car was fixed. He had recently received a promotion to foreman at work, but he was ambivalent—pleased with the promotion although uncertain of his readiness to accept the responsibility of a permanent job. Last, his best friend, a member of his motorcycle club, was out of town, and he felt that he had no one with whom to talk about his problems.

Further exploration with Bob revealed that his usual pattern of coping with stress was to ride his motorcycle with his friend "as fast and as far as we can go." They would stop someplace and "talk it out." He felt that this relieved his tension; things became clearer, and he could usually solve the problem.

Bob also expressed ambivalence in his relationship with Lauri. He loved her and wanted to marry her but was concerned because he thought that they had conflicting values; she was from a middle-class family with values that emphasized the importance of a steady job, conformity, and so forth, whereas he felt he belonged in the motorcycle club and liked their philosophy of, as he stated it, "to be free, take what you want, don't work." He was afraid that marriage to Lauri would inhibit his freedom and that to please her family he feared he would have to give up riding with his friends and working on his car and would have to trim his beard.

PLANNING THERAPEUTIC INTERVENTION

Because of the many problems presented, it was necessary for the therapist to sift through extraneous data and concentrate on major areas of difficulty. At this time, the therapist decided to assume the role of available situational support until other support could be found. This would give Bob the opportunity to use his prior successful coping device of "talking it out." As tensions decreased, other support would be provided for his attempts to solve his problems.

INTERVENTION

The goal of intervention was established by the therapist to assist Bob to recognize and cope with his feelings of ambivalence toward his job and Lauri and with the implications of making choices. The areas of difficulty were determined to be a conflict of values and Bob's need to feel that he belonged to something or someone.

In the next two sessions, while the therapist acted as a situational support, Bob's symptoms diminished. He was able to discuss and explore his feelings about Lauri and his job; he also began discussing his fears of "giving up so much" if they married. Because Bob's relationship with Lauri appeared to be a major problem area, the therapist suggested that she be included in the sessions.

In the subsequent sessions, which Lauri did attend, they began discussing areas of mutual concern and conflict. Lauri said that she did not expect him to give up riding his motorcycle. "He can do it on weekends, and I'll go along." Bob became angry, saying that he did not want her along because she was "too nice for that crowd." He then admitted he was not certain he would continue with them anyway, *but* he wanted it understood that he could go riding with his friend occasionally if he wanted.

Bob added that if they were married, he might not need them because he would have her (his need to belong).

When Bob spoke of her parents' comments about his shaggy beard, Lauri said that she liked his beard and that he was marrying her, not her family.

She insisted, however, that Bob spent too much time working on his car and not enough with her. Bob replied that the car was his hobby and said that he probably spent less time on his hobby than her father did on his golf.

In the concluding sessions, Bob apparently resolved his conflicts and stated firmly that he thought he would be gaining more than he might lose if he married Lauri and kept his job. At the last session, they made tentative plans to be married.

ANTICIPATORY PLANNING

The most important phase in anticipatory planning occurred when Bob agreed that Lauri be included in the therapy sessions. The necessity of choosing between present modes of behavior and gratifications and future expectations in his life led Bob to weigh the consequences involved. His decision to include Lauri in future planning indicated an orientation toward reality. In certain phases of life, it is necessary to give up certain pleasures of youth that appear to be consistent with freedom. An orientation toward the future, where maturity of decisions reflects not only an inner freedom but also a sense of self-fulfillment and a recognition of one's own strength, is consistent with a strong ego-identity.

CASE STUDY: BOB M

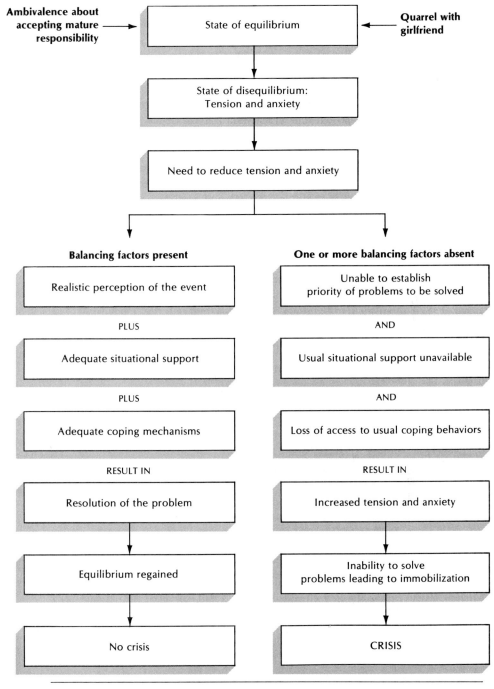

Figure 7-3

SUMMATION OF THE PARADIGM (Figure 7-3)

Bob M was forced to seek help because of increased symptoms of tension and anxiety. So many stressful events occurring in rapid succession had made it impossible for him to decide which problem should be solved first. His usual situational support, the friend from the motorcycle club, was out of town, and his normal method of coping with stress was unavailable. Ambivalent feelings about his job situation and his girlfriend, Lauri, increased his feelings of tension; he became immobile and unable to make decisions or to solve his problems.

Intervention focused on providing Bob with the situational support of the therapist, and Lauri was included as an active participant in the later sessions. When Bob was encouraged to ventilate his feelings, his anxiety decreased, and he was able to perceive relationships between the stressful events and his crisis situation more realistically. Previous successful coping skills were reintroduced and proved adequate in assisting him to solve his problem. Major focus of the last sessions was anticipatory planning to help him cope with future areas of stress as he made the transition to increased maturity.

Adulthood — Theoretical Concepts

Adulthood is the usual period in life when the responsibilities of life and/or of parenthood are assumed, involving the abilities of a man or woman to accept the strengths and weaknesses of one another and to combine their energies toward mutual goals. It is a crucial time for reconciliation with practical reality.

Maturity is always relative and is usually considered to develop in adulthood. Many adults who marry and have children never do achieve psychological maturity, whereas others who choose not to marry may show a greater degree of mature responsibility than many of their married peers.

Adult normality, like maturity, is also relative. Normality requires that a person achieve and maintain a reasonably effective balance, both psychodynamically and interpersonally. The normal adult must be able to control and channel his emotional drives without losing his initiative and vigor. He should be able to cope with ordinary personal upheavals and the frustrations and disappointments in life with only temporary disequilibrium; he should be able to participate enthusiastically in adult work and adult play, as well as have the capacity to give and to experience adequate sexual gratification in a stable relationship. He should be able to express a reasonable amount of aggression, anger, joy, and affection without undue effort or unnecessary guilt.

In actuality, it is unreasonable to expect to find perfect normalcy in any adult. Absolute perfection of physique and physiology are rare rather than normal, and an adult with a perfect emotional equilibrium is equally as exceptional.

This case study concerns a young woman whose lack of psychosocial maturity created problems when she was faced with the responsibility of motherhood. Her husband's competence and pleasure in caring for their baby increased her feelings of inadequacy and rejection.

Case Study   *Adulthood*

ASSESSMENT OF THE INDIVIDUAL AND THE PROBLEM

Myra and John, a young married couple, were referred by Myra's obstetrician to a crisis center because of her symptoms of depression. Myra said she was experiencing difficulty in sleeping, was constantly tired, and would begin to cry for no apparent reason.

Myra was an attractive but fragile blonde of 22 years whose looks and manners gave her the appearance of a 16-year-old. John, 28 years old, had a calm and mature demeanor. They had been married 1½ years and were the parents of a 3-month-old son, John, Jr. John was an engineer with a large corporation. Myra had been a liberal arts major when they met and married. John was the oldest of four children and was from a stable family of modest circumstances; Myra was an only child who had been indulged by wealthy parents.

When questioned by the therapist specifically about the onset of her symptoms, Myra stated that they had really begun after baby was born, with crying spells and repeated assertions that she "wasn't a good mother" and that taking care of the baby made her nervous. She said she felt inadequate and that even John was better with the baby than she. John attempted to reassure her by telling her she was an excellent mother and that he realized she was nervous about caring for the baby. He suggested that he get someone to help her. Myra said she did not want anyone because it was her baby, and she could not understand why she felt as she did. When questioned about her pregnancy and the birth of the child, she said there had been no complications and had added hesitantly that it had not been a planned pregnancy. When asked to explain further, she replied that she and John had decided to wait until they had been married about 3 years before starting a family. She went on to explain that she did not think she and John had had enough time to enjoy their life together before the baby was born.

After she recovered from the shock of knowing she was pregnant, she became thrilled at the thought of having a baby and enjoyed her pregnancy and shopping for the nursery. Toward the end of her pregnancy, she had difficulty sleeping and was troubled by nightmares. She began to feel uncertain of her ability to be a good mother and was frightened because she had not been around babies before.

When she and John brought the baby home, they engaged a nurse for 2 weeks to take care of the child and to teach Myra baby care. She thought that basically she knew how, but it upset her if the baby did not stop crying when she picked him up. When he was at home, John usually took care of the baby, and his competency made her feel more inadequate. The precipitating event was thought to have occurred the week before, when John had arrived home from work to find Myra walking the floor with the baby, who was crying loudly. Myra told him she had taken the baby to the pediatrician for an immunization shot that morning. After they returned home, he had become irritable, crying continuously and repeatedly refusing his bottle. When Myra said she did not know what to do, John told her the baby felt feverish. After they took the baby's temperature and discovered that it was 102° F, John called the pediatrician, who recommended a medication to reduce the temperature and discomfort. John got the medication and gave it to the baby; he also gave the baby his bottle. The baby went to sleep, but Myra went crying and upset to their bedroom.

PLANNING THERAPEUTIC INTERVENTION

Myra's mixed feelings toward the baby would be explored in addition to her feelings of inadequacy in caring for him. She apparently resented the responsibility of the parental role, which she was not ready to assume. Unable to express her hostility and feelings of rejection toward the baby, she turned them inward on herself, with the resulting overt symptoms of depression. Bringing these feelings into the open would be a necessary goal. Myra also needed reassurance that her feelings of inadequacy were normal because of her lack of contact and experience with infants and also because most new parents felt this same inadequacy in varying degrees. John obviously was comfortable and knowledgeable in the situation as a result of his experience with a younger brother and sisters; he would be used as a strong situational support.

INTERVENTION

The therapist, believing that a mild antidepressant would help to relieve Myra's symptoms, arranged a medical consultation. It was not thought that she was a threat to herself or to others, and intervention was instituted.

Myra's mention in the initial session that she and John had not had enough time to enjoy each other before the baby was born was considered to be an initial reference to Myra's negative feelings regarding her pregnancy and the baby. In subsequent sessions, through the therapist's use of direct questioning and the reflection of verbal and nonverbal clues, Myra was able to express some of her feelings about their life as a family with a baby in contrast to her feelings when there had been just she and John.

Their previous life pattern revealed much social activity before the birth of the baby and almost none afterward. Myra said that although this had not really bothered her too much at first, recently she had felt as if the walls were closing in on her. John appeared surprised to hear this and asked why she had not mentioned it to him. Myra replied with some anger that it apparently did not seem to bother him, because it was obvious that he enjoyed playing with the baby after he came home from work. The possibility of reinstating some manner of social life for Myra and John was considered essential at this point. John told her that his mother would enjoy the chance to babysit with her new grandson and that he and Myra should plan some evenings out alone or with friends. Myra brightened considerably at this and seemed pleased at John's concern.

The therapist also explored their feelings about the responsibilities of parenthood and Myra's feelings of inadequacy in caring for the baby. Myra could communicate to John and the therapist her feelings that the baby received more of John's attention than she and that she resented "playing second fiddle." John explained that he had originally assumed care of the baby so that she could get some rest and that he enjoyed being with her more than with the baby. He told her that he loved her and that she would always come first with him.

CASE STUDY: MYRA

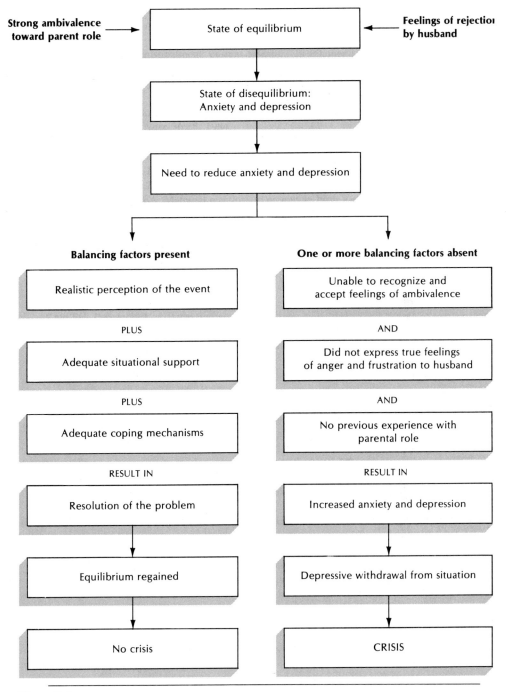

Figure 7-4

Myra was eventually able to see that she was being childish in resenting the baby and that she was competing for John's attention; as her social life expanded, her negative feelings toward the baby lessened, and she said she was feeling more comfortable in caring for him. After the fourth session, the medication was discontinued, and Myra's symptoms continued to decrease.

ANTICIPATORY PLANNING

Because of John's maturity, it was thought important that he should be aware of the possibility that Myra could occasionally have a recurrence of feelings of rejection. If the original symptoms returned, he would recognize them by the pattern they would take and would be able to intercede by exploring what was happening, discussing this openly with Myra. When the progress and adjustments they had made in learning to cope with the situation were reviewed with them, both expressed satisfaction with the changes that had occurred. They were told that they could return for further help if another crisis situation developed.

SUMMATION OF THE PARADIGM (Figure 7-4)

Myra was an only child who had rarely had to accept responsibility for others before her marriage. Because she had planned to wait 3 years before having a child, she had strong, mixed feelings about the responsibilities of motherhood before that time and felt unprepared. Her husband's adequacy in caring for the baby when she failed reinforced her mixed feelings. Loss of the social life shared with her husband, combined with the diversion of his attention from her to the baby, reinforced her strong feelings of rejection. Because she was unable to recognize and accept her feelings of ambivalence and was also unable to tell her husband of her anger and frustration, she turned them inward. Lack of previous experience in caring for infants made her unable to cope with the situation, increased her frustration and anger, and resulted in overt symptoms of depression and anxiety.

Late Adulthood—Theoretical Concepts

Late adulthood is the final stage of development discussed in Erikson's theory of maturation (1950, 1959, 1963, 1992). If a person has successfully negotiated the preceding stages, he or she should be mature enough to accept responsibility for his or her life-style without regrets.

To the average person, reaching late adulthood implies that life patterns have been fairly well set and are no longer open to choices for change. Anxiety results if a man or woman has not demonstrated some capacity for success in either family or career roles. Symptoms of this are frequently noted in such forms as excessive use of alcohol, psychosomatic symptoms, feelings of persecution, and depression (English and Pearson, 1955).

Our culture seems unable to place any firm boundary lines on phases of the aging process. The general tendency is to view life as uphill from infancy and over the hill and declining after reaching the peak of the middle years. With our cultural emphasis on youthfulness, it is not unusual for a person of 50 years to view his future with regret for things left unaccomplished. Hahn (1963) refers to this stage as "heads against the ceiling," a time when "the realization strikes home that the probability for appreciable advancement is remote. . . . The ceiling is encountered relatively early by some and at an amazing late time by others, but for all of us the ladder eventually ends at a ceiling." He further describes this as a period when "younger men and women are beginning to crowd into the competitive economic, political and social arenas." With the rapid technological changes affecting business and professions, younger persons are often better prepared to supply the necessary knowledge and skills.

Family life changes as children grow up and become involved with school, careers, and marriage. For parents, it is a time when specific tasks of parenthood are over, and they must return to the family unit of two, making reciprocal changes in role status in relation to their children and to the community. New values and goals must be developed in the marriage to replace those values no longer realistic in the present; failure to recognize this need can open the way to frustration and despair. The wife and mother now has freedom from parental responsibility, but, if her entire life-style was centered around the parental role, she may lack interests, skills, and abilities with which to make the role change.

Menopause, or the cessation of the menstrual cycle, is often thought of as a dividing point between young adulthood and middle age. The actual termination of menstruation, however, occurs over a wide age range, usually between 45 and 55. Menopause marks the abrupt loss of fertility in women, while in men the climacteric occurs gradually and at a later age.

Menopause can represent a hazard for women because of its psychological repercussions. For some, the end of fertility may represent the end of sexuality and the loss of role identity. For women who have chosen not to have children the loss of fertility may represent the closing of the door to bearing children, perhaps giving rise to doubts about their choice. Women who have been raised to view menopause as the beginning of middle age and the end of youth may well experience it as a negative event and be thrown into a crisis (Pruett, 1980).

There appears to be no definite evidence that sexual gland activity in the male undergoes similar rapid decline and cessation; however, men can experience symptoms similar to those of women at the same age period. Pruett (1980) considers these syndromes to be neuroses rather than a result of any changes in the sexual gland activity.

The unmarried person who has had thoughts of eventual marriage and family is now faced with the reality of advancing years. This is a particularly critical time for anyone who has relied strongly on physical attractiveness. He or she now faces the inevitability of physical decline. A person in this stage of life can continue to pursue career interests but may face limitations to further career advancements.

The following case study concerns a 40-year-old wife and mother whose planned changes in her family role after the marriage of her daughter seem to be threatened by the onset of early menopause.

Case Study   *Late adulthood*

ASSESSMENT OF THE INDIVIDUAL AND THE PROBLEM

Mrs. C, a 40-year-old, youthful-appearing mother of three daughters (ages 17, 20, and 22 years) was referred to a crisis center by her physician because of severe anxiety and depression, as evidenced by recent anorexia, weight loss, insomnia, crying spells, and preoccupation, which had begun after a visit to her physician 3 weeks earlier. At that time, she had been told that she was entering early menopause. Her youngest daughter was to be married in a month; the two older ones were already married and living out of state.

She described herself to the therapist as having always been socially active both in community affairs and in her husband's business and social life. Mr. C was employed as a senior salesman for a nationwide firm selling women's clothing. His work required frequent trips out of town and much business entertaining while at home. She seldom traveled with him (because of the children) but was deeply involved with planning and hostessing his in-town social engagements. She said that she enjoyed this and had always been confident of her ability to do it well. Part of her wife role was to wear the clothes of her husband's company as an unofficial model, and her husband had always expressed his pride in her attractiveness.

In recent weeks, she had begun to feel inadequate in this role, and strong feelings of doubt regarding her ability had begun to plague her. At the same time, she sensed that her husband was becoming indifferent to her efforts to keep herself and their home attractive to him. Her symptoms had overtly increased in the 2 days just past, until now she feared a complete loss of emotional control.

Mr. C was 2 years older than Mrs. C. He was socially adept, and her women friends frequently told her they thought he was "such a youthful, good-looking, and considerate person." She herself felt fortunate to have him for a husband. He was aggressive in business and could be sure of advancement. She said they had always been sexually compatible and shared interests and mutual esteem.

When asked about what had occurred in the past 2 days to increase her symptoms, she said that her husband had come home 2 nights ago and found her disheveled and crying and not ready to go to a scheduled business dinner for the second time in a week. He angrily told her that he did not know what to do and to "pull yourself together and find someone to help you because I've tried and I can't!" Then he left for the dinner alone. The next day he left town on a business trip after securing her promise to see a physician.

Mrs. C said that she had seen several physicians during the past few months because of various physical complaints. None had found any organic cause, but all had advised her to get more rest, and one even told her to find a hobby. The last physician, whom she saw 3 weeks ago, told her she was entering early menopause.

Mrs. C had not told her husband of this because she feared his reaction in view of her own negative feelings; her initial reaction had been disbelief. This was followed by fear of "change of life," as she had heard of so many unfortunate things that could happen to a woman during this time. In common with other women, she did not want to become old and unattractive and was angry that it could be happening to her so soon! She thought that she would no longer be an asset to her husband in his work because his clothes were not designed for middle-aged women.

Mrs. C had looked forward to traveling with her husband after their youngest daughter's marriage. They had planned such a future together enthusiastically, and she felt proud to have contributed to his success but was now afraid that he would not need her anymore and that all her plans were ruined.

Her expressed feelings of guilt and a fear of the loss of her feminine role were thought to be the crisis-precipitating events. She was not seen as a suicidal risk or as a threat to others, although she was depressed and expressed feelings of worthlessness. She was highly anxious but could maintain control over her actions.

PLANNING THERAPEUTIC INTERVENTION

Mrs. C had withdrawn from her previous pattern of social and family activities. Her husband was frequently out of town, and the last of the daughters living at home had transferred many of her dependency needs to her fiancé. Mrs. C in the past 3 months had felt physically ill and had narrowed her social activities to infrequent luncheons "when I felt up to it." Her peer group was in the 35- to 40-year age level and were all actively involved in community affairs, family activities, and so on. Conversation with women friends still centered around problems of raising children, and she believed that because her children were grown she no longer had much to offer to the conversation.

Her goals for a role change from busy parenthood to active participation with her husband in his business-social world were threatened, and she had no coping experiences in this particular situation. Previous methods of coping with stress were discussed. She related that she had always kept busy with their children and either forgot the problems or talked them out with close friends or her husband. She could not recall a close woman friend who had reached the menopausal stage and with whom she could discuss her feelings, and she was too fearful of the reaction she imagined her husband would have to discuss it with him. Her inability to communicate her feelings and the loss of busy work with her children eliminated any situational supports in her home environment, obviating the use of previously successful coping mechanisms. The goal of intervention established by the therapist was to assist Mrs. C to an intellectual understanding of her crisis.

INTERVENTION

It was obvious to the therapist that Mrs. C had little knowledge of the physiological and psychological changes that occur in menopause. She had no insight into her feelings of guilt and fear of the threatening loss of her feminine role. Unrecognized feelings about her relationship with her husband would be explored. During the next 5 weeks, through the use of direct questioning and reflection of verbal and nonverbal clues with Mrs. C, it became possible for her to relate the present crisis and its effect to past separations from her husband (business trips) and her previous successful coping mechanisms.

Mrs. C had married when she was 17 years old. She described herself as having been attractive and popular in school, busy at all sorts of school activities. Mr. C had been what everyone considered quite a catch. He came from a prosperous family, had been a high school football captain and class president, and was sought after by many of her girlfriends. At the time of their marriage he was a freshman in college.

She always had a high regard for her physical attractiveness and her ability to fulfill the social role Mr. C expected of her. Throughout the years when he traveled alone, she felt left out of a part of his life and had looked forward with great expectations to being able to be with him all of the time. Knowing that his business brought him in frequent contact with attractive women buyers and models, she regarded her own physical attractiveness as a prime requirement to "meet the competition." With Mr. C's frequent trips away from home, she had magnified her role in the husband-wife relationship to be more on the physical-social level than in the shared role of parental responsibilities.

ANTICIPATORY PLANNING

Mrs. C never questioned her physician after he informed her of his diagnosis of early onset of menopause, and obviously her knowledge was inadequate and based almost entirely on hearsay and myth rather than on fact. The physiological basis of the process of aging was discussed, and much of her fear was allayed. This was an important phase of anticipatory planning.

She was given situational support in which to talk out her feelings of insecurity in her marriage and to view it in much more realistic terms. Relationships between the precipitating events and the crisis symptoms were explored.

By the third week, Mrs. C had made significant progress toward reestablishing her coping skills. She no longer feared "getting old overnight" and was able to tell her husband that she was entering early menopause.

His response was, "What the hell! Is that why you have been acting so peculiar lately? You might have told me; the way you've been carrying on anyone would have thought you had just been told you had 6 months to live!" Although her first impulse was to interpret this as evidence of his indifference to her as a woman, she later saw it as positive proof of her own unrealistic fears. She returned to her medical doctor as advised for continuing care and planning for physical problems that might arise in the future.

By the fifth week, she expressed confidence in her ability to meet the goals that she and her husband had set for their future. Their daughter was married, and Mrs. C was ready to leave town with her husband on a business trip. Before termination, the adjustments she had made in coping with the crisis were reviewed and discussed with her.

SUMMATION OF THE PARADIGM (Figure 7-5)

Mrs. C had been unable to cope with the combined stresses of early menopausal symptoms and the need to change her family role. She avoided communicating her fears to anyone who might have given her situational support for fear they would confirm her own negative reactions. Increasing feelings of inadequacy, resulting in anxiety and depression, led to a crisis level of disequilibrium.

Initial intervention focused on the exploration of Mrs. C's knowledge of the physical and psychological changes that could occur in menopause. As she was encouraged to explore and ventilate her feelings about her relationship with her husband, her perception of the stressful situation became more realistic and her coping skills were reintroduced successfully.

Old Age—Theoretical Concepts

Erikson's formulation of the stages of human development stops with late adulthood. Unfortunately, he has not extended his analysis to crisis stages encountered by the retrenching organism.

CASE STUDY: MRS. C

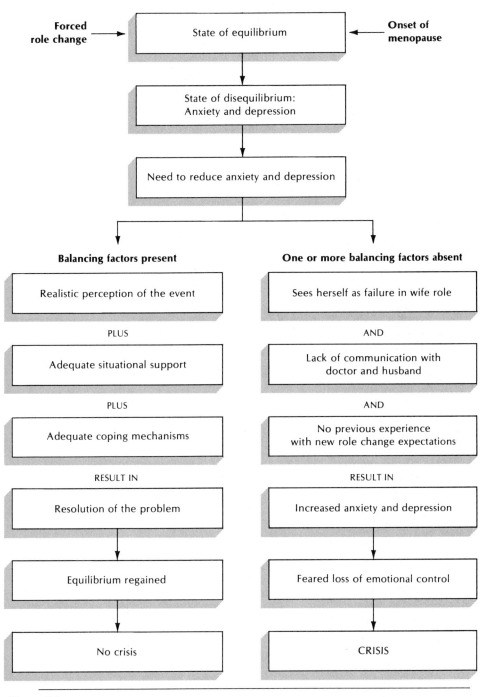

Figure 7-5

In human beings, the aging process must not be viewed only in terms of chronological years but also with regard for the complex interrelationships of biological, psychological, and sociological changes that occur during these years. There is no exact age of onset.

Aging will be the largest social issue in the United States in the next 50 years. In approximately 25 years, the baby boom will become the senior boom as the first of the 76 million baby boomers reach the age of 65. By the middle of the next century, 53% of the U.S. population will be senior citizens—double today's percentage (Larsen, 1988).

Generally, psychologists look on aging as a period of decline. The pace of physical decline is highly individual, occurring throughout life, yet it is most commonly attributed to the period loosely called *old age*. "Old age with respect to what?" is a most significant question. It could be one of many things—organic, sensory, or structural changes—and the significance of each is not fully understood.

Personality changes have been substantially investigated, but problems of interpretation have arisen because studies have been directed toward the segmentalized personality traits rather than the total organization or adaptiveness. Individual studies have found the aged to be "more set" in problem solving and "more stable" in their habits and tendencies than are younger subjects (Swan and other, 1991).

Abnormal behavior in the aged is difficult to diagnose because of the increase of organic damage with longevity. These abnormal patterns of experience and behavior develop along new lines with age and raise questions about the exact nature of endogenous psychosis and what part is played by reactive ill humor or somatically based psychosis. Abnormal mental attitudes may develop as reactions to loss of influence, destruction of or unfulfilled life goals, onset of human isolation, and threats to economic security.

Considerable research has been done concerning the social attitudes and forces creating the role of the aged in our culture. Goffman's (1961) denotative grouping of total institutions defines those for the aged as being established to care for people thought to be helpless and insecure—the blind, orphaned, indigent, and aged. In essence, this might define the negative attitudes of our society for the aged.

Our culture values mutual independence of the aged and their married children. Feelings of obligation on the part of adult children to support and care for their aging parents have declined with the establishment of the social insurance of medical and other community forces. An exaggerated premium is placed on the physical and psychological attributes of youth. When a culture assigns a role to the individual, acceptance and performance of it depend greatly on his conception of the role as it relates to his own self-concept.

Sullivan (1953) refers to the self as the reflected appraisal of others that comes into being as a dynamism to preserve the feelings of security. As new evaluations are reflected, the individual is obliged to reconcile these new concepts of self with those preexisting. Increasing conflictual appraisals may result in increased tension and anxiety, leading to a state tantamount to the acceptance of, or resignation to, old-age status.

As in the first years of adolescence, these later years of life are characterized by physical, emotional, and social crises. The onset of physical infirmities may require that the aged person turn to his milieu for a measure of care and security.

The presence or absence of environmental resources, as well as the degree to which help from others is required for survival, becomes of prime importance. The elderly who are economically secure, alert, and outgoing may be able to rise above social attitudes and be in the position of continuing to influence the lives of others, whereas those who are not in this position may be forced to play the roles designated by society's attitudes. Reisman's three ideal-typical outcomes of the aging process (1954) are as follows: (1) autonomous people with creative resources who use them to advantage in old age, (2) those who are adjusted and remain so, and (3) those who are neither and so decay.

A study of centenarians by Dunbar and Dunbar, as quoted by Solomon (1954), found a high correlation between longevity and a particular type of ego structure, and most of the subjects had chosen independence from their children as a way of life. In many cases, they contribute to the support of their dependents, many have an active sex life into the very late years, and few were found who retired to do nothing. They were not susceptible to feelings of uselessness and had maintained involvement in activities in which they took pride.

An apparent correlation between the degree of ego organization in early life and the degree maintained in the senescent years has been found. Those with strong ego organization seem better able to withstand the increased stresses and conflicts of later years. According to Palmore (1973), it is highly probable that much of the functional mental illness among the aged is chiefly the result of stresses caused by loss of income, loss of role and status, bereavement, isolation through disability, and loss of cognitive functioning.

Fear of death is not unique to the aged; its proximity is undeniably closer to some. This is verified as groups of contemporaries become smaller because of attrition by death. The old *are* living longer. Various studies and observations have noted that feelings of anxiety about death are most commonly coped with by the mechanism of denial, but it is not unusual to hear the very aged speak of "welcoming death" or saying that they "have lived a full life and have no fear of death." The social taboos that our culture places on frank discussion about death may lead to suppression of fear, to increased anxiety, and to resulting disequilibrium.

The aged are also faced with the fear of invalidism or chronic debilitating illness that might lead to dependency on society for survival. This may lead to a regression to earlier childlike levels of ego organization as a means of adjusting. According to Slater (1963), the increased powerlessness and loss of authority status of the aged weaken the respect of youth. This may be followed by anger at the reversal in dependency roles, the ultimate destruction of the child role, and the anticipation of desertion by death. As a means of handling guilt that may arise as a result of ambivalence, young people project their feelings onto others. It is the aged who become malevolent, isolated, and alienated and who are denied participation in society for all the evils for which they are blamed.

Cumming and Henry (1961) have noted two critical events that take place during this period of life: the loss of a spouse and retirement. Both represent conclusions of central tasks of the adult life.

The loss of a spouse is particularly traumatic for the aging person. For both widow and widower, this represents the loss of a primary source of need satisfaction. There is a loss of emotional security and a feeling of intense loneliness at a time in life when only the most resourceful may be able to find means to redistribute the cathexis. The surviving spouse loses those aspects of social identity that were solely dependent on a marital partner role. Both widow and widower must develop social identities of their own, based on their own interests, economic status, and social skills, as old social systems become closed to them and they are faced with finding and integrating into new ones.

Retirement is a highly critical time in a person's life. It is one thing if it occurs of one's own volition and planning; it becomes more complex when mandated by another. Losses include status identity based on identification with a productive and functional role in society. The retiree is also faced with the loss of a peer group.

Some people do not move easily into the role of pure sociability. Their focus of sociability has been directed toward their occupational peer groups, and loss of these groups through retirement leaves a void with few purely social skills to fill it.

Role reversal necessitated by a debilitating illness of a spouse is also a fertile area for the development of a crisis. Rarely is either spouse prepared socially, psychologically, or physically to assume all of the responsibilities of such a role change; the adjustments involved may be beyond the older individual's ability to cope and adapt.

It is evident that a continuation of maturational stages of development would be more difficult to define for the aged than for younger groups because the processes of decline and growth occur concomitantly but not in equal balance. The process is highly individualized in all cases, and the variability of physiological, psychological, and sociological factors makes definite chronological relationships highly improbable.

When an elderly person seeks help, his symptomatology requires particularly close scrutiny before an interpretation for intervention is undertaken. The therapist must first be aware of his own tendencies to stereotype the client's appearance and symptoms as a normal aging syndrome. Determining which of the crisis symptoms may be the result of organicity is particularly important because rapid onset of behavioral changes is not infrequently caused by cerebrovascular or other organic changes associated with longevity. A professional review of the current medical history of the individual must be part of the initial assessment phase.

Too often the individual, because of organic changes, cannot gain an intellectual understanding of the crisis or recognize his present feelings. It may also be that those who directed him to the therapist are themselves in crisis; if this is true, the therapist first may have to resolve the feelings of the referrer that have been projected toward the aged individual who seems to be in need of help.

In the aging process, the ego organization needs to withstand increasing biopsychosocial threats to its integrity; unfortunately, the individual's coping abilities may fail to adapt to meet the threats. The ability to accept new value systems and adapt to necessary changes in the achieved maturational development of earlier years without loss of achieved integrity may indeed be a developmental task for the aged.

The following case study concerns a couple, Sarah, 69 years of age, and John, 66, who could be considered members of the older age group.

Case Study

Old age

ASSESSMENT OF THE INDIVIDUAL AND THE PROBLEM

Sarah was accompanied to the crisis center by her husband, John, a former client who had come there for help when in crisis following the death of their only son about 10 years ago.

Sarah was 69 years of age, 3 years older than John. She was neatly dressed, appeared to be slightly apprehensive, and walked with obvious difficulty, supported by a Canadian crutch and her husband's arm. After being assisted into a chair in the therapist's office, she quickly asked that John be allowed to remain with her during the session. She stated that it "had really been John's idea that we both come here today. I'm sure that he can explain the problem better than I." After a slight pause and several hesitations John began to speak. Sarah sat tensely forward on her chair, never taking her eyes from his face as he spoke.

According to John, their problem "probably first began" about 3 months ago, when Sarah had fallen in the house and fractured her hip. After a month in the hospital, she had been sent home in his care. The plan was for her to continue physiotherapy as an outpatient. Despite all of the therapy and exercises at home, she was apparently not making the progress they had expected. "Look at her, she still can't walk alone! She still needs someone to help her about or she might fall again, and God knows what would happen to us then! It's been a worry for both of us."

As John continued to speak, it became quite obvious that he was avoiding any direct references to himself. He described Sarah as having recent symptoms of insomnia, anxiety, and depression and expressed the fear that she might be going into the same crisis symptoms that he had been treated for at the center 10 years ago. "It was sheer hell to feel the way I did then. She doesn't deserve to go through what I did then if she can be helped now."

As he spoke, he was becoming obviously more agitated. He avoided eye contact with Sarah, kept moving about restlessly in his chair, and was becoming increasingly tense and tremulous. His eyes frequently became tearful, and his voice broke on several occasions. In almost direct contrast to his behavior, Sarah had assumed a very supportive role, reaching out several times to pat his arm in a calming gesture and, finally, holding his hand tightly.

At the point when it seemed he might begin to cry openly, he abruptly stood up and said, "OK, Sarah, I've told her all about the problem. Now I'm going to go take a walk for a while and let you do some of the talking, too." With that, he said he would be back in about 20 minutes and left the office.

As soon as John had left, Sarah began to cry quietly. Then she gave several deep sighs and, for the first time, relaxed back into her chair. "Please," she asked the therapist, "can you help him again like you did the last time?" She stated that for the past week he had not slept more than an hour at a time during the night, paced constantly, cried easily and often for no apparent reason, and had reached the point where he now seemed too anxious and too preoccupied to make even the simplest of decisions.

According to Sarah, she and John had been married for 42 years. They had had only one son, who had died, unmarried, 10 years ago. Although Sarah had never held a salaried job, she had always been very actively involved in both civic and church organizations in their community. After John's retirement from federal service, she had withdrawn from several of these organizations in order to devote more time to activities that they could participate in together. They had developed many new social interests and maintained a fairly active social life. Sarah felt that the past 10 years had included some of the best times in their life together. They had always seemed to be planning something "for the future" and had acquired many new friends. Their home was completely paid for; they had planned wisely for financial security "in their old age," and, until her accident, they had had few health problems to worry about.

Even after her hip fracture, they had apparently been able to provide each other with the situational support needed to cope adequately with the many new changes arising in their daily lives. "After all," Sarah said, "it wasn't as though our world was going to come to an end because of this—only that it might have to slow down a bit until we could catch up again."

After a month in the hospital, Sarah went home and arranged to continue therapy as an outpatient. Despite regular visits to physiotherapy and John's rigidly imposed schedule of exercising at home, her recovery had been much slower than they had anticipated. Last week her physician, also not satisfied with the rate of her progress, recommended that she seriously consider admission as a full-time inpatient to a well-known rehabilitation center in a nearby city. He was unable to guarantee how long she might have to remain, estimating only that it would be a minimum of 1 month.

She stated that at the time John seemed to be as much in agreement as she with the idea, although, she recollected, he had seemed a bit preoccupied on the drive home. He took her out to dinner that night to celebrate her improved chances for a full recovery. That same night she was awakened several times by John getting out of bed and pacing about the house. When she mentioned it to him in the morning, he quickly apologized for disturbing her and blamed it on "too much coffee and food" the night before. She noticed, however, that he seemed very preoccupied that day, even to the point of having to be reminded when it was time for her exercises. Several times he asked if she felt confident that they were making the right decision, or if they should try to find another physician for her who might suggest "better treatments."

His tension and anxiety continued to increase over the next few days. He seemed unusually concerned with how she felt about the decision, and no amount of reassurance from her could convince him that she really wanted to go into the hospital for treatment. Several times yesterday, she found him looking at her sadly with tears running down his face. His only explanation was that he felt "so sorry for you, having to go to a strange place, and I might not be there when you need me!" Last night he had not gone to bed at all but had sat in the living room. She had not dared go to sleep for fear he would go outside and wander around.

Several times during the past few days, she had suggested he contact the crisis center to speak to his former therapist. At first, he ignored her, then finally yesterday he had countered with the proposal that they go together. "I'm sure," he told her, "that you must be feeling just as anxious as I am about all of this." She said that she agreed to this because she could think of no other way to convince him to come alone. "Of course, I'm upset about having to go back to a hospital," she told the therapist. "Anyone in my condition would like to have some sort of guarantee that they are going to improve, but my greatest concern is what this all has done to John." After discussing her feelings a bit longer with her, the therapist determined that Sarah appeared to be coping adequately with the recent events in her life and, although anxious and concerned about them, was indeed not in crisis.

Finding that John had returned from his walk, the therapist arranged to have Sarah wait outside and called him back into the office. He still appeared very tense, yet when confronted with his evident symptoms of depression and anxiety, he at first denied their severity. Then, after several evasive responses, he began to openly describe just how frightened and overwhelmed he had been feeling for the past week. "I just don't know what's going to happen to us next. I don't think I'll be able to handle much more. I was so sure she'd be back walking by this time. We did everything that the doctors told us to do—I worked so hard with her to keep up with the exercises and all of the appointments—and they haven't helped. Now she has to go back to the hospital. I feel that some of this is all my fault. Maybe I didn't work hard enough with her, or maybe I was doing the exercises the wrong way. She hates being crippled like this. Sometimes I think she must hate me because she has to be so dependent on me for doing everything."

After Sarah had come home from the hospital 2 months ago, John had been kept very busy and involved in driving her to appointments, arranging the household schedules, and helping her exercise at home. He found many rewards in this role, feeling that he was contributing greatly toward her eventual recovery. However, as the weeks and months passed without much apparent improvement in her condition, he was disturbed to find himself angry toward her, even at times blaming her for not trying harder. Lately, he had been finding it increasingly difficult to hide these feelings from her and found himself wishing that he could just get away from the situation for a while, to take a trip like they used to, even if it meant going off without her! Now, because of her decision to go into the rehabilitation center for treatment, he was being given the opportunity to "get away from it all" for a while, to turn the responsibility for her daily exercises and care completely over to others, and he felt very guilty. Perhaps he had not really tried hard enough to help her walk; maybe he should have found ways to encourage her more. The more he ruminated on these thoughts, the more he convinced himself that her lack of progress was entirely his fault. Therefore, it was his fault that she had to go back to a hospital, and it would be completely his fault if she were never able to return home again!

PLANNING THERAPEUTIC INTERVENTION

The goals of intervention were to help John obtain a realistic perception of the situation, to assist him to ventilate his feelings about the effects of Sarah's disability on his life, and to provide him with situational support to help him cope with the pending loss of Sarah, albeit temporary at this point. Before the next session and with his consent, his personal physician was contacted to determine if there were any organic bases for his behavioral changes. The physician's report was negative.

INTERVENTION

During the next two sessions, through questioning and reflection, John was helped to ventilate his feelings about his fears that Sarah might never recover beyond her present level of functioning. With situational support supplied by the therapist, he was able to begin to discuss openly the anger that he had felt toward Sarah for "threatening the security of their future" with her accident. All of the careful planning they had done for their "old age" seemed to be falling apart more each day. "It wasn't just the financial security," he said, "we have enough insurance to take care of our illnesses. Our plans were all made for the *two* of us, *together*—not for just *one* of us, *alone!*" His fears of losing her had been displaced into anger against her for being the cause of his very unpleasant feelings.

It became quite apparent during the first session that John really did not have any clear idea as to the nature of Sarah's injury. To him, a broken bone was just that, regardless of which one. It broke, therefore it should heal! He had never sat down with her orthopedic surgeon to ask questions, leaving it to her to keep him informed. He was advised to make an immediate appointment with this physician to get direct information about Sarah's expected progress rather than to continue to rely on his own uneducated conclusions.

By the next session, he reported that he had followed through, kept the appointment, and was relieved to learn that, although Sarah's progress was a bit slower than expected, the physician expected her to return to a fairly normal level of functioning. He was advised that it would take time, however, and he would be expected to help Sarah have patience. The recommendation that she enter the rehabilitation center in the next city was made in an effort to speed up her progress and was not to be construed by him as a sign that she might never recover. As John's anxiety and depression decreased, he began to view the events leading up to his crisis in a more realistic manner. He realized that his anger was a normal response to his situation with Sarah but that what he *did* with that anger was not normal. Rather than openly discussing his feelings with Sarah as he would have at any other time in their lives, he found himself "protecting" her from them, yet blaming her for all of his misery. Because he lacked any other available situational support, his anxiety and depression had increased, even further distorting his perceptions of the event.

When the suggestion was made that Sarah enter a rehabilitation center for further therapy, John's anxiety level interfered with his ability to perceive this as anything other than the beginning of a final loss of Sarah from his life. As he later described it to the therapist, "I guess this is always in the back of a person's mind once they get around my age. When you're young, you go to a hospital and the odds are good that you come home again, but when you get to be Sarah's and my age, the odds aren't so good that you come home again! And she was asking me to help her make the decision to go to that hospital—me, who was already mixed up in my feelings about having to take care of her like this the rest of my life!"

By the end of the third session, John's symptoms had lessened greatly, and he was now able to help Sarah pack and move into the rehabilitation center without any increase in anxiety. He realized now that, in overprotecting her from his true feelings, he had only created anxiety for her as well as a crisis for himself. He planned to visit her three times a week. They agreed that this would give her full time to concentrate on "being able to walk at home," and he would begin to reestablish contact with their old friends so that he would not feel so lonely while she was away.

ANTICIPATORY PLANNING

Exploration with John about his feelings concerning the possibility that Sarah might not improve beyond her current level of functioning helped prepare him for this eventuality. He was able to begin to consider alternative modes of life for the two of them. For example, he decided that they should seriously consider selling their two-story home. "After all," he said, "if it isn't her broken hip, sure enough it's going to be my arthritis in the next few years that is going to make those stairs seem like Mount Whitney!" Furthermore, John found himself faced with the realities of what he would have to be able to do for himself if Sarah ever left him forever. While she was in the rehabilitation center, he knew that he would have to begin learning how to plan a life for himself. Although she might outlive him, he recognized that this time without her was a sample for him of what life "might be for him—and only a complete idiot would not recognize that I had better learn what to do and learn pretty damned fast!"

SUMMATION OF THE PARADIGM (Figure 7-6)

Unprepared to assume his new role in caring for Sarah, John's increased anxiety distorted his perceptions of their stressful situation. When Sarah failed to make the progress that he had expected, he became frustrated and angry and saw himself as a failure in his new role. Unable to communicate these feelings appropriately, he displaced his anger on Sarah. When asked to help her decide about reentering a hospital, he felt threatened by a permanent role reversal and the eventuality of her loss. He lacked adequate coping mechanisms to deal with the increasing stresses of the situation; he became immobile and unable to make any decisions for their future.

Intervention focused on helping John ventilate his feelings and obtain a realistic perception of the event. As his anxiety and depression decreased, he became able to anticipate and plan for their future. The major focus of the last session was to help him recognize and accept that with increasing age there could be future threats to his biopsychosocial integrity and that he should learn to seek help as problems arose and not try to assume all of the responsibility himself.

ADDENDUM

Two months later, the therapist received a telephone call from John. Sarah had come home from the rehabilitation center about 2 weeks before. Her progress, unfortunately, was not what they had expected. However, according to John, she was at least able to stand in the kitchen and make the "best damned dinner I have eaten in a month" and that was "good enough for me!" They had already put their home up for sale and were looking for a large mobile home into which they could move and then travel around the country to begin living the retirement they had planned.

CASE STUDY: JOHN

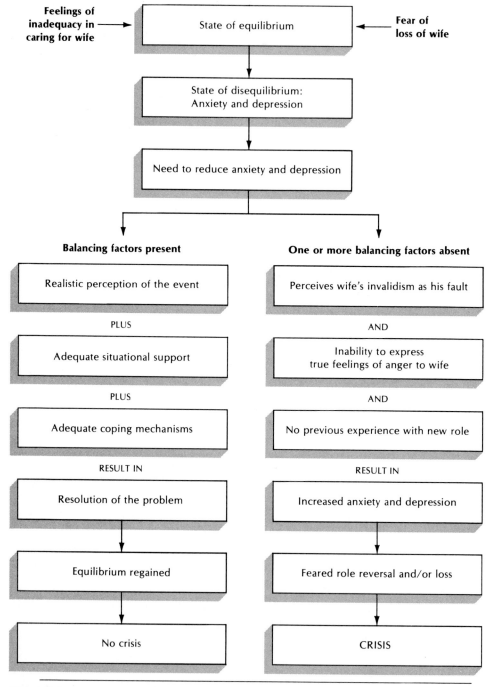

Figure 7-6

REFERENCES

Adler ES and Clark R: Adolescence: a literary passage, *Adolescence* 26:757, 1991.

Baack D: The personal impact of company policies: a social penetration theory perspective, *J Managerial Issues* 3:196, 1991.

Cameron N: *Personality development and psychopathology,* Boston, 1963, Houghton Mifflin.

Carter B, McGoldrich M: *The changing family life cycle,* ed 2, Boston, 1989, Allyn & Bacon.

Cassel RN: The child "at risk" for drug abuse rating schedule (DARS), *Psychol A J Human Behav* 28:52, 1991.

Cumming E, Henry WE: *Growing old,* New York, 1961, Basic Books.

Dunbar F, Dunbar F: A study of centenarians. Quoted in Solomon JC: *A synthesis of human behavior,* New York, 1954, Grune & Stratton.

English OS, Pearson GHJ: *Emotional problems of living,* New York, 1955, W W Norton & Co.

Erikson EH: Growth and crises of the health personality. In Senn MJE, editor: *Symposium on the healthy personality,* New York, 1950, Josiah Macy, Jr, Foundation.

Erikson EH: Identity and the life cycle. *Psychological issues,* vol 1, No 1, monograph 1, New York, 1959, International Universities Press.

Erikson EH *Childhood and society,* ed 2, 1963, WW Norton.

Erikson EH: Maturational crisis. In Stantrock JW, editor: *Life-span development,* ed 4, Dubuque, 1992, WC Brown.

Goffman E: *Asylums,* New York, 1961, Doubleday & Co.

Hahn ME: *Psychoevaluation: adaptation, distribution, adjustment,* New York, 1963, McGraw-Hill.

Homonoff EE, Maltz PF: Developing and maintaining a coordinated system of community-based services to children, *Community Ment Health J* 27:347-358, 1991.

Larsen G: Graying, *Los Angeles Times,* October 4, 1988.

Lau S: Crisis and vulnerability in adolescent development:erratum, *J Youth Adoles* 20:561, 1991.

Palmore EB: *Social factors in mental illness of the aged.* In Busse EW and Pfeiffer E, editors: *Mental illness in later life,* Washington, DC, 1973, American Psychiatric Association.

Piaget J: *The child's conception of the world,* Totowa, NJ, 1963, Littlefield, Adams & Co.

Piaget J: The life cycle. In Carter B, McGoldrick M, editors: *The changing family life cycle,* ed 2, Boston, 1989, Allyn and Bacon.

Pruett H: Stressors in middle adulthood, *Family & Community Health,* 2(4):53-60, 1980.

Reisman D: *Individualism reconsidered,* New York, 1954, Free Press.

Rose-Gold MS: Intervention strategies for counseling at-risk adolescents in rural school districts, *School Counselor* 39:122, 1991.

Slater P: Cultural attitudes toward the aged, *Geriatrics* 18:308, 1963.

Stantrock JW: *Life-span development,* ed 4, Dubuque, 1992, WC Brown.

Sullivan HS: *Conceptions of modern psychiatry,* New York, 1953, WW Norton & Co.

Swan GE, Dame A, Carmelli D: Involuntary retirement, type A behavior, and current functioning in elderly men: a 27-year follow-up of the western collaborative group study, *Psychol Aging* 6:384, 1991.

Zachry CB: *Emotion and conduct in adolescence,* New York, 1940, Appleton-Century-Crofts.

ADDITIONAL READINGS

Aguilera DC: Stressors in late adulthood, *Fam Community Health* 2(4):61, 1980.

Barry VC: Maturation, integration, and psychic reality, *Annu Psychoanal* 15:3, 1980.

Beyene Y: Cultural significance and physiological manifestations of menopause: a biocultural analysis, *Cult Med Psychiatry* 10:47, 1986.

Bishop S, Shoemaker Y: Married couples in later life: the ecologic transition of retirement. *Fam Community Health* 9:22, 1987.

Branyon D: Career and life planning: no magic answers, *J College Student Personnel* 28:187, 1987.

Brighton-Cleghorn J: Formulations of self and family systems, *Fam Process* 26:185, 1987.

Broughton JM: *Critical theories of psychological development,* New York, 1987, Plenum.

Calabrese L: Adolescence: a growth period conducive to alienation, *Adolescence* 34:226, 1987.

Clark CB: Geriatric abuse intervention team in a family practice setting, *J Tenn Med Assoc* 77:535, 1984.

Corr A, McNeil JN: *Adolescence and death,* New York, 1986, Springer.

Dawson HB and others: Regulation of growth hormone and somatomedin-C secretion in postmenopausal women: effect of physiological estrogen replacement, *J Clin Endocrinol Metab* 63:424, 1986.

Dilworth-Anderson P: Effectiveness of family support group involvement in adult day care. *Fam Relations J Appl Fam Child Studies* 36:78, 1987.

Dowrick PW: *Social survival for children: a trainer's resource book,* New York, 1986, Brunner/Mazel.

Duncan PD and others: The effects of pubertal timing on body image, school behavior and deviance. *I J Youth Adolesc* 14:227, 1985.

Dusek JB: *Adolescent development and behavior,* Englewood Cliffs, NJ, 1987, Prentice Hall.

Eisen P: Adolescence: coping strategies and vulnerabilities. Seminar on psychiatric vulnerability in adolescence, *Int J Adolesc Med Health* 2:107, 1986.

Essa M: Grief as a crisis: psychotherapeutic interventions with elderly bereaved, *Am J Psychother* 40:243, 1986.

Fajardo B: Neonatal trauma and early development, *Annu Psychoanal* 15:233, 1987.

Fogel A, Melson GF: *Origins of nurturance: developmental, biological and cultural perspectives on caregiving,* Hillsdale, NJ, 1986, Lawrence Erlbaum.

Fortenberry JD, Kaplan DW, Hill RF: Physicians' values and experience during adolescence: their effect on adolescent health care, *J Adolesc Health* Care 9:46, 1988.

Gatz M, Pearson C, Fuentes M: Older women and mental health. *Issues Men Health Nur* 5:273, 1983.

Giblin PT, Poland ML, Ager JW: Clinical applications of self-esteem and locus of control to adolescent health, *J Adolesc Health Care* 9:1, 1988.

Gindis B: Remembering the future: contemporary school psychology in the Soviet Union, *School Psychol Intl* 12:165, 1991.

Goethals GW, Klos DS: *Experiencing youth: first person accounts,* ed 2, Lanham, Md, 1986, University Press of America.

Goodson CS, Jamison PL: The relative rate of maturation and its psychological effect, *J Biosoc Sci* 19:73, 1987.

Gray RE: Adolescent response to the death of a parent, *J Youth Adolesc* 16:511, 1987.

Hansson RO, Remondet JH: Relationships and the aging family: a social psychological analysis, *Appl Soc Psych Annu* 7:262, 1987.

Hart D: The development of personal identity in adolescence: a philosophical dilemma approach, *Merrill-Palmer Q* 34:105, 1988.

Johnson BB: Sexual abuse prevention: a rural interdisciplinary effort, *Child Welfare* 66:165, 1987.

Johnson RJ and others: Stress, self-esteem and coping during bereavement among the elderly, *Soc Psych Q* 49:273, 1986.

Kastenbaum R: The search for meaning: when a long life ends. *Generations* 11:1, 1987.

Keith PM: The social contest and resources of the unmarried in old age, *Int J Aging Hum Dev* 23:81, 1986.

Kelly PC, Weir MR, Fearnow RG: Pediatricians' views: "latchkey" children, corporal punishment, *Tex Med* 83:40, 1987.

Kessler GR, Ibrahim FA, Kahn H: Character development in adolescents, *Adolescence* 21:1, 1986.

Kobak R, Rogers G, Sceery A: Attachment in late adolescence: working models, affect regulation, and representations of self and others, *Child Dev* 59:135, 1988.

Kouri MK: A life design process for older adults. *J Career Dev* 13:6, 1986.

Lerner RM, Foch TT: *Biological-psychological interactions in early adolescence,* Hillsdale, NJ, 1987, Lawrence Erlbaum Associates, Inc.

Levin RN, Johnston RE: Social mediation of puberty: an adaptive female strategy? *Behav Neural Biol* 46:308, 1986.

Lezak MD: Norms for growing older, *Dev Neuropsychol* 3:1, 1987.

Littwir S: *The postponed generation: why America's grown-up kids are growing up later,* New York, 1986, William Morrow.

Manning ML, Allen MS: Social development in early adolescence: implications for middle school educators, *Child Education* 63:172, 1987.

Marini MM: Measuring the process of role change during the transition to adulthood, *Soc Sci Res* 16:1, 1987.

Moore RC: *Childhood's domain: play and place in child development,* London, 1986, Croom Helm.

Myers LS, Morokof PJ: Physiological and subjective sexual arousal in pre- and postmenopausal women and postmenopausal women taking replacement therapy, *Psychophysiology* 23:283, 1986.

Nahemow L, McCluskey-Fawcett KA, McGhee PE: *Humor and aging,* San Diego, 1986, Academic Press.

Newcomb MD, Bentler PM: Impact of adolescent drug use and social support on problems of young adults: a longitudinal study, *J Abnorm Psychol* 97:64, 1988.

Newman RG: Consultation: Redl's influence, *Residential Treatment for Children and Youth* 8:83, 1991.

O'Neil MK, Mingle P: Life stress and depression in university students: clinical illustrations of recent research, *J Am Coll Health* 30:235, 1987.

Paisley PO: Prevention of child abuse and neglect: a legislative response, *School Counselor* 34:226, 1987.

Papalia DE, Wendkosolds S: *A child's world: infancy through adolescence,* ed 4, New York, 1987, McGraw-Hill.

Paulson RI: Addressing the public mental health personnel crisis through systemic reform and public-academic linkages, *Community Ment Health J* 27:393, 1991.

Perlman D, Rook KS: Social support, social deficits and the family: toward the enhancement of well being, *Appl Soc Psych Annu* 7:17, 1987.

Pierce RL, Trotta R: Abused parents: a hidden family problem, *J Fam Violence* 1:99, 1986.

Pietropinto A: Effect of unhappy marriages on children, *Med Asp Hum Sexual* 19:173, 1985.

Rajabally MH: Instruction in developmental psychology and its influence on self-concept, *Adolescence* 22:545, 1987.

Rice F: *The adolescent: development, relationships and culture,* ed 5, Boston, 1987, Allyn & Bacon.

Richardson V, Sands R: Death attitudes among mid-life women, *Omega J Death Dying* 17:327, 1986-87.

Rogers D: *The adult years: an introduction to aging,* ed 3, Englewood Cliffs, NJ, 1986, Prentice Hall.

Rosenkoetter MM: Is your older client ready for a role change after retirement? *J Gerontol Nurs* 11:21, 1985.

Rowland R: The childfree experience in the aging context: an investigation of the pro-natalist bias of life-span developmental literature, *Aust Psychol* 17:141, 1982.

Rybash JM, Hoyer WJ, Roodin PA: *Adult cognition and aging: developmental changes in processing knowing and thinking,* New York, 1986, Pergamon.

Saito S: The relationship between pubertal growth and sex-role formation, *Jpn J Educational Psychol* 33:336, 1985.

Sarafino EP: *The fears of childhood: a guide to recognizing and reducing fearful states in children,* New York, 1986, Human Sciences Press.

Savin-Williams RC: *Adolescence: an ethological perspective,* New York, 1987, Springer-Verlag.

Savin-Williams RC, Small SA: The timing of puberty and its relationship to adolescent and parent perceptions of family interactions, *Dev Psychol* 22:342, 1986.

Solan HA, Mozlin R: The correlations of perceptual-motor maturation to readiness and reading in kindergarten and the primary grades, *J Am Optom Assoc* 57:28, 1986.

Sorensen AB, Weinert FE, Sherrod LR: *Human development and the life course: multidisciplinary perspectives,* Hillsdale, NJ, 1986, Lawrence Erlbaum Associates.

Steinberg L: Impact of puberty on family relations: effects of pubertal status and pubertal timing, *Dev Psychol* 23:451, 1987.

Steinberg L: Reciprocal relation between parent-child distance and pubertal maturation, *Dev Psychol* 24:122, 1988.

Strain PS, Guralnick MJ, Hill MW: *Children's social behavior: development, assessment, and modification,* Orlando, 1986, Academic Press.

Sugarman S, Masheter C: The family crisis intervention literature: what is meant by crisis?, *Int J Fam Psych* 7:359, 1986.

Sullivan T and Schneider M: Development and identity issues in adolescent homosexuality, *Child Adolesc Soc Work J* 4:13, 1987.

Susman EJ and others: The relation of relative hormonal levels and physical development and social-emotional behavior in young adolescents. *J Youth Adolesc* 14:245, 1985.

Thomson B, Vaux A: The importation, transmission and moderation of stress in the family system, *Am J Community Psychol* 14:39, 1986.

Yaffe SJ: Commentary, *J Adolesc Health Care* 8:3, 1987.

Chapter 8

Acquired Immune Deficiency Syndrome (AIDS)

The late twentieth century will be remembered as the time in which acquired immune deficiency syndrome (AIDS) changed attitudes and beliefs of people around the world. We are faced with many unknowns. When will a cure be discovered? Will scientists be able to create a vaccine against it? How many men, women, and children will die from AIDS and its opportunistic infections? No infectious condition of recent times has had the psychosocial impact of this human immunodeficiency virus (HIV) disease. A near "AIDS hysteria" has developed throughout the world, as the informative as well as the sensationalistic media have bombarded the public with reports about AIDS. AIDS patients must cope not only with their own adjustment to a terminal diagnosis but also with discrimination caused by society's fear of them (Johnson, 1988).

As many as 40,000 Americans in 1992 who were defined *only* as HIV positive woke up on New Year's Day, January 1, 1993, with a diagnosis of AIDS, the consequence of a new and more inclusive official definition that is likely to place a strain on already strapped social service agencies and add to the emotional trauma of many who are infected.

The broader definition, drafted by the U.S. Centers for Disease Control and Prevention (CDC) after a year of debate, is intended to give public health officials a truer picture of the scope of the disease by adding three diseases often found in women and intravenous drug users, who have been undercounted in the past. The diseases are cervical cancer, pulmonary tuberculosis, and recurrent pneumonia. Although including these three diseases is expected to push caseload counts higher, the real boost in numbers will come from the addition of a fourth indicator: a dip in the level of the immune cells that are the main target of HIV.

"The current definition is falling out of step with the times," said Dr. John Ward, acting chief of the AIDS Surveillance Branch of the CDC. "This will help us more completely represent the HIV epidemic."

The CDC predicts that the new policy will increase the nation's roster of new AIDS patients by about 75% in 1993, with 90,000 people newly diagnosed as compared with an average of 50,000 in previous years. In some cities, authorities are estimating that the AIDS population will more than double; San Francisco officials say their AIDS caseload will jump from 3600 to 8800. (Stolberg, 1992).

Background

The U.S. Centers for Disease Control and Prevention, which monitor the AIDS epidemic, uses a so-called surveillance definition to determine when an HIV-positive person has developed full-blown AIDS. Under the current definition, a person who is infected with HIV is diagnosed as having AIDS when he or she develops one of 23 indicator illnesses. On Jan. 1, 1993, the definition was expanded to include three diseases common to HIV-infected women and intravenous drug users: cervical cancer, pulmonary tuberculosis, and recurrent pneumonia. The expanded definition also included a fourth new indicator: a drop in the level of CD4 immune cells, also called T-cells, to 200 per cubic milliliter of blood, about one fifth the level of a healthy person. More so than most other diseases, AIDS also has an emotional impact on physicians who are called on to treat their AIDS patients' social, emotional, and medical problems, many of which can be overwhelming. Physicians frequently may have feelings to resolve about caring for these patients because of their own fears of contagion, homophobia, or other negative attitudes (Johnson, 1987).

Patients with AIDS, as well as those who perceive themselves to be at risk (the "worried well"), face a range of fears and concerns about AIDS (Faulstich, 1987; Holland and Tross, 1985; Johnson, 1987; Nichols, 1985). HIV infection can have devastating effects on a person's interpersonal relationships—isolation, rejection, and overall loss of social support. Health consequences from the virus can make the basic activities of daily life difficult by causing weakness, physical debilitation, and dementia. Financial problems result from loss of job, numerous hospital and medical bills, and exhausted medical insurance. The patient may experience multiple psychological effects, including depression, anxiety, and loss of hope for the future; issues of death and dying also surface (Perry and Markowitz, 1986).

Physicians who care for these patients may feel beset by the medical, psychological, social, and other problems and may not be able to address all of these issues in a busy practice. Many communities, even smaller ones in rural areas, offer resources to which the patient can be referred for specialized AIDS-related psychosocial support. Local health departments and community mental health centers frequently can provide lists of these community services. Some health departments also provide AIDS testing. These are usually termed *alternate test sites,* and the tests and results are confidential and anonymous (AIDS Project Los Angeles, 1993).

Antibody Testing

HIV antibody testing was approved by the U.S. Food and Drug Administration in March 1985 for the screening of donated blood (CDC, 1987). Since then, the test has also been used to screen persons at risk for and those showing signs of HIV infection.

HIV antibody serological testing generally refers to a two or three test sequence. The first is an enzyme-linked immunosorbent assay (ELISA) test; if this is reactive (positive), a Western Blot test is indicated for more specificity. If this second test is also reactive, the patient should be given the Immuno-Fluorescent Acid (IFA) test. If the IFA test is positive, the individual is considered infectious and able to transmit the disease (APLA, 1993).

To protect the patient's confidentiality, some laboratories process HIV antibody tests differently from other laboratory work. Frequently, specimens submitted with the patient's name are not accepted; only those specimens labeled with a code number are accepted. To further protect the patient's identity, many laboratories do not directly bill insurance companies for the test. Many laboratories do not report test results over the telephone, even to the physician who ordered the test. Physicians should also arrange their office or hospital practice (e.g., record keeping, staff attitudes) so that patient confidentiality is maintained (Johnson, 1988).

Patient counseling, both before and after HIV antibody testing, has become the standard medical practice in many clinical situations. This can be done by the patient's individual physician, a specially trained counselor, or, before the tests, in a group setting (CDC, 1992).

All counseling involves educating the patient about HIV antibody testing. In most situations, HIV testing should be performed with informed consent, which means the patient understands that the testing is being done, the reasons for the test, and the possible implications (medical, social, and legal) of both positive and negative results. In addition, counseling should offer an environment that encourages the patient to discuss fears and feelings about AIDS. Test results should also be discussed. The clinician should assess the patient's emotional ability to handle positive or negative results and then, together with the patient, make a final decision about whether to test (Johnson, 1987).

The functions of pretest counseling are to educate the patient about AIDS and its prevention and to help the patient decide whether the test is indicated and desired.

The primary purposes of posttest counseling are to inform the patient of test results and to provide emotional support. The patient should be encouraged to express feelings about the results but not be allowed to become so depressed that he can no longer function and pose a danger to himself. Some patients require a referral to mental health professionals to help them work out their feelings (Johnson, 1987).

In working with AIDS, therapists need to understand that the concept of family has a broader meaning than is traditionally understood. We see, on one hand, the traditional family composition that is the nuclear family, the family of origin, or both. On the other hand, we see the family of choice, which is also very significant and may be included at different points in treatment. In working with the family of choice, we may find that the definition of family includes lover or life partner and close friends who may be the most significant relationships and source of support. Blending the family of choice with the family of origin is therapeutic. In doing this blending, we serve as models, showing that this is appropriate and needed (Appell and Blatt, 1992).

Role of the Therapist

In working with AIDS, the therapist's flexibility is crucial. For those of us who have had more traditional training as therapists, AIDS can challenge our thinking. In addition to working on relationship and family issues, both past and present, we need to serve as educators, crisis counselors, and referral sources. Our comfort with moving between different roles helps our clients.

Many families have no experience or prior knowledge about AIDS; we become their source of information in the beginning. We need to educate families about transmission and address their fears about risks of contagion. The families' fears are real. Validating those fears and concerns is an essential step in joining with the family and helping them understand AIDS. As we educate the family, we demystify AIDS.

Being available to the family is critical. Every time we discuss AIDS openly and nonjudgmentally, we serve as role models to the family about open communication in a subtle, powerful way. Referral to support groups, helpful books, and AIDS-related agencies is part of our job that often gives the family their first connection to information about AIDS. For our own well-being, we need to help our family find as many other forms of support as possible so that we are not the only resource for them.

We can also use our role to empower our clients and enhance their assertiveness or sense of control by allowing them to take the lead in bringing up issues that need to be addressed. Although there are times when this would not be appropriate— such as in a case of unhealthy denial that created obstacles to needed treatment— generally this attitude helps preserve the autonomy of the client, an important issue in AIDS.

BOUNDARIES OF THE THERAPIST

We need to define boundaries in a way that works both ethically and therapeutically. When we work with persons living with AIDS, we need to be open to seeing the individual in the context of the family or subgroups within the family.

Our flexibility will often be challenged. There will be times that clients will not be able to keep appointments and cancel at the last minute because of illness or medical appointments. Will you charge? Is your schedule open enough to reschedule in the same week? Are you willing to do home visits when the client becomes too ill to travel? It is a judgment call; it is important that we not do a house call out of our own anxiety, but rather out of the client's needs (Appell and Blatt, 1992).

Working with AIDS can be integrated into most theoretical frameworks. However, it is also important to focus on some of the specific issues regarding family functioning in order to meet effectively the unique needs of the AIDS affected. Some family subgroups have issues that differ from those of other family subgroups. Assessing family functioning can help us to develop appropriate treatment plans and goals.

We have yet to work with someone who has not wished for the family to be there and be supportive. We need to assess how realistic that hope is, and how likely it is that it will be fulfilled. Sometimes the disclosure of AIDS status is the first time the family has heard that the person is gay, if the person happens to be gay. Disclosure needs to be tailored to the specific dynamics of the family and the needs of the individual (Appell and Blatt, 1992).

Enmeshment

When working with families, whether we begin with an individual or a larger group, we find it useful to look at the boundaries in the family system. We need to understand what those boundaries are and how they have operated in the past as well as the present.

People from enmeshed families may have blurred boundaries. In such families, premature disclosure of the AIDS status may occur when family members are not emotionally ready to deal with it. We can assist the HIV-positive client in containing anxiety long enough to think through the process of disclosure, including each family member's emotional preparedness and the appropriate timing for disclosure. It would not be unusual for members of an enmeshed family to become too involved too quickly.

Understanding this style and makeup of the family system is vital for assessment and treatment. In over-involved or enmeshed families, unity is stressed and autonomy is discouraged. Because autonomy is so important for the person who has AIDS, family members need to resist a natural tendency to overprotect the patient. The more they protect, the more helpless the patient may feel, and the less able to mobilize strength and resources. We need to teach family members that there is a difference between helping and rescuing. Rescuing behavior starts with the view that the patient is a victim who is hopeless and helpless. If the family behaves as rescuers, we need to talk about that. Unattended, rescuing behavior has the effect of infantilizing the client (Appell and Blatt, 1992).

Disengaged Families

If in a family there are few if any emotional connections, or if the family is emotionally cut off, the family is disengaged. Often in this system, AIDS disclosure may not have taken place. If it has, and if the AIDS-infected person has historically been the identified patient in the family, this may be one more reason for family members to see him or her as the identified patient and further blame the person. Because of the shame connected with HIV, this could have a devastating effect.

Depending on the dysfunction of the family and the emotional stability of the individual, disclosure may or may not be appropriate. As therapists, we have to pay attention to our need for our clients to disclose. We may hold a bias that disclosure can be helpful, but it may not be possible. The individuals from this system are more likely to erect rigid boundaries around themselves under the stress of an AIDS diagnosis. They then might isolate themselves in unhealthy ways or may undermine, distance, or cut off relationships prematurely. If a person in this type of system wants to disclose, the therapist can help the client prepare for disclosure by assisting the client in gathering other support systems and creating a more positive image. Also, repeatedly separating the virus from personhood helps take away the moral judgment that contributes to shame. If the individual who has been through this process decides to disclose, he or she may be more emotionally able to handle the family's response. Sometimes in these situations, selective disclosure may work better: The person picks the safest member in the family to tell first. As in the enmeshed system, timing of disclosure is important (Appell and Blatt, 1992).

DENIAL WITHIN THE FAMILY

How families deal with stress and difficult news can be assessed in their level of denial. There is a difference between healthy and unhealthy denial that can be reflected in a family's difficulty in taking in the reality of the situation, struggling with their many feelings, and eventually accepting the roller coaster ride they are about to begin. Unhealthy denial needs to be confronted, in a gentle and supportive way. Families do not unlearn denial overnight. Communication is necessary for the family to overcome their denial; otherwise, it will sabotage their chances of success in supporting one another. For us as therapists, confronting denial is a walk on a tightrope at best. However, not to pay attention to it is doing all a disservice.

RELIGIOUS BACKGROUND OF THE FAMILY

The religious influences and beliefs of the individual and the family need to be taken into consideration. Sometimes the family and the individual are in conflict about these influences. Many gays have been cut off from their families of origin due to religious differences. Can these families come together and accept their differences? Not always.

Clients who are AIDS infected sometimes want to reconnect with their original faith or find a new sense of spirituality. Some may want to explore other avenues, such as listening to meditation tapes, using crystals, or participating in alternative religious or spiritual organizations. We must keep our personal biases out of their decisions and explore religion from their point of view. Our job is helping them define what is right for them and helping the family to accept the client's perspective (Stribling, 1990).

Isolation

When evaluating family systems, look for isolation. This isolation can be adaptive and part of the adjustment process of accepting and incorporating new information. For example, after an AIDS disclosure, some family members may distance or withdraw for a short time. We need to normalize this reaction so that our clients do not overreact and assume that this is a permanent state.

However, isolation and withdrawal by the family may not be adaptive. People isolate for many reasons; one may be fear of contagion. Sometimes families withdraw because they feel helpless. Often family members ask, "What do I do? What do I say?" Fearing that they'll make a mistake, they withdraw.

Family members may also withdraw from the AIDS member because they find it difficult to be close when they fear losing someone. They may see AIDS as an immediate death. A spouse or lover who also has AIDS may withdraw because of fears about facing their own mortality. Finally, family members may experience isolation and withdrawal in their own social circles because of the stigma of HIV.

This adds much stress at a time when support is especially important. In all of these cases, we as therapists must educate, support, normalize, and validate feeling and fears. It is important to identify isolation and intervene when we see it. It is also important for us to encourage open communication among family members to increase intimacy and decrease isolation (Appell and Blatt, 1992).

Grief

Grief is ongoing in working with AIDS. It is a constant adjustment process. The losses are both real and symbolic. In addition to the many losses that the individual suffers, the family experiences loss as well. Parents may be faced with losing a child. Spouses and lovers face the potential loss of a life partner. These losses are tremendous, particularly because HIV so often infects people who are quite young. So these threatened losses also challenge the hopes and future dreams of the individual and the family. Physical limitation caused by AIDS can also limit the activities the family has shared in the past. The person with AIDS and family members may also have lost other loved ones to AIDS, which decreases their support system and compounds their loss.

We can help people grieve by assisting them in expressing their feelings and by normalizing their feelings. People often do not know how to grieve or what is normal. People often feel angry during grief; without knowing that this is normal, they may experience much guilt.

We can help them talk about their feelings individually and together, as well as express regrets and remembered joys when appropriate. Not only does this help the ongoing grief process but also in the event death occurs the grief will be much less conflicted. Guilt over things unsaid make the grief process more difficult. However, talking about loss as it occurs and death before it happens is important and healthy.

We must not forget our own grief. As we work with people with HIV, we care, we get attached, and we also have to let go. It is important for us as caregivers to give ourselves permission to grieve and get support (Appell and Blatt, 1992).

Death

We live in a death-phobic society. The person who may be dying does the family the favor of not discussing it. The partners, in an attempt not to upset the person with AIDS, do not talk about it either. Often both parties want to talk about their feeling regarding death but are afraid. One of the most important things we can do is to help people have a peaceful closure in life. If people are not able to acknowledge or discuss death, it is very difficult to say good-bye when the time comes. If we successfully facilitate these discussions, people have the opportunity to stay connected and to say a healthy good-bye. The value of this cannot be overestimated.

Psychiatric treatment must include psychological, biological, and social approaches. The psychological sequelae of AIDS affect all individuals at known risk, such as homosexual men with generalized lymphadenopathy, as well as those already diagnosed with AIDS. In the AIDS patient, the impersonal aspects of the disease may be cruel and devastating. Malaise, fatigue, severe infectious processes, and loss of control over excretory functions promote profound depression. This complements the intrapsychic effects of AIDS, which promote depression and anxiety, and the cognitive dysfunction, which occurs as delirious states resulting from febrile illness, meningitis, and the toxic side effects of various chemotherapeutic agents (Wise, 1986).

AIDS in The United States

AIDS is *not* a disease of homosexuals or intravenous drug users (IDUs) alone; it threatens millions of sexually active individuals regardless of age, gender, race, or place of residence. The disease is insidious. Transmitted during sex or through the exchange of blood (sharing needles, for example), it invades the genetic core of specific cells in the immune system. Because it directly attacks the immune system, AIDS is both daunting and deadly. Although the epidemic has spread worldwide, AIDS is an especially acute problem for all—a social and medical crisis and, according to some of the best scientific minds in the nation, a national catastrophe in the making (Conant, 1993).

The official projections for the next 10 years of the epidemic—179,000 deaths and 270,000 cumulative cases of AIDS—have been widely publicized. By the year 2000, an estimated 10 million Americans may be carrying the AIDS virus. What is less well known, but vitally important, is that these projections are almost certainly low. They do not include any estimates of AIDS-related complex (ARC), a disease syndrome that is sometimes fatal in itself and almost invariably a precursor of AIDS; by most estimates, there are 10 times as many cases of ARC as there are cases of AIDS. Most experts in the field believe that the government's estimates of AIDS are skewed by pervasive underreporting (Conant, 1993); the real total of AIDS cases will be as much as 75% higher than the official figures. Another reason the 10-year projections may be low is that they are based on estimates of the *current* extent of the epidemic. The projections assume, perhaps unrealistically, that only those individuals who are already infected will develop AIDS by the year 2000 (APLA, 1993).

Who will have AIDS 10 years from now? More than 90% of the victims will be members of the two main risk groups, male homosexuals and intravenous drug users. However, the nation's heterosexual, drug-free majority cannot be reassured by that fact because AIDS can be transmitted through conventional sex. Heterosexual transmission is believed to have accounted for 1100 of the AIDS cases in 1986. By the year 2000, that total will probably have risen to about 7000 cases, or 9% of the epidemic caseload. Tragically, there will also be a total of 3000 infants born with AIDS. Babies infected with the disease at or before birth will lead short and painful lives (Frierson and Lippmann, 1987).

Many Americans have shrugged off the AIDS epidemic because it is primarily identified with homosexuals and drug addicts, an attitude that is now changing. Another reason for the nation's generally complacent attitude may be the belief that science will quickly find a cure. That belief may not be warranted. Despite the optimism of many researchers and despite gains against the disease, AIDS is one of the most difficult challenges ever faced by modern medicine.

Apparently, many Americans remain confused about two key aspects of the disease. One is the relationship between infection with the AIDS virus and the onset of AIDS symptoms. For many reasons, not the least of which are human decency and compassion, many of those who are infected with the virus are told that they have a 1 in 10 to a 1 in 3 chance of contracting AIDS. The odds may be much worse; experts now believe that half of all those infected will eventually develop and die of AIDS, and the actual percentage may be even higher (CDC, 1992b). The second crucial issue is transmissibility. AIDS is not easily transmitted from one person to another, but it is transmitted through unprotected sexual contact, the sharing of needles, and the transfusion of infected blood. Every person who has the virus is capable of giving AIDS to someone else (Conant, 1993).

The present concern is that AIDS is on the verge of breaking out into the population at large. The source of the contagion probably will be intravenous drug users, a submerged and secretive subpopulation totaling about 1.5 million people nationwide. Intravenous drug users, most of whom are heroin addicts, are least likely to learn about controlling the spread of AIDS. Most addicts are young men with limited education, a history of criminal behavior, and only tenuous ties to the community or their families. In New York, which has the greatest concentration of heroin addicts in the nation, 60% of those addicts are believed to be infected with the AIDS virus. Assuming that most addicts are heterosexual, the next risk group will be their girlfriends and wives; the infection rate among women is rising and will pass the rate of men by the year 2000 (Conant, 1993).

Those fighting against AIDS face two enemies: the epidemic itself and fear. AIDS poses profound questions to American society, and it definitely tests the nation's reserves of compassion and common sense. It has already forced millions of people to reconsider their sexual behavior and has brought the sexual revolution of the 1960s and 1970s to an abrupt halt. AIDS is raising a host of difficult legal issues about discrimination, and it may yet cause an upheaval in national politics.

The struggle against AIDS is evident daily within the nation's homosexual minority. With the disease toll mounting rapidly, homosexuals in New York, Los Angeles, San Francisco, and other cities have rallied to fight the epidemic. They have reduced their high-risk behavior—promiscuous anal sex—to a remarkable degree, and they are providing important support for AIDS victims and the worried well. At the same time, the pall of death is omnipresent, and many homosexuals are suffering from bereavement overload (Morganthau, 1986). Canada is far ahead of the United States in recognizing gay rights. In recent years and months, Canadian progress on homosexual rights has proceeded at such a clip that some gay activists, as well as legal scholars, say the foundations are being laid for a wholly new definition of "the family" under Canadian law, one in which men may legally marry men and women marry women, one in which same-sex couples may adopt children, receive spousal pension benefits, and generally be treated the same in all respects as traditional heterosexual couples.

"Canada is just light-years ahead of [gay-rights legal activities] in the United States," said David Pepper, an assistant to Svend Robinson, Canada's only openly gay member of Parliament. Consider the following:

• Seven of Canada's 12 provinces and territories have explicitly prohibited sexual orientation as grounds for discrimination, a high percentage compared with the 7 of the 50 U.S. states that have done so.

• At a national level, Justice Minister Kim Campbell said recently that she would introduce a bill amending the Canadian Human Rights Act to proscribe discrimination against gays and lesbians. (The act had already effectively been amended by a federal court ruling.) There is no comparable proscription at the federal level in the United States, although U.S. gay activists hope that President Clinton's election heralds a long-awaited amendment of the Civil Rights Act of 1964.

• A 1990 court ruling has apparently made Canada the first country in the world to offer gays and lesbians antidiscrimination protection under a national constitution.

• In October, the Canadian military lifted its ban on homosexual bias in the armed forces and provided sensitivity training sessions similar to those now given recruits on the sexual harassment of women.

By ending its ban on homosexuals in the military, Canada has come into step with the vast majority of armies in the Western world. It has also heightened the pressure on President Clinton to make good on his campaign promise to end the Pentagon's ban on gays and lesbians in uniform (Walsh, 1992).

Homosexuals fear backlash as well. They are clinging to their gains in civil rights against an anticipated wave of prejudice, scapegoating, and stigmatization. Acutely conscious of the limits of the heterosexual majority's tolerance in the best of times, they are well aware that AIDS has reinforced their pariah status. However, the homosexual community's offensive against discrimination is going well: 33 states now include AIDS victims under laws protecting the handicapped, and others are moving in that direction. Legal experts foresee an explosion of AIDS-related lawsuits in the next 5 years (Aguilera, 1993).

AIDS undoubtedly will become politicized; in many respects, it is the ultimate social issue, and the potential for demagogy is vast. In California, followers of the extremist Lyndon La Rouche forced an AIDS issue onto the ballot as Proposition 64, a referendum item that could have forced state public health officials to quarantine some AIDS patients. The referendum failed by better than 2 to 1, a margin that left AIDS activists cheering. However, the battle is not over. On November 8, 1988, Californians voted on two propositions whose passage may have negated the progress made against AIDS discrimination. Proposition 96, which passed, read:

> Requires courts in criminal and juvenile cases, upon finding of probable cause to believe bodily fluids were possibly transferred, to order persons charged with certain sex offenses, or certain assaults on peace officers, firefighters, or emergency medical personnel to provide specimens of blood for testing for AIDS. . . .

Proposition 102, which was defeated, would have required the medical community to report patients and blood donors believed to have been infected or tested positive for the AIDS virus to local health authorities.

Proposition 96 could cripple the efforts of physicians, researchers, and public health officials to halt the spread of AIDS. It would only make the epidemic worse (Conant, 1993). Raising the level of public concern is essential, but it must be done without touching off hysteria.

THE AMERICANS WITH DISABILITIES ACT OF 1990

The Americans with Disabilities Act (ADA) addresses the concern that society has been inclined to segregate individuals with disabilities. The ADA is a mandate to eliminate discrimination against those with physical and mental disabilities in *all* aspects of their lives. An employer, program, or health care provider must evaluate each person's ability to perform a given task and make *reasonable* accommodations that would allow the disabled person to perform.

Most health care institutions have had disability nondiscrimination. Nondiscrimination obligation can be found in Section 504 of the Vocational Rehabilitation Act passed in 1973. The ADA is modeled after Section 504 and, for the most part, the difference between Section 504 and the ADA is a change in terminology from "otherwise qualified handicapped individual" to "otherwise qualified individual with a disability."

Every court case deciding on the HIV-AIDS discrimination issue has found that individuals with AIDS are protected as handicapped under Section 504. Section 504 and the ADA protect not only people with actual impairments but also those with a past history of an impairment and those perceived by others as being impaired, despite the fact that the individual has no past or present impairment at all (Palma, 1992). To demonstrate the extent of coverage in Section 504, Palma cites a recent AIDS discrimination case against Beth Israel Hospital. A resident teaching physician of a hospital refused to perform surgery on an HIV-infected patient. The court held that because the hospital received Medicare and Medicaid funds for services rendered, the hospital was liable under Section 504. However, the court dismissed the claim against the physician because he could not receive federal funds as a resident teaching physician. The ADA will eliminate such exclusions (Stine, 1993).

The ADA is the most sweeping piece of civil rights legislation since 1964. The goal is to remove barriers to employment, shopping, travel, and entertainment for the nation's 43 million disabled people.

The guidelines cover more than 5 million public facilities. Companies have begun making changes to their premises. They must do so as long as the changes can be done without excessive expense. The act is estimated to cost business as much as $2 billion.

Here are the highlights of its first phase, which began on January 26, 1992.
- Public accommodations may not discriminate on the basis of disability.
- Physical barriers in existing facilities must be removed if possible. If not, other methods of providing services must be offered. Alterations to existing facilities must be accessible.
- Public transit systems must provide comparable paratransit, such as vans, to people who cannot use a fixed-route bus service. New buses and rail vehicles must be accessible.

THE ADA ACCESS TIME LINE

- January 26, 1992: Organizations must take steps to assure that people with disabilities have access to existing public areas so long as such accommodations would not pose an unreasonable hardship. New buildings and renovations undertaken after this date must meet more stringent guidelines.

- July 26, 1992: Employers with 25 or more people on the payroll must make sure that persons with disabilities are not discriminated against in any employment practice. This rule takes effect July 26, 1994, for companies with 15 or more employees; those with fewer than 15 are exempt.
- July 26, 1993: Requires that states provide unrestricted telephone service for individuals who use telecommunications devices for the deaf.
- July 26, 1995: Providers of commuter rail transportation must have at least one passenger car per train readily accessible to individuals with disabilities.

The ADA will eventually apply to all employers with 15 or more employees. It will impact nearly every local government. For large cities, the impact began in January 1992; for smaller towns, 1994. ADA will underscore the rights of the AIDS worker by utilizing the same criteria for coverage that is currently used in Section 504 of the 1973 Vocational Rehabilitation Act, but ADA goes beyond existing legislation and strengthens the rights of AIDS-infected employees in several ways. First, it is the specific intent of Congress to include HIV and AIDS as a handicap covered by ADA. Second, the legislation provides concrete examples of reasonable accommodation. Third, with the exception of drug testing, ADA will also prohibit employers from using preemployment medical examinations as a screening device. Employers will still be able to impose job-related physical examinations, but only after they have extended job offers to applicants. Moreover, AIDS-infected people will benefit from the heightened stature of ADA in that its implementation and monitoring will now fall under the auspices of the Equal Employment Opportunity Commission (Stine, 1993).

The expanding AIDS epidemic poses gargantuan challenges for one American institution in particular, the nation's health care system. Even the most conservative estimate of the 5-year outlook for active AIDS cases proves the need for changes in the delivery, financing, and character of health care provided to the epidemic's victims. Virtually every big city hospital in America will be treating AIDS cases by 2000, and major cities, such as New York, will be compelled to restructure their existing hospital systems to meet the rising need. At this point, real planning for the crisis that lies ahead has barely begun (Hager, 1986).

AIDS is already taking a disproportionate toll among the estimated 35 million Americans who have no medical insurance. Given the enormous expense of treating AIDS patients in the terminal phase of the disease, this gap poses three unsettling possibilities: (1) an explosive increase in billings to Medicaid, the federal safety net for the medically indigent; (2) a budget crisis for the most severely affected tax-supported big city hospitals; and (3) a drastic reduction in the level of care for most, if not all, AIDS patients (Cohen, 1986).

Health care planners foresee much wider use of alternative-care facilities by AIDS patients—hospices, nursing homes, and in-home care by visiting nurses. Hospital care would be reserved for AIDS patients in acute medical crises; the epidemic's other victims would receive less intensive care. Alternative care does have its flaws. Few cities have yet established the elaborate outpatient system that will be necessary; doing so will take time, money, and effort. Nursing homes offering custodial care for the elderly are no place for young AIDS patients with

Kaposi's sarcoma, and the visiting nurse programs in many cities are not equipped for the immense needs of a patient dying of AIDS-related toxoplasmosis. Many AIDS patients require 24-hour care by skilled professionals no matter where they are housed; severe nervous system impairment and dementia are commonplace when the AIDS virus invades the brain (Reese, 1986).

AIDS may well become the dominant social and political issue of the next decade, but it is first and foremost a crisis in public health, an epidemic that may be out of control. AIDS differs from other epidemic diseases in two important respects. First, as far as we know, it is fatal in every case; it may remain dormant in the body from 5 to 15 years. Second, it utterly disables the human immune system, which has always been the base of medical and public health strategies. If science cannot solve this puzzle or cannot solve it fast enough, the death toll will be enormous. Thousands have already died and thousands more will probably follow: very soon, millions of Americans will know someone who has succumbed to the disease. Without a medical miracle, tough decisions and a full measure of compassion are needed to fight this disease (Ernsberger, 1986).

Heterosexual AIDS Transmission

The proportion of HIV infection and AIDS cases among the heterosexual population in the United States is now increasing at a greater rate than the proportion of HIV infections and AIDS cases among homosexuals or intravenous drug users (IDUs) (Friedland, 1987). In 1985, fewer than 2% of AIDS cases were from the heterosexual population; by 1989, 5% were from the heterosexual population. In 1991, 7% of AIDS cases were heterosexually transmitted; that is, AIDS was transmitted during heterosexual sexual activities.

In contrast to these findings, studies in Africa, Haiti, and other Caribbean and Third World countries indicate that AIDS transmission is most prevalent among the heterosexual population. The male-to-female ratio in Africa is 1:1. In late 1991, the World Health Organization stated that 75% of worldwide AIDS transmission occurred heterosexually. By the year 2000, up to 90% will occur heterosexually. Homosexuality and injection drug use occur in Africa, but the incidence is reported to be very low. The high frequency of AIDS cases in Third World countries is thought to be due to poor hygiene, lack of medicine and medical facilities, a population that demonstrates a large variety of sexually transmitted diseases (STDs) and other chronic infections, unsanitary disposal of contaminated materials, lack of refrigeration and the reuse of hypodermic syringes and needles because of supply shortages.

Transmission from men to women in Nairobi has been shown to be facilitated by common genital ulcers, the use of oral contraceptives rather than condoms, and the presence of *Chlamydia*, which probably increases the inflammatory response in the vaginal walls and increases the likelihood of having lymphocytes there that can attach to the virus and allow transmission. The damage that sexually transmitted ulcerative diseases cause to genital skin and mucous membranes may facilitate AIDS transmission. If coexisting sexually transmitted infections increase the transmission rate of AIDS, then populations with high rates of these infections are at higher risk for AIDS. Prevention and early treatment of STDs could slow AIDS transmission in the United States and in other countries.

Vaginal and anal intercourse. Among the routes of AIDS transmission, there is overwhelming evidence that AIDS can be transmitted via anal and vaginal intercourse. In vaginal intercourse, male-to-female transmission is much more efficient than the reverse. This is believed to be due to (1) a consistently higher concentration of AIDS in semen than in vaginal secretions; and (2) abrasions in the vaginal mucosa. Such abrasions in the tissue allow HIV to enter the vascular system in larger numbers than would occur otherwise, and perhaps at a single entry point.

The same reasoning explains why the receptive rather than the insertive homosexual partner is more likely to become HIV-infected during anal intercourse. It appears that the membranous linings of the rectum are more easily torn than are those of the vagina. In addition, recent studies indicate the presence of receptors for HIV in rectal mucosal tissue.

It appears that of all sexual activities, *anal intercourse* is the most efficient way to transmit AIDS (De Vincenzi and others, 1989). Information collected from cross-sectional and longitudinal (cohort) studies has clearly implicated receptive anal intercourse as the major mode of acquiring AIDS. The proportion of new AIDS infections among gay males attributable to this single sexual practice is about 90%.

Major risk factors identified with regard to AIDS transmission among gay males include anal intercourse (both receptive and insertive), active oral-anal contact, number of partners, and length of homosexual life-style (Kingsley and others, 1990).

Teenage Perception about AIDS

A recent survey run by *People* magazine indicated that 96% of high school students and 99% of college students knew that HIV is spreading through the heterosexual population; but the majority of these students stated that they continued to practice unsafe sex. Combined data from surveys performed in 1988 and 1989 indicate that among sexually active teenagers, only 25% used condoms. Peter Jennings stated in a February 1991 "AIDS Update" television program that 26% of American teenagers practice anal intercourse. Data such as these have prompted a number of medical and research people to express concern for the next generation. If AIDS becomes widespread among today's teenagers, there is a real danger of losing tomorrow's adults. Available data suggest that teenagers have not appreciably changed their sexual behaviors in response to HIV and AIDS information presented in their schools or from other sources (Stine, 1993).

Teenagers at high risk include some 200,000 who become prostitutes each year and others who become IDUs. About 1% of high school seniors have used heroin, and many from junior high on up have tried cocaine (Stine, 1993). A large number of children from age 10 consume alcohol. Is it possible that too much hope is being placed on education to prevent the spread of AIDS? Through the end of June 1992, teenagers made up about 0.5% of 225,000 AIDS cases, or about 1125 cases. Teenagers must be convinced that they are vulnerable to AIDS infection and death. Until then, it only happens to someone else. Jonathan Mann, past director of the

World Health Organization, estimates there are between 1 and 2 million AIDS-infected teenagers worldwide.

Teenagers, like adults, must be convinced of their risk of infection but not with scare tactics. Behavior modification as a result of a scare is short-lived. However the information is given, it must be internalized if it is to be of long term benefit (Stine, 1993).

Common Questions About AIDS

AIDS is a frightening disease, but it is hard to catch and can be avoided. The following questions and answers will provide a working knowledge of the disease and how individuals can protect themselves, their families, and their friends from AIDS (APLA, 1993).

Are These Symptoms Familiar?

For some people, the following are symptoms of AIDS:
- Dizziness
- Night sweats
- Extreme fatigue
- Chronic coughing
- Unusual bruising
- Coated mouth
- Swollen glands
- Shortness of breath
- Chronic diarrhea
- Headaches
- Unusual bleeding
- Unusual weight loss
- Purplish growths on the skin

Anyone who has had any of these symptoms for more than a month and who has had sexual relations in the last 8 years with anybody whose sexual, drug, and medical histories were unknown to them or who shared a needle when using intravenous drugs should see a doctor.

What is AIDS?

AIDS is the acronym for acquired immune deficiency syndrome, which results from a viral infection and most often causes death. The AIDS virus does its damage by breaking down the body's shield against disease, its *immune system.* Because they have lost this natural shield against disease, people with AIDS contract diseases that usually do not seriously harm those with intact immune systems. These diseases are called *opportunistic diseases.* Some of the opportunistic diseases occurring most often in people with AIDS are
- Kaposi's sarcoma (KS), a type of skin cancer
- *Pneumocystis carinii* (PC), an organism that causes a kind of pneumonia
- Toxoplasmosis, a disease caused by a parasite that infects the brain and the central nervous system and can cause pneumonia
- Cryptosporidiosis, caused by an intestinal parasite that causes extreme diarrhea

- Candidiasis, caused by a fungus that coats the intestinal tract and is seen most often in the throat as hard, white patches of growth
- Cytomegalovirus (CMV), a virus of the digestive tract
- Herpes simplex, a virus causing the ulceration of mucous membranes as well as of the digestive and circulatory systems
- Lymphoma, a cancer that, in AIDS, affects the brain
- Cryptococcal meningitis

WHAT CAUSES AIDS?

The AIDS virus is a newly discovered type of virus called a *retrovirus*. Retroviruses are difficult for scientists to understand because they continually develop new structures. The ability of retroviruses to change structure complicates the development of medical treatment for AIDS and frustrates the search for a vaccine to prevent it. It is not yet known whether the HIV virus is the direct cause of AIDS or if its ability to produce an AIDS infection results from a damaged immune system. One or both of these possibilities may be true.

Scientists do not know why most of the people exposed to the AIDS virus have not yet developed symptoms. In fact, scientists believe that most of those exposed may never develop symptoms. However, scientists think that those who have no symptoms (are asymptomatic) may carry the virus for many years following their exposure to it. Some people who are exposed to the AIDS virus but do not develop full-blown cases of AIDS may develop a less life-threatening condition called *AIDS-related complex (ARC)*.

How is AIDS Spread?

The AIDS virus does not survive easily outside the human body, and it is not transmitted through air, food, or water. People can contract the virus only by having certain bodily fluids (blood and semen) that are contaminated with the virus come into contact with their own bloodstreams. Infection most commonly occurs by

- Having sexual intercourse with a person who carries the AIDS virus (this includes anal intercourse, oral-anal contact, and oral-genital contact)
- Sharing hypodermic needles and syringes with people who carry the AIDS virus
- Receiving transfusions of blood or blood products donated by someone who carries the AIDS virus
- Being born to a woman who contracted the AIDS virus before or during pregnancy
- Contaminating open wounds or sores with HIV-infected bodily fluids
- Receiving organs from an HIV-infected donor

WHO GETS AIDS?

The populations that are at risk for AIDS currently vary from country to country and, in some cases, from city to city. In some parts of the world, AIDS is largely a STD that is spreading throughout heterosexual populations. In the United States, AIDS has not yet established itself as a major threat to the heterosexual population. Currently only 7% of the AIDS cases in the United States can be traced to heterosexual intercourse, but this percentage is likely to increase in the next 10 years if the spread of the disease remains unchecked.

In the United States, the population most at risk for AIDS includes homosexual and bisexual men who have more than one sex partner and who engage in sexual activities that result in the exchange of bodily fluids. This population accounts for 64% of the nation's cases.

The second-largest group of people at risk for AIDS in the United States consists of intravenous drug users who become infected by sharing hypodermic needles. These men and women account for 23% of the AIDS population. The remaining AIDS cases in the United States break down as follows: (1) 2% have been caused by the transfusion of HIV-infected blood or the transplantation of HIV-infected organs and (2) 3% include children born with AIDS and patients with AIDS who die before their complete medical histories can be taken (APLA, 1993).

What are the Symptoms of AIDS?

Symptoms of the opportunistic diseases associated with AIDS may include
- Swelling or hardening of the glands located in the throat, groin, or armpit
- The appearance of hard, discolored, or purplish growths on the skin or inside the mouth
- The appearance of a thick, whitish coating on the tongue or mouth, called *thrush* which may also be accompanied by a sore throat
- Increasing shortness of breath
- Periods of continued deep, dry coughing that are not the result of other illnesses or smoking
- Periods of extreme and unexplainable fatigue that may be accompanied by headaches, light-headedness, or dizziness
- Recurring fevers or night sweats
- Rapid loss of more than 10 pounds of weight that is not the result of increased physical exercise or dieting
- Bruising more easily than normal
- Unexplained bleeding from growths on the skin, from mucous membranes, or from any opening in the body
- Repeated occurrences of diarrhea

Whether or not such symptoms prove to be AIDS related, a doctor should be consulted if any of these symptoms occur.

HOW IS AIDS DIAGNOSED?

Diagnosis is based on factors that include the state of a person's immune system, the presence of AIDS antibodies, and the presence of opportunistic infections and diseases associated with AIDS.

How Can People Avoid Getting AIDS?

To avoid getting AIDS, take the following precautions:
- Abstinence
- When having sex, follow "safe sex" guidelines.
—Know your partner's health status and whether he or she has other sex partners.

—Do not exchange blood and semen.

—Limit your number of sex partners (preferably to one person who also has no other sex partners).

—Use latex condoms.

• Never share needles when using intravenous drugs. (Boiling does not guarantee sterility.)

• Do not share toothbrushes, razors, or other personal items that could be contaminated with blood.

• Maintain a strong immune system.

—Eat well.

—Get enough rest and exercise.

—Avoid recreational use of illicit drugs.

—Avoid heavy use of alcohol and tobacco.

—Have regular medical checkups.

People with AIDS, people who are at risk for AIDS, and people who carry the AIDS virus must not donate blood, plasma, sperm, body organs, or other tissues.

How Do Women Get AIDS?

Like men, women can get AIDS by sharing needles with intravenous drug users or by having sexual intercourse that involves the exchange of bodily fluids with a person who has AIDS or who is infected with the AIDS virus. A few women have developed AIDS following transfusions of contaminated blood.

Any pregnant woman who knows or thinks she may carry the AIDS virus should immediately consult a health care provider who is knowledgeable about AIDS. It is also important to do so if her partner has AIDS, if she or her partner is an intravenous drug user, or if either is having other sexual relationships. Because the AIDS virus may spread from her to the fetus during pregnancy and because AIDS is fatal to children born with the disease, a pregnant woman who tests positive for the AIDS virus may want to consider terminating her pregnancy.

Should Mothers Exposed to the AIDS Virus Breastfeed Their Infants?

No. Breastfeeding may spread AIDS from the mother to her child.

Is There a Test to Determine if a Person Has Been Exposed to AIDS?

Blood tests that determine whether or not a person has been exposed to the AIDS virus are available through private physicians, hospital clinics, and blood banks, as well as most local, state, and federal health departments. The tests are designed to detect antibodies to the AIDS virus. The presence of AIDS antibodies in a person's blood means that he or she has been exposed to the AIDS virus; it does not mean that the person has or will have AIDS. Although they are highly accurate, AIDS antibody tests are not reliable in detecting infections that have been present for less than 4 months.

Who Should be Tested for Antibodies to AIDS?

There are several things to consider before deciding to be tested for antibodies to AIDS. For example,

- Testing positive for AIDS antibodies does not mean that a person has or will develop AIDS.
- Test results cannot distinguish persons who have developed an immunity to AIDS from those who have not.
- Positive test results, if leaked to an employer or insurance company, can lead to serious and prejudicial consequences.
- Because there is no medical treatment for a positive result, testing might lead to overwhelming anxiety and psychological distress.
- Use of birth control pills, alcoholism, and other factors may cause false-positive results.

However, confidential testing may be appropriate for people at risk for AIDS and/or for their partners who:

- Are considering parenthood
- Are considering enlistment in the armed forces
- Have been exclusively monogamous for a number of years and wish to disregard safer sex guidelines

Is There a Risk of Getting AIDS Through a Blood Transfusion?

Since May 1985, all blood donations have been screened for antibodies to AIDS. Blood that tests positive for AIDS antibodies is not used for transfusions. However, because it takes time for the body to develop antibodies, there is a very small chance that a newly infected blood donor may not have developed AIDS antibodies between the time of exposure to the virus and the donation of blood. Nevertheless, when a blood transfusion is deemed essential, the benefits outweigh the small risk of contracting AIDS.

Is There a Chance of Getting AIDS by Donating Blood?

No. Blood banks and other blood collection centers use sterile, disposable needles and syringes that are used only once.

How is AIDS Treated?

Currently, there is no cure for AIDS and no vaccine to prevent it. Therapies are available to treat each of the many opportunistic diseases affecting patients with AIDS; success of these therapies varies from one patient to another.

It is possible to ease the burdens of this frightening, tragic, and often lengthy illness. Many people with AIDS, their families, friends, neighbors, and health care workers have made major strides by coming to terms with the feelings of fear, helplessness, and inadequacy that surround AIDS. Learning to cope with the overwhelming personal catastrophe of AIDS has also led to the recognition that there are other nonmedical elements that are essential in the treatment of AIDS victims.

People with AIDS require not only the most advanced medicines and chemical therapies but also psychologically positive environments. The latest medical research indicates a direct relationship between a person's psychological outlook and the function of his or her immune system. The ingredients for maintaining the healthy outlook of a person with AIDS are those of any normal and healthy life. They include

- Companionship
- Access to a job
- Access to social, educational, and recreational facilities
- Access to a place of worship in the community

Members of the community need to realize that no one has contracted AIDS in any way other than those listed previously.

Is It Possible to Get AIDS through Casual Contact with AIDS Patients?

No. It is not possible to get AIDS by visiting, socializing, or working with someone who has the disease. It is not possible to get AIDS by being sneezed on, coughed at, or breathed on by anyone who has it. It is also not possible to get AIDS by touching or sharing anything that a person with AIDS has touched, for instance, doorknobs, bed linens, clothing, towels, toilets, telephones, showers, swimming pools, eating utensils, or drinking glasses. None of these items has been found to carry AIDS. It is not possible to get AIDS by crying with, sweating with, or hugging people with AIDS.

WHAT DOES THE FUTURE HOLD?

The National Institutes for Health and the CDC report that millions of Americans have already been exposed to the AIDS virus. They project that in the next several years the number of people in the United States with AIDS will rise from the current estimate of tens of thousands to hundreds of thousands. In some parts of the world, the projections are even higher (APLA, 1993).

There are no vaccines or treatments on the horizon that will prevent or permanently cure AIDS, ARC, or any of the many opportunistic infections associated with these diseases. The U.S. government has targeted AIDS as its number one public health priority and has established funding for research programs designed to develop vaccines and cures. Research scientists cannot project when vaccines or cures will be developed.

What Can Be Done?

People must be helped to understand the nature of AIDS in order to avoid contracting it. AIDS poses a particular danger to

- Young people, who do not always consider the consequences of their sexual decisions
- The uninformed, who do not understand AIDS or how it is transmitted
- The misinformed, who are led to believe they cannot get AIDS because they do not belong to one of the dominant risk groups or who believe the myth, for example, that AIDS is God's punishment for a select group of "sinners"
- The secretive, who believe they must hide their sexual preferences from the people with whom they live and work and who are more likely to have sexual relations with a variety of anonymous partners whose medical histories and circumstances are unknown to them

What Can I Do?

The first thing is abstinence. The second thing you can do is practice safer sex. Know your partner's health status and whether he or she has other sex partners.

Limit the number of your sexual partners, and always use condoms. A wide range of lubricants commonly used in conjunction with condoms—including Wesson Oil, Nivea hand cream, Vaseline Intensive Care Lotion, and baby oil—can cause condoms to break within 60 seconds. Safe lubricants include water-based preparations such as KY jelly and generic contraceptive gels that contain the spermicide nonoxynol-9 (Parachini, 1989).

Help prevent families, friends, and neighbors from contracting AIDS by making sure that they are informed about the disease and the way in which it is spread. For friends, neighbors, or family members who already have AIDS, do everything possible to make the rest of their lives dignified and rewarding (APLA, 1993).

The following case study is of a 32-year-old heterosexual woman. Judy is married, and she and her husband, Grant, have a 4-year-old daughter, Candice. Judy came to a crisis center after a referral call from the AIDS hot line and was assigned to the author.

Case Study   *AIDS (Heterosexual)*

ASSESSMENT OF THE INDIVIDUAL AND THE PROBLEM

After reading Judy's chart, in which she had written, "I have AIDS and I don't know what to do! Please help me!" the therapist went to the reception area, introduced herself, and shook hands with Judy. They walked the office, and the therapist asked Judy to sit down and said, "Judy, I read your chart. I know you have AIDS. I'm so sorry, I'll do everything I possibly can to help you. Please tell me anything you want to."

Judy started to cry and was handed tissues by the therapist, who said, "Go ahead and cry. I know I would." Judy was slim, attractive, and very well dressed. She stopped crying, smiled wanly, and said, "That's the first time I've cried since I found out I had AIDS." The therapist asked, "Would you like to tell me how you got AIDS?"

Judy said, "I've got to talk to someone or I'll lose my mind." The therapist nodded for her to continue. She took a deep breath and said, "First, I want you to know that my getting AIDS is a 'fluke,' something that should *never* have happened, but it did. Eight months ago I had a tubal pregnancy and had to have surgery. I bled out for some unknown reason, and I was given seven blood transfusions. After I was able to go home, I felt tired all the time. I just couldn't seem to get my strength back. I had no problems after Candy was born. I bounced right back. Then about 3 months ago, I began to get severe headaches and night sweats. I just thought I had the flu. I noticed that I began to bruise easily. I've always been very healthy, I've never had headaches, and I seldom had a bruise. Finally, I made an appointment with my doctor 2 weeks ago. I had to find out what was wrong with me. He did all kinds of tests, blood work, urinalysis, chest x-rays, everything! He said he would call me when all the results were in. His office called me 3 days ago and asked me to come in. Of course, I did.

"He asked me to come to his office and have a seat, which I did. He then said, very seriously, 'Judy, I hate to tell you this, but your blood work came back positive HIV. You have AIDS.' I remember feeling cold all over, and I said, 'You have got to be crazy, I have *never* been with any man but Grant. I am *not* promiscuous!'

He responded, 'Judy, I believe you, it must have been contaminated blood. You *did* have seven transfusions. I checked the hospital record.' I told him that I thought all the blood was tested for AIDS. He said that it is, but that occasionally—*rarely*—one does get contaminated."

Judy said, "I was in a complete state of shock. I just sat there and stared at him. He kept talking but I didn't hear a word he said until he stood up and handed me appointment cards for Grant and Candy! I remember that I screamed, 'No! No! I haven't given it to them, have I?' He tried to calm me but I kept saying, No! He took the appointment cards, tore them up, and said that he'd call Grant. He handed me a card with the AIDS hot line number and asked me to call and talk to them. I couldn't answer; I put the number in my purse. I don't even remember leaving his office *or* driving home! I could have killed someone!" She sank back in the chair, looking very pale and tired.

The therapist asked, "Judy, how do you feel?" She answered, "I am physically and emotionally exhausted. I haven't told you Grant's reaction, but I really think I should go home and take a nap. Do you mind?" The therapist replied, "Of course not. Let's make an appointment for next week. In the meantime I would like to find an AIDS support group for you and possibly a 'buddy.' I would also like to talk to your doctor. May I have his name and telephone number?" Judy looked surprised and answered, "Of course, here is his card. You are going to do all of that for me?" The therapist smiled and replied, "Yes, I am. Now give me a hug and I'll walk you out." Judy's eyes filled with tears and she said, "You aren't afraid I'll give it to you?" The therapist answered, "Judy, of course not. You need to know more about AIDS. You can't get it from tears." She gave her a hug that was strongly returned and kept her arm around Judy's shoulder as they walked out.

PLANNING THERAPEUTIC INTERVENTION

It was obvious that Judy needed factual information about AIDS. Her physician needed to be contacted to determine what he had told Grant and how he had responded to Judy's diagnosis of AIDS. It would be necessary to find out if he was referring Judy to a specialist. The local AIDS project would be contacted to find out if there was a woman's support group available and the possibility of getting a "buddy" for Judy. It would be vital if Grant would consider entering therapy with Judy. Grant would be contacted to discuss this possibility. One goal of intervention would be to give Judy and Grant as much situational support as necessary.

INTERVENTION

The therapist called Judy's physician, explained who she was, and asked if he had talked with Grant. He said that he met with Grant and tested him and Candice for HIV. He continued, saying that Grant was not concerned about himself, only about Judy and Candy. He added that he had ordered "stat" for their tests and should have the results the next day. He agreed to call the therapist and let her know the results as soon as he received them. When asked about the treatment planned for Judy, he said that he had already talked with a colleague who specialized in the treatment of persons with AIDS and that he was seeing Judy the next day.

The therapist then called the AIDS project and talked with one of the case managers. She told the case manager about Judy and how little she and Grant knew about AIDS and made arrangements to pick up brochures for Judy and Grant. She asked about the availability of a support group for women. Unfortunately, there was not a group ready to start at that time. The therapist asked about the possibility of a "buddy" for Judy. (A buddy is a volunteer, without AIDS, who has had extensive and thorough training and is carefully screened before he or she can qualify as a buddy. The buddy should be approximately the same age, race, marital status, economic status, and so on as the person with AIDS.) This fosters a strong supportive relationship that continues until the person with AIDS either dies or lapses into a state of dementia. The buddy system is a vital part of any well-organized AIDS project. The therapist told the case manager some specifics about Judy: her age, race, marital status, number of children, economic status, educational background, and occupation. The case manager said that he would go through the file and see if he could find someone suitable for Judy.

The therapist then called Judy's husband. Grant answered the phone and said, "Thank you so much for calling. Judy told me about her therapy session. May I see you as soon as possible? I want to do everything I can to help Judy, but I don't *know* what to do!" The therapist said that she could see him in approximately 2½ hours. The therapist arrived at the AIDS project location and picked up the pamphlets. While there, she went to the case worker's office to see if he'd found a buddy for Judy. The case manager was pleased to tell her that he had indeed found someone—a woman named Dotty. The therapist responded, "Dotty! Of course! She's been with the buddy program for over a year. Is she ready for another buddy?" The case worker replied, "Yes, she says she is. It's been 6 months since her last."

The therapist read her folder and was pleased to note that Dotty was close to Judy's age, had the same educational background and marital status, had two children, and worked in the same field as Judy. The therapist said, "I remember her. I was impressed with her commitment and sense of humor. Have you talked to her about Judy?" The case worker said that Dotty would like to meet Judy. They then made arrangements for the two women to meet.

The therapist returned to the counseling center to keep her appointment with Grant. The therapist took him to her office. He was tall and very well dressed but looked tired and depressed. He thanked the therapist for agreeing to see him and added, "Please tell me what I can do to help Judy. She won't let me touch her; she is isolating herself in one of the guest rooms. She won't let Candy come near her. She told Candy that she had a cold and didn't want her to get it. I feel so helpless."

The therapist asked Grant what he knew about AIDS, and he replied, "Only what I see on the news. That you get it from having sex and that it's a 'gay' disease." The therapist responded, "You're wrong, Grant. It is not a 'gay' disease, it is our disease." She handed him two packages of pamphlets and said, "One is for you and one is for Judy. Don't read them now. Take them home, and you and Judy read them together. What I would like to tell you is how you can't get AIDS, and how we can help Judy."

The therapist continued, "Grant, the AIDS virus is a very weak and fragile virus. You can't get it by touching Judy, or by holding her close or by lightly kissing her. You can't get it from drinking from the same glass as Judy or by eating food on her plate. You can't get it from her tears. The virus can easily be destroyed with a solution of 1 part household bleach to 10 parts of water. The only way you can get AIDS is through unprotected sex, contaminated blood from needles, or, in Judy's case, from a contaminated blood transfusion, which is very rare. Do you have any questions so far?" Grant answered, "What about this unprotected sex?" The therapist replied, "That's all explained in the pamphlets. If you or Judy have *any* questions, please call me."

She then asked, "Grant, do you feel uncomfortable being with Judy? Are you afraid you'll get AIDS from her?" Grant looked shocked and said, "Good Lord, No! I love her. I would die for her or Candy. She's the one that won't let me get near her." The therapist smiled and said, "I hoped you would feel that way. What I would like you to do is take those pamphlets home, make Judy sit with you, and both of you read them. They should tell you everything we know about AIDS. I think you'll be surprised to learn the 'true' facts, not myths, about AIDS and what is being done to control the symptoms and help victims of AIDS."

Grant looked thoughtful for a minute and responded, "I will, I promise. I've already learned so much from you today." The therapist said, "I'm glad. After you and Judy have read and discussed the information in the pamphlets, give her a big hug and kiss, and ask her out to dinner. Do you think you can convince her?" Grant smiled and said, "If I can't, no one can, and I know I can!"

The therapist made arrangements with Grant for him to call and let her know how the evening went. They also made arrangements for Grant to accompany Judy to the next therapy session on Tuesday. As the therapist walked out with Grant, she said, "I think I've found a 'buddy' for Judy. Someone who understands what she is going through and will be available for her to talk to—to ventilate her feelings, provide a shoulder to cry on, whatever Judy needs to do. She'll be calling her soon. Her name is Dotty." Grant said, "That sounds wonderful—thanks!"

ANTICIPATORY PLANNING

The diagnosis of AIDS had left Judy and Grant in a state of shock and disbelief. The next sessions were spent with both Judy and Grant.

Fortunately, neither Grant nor Candice tested positive for AIDS. Judy and Dotty had met several times and shared feelings of trust and respect for each other. This relationship was encouraged by the therapist. Judy had seen the specialist frequently and was responding well to a new experimental drug. Judy and Grant were encouraged to maintain contact with the AIDS project and with the therapist, as needed.

SUMMATION OF THE PARADIGM (Figure 8-1)

Judy had little knowledge of AIDS. When she was diagnosed, she isolated herself from her family; she was afraid that she would give them AIDS. Because she isolated herself, she had no situational support available. The diagnosis of AIDS made Judy face the inevitability of death. This was a new experience, and Judy had no available coping mechanism. She entered a state of panic and had disorganization of her thought processes. She went into a crisis. The following case study concerns Douglas, a homosexual who had been HIV positive for 9 months.

CASE STUDY: JUDY

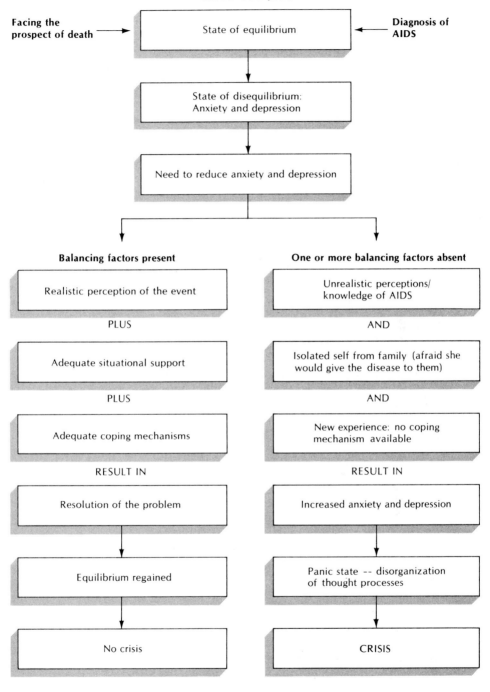

Figure 8-1

Case Study   *AIDS (Homosexual)*

ASSESSMENT OF THE INDIVIDUAL AND THE PROBLEM

Douglas was referred to the crisis center by the AIDS project. He was a 41-year-old gay attorney with AIDS. He was on medication and appeared to be responding well to it and to the diagnosis of AIDS. Three days ago, his lover, Mark, 32 years of age, moved out of the apartment they had shared for 4 years. Douglas became very depressed and had talked about suicide.

The therapist went to the reception area, introduced herself to Douglas, and invited him to her office. He sat down and slumped in the chair. He was a very attractive, well-dressed man who looked younger than his stated age of 41. He looked healthy, yet his eyes were sad and his slumped posture indicated that he was depressed.

The therapist began, "I read your chart, Douglas, and I know that you're gay, have AIDS, and that Mark moved out of your apartment 3 days ago. You stated in your chart that you're depressed and thinking of suicide. Is that correct?" He looked up and said, "Yes. Would you call me Doug? Everyone else does." She replied, "Of course, Doug. Would you like to tell me why Mark moved out?" He glanced over at the coffee pot and said, "Could I please have a cup of coffee?" The therapist poured coffee for both of them. She noticed that Doug's hand trembled as he took the cup. She sat down and asked if he felt like continuing.

He took a sip of coffee, sighed, and responded, "Yes, I may as well. Not that it will change anything." The therapist said, "Doug, don't stall, I can't help you if you won't tell me why Mark left you." Doug shrugged and sat up in the chair saying, "I'm sorry. You're right. I did come here for help." He began to talk. He said that he did not blame Mark for leaving him, that he deserved it. He went on to explain that he and Mark had a wonderful monogamous relationship and that they truly loved each other until "I loused up." The therapist asked how he had loused up.

Doug stood up and started pacing as he continued. He said that a year ago Mark had had to go out of town for 2 weeks on business. Doug could not go because he had cases that were due to go to trial. Usually he could arrange for his partner to cover for him, but his partner's wife had just given birth to a premature infant, and he had his hands full coping with his family. Doug went on to say that one night a friend of his invited him to dinner and then a party. When they arrived at the party, Doug was pleasantly surprised to see a former lover, Jeff. He and Jeff had not seen each other for at least 10 years. They talked, drank, and reminisced about their time together. The party was getting noisy, and Jeff suggested that they go to his hotel to continue their conversation. Doug agreed because he really enjoyed seeing Jeff again.

He drove Jeff to the hotel. When they got to the suite, Jeff said to Doug, "Take off your tie and shoes and relax while I fix you a drink. I have your favorite Scotch." Doug did as Jeff asked and relaxed on the couch. Jeff handed him his drink and sat down on the couch. They continued to talk about the time they had spent together. Doug said that after he had had another drink Jeff looked at him and said, "I should never have let you go, I still love you." He leaned over Doug and kissed him very gently. Doug said, "I was surprised, but I found myself returning his kiss. Maybe

I had too much to drink; I don't really know. I only know that we ended up in bed, making love. It was wonderful—just like it was before. Funny, I knew that I loved Mark, but I was still attracted to Jeff."

Doug sat down on the chair and continued talking. He said that when he left Jeff that night he agreed to meet him for dinner the next evening. They had met at Jeff's hotel, had dinner, and then went to Jeff's suite and made love again. Doug said that he told Jeff about Mark and he said, "I understand. Don't tell him about us." Doug asked, "Why? It happened but it won't happen again. Mark will understand—we've been together 4 years." Jeff responded, "Well, you know him and I don't. Use your own judgment."

The therapist asked Doug if he had told Mark. Doug said, "Yes. I picked him up at the airport. Damn, it was so good to see him. That's when I began to feel guilty. I told him that I was taking him to dinner at his favorite restaurant. He was very pleased. We went to dinner, and he told me about his successful business trip. We went home, and I fixed us a drink and told him that I had something to tell him."

Doug continued, saying that he had told Mark everything. Mark was hurt but said that he understood and that he would not go on another business trip unless Doug came with him. Doug agreed, but they did not make love that night. He added that he did not want to press the issue because he was the guilty party. He said that it was about 5 days before Mark approached him to make love. Their relationship continued as it had before for about 3½ months.

Doug began to pace again and said, "I thought I had the flu. I had headaches, night sweats. I was dizzy. I took 3 days off from work, but it didn't leave. I went to my doctor. I thought he would give me a shot to knock it out but . . . he checked me out completely and found that I had some swollen lymph glands. He ordered some blood tests."

The therapist asked, "Does your doctor know you're gay?" Doug said, "Yes, of course, I've always told him the truth." He laughed bitterly and added, "If you can't be honest with your doctor, who can you be honest with? I'm not stupid. I knew he was testing for AIDS! That's exactly what he found. I had tested HIV positive!"

The therapist stood up, walked over to Doug, put her hand on his shoulder, and said, "Doug, I'm so sorry." He started to cry softly. After about 2 minutes, he stopped crying and they continued. The therapist asked, "Doug, has Mark been tested for AIDS?" He replied, "Yes, and he was negative, thank God! But he will have to be retested later." The therapist asked him why Mark left. He looked sad and replied, "I don't blame him for leaving. He was afraid he might get AIDS, too. Don't forget, he is only 32. He has his whole life ahead of him. We talked about using safer sex methods but he was too afraid . . . afraid he wouldn't really be protected. I might feel the same way if he had it. I really don't know."

The therapist asked, "Doug, are you really thinking about suicide?" He replied, "Yes. I have been thinking about killing myself. I miss Mark so much, and even though the new drug seems to be working, let's face it, I do have AIDS."

The therapist asked, "How would you kill yourself?" He grinned and said, "I don't know. Besides, I'm 'chicken' when it comes to pain. I can talk about it, but I honestly don't believe I could do it. I really wanted Mark to think I would so that he would come back, but it didn't work. Don't worry, I won't commit suicide."

The therapist smiled and said, "That I am very glad to hear." The therapist asked Doug if he was familiar with the AIDS project and if he would like to get involved with a support group and possibly a buddy. Doug agreed, saying that he could use all the support he could get.

The therapist told Doug that she would begin working to find him a support group and a buddy and that she would have some information for him at his next session. She told him to call her on the exchange if he needed to talk. He agreed, and they made an appointment for the following week.

PLANNING THERAPEUTIC INTERVENTION

The therapist believed that Doug needed contact with other people with AIDS to reinforce the facts that he was not alone and that his situation was not unique. He could get this through a support group and a buddy from the AIDS project.* Although he was depressed, he was not believed to be a high suicidal risk for several reasons: He had no specific method, plan, or time selected, and he had a fear of pain.

INTERVENTION

The therapist contacted the AIDS project and the case manager. She told the manager about Doug and asked about a support group and buddy for him. The case manager informed her that there were several support groups available and that he would meet with Doug to see which would be the most appropriate. (There are usually several support groups for men with AIDS but few for women. This is because, at this point in time, there are more men than women with AIDS.) The case manager believed that he would have no problem finding a buddy for Doug.

ANTICIPATORY PLANNING

The main goal was to maintain contact with Doug, to give him situational support, and to see how he was doing physically. The therapist also believed that it would be important to find out how he was getting along in the support group and with his assigned buddy.

SUMMATION OF THE PARADIGM (Figure 8-2)

After testing positive for AIDS, Doug was faced with the loss of his lover. He felt rejected, had no situational support, and lacked adequate coping mechanisms. He became depressed and had suicidal ideation.

---

*AIDS Project Los Angeles (APLA) has many resources available to the community. It is staffed with professionals and numerous volunteers. The author is a volunteer with the Speaker's Bureau. Speakers are requested by various groups, such as schools, universities, and employers. The AIDS project also provides food, transportation, the buddy program, a dental clinic, household visitation, insurance counseling, telephone buddies, mental health services (support groups and crisis intervention), pastoral counseling, home health care, temporary shelters, transition shelters, and financial counseling. APLA also maintains three 800 AIDS hot lines: one in English, one in Spanish, and one for the hearing impaired. Not all AIDS projects have all of these services. Los Angeles is a large metropolitan city that is second only to New York in the number of AIDS cases. San Francisco ranks third. The main focus of APLA is to educate the public about AIDS.

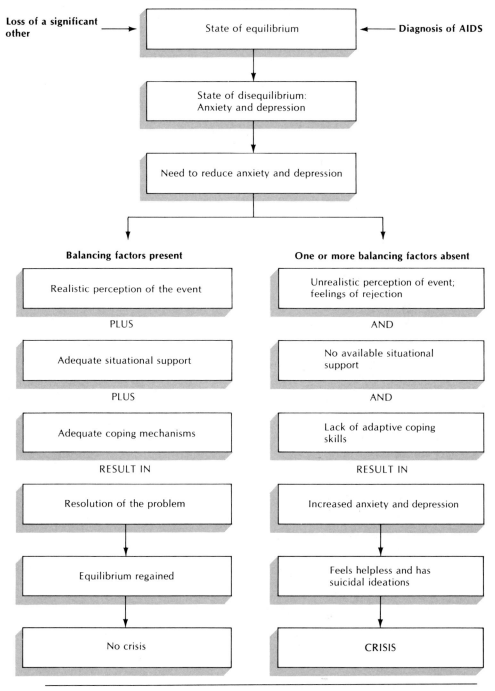

Figure 8-2

Teenagers feel invulnerable. Their hormones are flooding their systems, and they are inclined to believe that they know it all. Too young to indulge legally in drinking, smoking, and having sex, they still indulge in these behaviors. It makes them feel mature, grown-up, and very macho. They brag to their peers about how many beers they had, how many cigarettes they have smoked, and how many girls they "made it with." Ironically, smoking is increasing in the younger population as it is decreasing in the older population.

Statistics indicate that even though sex education classes in schools stress abstinence and the use of condoms, this education is ignored. Adolescents want to test their limits in the forbidden areas of life to prove to themselves and their peers that they are not afraid of anything (even AIDS) or anyone. The majority of teenagers do not use condoms. Why should they? After all, they know the people they are having sex with; they have been going to school together for years. Even though they may have a condom with them at the time, perhaps that last beer clouded their judgment, and they do not use it. Then they develop strange and uncomfortable symptoms, they begin to miss school, and their friends tell them they are not looking too good.

The following case study is how Jack, age 14, contracted AIDS. He trusted his older brother, Bill, so he discussed his symptoms and asked for his advice. Bill called the AIDS hot line and got the address of an anonymous test site. Jack was tested, and the test came back HIV positive. The test center sent him to the crisis center for assessment.

Case Study   *AIDS (Adolescent)*

ASSESSMENT OF THE INDIVIDUAL AND THE PROBLEM

The therapist was given Jack's chart and went to the reception area to meet him. Jack's brother Bill was with him. They both looked as if they were in a complete state of shock. The therapist introduced herself to Jack; he nodded and asked if his brother Bill could go to her office with them. She replied, "Of course." They walked to the therapist's office.

After Jack and Bill sat down, the therapist said to Jack, "I see that you were referred to the crisis center by the AIDS hot line. Have you been tested?" Jack replied that he had been tested for AIDS and he was HIV positive. He was asked if he knew the source of his infection. Jack answered, "It could only be one of three girls. I haven't been with any more." He was told that they should be notified by the health department so they could be tested for AIDS.

His brother Bill had been quiet, but he spoke up and in anger and sadness said to Jack, "How many times have I told you to *always* protect yourself. That's what condoms are for! How are we going to tell Mom and Dad?"

Jack answered, "I know I have been stupid, but I've known all three of the girls for years. I also always have a condom with me but I *hate* using the damn thing. Most of the time, I've had a few beers and the girls don't like me to use condoms anymore than I like to—so I don't!" Bill replied in anger, "Yeah, and look where it got you!"

The therapist interrupted them and said to Jack, "What do you know about being HIV positive?" He looked puzzled and said, "It means I've got AIDS and there is no cure." The therapist said, "You are HIV positive but you don't have any of the ARC symptoms. You could go 15 years and never get AIDS. This means that you can pass the AIDS virus to someone else so you will have to always use a condom or abstain."

It was obvious that he had tuned out his sex education classes. He obviously needed more in-depth knowledge of AIDS.

PLANNING THERAPEUTIC INTERVENTION

Because Jack apparently had problems believing "adults" or authority figures, the therapist believed he could learn more and relate better to his own peer group. His brother Bill was trusted by Jack, and he could be an important supporter and mediator with their parents. She planned to meet with their parents.

INTERVENTION

The therapist contacted the AIDS project and the case manager. She discussed Jack's situation and asked about informal classes with a peer support group for him. The case manager told her that he had two ongoing support groups and one that was starting the next day that sounded perfect for Jack. He added that they were all approximately Jack's age and all were still in a state of shock and disbelief.

ANTICIPATORY PLANNING

The main goal was to maintain contact with Jack and Bill to determine if Jack was following through with the peer group classes at the AIDS project. She would be available to him if he had any questions. She would also meet with his family, have them come for therapy, and be their situational support.

SUMMATION OF THE PARADIGM (Figure 8-3)

Jack was a 14-year-old adolescent with a recent diagnosis of AIDS. He had little knowledge of AIDS. He did not know anyone his age who had AIDS. This was a totally new situation and he had no coping skills. His anxiety and depression increased, and he entered a state of crisis.

There is no vaccine, no cure, and not even an indisputable effective treatment. Although AIDS education has slowed the epidemic in developed countries, the disease continues to spread rapidly in many poorer nations. The World Health Organization says at least 30 million people around the world could be infected with the AIDS virus by the year 2000. Other experts think the number could reach 110 million.

Despite dogged detective work by the world's best researchers, AIDS remains one of the most mysterious maladies ever to confront medical science. The more researchers learn about the disease, the more questions they have. AIDS has proved to be a fast-moving target, able to mutate its structure to elude detection, drugs, and vaccines. No one knows for sure how AIDS destroys the human immune system, but it does (Gorman, 1992).

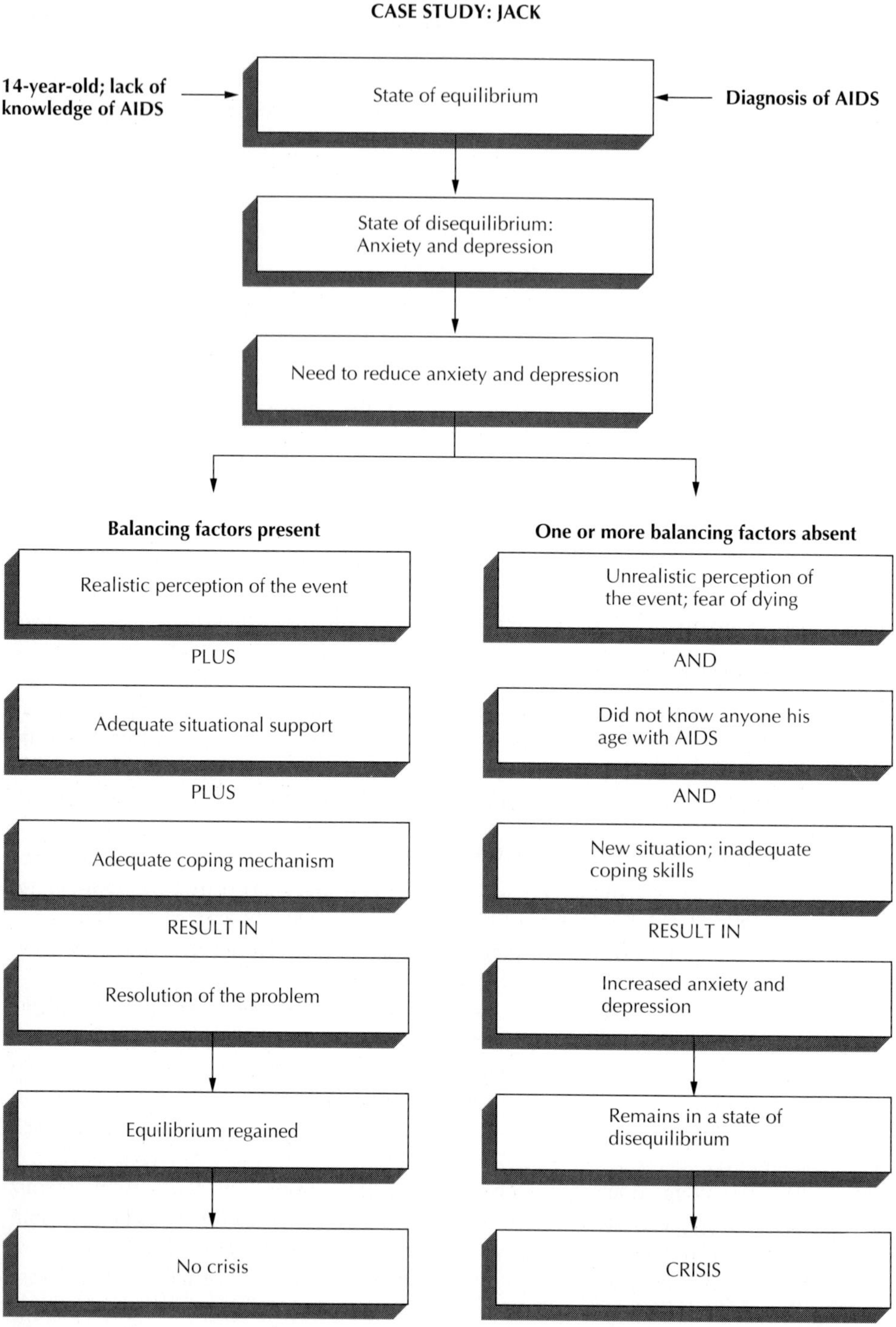

CASE STUDY: JACK

14-year-old; lack of knowledge of AIDS → State of equilibrium ← **Diagnosis of AIDS**

State of disequilibrium:
Anxiety and depression

Need to reduce anxiety and depression

Balancing factors present	**One or more balancing factors absent**
Realistic perception of the event	Unrealistic perception of the event; fear of dying
PLUS	AND
Adequate situational support	Did not know anyone his age with AIDS
PLUS	AND
Adequate coping mechanism	New situation; inadequate coping skills
RESULT IN	RESULT IN
Resolution of the problem	Increased anxiety and depression
Equilibrium regained	Remains in a state of disequilibrium
No crisis	CRISIS

Figure 8-3

The following case study concerns Diane, a heterosexual female, 25 years old; she tested HIV positive and was infected by her live-in lover, Dave.

Case Study   *AIDS (Heterosexual Female)*

ASSESSMENT OF THE INDIVIDUAL AND THE PROBLEM

Diane walked into a community mental health center and asked to see a therapist. She was given a brief chart to fill out and was assigned to a therapist in approximately 1½ hours.

The therapist went out to the reception area, after reading Diane's chart, with a feeling of anger, frustration, and hopelessness, and *hoping* that it would not show. She called Diane's name, and a very attractive young woman wearing dark glasses, approximately 5′ 7½″ tall, slim, well dressed, with a lovely figure, stood up, walked over to the therapist, and held out her hand. They shook hands; Diane's hand was cold and slightly damp. The therapist managed to maintain her composure because she recognized her! She was a former well-known model who was doing a few small but good parts in movies and television. She asked Diane to come to her office. Diane followed her to her office.

In the office, the therapist asked Diane to have a seat and offered her a cup of coffee, which she accepted. The therapist said to Diane, "I have read your chart, and it makes me angry and sad. I must let you know that I recognized you. Maybe another therapist might not know you. You may change to another therapist now if you wish."

Diane took off her dark glasses and sighed. "I really didn't think anyone would remember me. I haven't done any modeling for years, and I have only had a few very small parts in TV and a couple of movies." The therapist answered with a smile, "But you were my favorite model, your gorgeous green eyes, flowing streaked blonde hair riding a horse down a beach. I love horses!" We both laughed.

Remembering why they were there, they immediately sobered. The therapist asked Diane again, "Would you like to change to another therapist?" Diane looked at the therapist and shook her head. "No, I feel very comfortable with you and I think you like me. I don't know if anyone can help me, but if anyone can I believe it would be you." The therapist nodded her thanks and said to Diane, "Just in case someone at the clinic recognizes you we have a room upstairs where I can lock your chart so no one can ever see it but me, and don't forget we have a fiduciary relationship." Diane smiled slightly and said, "Thanks."

The therapist asked, "How did you get AIDS? Didn't you use protection? Surely you know how it is transmitted." Diane said, "Let me tell you how it happened. Then maybe you won't think I'm really stupid and careless." She began talking.

She and Dave, who was also a model when they met, had been living together. She said that it was really "hate" at first sight. She felt he was conceited, all the girls chased him, and he dated first one and then another. They had a "shoot" in the Caribbean for a well-known magazine that would involve many weeks. She was thrilled that she was one of the three female models selected and Dave was one of the two men selected to go. She smiled and said that from that trip came the shot of her riding the horse on the beach. She said that when they were in the

Caribbean Dave seemed so different. He was very relaxed, and he teased her. They went swimming and horseback riding, had dinner together, and were really getting to know each other. Her "hate" turned to "like" and then to "love." By the time they finished the "shoot," they were talking about living together. She said she was truly happy and he seemed happy.

When they talked about where they would live, she wanted them to live in her townhouse, but he wanted them to live in his townhouse. They were only about three blocks apart. Finally, Dave said that they could *live* in her townhouse but that he wanted to keep his townhouse. His reasons were that the "real estate market was down" and "that occasionally he liked to have his privacy." Diane said that she accepted his conditions. They moved into her townhouse, but occasionally he would spend the night in his townhouse when he had an early morning "shoot" and she did not. They lived together in what they had agreed upon, a monogamous relationship (at least she thought they were), for a little over a year. They both were very happy. He was working more than she was. (Men can model longer than women because "they just get distinguished looking as they get older; women just get older.")

Diane said that she made an appointment with her physician because she had a discharge and it was beginning to itch. Her doctor did several lab tests on her, told her to use the suppositories he gave her, and said he would call her the next day. The next day, his nurse called her and said that the physician wanted to see her. She said that she went to his office and he told her as gently as he could that she had a yeast infection but that her blood work showed that she was HIV positive. Diane said that she could not believe it—she *knew* that she had been with only Dave.

She said she drove to her townhouse and then changed her mind and drove to Dave's. His car was in the garage, and she used her key to get in his townhouse. He was in bed with one of the new young models. "I just looked at him. Then I said, 'You bastard, you gave me AIDS.' I looked at the girl and said, 'You better get tested too!'" She said Dave got out of bed and tried to talk to her, but she said all she could think of was how stupid she had been to believe him. She said, "I really trashed his house, screaming obscenities all the time. Then I went home and started crying. I knew I had to know more about AIDS. I remembered this crisis center and I came here."

PLANNING THERAPEUTIC INTERVENTION

Diane needed information on AIDS. She also needed to have a buddy. Because she was probably better known than she realized, the therapist would delay getting her in a support group. She would probably intimidate the other members. She would continue seeing her in therapy until she stabilized more.

INTERVENTION

The case manager at the AIDS project was contacted and agreed to find a buddy for Diane. He also agreed with the therapist that she would probably intimidate a support group. He agreed to send all the new literature over so Diane could learn about HIV and AIDS. The therapist would remain her situational support.

MAGIC' S MESSAGE

Magic Johnson is still a much-loved sports hero and a role model for hundreds of thousands of children and young adults worldwide – so much so that his announcement that he had tested HIV positive overshadowed all other sports stories in 1991. It was the Associated Press sports story of the year. Perhaps his story was of such importance because he was in the prime of life, wealthy, and popular, and he appeared to be invincible. His announcement made people suddenly feel vulnerable. His message was valuable in that it stressed prevention, but his message also carried an unnerving element; he said to the young, "I slept around and you can, too. Just don't make the same mistake I did. Use a condom." This statement created a great deal of controversy. First of all, condoms do not guarantee safe sex, but most compelling are the arguments that his announcement carelessly encouraged young people to imitate his promiscuity, just use a condom. He made no reference to abstinence before marriage or faithfulness within marriage (Stine, 1993).

ANTICIPATORY PLANNING

The main goal was to be a constant resource person to Diane, available through the exchange, day or night. She had no family and, being so beautiful, it was not easy for her to make friends.

SUMMATION OF THE PARADIGM (Figure 8-4)

Diane had a diagnosis of AIDS. She had been betrayed by her live-in lover. She had no situational support, this was a new situation, and she had no coping skills. She went into crisis.

CASE STUDY: DIANE

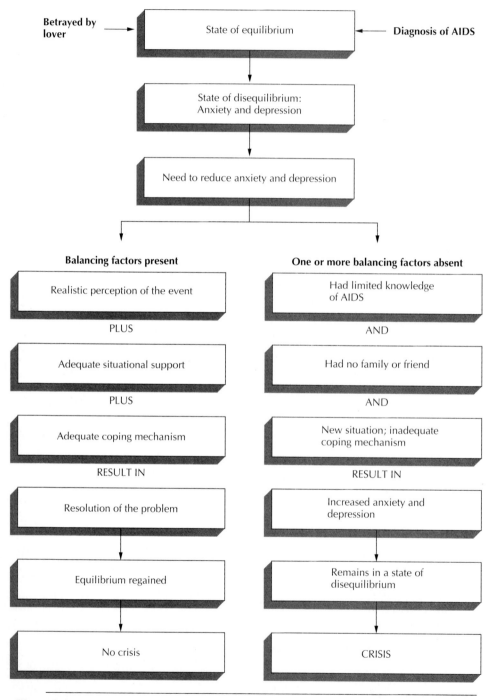

Figure 8-4

REFERENCES

Aguilera B (Vice President/General Counsel, The Mirage, Las Vegas): Personal communication, January 1993.

Aguilera C (Chief Investigator, Orange County Health Care Agency, Public Health and Medical Services): Personal communication, January 1993.

AIDS Project Los Angeles: Personal communication, January 1993.

Appell T, Blatt T: How HIV has changed traditional therapy, *Pacific Center J* 4:1, 1992.

Buckman R: *I don't know what to say,* Vintage Books, 1988.

Centers for Disease Control: Update: acquired immunodeficiency syndrome—United States, *MMWR* 34:245, 1987.

Centers for Disease Control: Personal communication, December 1992a.

Centers for Disease Control: Public health service guidelines for counseling and antibody testing to prevent HIV infection and AIDS, *MMWR* 36:509, 1992b.

Cohen B: The AIDS epidemic: future shock, *Newsweek,* Nov 24, 1986.

Conant M (Chairperson, AIDS Leadership Committee, State of California): personal communication, January 1993.

De Vincenzi I and others: Risk factors for male to female transmission of HIV, *BMJ* 298:411, 1989.

Ernsberger R Jr: The AIDS epidemic: future shock, *Newsweek,* Nov 24, 1986.

Faulstich ME: Psychiatric aspects of AIDS, *Am J Psychiatry* 144:551, 1987.

Friedland G: Fear of AIDS, *NY State J Med* 87(5):260, 1987.

Frierson R, Lippmann S: Psychologic implications of AIDS, *Am Fam Physician* 35:109, 1987.

Gorman C: Invincible AIDS, *Time,* p. 30, Aug 3, 1992.

Hager M: The AIDS epidemic: future shock, *Newsweek,* Nov 24, 1986.

Holland JC, Tross S: The psychosocial and neuropsychiatric sequelae of the acquired immunodeficiency syndrome and related disorders, *Ann Intern Med* 103:760, 1985.

Hostetler HM: *A time to love,* 1989, Scottdale, Pa, Herald Press.

Johnson J: Psychiatric aspects of AIDS: overview for the general practitioner, *JAOA* 87:99, 1987.

Johnson J: AIDS-related psychosocial issues for the patient and physician, *JAOA,* 88, 1988.

Kingsley LA and others: Sexual transmission efficiency of hepatitis B virus and human immunodeficiency virus among homosexuals, *JAMA* 264:230, 1990.

Levine S: *Who dies? An investigation of conscious living and conscious dying,* New York, 1982.

Moffatt B and others, editors: *AIDS: a self-care manual,* Los Angeles, 1992, AID Project Los Angeles.

Morganthau T: The AIDS epidemic: future shock, *Newsweek,* Nov 24, 1986.

Nichols SE: Psychosocial reactions of persons with the acquired immunodeficiency syndrome, *Ann Intern Med* 103:765, 1985.

Palm LL: Americans with disabilities Act (ADA): take the first steps now, *AIDS Newsline: Mountain Plains Regional AIDS Education and Training Center,* 3:8, 1992.

Parachini A: Condom failure stressed by panel, *Los Angeles Times,* Feb 28, 1989.

Perry SW, Markowitz J: Psychiatric interventions for AIDS-spectrum disorders, *Hosp Community Psychiatry* 37:1001, 1986.

Reese M: The AIDS epidemic: future shock, *Newsweek,* Nov 24, 1986.

Salisbury D: AIDS psychosocial implications, *J Psychosoc Nurs Ment Health Serv,* 24, 1986.

Shilts R: *And the band played on,* New York, 1987, St Martin's Press.

Simonton SM: *The healing family: the Simonton approach for families facing illness,* New York, 1984, Bantam.

Stine GJ: *Acquired immune deficiency syndrome*, Englewood Cliffs, NJ, 1993, Prentice Hall.

Stolberg S: New AIDS definition to increase tally, *Los Angeles Times*, p 1, Dec 31,1992.

Stribling TB: *Love broke through: a husband, father, and minister tells his own story*, Zondervan Books, 1990.

Walsh M: *Los Angeles Times*, p 1, Dec 29, 1992.

Wise TN: Psychiatric aspects of acquired immunodeficiency syndrome, *Psychiatr Med* 4:79, 1986.

ADDITIONAL READINGS

Adams T: HIV-related dementia, *Nurs Times* 84:45, 1988.

Allison WW: AIDS problem calls for education, *Occup Health Saf* 56:43, 1987 (letter).

Alroe CJ: AIDS paranoia, *Med J Aust* 148:369, 1988 (letter).

Athy D: AIDS—a New York view, *Ohio Med* 84:15, 1988.

Bail JP: AIDS and the hidden epidemic of grief: a personal experience, *Am J Hosp Care* 5:25, 1988.

Bennett K: AIDS: a generation of children at risk, *J Psychosoc Nurs Ment Health Serv* 25:32, 1987.

Benson DF: The spectrum of dementia: a comparison of the clinical features of AIDS/ dementia and dementia of the Alzheimer type, *Alzheimer Dis Assoc Disor* 1:217, 1987.

Bickelhaupt EE: Psychosocial aspects of AIDS, *Kans Med* 87:66, 1986.

Blaney RL, Piccola GE: Psychologic issues related to AIDS, *J Med Assoc Ga* 76:28, 1987.

Bor R, Miller R, Salt H, Scher I: The relevance of a family counseling approach in HIV/ AIDS: discussion paper, *Patient education counseling* 17:235, 1991.

Boyd KM: The moral challenge of AIDS, *J R Soc Med* 80:281, 1987.

Boyton R, Scambler G: Survey of general practitioners' attitudes to AIDS in the North West Thames and East Anglian regions, *Br Med J (Clin Res)* 296:538, 1988.

Bretile RP and others: Human immunodeficiency virus and drug misuse: the Edinburgh experience, *Br Med J (Clin Res)* 295:421, 1987.

Bridge TP: AIDS and HIV CNS disease: a neuropsychiatric disorder, *Adv Biochem Psycho- pharmacol* 44:1, 1988.

Bridge TP: Legal and ethical issues in the neuropsychiatric research in AIDS, *Adv Biochem Psychopharmacol* 44:241, 1988.

Britton S: Psychosocial aspects of HTLV-III infections, *Scand J Soc Med* 14:211, 1986.

Broadbent J: Assessing the counselling of HIV positive clients, *Health Visit* 60:262, 1987.

Brosnan S: Our first home care A.I.D.S. patient: Maria, *Nursing* 16:37, 1986.

Brown DS: HIV infection in persons with prior mental retardation, *AIDS Care* 3:165, 1991.

Buckingham SL, Rehm SJ: AIDS and women at risk, *Health Soc Work* 12:5, 1987.

Burton SW: The psychiatry of HIV infection, *Br Med J (Clin Res)* 295:228, 1987, (editorial).

Cameron P, Playfair WL: AIDS: intervention works; "education" is questionable, *Psychol Rep* 68:467, 1991.

Campbell CA: Prostitution, AIDS, and preventive health behavior, *Social Sci Med* 32:1367, 1991.

Carlson MJ: AIDS testing, *Ohio Med* 83:836, 1987.

Chodoff P: Fear of AIDS, *Psychiatry* 50:184, 1987.

Cohen MA, Weisman HW: AIDS program update, *Psychosomatics* 28:137, 1987 (letter).

Cohen SI: Voodoo death, the stress response, and AIDS, *Adv Biochem Psychopharmacol* 44:95, 1988.

Coles P: AIDS and public opinion in France, *Nature* 332:295, 1988.

Covell RG: HIV infection and adoption in Scotland, *Scott Med J* 32:117, 1987.

Cummings MA and others: Acquired immunodeficiency syndrome presenting as schizo- phrenia. *West J Med* 146:615, 1987.

Dane BO: Anticipatory mourning of middle-aged parents of adult children with AIDS, *Fam Soc* 72:108, 1991.

D'Anzi FA: AIDS in Louisiana: transference and countertransference issues in the treatment of persons with AIDS, *J La State Med Soc* 139:80, 1987.

Davidson DE: Psychiatric aspects of HIV infection, *Kans Med* 89:112, 1988.

Decker MD: The use of HIV antibody testing by physicians, *JAMA* 259:2994, 1988 (letter).

DiClemente RJ, Boyer CB, Moreales ES: Minorities and AIDS: knowledge, attitudes, and misconceptions among black and Latino adolescents, *Am J Public Health* 78:55, 1988.

Di Giovanni C: Update on HIV infection: psychiatric aspects, *Md Med J* 36:35, 1987.

Dorman JM: A physician's experience: taking care of Ralph, *J Am Coll Health* 36:243, 1988.

Edwards KS: Snapshots: an ethical look at AIDS, *Ohio Med* 84:43, 1988.

Ellis NK, Kroh-Cole E: Providing a therapeutic milieu experience for a patient diagnosed with acquired immune deficiency syndrome, *Arch Psychiatr Nurs* 1:436, 1987.

Eustace JC: Infected patients: psychosocial-psychiatric needs, *J Fla Med Assoc* 75:299, 1988.

Evans KM: The female AIDS patient, *Health Care Women Int* 8:1, 1987.

Faulstich ME: Psychiatric aspects of AIDS, *Am J Psychiatry* 144:551, 1987.

Fehrs LJ and others: Trial of anonymous versus confidential human immunodeficiency virus testing, *Lancet* 2:379, 1988.

Fisher DW: The cruel paradox of AIDS: a letter and reply, *Hosp Pract [Off]* 22:13, 1987 (editorial).

Fisher EJ: Consider the psychosocial consequences of AIDS, *Mich Med* 85:95, 1986.

Flaskerud JH: AIDS: psychosocial aspects, *J Psychosoc Nurs Ment Health Serv* 25:8, 1987.

Flavin DK, Frances RJ: Risk-taking behavior, substance abuse disorders, and the acquired immune deficiency syndrome, *Adv Alcohol Subst Abuse* 6:23, 1987.

Fox R and others: Effect of HIV antibody disclosure on subsequent sexual activity in homosexual men, *AIDS* 1:241, 1987.

Friedland G: AIDS and compassion, *JAMA* 259:2898, 1988.

Friedland G: Fear of AIDS, *N Y State J Med* 87:260, 1987.

Friedlander AH, Arthur RJ: A diagnosis of AIDS: understanding the psychosocial impact, Brentwood Division, West Los Angeles Veterans Administration Medical Center, *Oral Pathol* 65:680, 1988.

Frierson RL, Lippmann SB: Psychologic implications of AIDS, *Am Fam Physician* 35:109, 1987.

Frierson RL, Lippmann SB: Suicide and AIDS, *Psychosomatics* 29:226, 1988.

Frierson RL, Lippmann SB, Johnson J: AIDS: psychological stresses on the family: recommendations for counseling relatives of the AIDS patient, *Psychosomatics* 28:65, 1987.

Frolkis JP: AIDS anxiety: new faces for old fears, *Postgrad Med* 79:265, 1986.

Furst ML: The short and long of stress: AIDS; Challenger; terrorism; meltdown, *Int J Psychosom* 33:60, 1986.

Gallagher M: HIV infection in a rehabilitation unit, *J R Coll Gen Pract* 37:131, 1987 (letter).

Ghodse AH, Tregenza G, Li M: Effect of fear of AIDS on sharing of injection equipment among drug abusers, *Br Med J (Clin Res)* 295:698, 1987.

Glass RM: AIDS and suicide, *JAMA* 259:1369, 1988 (editorial).

Goldmeier D: Psychosocial aspects of AIDS, *Br J Hosp Med* 37:232, 1987.

Goodhope RC and others: What teachers think about AIDS, *S D J Med* 41:29, 1988.

Goodwin MP, Roscoe B: AIDS: students' knowledge and attitudes at a midwestern university, *J Am Coll Health* 36:214, 1988.

Gordon FM and others: Knowledge of AIDS among hospital workers: behavioral correlates and consequences, *AIDS* 1:183, 1987.

Grant D: Support groups for youth with the AIDS virus, *Int J Group Psychother* 38:237, 1988.

Grant D, Anns M: Counseling AIDS antibody-positive clients: reactions and treatment, *Am Psychol* 43:72, 1988.

Grief GL, Porembski E: Significant others of I.V. drug abusers with AIDS: new challenges for drug treatment programs, *J Subst Abuse Treat* 4:151, 1987.

Grimshaw J: ABCs of AIDS: being HIV antibody positive, *Br Med J (Clin Res)* 295:256, 1987.

Guinan JJ and others: Stressors and rewards of being an AIDS emotional-support volunteer: a scale for use by care-givers for people with AIDS, *AIDS Care* 3:127, 1991.

Hall JM, Stevens PE: AIDS: a guide to suicide assessment, *Arch Psychiatr Nurs* 2:115, 1988.

Hansen B and others: Workers with AIDS: attitudes of fellow employees, *AAOHN J* 36:279, 1988.

Harowski KJ: The worried well: maximizing coping in the face of AIDS, *J Homosex* 14:29, 1987.

Hastings GB, Leather DS, Scott AC: AIDS publicity: some experiences from Scotland, *Br Med J (Clin Res)* 294:48, 1987.

Hastings GB, Leather DS, Scott AC: Scottish attitudes about AIDS, *Br Med J (Clin Res)* 296:991, 1988.

Hays LR, Lyles MR: Psychological themes in patients with acquired immune deficiency syndrome, *Am J Psychiatry* 143:551, 1986 (letter).

Helbert M: AIDS and medical confidentiality, *Br Med J (Clin Res)* 295:552, 1987 (letter).

Henry K, Willenbring K, Crossley K: Human immunodeficiency virus antibody testing: a description of practices and policies at US infectious disease teaching hospitals and Minnesota hospitals, *JAMA* 259:1819, 1988.

Holland JC, Tross S: Psychosocial considerations in the therapy of epidemic Kaposi's sarcoma, *Semin Oncol* 14:48, 1987.

Holmes SW, Peel J: Meeting the mental health challenge of AIDS and related disorders, *J Med Assoc Ga* 76:33, 1987.

Horejsi GA: Support for AIDS staff, *Health Soc Work* 12:229, 1987.

Hull HF and others: Comparison of HIV-antibody prevalence in patients consenting to and declining HIV-antibody testing in an STD clinic, *JAMA* 260:935, 1988.

Hunter CE, Ross MW: Determinants of health-care workers' attitudes toward people with AIDS, *J Appl Soc Psychol* 21:947, 1991.

Hutton MJ: AIDS and our attitudes—from a nursing perspective, *J Palliat Care* 3:48, 1987 (letter).

Imperato PJ and others: Medical students' attitudes towards caring for patients with AIDS in a high incidence area, *N Y State J Med* 88:223, 1988.

Jacob KS and others: AIDS-phobia, *Br J Psychiatry* 150:412, 1987 (letter).

Jason JM: Abuse, neglect, and the HIV-infected child, *Child Abuse Negl* 15:79, 1991.

Joffe RT and others: Neuropsychiatric aspects of AIDS, *Psychopharmacol Bull* 22:684, 1986.

Johnson JM: Psychiatric aspects of AIDS: overview for the general practitioner, *J Am Osteopath Assoc* 87:99, 1987.

Johnson JM: AIDS-related psychosocial issues for the patient and physician, *J Am Osteopath Assoc* 88:234, 1988.

Judson FN, Vernon TM Jr: The impact of AIDS on state and local health departments: issues and a few answers, *Am J Public Health* 78:387, 1988.

Kaminski MA, Hartmann PM: HIV testing: issues for the family physician, *Am Fam Physician* 38:117, 1988.

Kaplan HB and others: The sociological study of AIDS: a critical review of the literature and suggested research agenda, *J Health Soc Behav* 28:140, 1987.

Katz I and others: Lay people's and health care personnel's perceptions of cancer, *Psychol Rep* 60:615, 1987.

Kelly K: AIDS and ethics: an overview, *Gen Hosp Psychiatry* 9:331, 1987.

Kessler RC and others: Stressful life events and symptom onset in HIV infection, *Am J Psychiatry* 148:733, 1991.

Kraft P and Rise J: AIDS—public knowledge in Norway 1986, *NIPH Ann* 11:19, 1988.

Krasinski K and others: Failure of voluntary testing for human immunodeficiency virus to identify infected parturient women in a high-risk population, *N Engl J Med* 318:185, 1988 (letter).

Kristal AR: Sexual behavior and risks of HIV infection, *Am J Public Health* 78:91, 1988 (letter).

Levenson RL and others: Equivalence of Peabody Picture Vocabulary Test—Revised, Forms L and M for *children* with acquired immune deficiency syndrome (*AIDS*), *Percept Mot Skills* 72:99, 1991.

Levine SS, Helm ML: An AIDS diagnosis used as focus of malingering, *West J Med* 148:337, 1988.

Lewy R: AIDS in the workplace: guidelines, *J Occup Med* 30:578, 1988.

Lim MS: AIDS: dealing with a pandemic problem, *Postgrad Med* 1:24, 1988 (letter).

Link RN and others: Concerns of medical and pediatric house officers about acquiring AIDS from their patients, *Am J Public Health* 78:455, 1988.

Linn R: When an AIDS child enters the classroom: moral-psychological research questions, *Psychol Rep* 61:191, 1987.

Livingston IL: Co-factors, host susceptibility, and AIDS: an argument for stress, *J Natl Med Assoc* 80:49, 1988.

Lyter DW and others: The HIV antibody test: why gay and bisexual men want or do not want to know their results, *Public Health Rep* 102:468, 1987.

Madeley T: ABCs of AIDS: having AIDS, *Br Med J (Clin Res)* 295:320, 1987.

Mallory MA: For A.I.D.S. patients, little things can mean a lot. Sharing Lloyd's pain: a sister's story, *Nursing* 18:62, 1988.

Martin JL: The impact of AIDS on gay male sexual behavior patterns in New York City, *Am J Public Health* 77:578, 1987.

Marzuk PM and others: Increased risk of suicide in persons with AIDS, *JAMA* 259:1333, 1988.

Massie MJ and others: Neuropsychological and psychosocial sequelae of AIDS, *Antibiot Chemother* 38:132, 1987.

Mastroianni CM, Liuzzi GM, Riccio P: AIDS dementia complex: on the relationship between HIV-1 infection, immune-mediated response and myelin damage in the brain. *Acta-Neurol (Napoli)* 13:184, 1991.

Mathews SJ: Nothing to fear but fear, *Nurs Times* 84:35, 1988.

Mays VM, Cochran SD: Acquired immunodeficiency syndrome and black Americans: special psychosocial issues, *Public Health Rep* 102:224, 1987.

McCarthy MS, Albright PA: AIDS. Hospital lawyer responds: a case for confidentiality, *J Christ Nurs* 4:7, 1987.

McClatchey WM: AIDS. A physician responds: confidentiality may kill, *J Christ Nurs* 4:8, 1987.

McCormick B: Workers who get AIDS: combating coworkers' fears, *Hospitals* 60:110, 1986.

McCusker J and others: Behavioral risk factors for HIV infection among homosexual men at a Boston community health center, *Am J Public Health* 78:68, 1988.

McKusick L and others: The psychological impact of AIDS on primary care physicians, *West J Med* 144:751, 1986 (letter).

Menenberg SR: Somatopsychology and AIDS victims, *J Psychosoc Nurs Ment Health Serv* 25:18, 1987.

Metzger D and others: Risk factors for needle sharing among methadone-treated patients, *Am J Psychiatry* 148:636, 1991.

Miller D: ABCs of AIDS: counselling, *Br Med J (Clin Res)* 294:1671, 1987.

Miller D: HIV counselling: some practical problems and issues, *J R Soc Med* 80:278, 1987.

Mirsky AF: Neuropsychological manifestations and predictors of HIV disease in vulnerable persons, *Adv Biochem Psychopharmacol* 44:117, 1988.

Mirsky H: A pinch of will is better than a pound of perhaps, *Am Pharm* 27:26, 1987.

Mitchell C, Smith L: If it's AIDS, please don't tell, *Am J Nurs* 87:911, 1987.

Mondragon D, Kirkman-Liff B, Schneller ES: Hostility to people with AIDS: risk perception and demographic factors, *Soc Sci Med* 32:1137, 1991.

Moore SM, Barling NR: Developmental status and AIDS attitudes in adolescence, *J Genet Psychol* 152:5, 1991.

Morgen KB: Update on HIV infection: counseling and HIV: test results and risk reduction, *Md Med J* 36:44, 1987.

Morrison V: The impact of HIV upon injecting drug users: a longitudinal study, *AIDS Care* 3:193, 1991.

Morton AD, McManus IC: Attitudes to and knowledge about the acquired immune deficiency syndrome: lack of a correlation, *Br Med J (Clin Res)* 293:1212, 1986.

Murphy P: Pastoral care and persons with AIDS: a means to alleviate physical, emotional, social, and spiritual suffering, *Am J Hosp Care* 3:38, 1986.

Nelson LP, Album MM: AIDS: children with HIV infection and their families, *ASDC J Dent Child* 54:353, 1987.

O'Brien LS: Not a case of pseudo-AIDS, *Br J Psychiatry* 151:127, 1987 (letter).

O'Dowd MA and others: Characteristics of patients attending an HIV-related psychiatric clinic, *Hosp Community Psychiatry* 42:615, 1992.

Oerlemans-Bunn M: St. Vincent's Hospital, New York City, On being gay, single, and bereaved, *Am J Nurs* 88:472, 1988.

Olsen JA, Jensen LC, Greaves PM: Adolescent sexuality and public policy, *Adolescence* 26:419, 1991.

Ostrow DG: Psychiatric consequences of AIDS: an overview, *Int J Neurosci* 32:647, 1987.

Ostrow DG: Models for understanding the psychiatric consequences of AIDS, *Adv Biochem Psychopharmacol* 44:85, 1988.

Ostrow DG, Gayla TC: Psychosocial and ethical issues of AIDS health care programs, *QRB* 12:284, 1986.

Ostrow DG and others: Psychosocial aspects of AIDS risk, *Psychopharmacol Bull* 22:678, 1986.

Owen N, Mylvaganam A: AIDS prevention: epidemiologic and behavioural perspectives, *Aust Psychol* 26:11, 1991.

Oxley S: AIDS and counselling, *Occup Health (Lond)* 39:291, 1987.

Papathomopoulos E: An attempt to commit suicide by contracting AIDS, *Am J Psychiatry* 145:765, 1988 (letter).

Pearson SD: A piece of my mind: immune response, *JAMA* 256:3088, 1986.

Perkins AC: AIDS: a sister's experience, *J Am Coll Health* 36:245, 1988.

Perry S, Marotta RF: AIDS dementia: a review of the literature, *Alzheimer Dis Assoc Disord* 1:221, 1987.

Plotkin MS, Domanski MD: The AIDS challenge: a psychosocial perspective, *Henry Ford Hosp Med J* 35:47, 1987.

Pohl MI: Neurocognitive impairment in alcoholics: review and comparison with cognitive impairment due to AIDS, *Adv Alcohol Subst Abuse* 7:107, 1987.

Power R, Dale A, Jones S: Towards a process evaluation model for community based initiatives aimed at preventing the spread of HIV amongst injecting drug users, *AIDS care* 3:123, 1991.

Puschel K and others: HIV-infection in forensic autopsy cases, *Forensic Sci Int* 34:169, 1987.

Qualand MC, Shattls WD: AIDS, sexuality, and sexual control, *J Homosex* 14:277, 1987.

Rhyne M: The source of a patient's strength, *Ala Med* 57:37, 1988.

Richards T: "Don't tell me on Friday," *Br Med J (Clin Res)* 292:943, 1986.

Richardson JL and others: Physician attitudes and experience regarding the care of patients with acquired immunodeficiency syndrome (AIDS) and related disorders (ARC), *Med Care* 25:675, 1987.

Rickert VI, Jay MS, Gottlieb A: Effects of a peer-counseled AIDS education program on knowledge, attitudes, and satisfaction of adolescents, *J Adolesc Health* 12:38, 1991.

Riesenberg DE: AIDS-prompted behavior changes reported, *JAMA* 255:171, 1986.

Riffer J: Blood banks still cope with AIDS fears and myths, *Hospitals* 60:74, 1986.

Robinson EN Jr, Latham RH: A factitious case of acquired immunodeficiency syndrome. *Sex Transm Dis* 14:54, 1987.

Rogers DE: Caring for the patient with AIDS, *JAMA* 259:1368, 1988.

Rolf J and others: Substance misuse and HIV/AIDS risks among delinquents: a prevention challenge, *Int J Addict* 25:533, 1991.

Rosner F: Acquired immunodeficiency syndrome: ethical and psychosocial considerations, *Bull N Y Acad Med* 63:123, 1987.

Ross JA: AIDS: public panic, *J R Soc Med* 81:370, 1988 (letter).

Ross M, Herbert P: Responses of homosexual men to AIDS, *Med J Aust* 146:280, 1987 (letter).

Royse D, Birge B: Homophobia and attitudes towards AIDS patients among medical, nursing and paramedical students, *Psychol Rep* 61:867, 1987.

Royse D, Dhooper SS, Hatch LR: Undergraduate and graduate students' attitudes towards AIDS, *Psychol Rep* 60:1185, 1987.

Rubinow DR and others: Neuropsychiatric impairment in patients with AIDS, *Adv Biochem Psychopharmacol* 44:111, 1988.

Rundell JR, Wise MG, Ursano RJ: Three cases of AIDS-related psychiatric disorders, *Am J Psychiatry* 143:777, 1986.

Ryan MS: Neglected survivors, *Am J Nurs* 88:1070, 1988.

Salisbury DM: AIDS: psychosocial implications, *J Psychosoc Nurs Ment Health Serv* 24:13, 1986.

Saunders JM, Buckingham SL: Suicidal AIDS patients: when the depression turns deadly, *Nursing* 18:59, 1988.

Schaffner B: Some thoughts about AIDS, *J Subst Abuse Treat* 4:141, 1987.

Schoen K: Psychosocial aspects of hospice care for AIDS patients: addressing these issues is a key aspect of treatment, *Am J Hosp Care* 3:32, 1986.

Seeley J and others: The development of a community-based HIV-AIDS counselling service in a rural area in Uganda, *AIDS Care* 3:207, 1991.

Selwyn PA: AIDS: what is now known. IV. Psychosocial aspects, treatment prospects, *Hosp Pract [Off]* 21:125, 1986.

Selwyn PA and others: Knowledge about AIDS and high-risk behavior among intravenous drug users in New York City, *AIDS* 1:247, 1987.

Shaffer HJ, Costikyan NS: Cocaine psychosis and AIDS: a contemporary diagnostic dilemma, *J Subst Abuse Treat* 5:9, 1988.

Sherer R: Physician use of the HIV antibody test: the need for consent, counseling, confidentiality, and caution, *JAMA* 259:264, 1988.

Shetty GC: Depressive illness with delusions of AIDS, *Am J Psychiatry* 145:765, 1988 (letter).

Shoemaker P, Lasorsa D, and McAlister A: AIDS related knowledge, attitudes and behavior in Travis county, *Tex Med* 84:47, 1988.

Silberman JM, The AIDS epidemic: professional and personal concerns of graduate social work students in field placement, *Soc Work Health Care* 15:77, 1991.

Simkins L, Kushner A: Attitudes toward AIDS, herpes II, and toxic shock syndrome: two years later, *Psychol Rep* 59:883, 1986.

Skinner A, Walls L, Brown LS: AIDS related behavioral research and nursing, *J Nat Med Assoc* 83:585, 1991.

Slonim-Nevo V, Ozawa MN, Auslander WF: Knowledge, attitudes and behaviors related to AIDS among youth in residential centers: results from an an exploratory study, *J Adolesc* 14:17, 1991.

Smiley ML, Meriwether R: Human immunodeficiency virus antibody testing and counseling, *N C Med J* 49:5, 1988.

Smith DH: Ethics in the care of AIDS patients, *J Fla Med Assoc* 75:305, 1988.

Snell WE, Finney PD: Interpersonal strategies associated with the discussion of AIDS, *Ann Sex Res* 3:425, 1990.

Solomon GF: Psychoneuroimmunologic approaches to research on AIDS, *Ann N Y Acad Sci* 496:628, 1987.

Sonnex C and others: HIV infection: increase in public awareness and anxiety, *Br Med J (Clin Res)* 295:193, 1987.

Spence C: Community response to the challenge of AIDS, *Midwife Health Visit Community Nurse* 24:85, 1988.

Stamford J: AIDS/HIV: how do you react? *Prof Nurse* 3:292, 1988.

Stamm WE and others: The association between genital ulcer disease and acquisition of HIV infection in homosexual men, *JAMA* 260:1429, 1988.

Steinbrook R and others: Preferences of homosexual men with AIDS for life-sustaining treatment, *N Engl J Med* 314:457, 1986.

Szapocznik J, Millon C, Eisdorfer C: Conference on psychoimmunological aspects of HIV infection: planning for comparative research, *AIDS* 1:255, 1987.

Taylor GW: AIDS: the art of debate, *Br Med J (Clin Res)* 295:610, 1987 (letter).

Taylor-Brown S: The impact of AIDS on foster care: a family centered approach to services in the United States, *Child Welfare* 70:193, 1991.

Temoshok L: Malignant melanoma, AIDS and the complex search for psychosocial mechanisms, *Advances* 7:20, 1991.

Thomas CS: HIV and informed consent, *Br J Psychiatry* 151:410, 1987 (letter).

Thomas CS, Szabadi E: Paranoid psychosis as the first presentation of a fulminating lethal case of AIDS, *Br J Psychiatry* 151:693, 1987.

Thompson C, Riccio M: AIDS phobia, *Br J Hosp Med* 38:167, 1987 (editorial).

Thompson C and others: AIDS: dilemmas for the psychiatrist, *Lancet* 1:269, 1986 (letter).

Tovey LA: Why women are not receiving anti RH prophylaxis, *Br Med J (Clin Res)* 294:1485, 1987 (letter).

Trice AD, Price-Greathouse J: Locus of control and AIDS information-seeking in college women, *Psychol Rep* 60:665, 1987.

Tross S and others: Neuropsychological characterization of the AIDS dementia complex: a preliminary report, *AIDS* 2:81, 1988.

Turnbull O and others: Neuropsychological deficit in haemophiliacs with human immuno-deficiency virus, *J Neurol Neurosurg Psychiatry* 54:175, 1991.

Underwood CR: A plague amongst us? *J Med Assoc Ga* 76:14, 1987.

Underwood CR: On loneliness, *J Med Assoc Ga* 77:144, 1988.

Valdiserri EV: Fear of AIDS: implications for mental health practice with reference to ego-dystonic homosexuality, *Am J Orthopsychiatry* 56:634, 1986.

Viney L and others: Psychological frailness and strength in an AIDS affected community: a study of seropositive gay men and voluntary caregivers, *Am J Community Psychol* 19:279, 1991.

Vollmer J: AIDS in Arkansas. AMS Special Committee on AIDS. Update: December, 1987. Self-help for seropositive patients, *J Arkansas Med Soc* 84:270, 1987.

Wachter RM and others: Attitudes of medical residents regarding intensive care for patients with the acquired immunodeficiency syndrome, *Arch Intern Med* 148:149, 1988.

Wallack JJ and others: An AIDS bibliography for the general psychiatrist, *Psychosomatics* 32:243, 1991.

Walsh ME, Bibace R: Children's conceptions of AIDS: a developmental analysis, *J Pediatr Psychol* 16:273, 1991.

Weisman E: Current issues in hospice care, 13:349, 1987.

Weitz R: The interview as legacy: a social scientist confronts AIDS, *Hastings Cent Rep* 17:21, 1987.

Wetterau PD, Stegelin DA, Day care providers' knowledge and attitudes about AIDS: A needs assessment, *Children's Health Care* 20:108, 1991.

Whiteford HA, Csernansky JG: Psychiatric aspects of acquired immune deficiency syndrome (AIDS), *Aust N Z J Psychiatry* 20:399, 1986.

Widen HA: The risk of AIDS and the defense of disavowal: dilemmas for the college psychotherapist, *J Am Coll Health* 35:268, 1987.

Wilkie PA: Counselling in HIV infection, *Scott Med J* 32:114, 1987.

Wilkinson R, Powills S: Education: a forum for attacking fear, *Hospitals* 60:60, 1986.

Williams RJ, Stafford WB: Silent casualties: partners, families and spouses of persons with AIDS, *J Counsel Dev* 69:423, 1991.

Windgassen E, Somi SD: AIDS panic, *Br J Psychiatry* 151:126, 1987 (letter).

Woolley PD, Bowman CB, Kindhorn GR: Fear of HIV infection and reduction in heterosexual gonorrhoea, *Br Med J (Clin Res)* 296:1199, 1988.

Zimet GD and others: Knowing someone with AIDS: The impact on adolescents, *J Pediatr Psychol* 16:287, 1991.

Chapter 9

Burnout Syndrome

In this text, *burnout* refers to a progressive loss of idealism, energy, and purpose experienced by people in the helping professions as a result of the conditions of their work. These conditions may include insufficient training, client overload, too many hours, too little pay, inadequate funding, ungrateful clients, bureaucratic or political constraints, and the gap between aspiration and accomplishment.

The word *burnout* came into professional literature in 1974 with the first of Freudenberger's articles on staff burnout in alternative help-giving facilities, such as free clinics, that exist outside the established institutional structures of society and depend on dedicated volunteer help. It was then recognized that the concept applied equally well to the salaried or self-employed professional in an "establishment" position.

Stressors in Hospice Home Care

Stressors include those factors that are part of the work environment as compared with *stressors* that are a function of the individual's own experience. They include five important facts: (1) All hospice patients are dying, (2) their disease process presents staff with many distressful symptoms, (3) the work itself is physically and emotionally demanding, (4) many aspects of care cannot be controlled in the home because of the inability of the family, and (5) the process of integration of hospice into a health care system.

Nature of terminal illness. The most obvious stressor is the nature of terminal illness itself. There is no question that dying patients and their families are under a tremendous amount of stress, which significantly affects the hospice staff. Most families have little experience in caring for a gravely ill person and are, therefore, apprehensive, unsure, anxious, and in need of a tremendous amount of support and assurance from the hospice caregiver. In addition, their own feelings about the impending death of a family member generates many emotions and potential difficulties with interpersonal relationships.

Although death is the ultimate loss, in the course of a terminal illness the patient and family experience many other losses. Coping with each successive one often becomes increasingly difficult for the family, as well as for the patient. Their emotional reactions are often exacerbated by previous experiences with grief and loss that may or may not have been resolved (Friel and Tehan, 1980). The needs of the patient at the terminal stage are also great. Not only are there physical symptoms to alleviate but also psychological, spiritual, emotional, and financial needs to relieve.

It is essential, therefore, to recognize the impact of working with patients at only one end of the health-illness continuum. The staff know and interact with families at a most difficult time in their lives. They have had no opportunity to participate in the curative treatment phase when a more positive or hopeful atmosphere prevailed. In short, the staff has no other perspective from which to work with this family. Although many rewards are associated with this work, the pain and suffering of patients and families occupy a significant portion of the staff's day. Consequently, the innumerable problems a staff member faces in caring for a terminally ill patient become major contributors to burnout in hospice care.

Organizational factors. Organizational factors may also be considered as stressors. Hospice care requires the availability of 24-hour coverage, 7 days a week. The work is never predictable; although a team member schedules regular visits, emergencies and crises are a way of life. This translates into long workdays in order to accommodate unexpected needs. Flexibility and adaptability are essential personal characteristics of hospice team members.

In most home care situations, the patient is cared for by family members who, for the most part, are inexperienced and untrained. Although hospice care is predicated on the team approach, the nurse remains responsible for the coordination of care; there is no other shift taking over after she leaves the home. All aspects of care, including supplies and personnel, must be arranged by the staff.

The number of patients assigned to a hospice staff member, as well as the acuity level of each patient-family unit, influences the amount of stress a hospice staff member experiences. In short, the size of the caseload must be considered in relation to the severity of the needs and problems of each particular family unit.

INDICATORS OF BURNOUT

Those circumstances related to hospice work that are a source of stress for staff in a hospice home care program have been explained. No one stressor is apt to cause burn-out. One must look instead at the number of stressors experienced by a staff member and the extent to which individual stressors impact the caregivers. One does not suddenly "burn out"; rather, he undergoes a process marked by physical, emotional, and behavioral indicators that can be easily recognized. *Physically,* the individual may describe a never-ending sense of exhaustion and fatigue; often, he shows symptoms of frequent headaches, gastrointestinal disturbances, respiratory problems, loss of appetite, weight changes, sleeplessness, and continual colds. He may also increase the normal use of alcohol, cigarettes, or drugs.

Emotionally, the person may be described as depressed, irritable, or paranoic. The individual often has a negative self-image because he does not like what is happening or how he feels. A person may describe a sense of powerlessness and a lack of appreciation. There is an overall feeling of negativity about changes that may be occurring within the job or about the work in general. Overall, there is decreasing job satisfaction, for the rewards do not nearly balance the problems.

There are also observable *behavioral* changes that include increased absenteeism, inability or unwillingness to be as productive as previously, irritability with patients and other staff members, and an attitude of omnipotence or "I can do it alone," accompanied by increasing isolation from co-workers. There may be nightmares about patients or about the job to the point where it interferes with sleep.

In the individual's personal life, spouse, friends, or children may complain about being ignored. There may also be a major change in these relationships. Often, the burned-out person complains about not being able to relax (Friel and Tehan, 1980).

A number of factors in the hospice routine appear to be important for grief resolution of the bereaved: (1) awareness of imminent death on the part of the patient, the spouse, and other family members; (2) adequate palliation (pain relief) of the patient: (3) a rehearsal of the tasks to be faced after the death of the patient; (4) greater family engagement with the spouse likely to play a major part in the care of the patient; (5) bereavement support of the spouse likely to be in close contact with the staff before and after the death of the patient (Ransford and Smith, 1991).

Awareness of imminent death permits anticipatory grief. The evidence indicates that it usually leads to greater calm and acceptance of the ensuing death (Fulton, 1971) and that it permits the bereaved person to regain full capacity for effective functioning and subsequent happiness more rapidly. In a hospice, instances in which the patient and family talk about a time when the person will not be there may help the hospice survivor get a head start on dealing with the painful loss of a loved one (Rando, 1986).

Adequate palliation for the patient is another important factor. To see one's spouse in pain may negatively affect grief resolution (Cameron, 1981). In a hospice, pain relief is typically achieved by meticulous attention to the individual needs of each patient, continuous monitoring of drug responses, and smaller, more frequent dosages of narcotic drugs. When analgesic dosages are administered in this manner, the patient is able to remain alert and mobile (Hinton, 1979; Parkes, 1979). It is interesting that current research indicates that now some hospitals are as good as hospices at pain relief (Rando, 1986; Parker, 1984). Perhaps hospice care has set an example for hospitals.

Successful palliation (a pain-free and alert patient), combined with hospice's encouragement of open expression of grief and mourning with the patient, permits resolution of unfinished family business and a rehearsal of the problems to be faced by the family after the death.

In its ideal form, hospice enables the spouse to view a mate dying with dignity, with power and control over his or her life until the end. Viewing one's spouse in control should reduce some of the bereaved's stress and anxiety in the last months of the patient's life, as well as encourage favorable memories of the patient, factors that should translate into more rapid grief resolution.

With the prevalence of AIDS in the United States today, health care providers are at great risk for experiencing burnout. There are many reasons for this. Stressors include (1) fear of contagion and mortality, (2) the young age of those afflicted, (3) the inevitability of the patient's death, (4) deterioration of the patient's physical condition and psychological state, (5) the need for extra precautions, and (6) being the target of the patient's anger. The emotional and educational needs of the patient's significant others also place a burden on the health professional. Additional stress may be experienced if the health care worker becomes placed in the role of mediator between the patient, the patient's family, and the patient's lover (Salisbury, 1986).

Health care workers who have adverse feelings toward homosexuality, bisexuality, or AIDS experience additional stress. The strain is compounded when the professional tries to suppress personal feelings and attitudes in order to deliver care in a nonjudgmental fashion. Health care providers may be shunned by their families, friends, the community, and other professionals for their work with AIDS patients. They may try to protect their personal and professional lives by concealing the nature of their jobs from others. The combined stressors involved in working with AIDS patients result in an increased potential for burnout among health professionals (Nichols, 1985).

Causes of Burnout

Burnout, often described as the emotional exhaustion caused by stress, occurs at high levels among health professionals, and antibody test counselors are especially vulnerable to it because of the nature of their jobs, the nature of AIDS, and worksite conditions. Therapists develop therapeutic relationships with a wide range of clients to whom they must offer education and support during short, one-time sessions. These sessions can become highly personal, as clients discuss drug using and sexual behaviors and express a broad range of emotional reactions that require therapists themselves to invest emotional energy. As a result, antibody test counseling often presents a complex mix of high-intensity encounters of a repetitive nature, leading to both exhaustion and feelings of boredom and apathy. This situation is aggravated by the fact that one-time antibody test counseling is essentially limited in resolving the emotional and practical issues that test results raise, and therapists who seek to provide appropriate referrals to more specific resources often find none available (Tighe, 1991).

The daunting nature of AIDS itself also leads to burnout. HIV-related counseling requires knowledge of complicated medical and social topics. Counselors must be prepared to deliver this information in a variety of ways to clients—from those who may know more about AIDS than counselors to those who may not understand even the most basic information about health. Beyond the "facts," the realities of AIDS are grim, and knowing that AIDS leads to death can anger and discourage therapists. For therapists who have friends or partners with AIDS, particularly those for whom they provide care, the pressure of these realities may extend beyond work hours.

Worksite conditions can exacerbate these factors by limiting on-the-job support. Supervisors and colleagues may offer little emotional or professional support for therapists, and therapists may fear that talking about their emotional concerns may make them seem weak and ineffective. High turnover rates may lead to inadequate staffing and an interruption of relationships among staff. Conscientious work habits may be "rewarded" with increased work loads; for example, the most capable therapist may be given responsibility for the most emotionally draining tasks, such as disclosing all of the positive results at a site or providing posttest counseling. Therapists, who may find some relief in offering more personalized attention regardless of an individual's antibody status, may be criticized for spending too much time with clients (Knox, 1991).

Burnout Progression

Two factors are most likely to create conditions under which burnout may progress. First, therapists are vulnerable when they fail to adhere to the psychological boundaries that separate their lives from their clients' lives or when these boundaries are poorly or unrealistically defined. When boundaries fail, therapists adopt into their personal lives the emotional responses—grief, anger, fear—that clients bring to the counseling session. Although identifying with their work is often productive for therapists, psychological boundaries also protect their personal lives from being substituted by work (Tighe, 1991). Second, unrealistic goals and expectations set the stage for frustration and burnout. Therapists are limited in what they can achieve at antibody test sites during one session; for example, if they see success as entirely changing an individual's risk-taking behaviors or totally eliminating the transmission of AIDS, they will fail. A related factor is the perception that an inadequate health care system can never fully satisfy client needs and therefore leaves them to therapists to resolve. By contrast, expectations of failure—for example, thinking that clients will not be able to get appropriate treatment despite referrals offered by therapists— may lead therapists to feel hopeless and powerless (Stine, 1993).

A therapist's emotional state and job performance may offer warning signs of burnout. During the early stages of burnout, therapists often report that outside work, they are listless and inactive, inclined to meet only minimal responsibilities imposed on them by friends and family, and apt to sleep longer. They are more likely to participate in addictive behaviors, such as eating, smoking, drinking, and recreational drug use.

Avoiding Burnout

A first useful step to managing or avoiding burnout is to acknowledge the difficulties and limitations of the therapist's job: seeing clients for short periods of time, soliciting information that many consider private, and being charged with providing risk-reduction education and counseling as well as emotional support. The second step is to acknowledge the complexity of clients' lives, the fact that all of their needs and emotional concerns cannot be resolved during a single session, and the fact that therapists cannot compensate for all of the inadequacies of the health care and social service systems. Therapists should not excessively scrutinize themselves about what they are unable to do. Instead, they should give themselves credit for the positive work they can accomplish (Miller and others, 1990).

Therapists state that "taking care of yourself" is the most important way to maintain a healthy approach to work. This requires satisfying personal needs, which may include independence, acceptance, support, and emotional expression, as well as feeling good about oneself and one's work. Clients' needs for social services, emotional support, and information are important during therapy, but therapists should not carry their clients' burdens away from the test site. To accomplish this, it is essential for therapists to set explicit psychological boundaries and to review their work and behavior to make sure that they are not exceeding these boundaries.

Institutions and organizations that deal with AIDS patients have a responsibility to be aware of these stressors and to take action to prevent burnout. Weekly meetings with the staff can assist in stress management by encouraging members to express their feelings. The meetings can decrease anxiety, provide for an exchange of mutual support, and allow acceptance of the situation. The sessions can occur in the form of staff meetings or support groups. Other techniques that may prove useful in preventing burnout include relaxation exercises, assignment rotation, and scheduled time off for "mental health days."

Educational needs of health care workers should be strongly considered. Access to current information about AIDS and instructions on mental status examinations should be readily available. Institutions and organizations caring for AIDS patients can only provide optimal care when they take optimal care of their health professionals (Salisbury, 1986).

Articles have been published on burnout among teachers, police officers, attorneys, nurses, mental health workers, and day care staff (Ellison and Geng, 1978; Hendrickson, 1979; Maslach and Jackson, 1979; Maslach and Pines, 1977; Pines and Maslach, 1978; Shubin, 1978).

The most definitive work on burnout syndrome is the text by Edelwich and Brodsky (1980). According to the authors, the four stages of disillusionment that occur are (1) enthusiasm, (2) stagnation, (3) frustration, and (4) apathy. Each of these stages of disillusionment is discussed briefly, and a fifth stage, that of hopelessness, is included, as well as some intervention techniques.

Stages of Disillusionment

ENTHUSIASM

Enthusiasm is the initial period of high hopes, high energy, and unrealistic expectations. During this period, the person does not need anything in life but the job because the job promises to be everything. Overidentification with clients and excessive and inefficient expenditure of one's own energy are the major hazards of this stage.

People go into the human services to make a living but not to make money. Although the full extent of the inequities in salaries between publicly funded service positions and jobs in the private sector may become apparent only after a person has invested years of training and work in a helping profession, the person is generally aware that such professions do not pay especially well. The motivation is a desire to "help" people. Individuals become "helpers" because they really enjoy working with people and they want to make a difference in people's lives. Those who are genuinely involved far outnumber those who are cynical and self-seeking.

An important factor in bringing people into the human services is the example of others. People want to be like the people who have helped them. This is especially common in teaching and medicine because every young person is exposed to teachers and physicians, some of whom are inspiring models.

In other human services fields, the experience of being a client often engenders the desire to be a helper (Edelwich and Brodsky, 1980). The experience of being helped provides the strongest demonstration of the value of helping. At the same time, it creates expectations of what it would be like to assume the role of helper.

People who have been counseled unsuccessfully do not become counselors. The people who become counselors are those who have been counseled successfully, and their experiences as cooperative clients who have benefited from the services offered them may give them unrealistic expectations. They may expect all clients to be as receptive and resourceful as they were and all counselors to be as competent and caring as those who counseled them.

Enthusiasm comes not only from high initial motivation but also from early successes and satisfactions on the job. The new counselor or social worker, needing a certain amount of structure and supervision, tends to be put to work in environments that are safer and more rewarding than those they will face later. When the social worker has moved out into tougher, more demanding environments and has exhausted the capacity for self-reinforcement as well, he tends to look back on those halcyon days with a certain wistful nostalgia. In the stage of enthusiasm, it is commonly believed that the job is the person's whole life and that all gratifications are coming from the job. This unbalanced existence comes about by a kind of vicious cycle. On the one hand, an inflated conception of the job tends to obliterate personal needs and concerns. On the other hand, glorification of work may arise from deficiencies in an individual's personal life. The cycle of overcommitment is self-fulfilling because the longer the personal life is neglected, the more it deteriorates. The helper is thus left in a highly vulnerable position when the job ceases to furnish the rewards it once did (Edelwich and Brodsky, 1980).

Overidentification with clients is a major link in the chain that stretches from enthusiasm to burnout, both because it leads the helper to act in ways that are detrimental to clients and because it makes the helper's emotional well-being dependent on the client's living up to unrealistic expectations. Overidentification stems from an excess of energy and dedication, a lack of knowledge and experience in the field, and a confusion of personal needs with those of clients. It manifests itself as a lack of clarity in role definitions between client and helper. It leads well-meaning professionals and paraprofessionals to make themselves available to receive telephone calls at home at all hours of the night, a degree of accessibility that can have damaging effects on the helper's life.

The problem facing those who are dedicated to human services is to be realistic enough to cope with discouraging conditions without suffering a total loss of idealism and concern. This is also the lesson that needs to be conveyed to students and trainees. This is the area where intervention is the most crucial, especially when a person reflects that an initial lack of realism is what leaves him most vulnerable to eventual disillusionment.

STAGNATION

According to Edelwich and Brodsky (1980), *stagnation* refers to the process of becoming stalled after an initial burst of enthusiasm. It is the loss of the momentum of hope and desire that originally brought the person into the helping professions.

No sharp distinction can be drawn between stagnation and frustration or, indeed, between any two of the four stages of burnout. The progression through the four stages can not be traced in precise chronological sequence in any given instance.

When accomplishments are reduced to a human scale, minor annoyances such as low pay and long hours begin to be noticed. The frustrations that occur at this point are not enough to question doing the job, but they are enough to question doing nothing but the job. In stagnation a person is still doing the job, but the job can no longer make up for the fact that personal needs—to earn a decent living, to be respected on and off the job, to have satisfying family and social relationships, and to have some leisure time in which to enjoy them—are not being met. If those needs remain unmet, that person will not be able to keep on doing the job for very long.

Stagnation often begins with the discovery that it is not as easy as anticipated to see, let alone assess, the results of one's labors. Initially, it is experienced not as a source of active discontent but as a kind of bewilderment that leaves a person wondering why the job is not quite what it appeared to be. At the heart of stagnation lies the feeling that one's career is at a dead end (Edelwich and Brodsky, 1980).

FRUSTRATION

In the stage of frustration, individuals who have set out to give others what they need find that they themselves are not getting what they want. They are not doing the job they set out to do. In essence, they are not really "helping." Besides the low pay, long hours, and low status, there is a more basic frustration in the helping professions. It is extremely difficult to change people, and it is even more difficult under negatively perceived working conditions.

The sensation of powerlessness is felt at many levels by people in the helping professions. Most obvious is the powerlessness felt by front-line workers who occupy the lowest positions in the decision-making hierarchy, for example, the therapist who has no way to compel his crisis patients to keep their appointments with him. Powerlessness is relative to a person's position. A frequent complaint of supervisors is that their subordinates credit them with more power than they actually have (Larson, 1978).

The feeling of powerlessness is universal; it goes beyond hierarchical status. Its broader implications are the inability to change the system and the inability to control patients, subordinates, superiors, or the agency. This is the frustration that leads directly to burnout.

Notwithstanding the idealism that motivates people to enter the helping professions, the issues of power and control are central to the helping relationship. Some people complain that they do not have enough power; others complain that they have too much power. The unresponsiveness of the system to the people working in it is seen as a lack of appreciation. Individuals who are not given responsibility, are not consulted about decisions, and are generally overlooked by the bureaucratic system will certainly believe they are not appreciated by their supervisor or by the organization as a whole.

Appreciation from clients is what enables the individual to go on despite lack of institutional support. A person can take the stress from the supervisor when he is appreciated and receives positive feedback from clients. When they, too, are unappreciative, it makes that person question the whole purpose in being there. Helping people is what it is all about.

The effects of frustration—and of stagnation, as well—on the quality of services rendered to individuals are all too evident. Implicit and explicit in the accounts of overwork, inadequate funding, staff polarization, bureaucratic sluggishness, and other sources of discouragement and demoralization among staff members is the almost inevitable conclusion that the client is the one who suffers.

The importance of frustration for burnout lies in what a person does with it. Reaction to frustration has a great deal to do with whether he will fall deeper into burnout and, ultimately, whether he can stay in the field. A person can respond to frustration in three ways: (1) use it as a source of negative energy, (2) use it as a source of positive energy, or (3) just withdraw from the situation.

There is no doubt that frustration creates energy. When it is an energy of willful denial, a frenzy of activity aimed at evading the reality of frustration or doing away with the causes of frustration that are among the givens of the situation, then it is a self-destructive, negative energy. The energy of frustration can also be directed into a constructive effort. By taking responsibility, confronting issues, and taking actions that may bring about change, a person can release some of the emotional tension created by frustration. Frustration can be a major turning point in the progression through the stages. An individual who misses this turn is likely to descend into apathy.

Probably the most common response to frustration is not to express it at all, but to internalize it and withdraw from the threatening situation. The helper avoids clients because he has come to dislike or resent them, despairs of being able to do anything for them, or is physically exhausted. Some individuals walk away from their jobs and from their idealism and concern. Then they may get angry, assert themselves, and get back into the center of things. Others, unfortunately, drift into the fourth and last stage of burnout—apathy (Edelwich and Brodsky, 1980).

APATHY

Apathy takes the form of a progressive emotional detachment in the face of frustration. The starting point is the enthusiasm, the idealism, and overidentification of the beginner. If one is to come down from the clouds and work effectively, some detachment is desirable and inevitable, but most individuals do not have ideal learning conditions and sympathetic guidance to help them reach an optimum level of detachment. Frustration comes as it will, sometimes brutally, and the detachment that develops in its wake is less a poised emotional distancing than a kind of numbness. In turning off to frustrating experiences, a person may well turn off to people's needs and to his own caring. Apathy can be felt as boredom. The once-idealistic helper can trace the erosion of the desire to help and the feeling of involvement with patients that he used to have. People who started out caring about others end up caring mainly about their own health, sanity, peace of mind, and survival.

The most severe and saddest form of apathy is experienced when a person remains at a job for one reason only—because the job is needed for survival. The person has seen what is going on but has no inclination to try to change it. Certainly, no risks will be taken when the individual can just go along, protecting the position while doing as little as possible. Security has become the prime concern. Of all the stages of burnout, apathy is the hardest to overcome and the one against which it is most difficult to intervene successfully. It is the most settled, the most deep-seated, and the one that takes the longest to arrive at, and it lasts the longest. It stems from a decision, reached over a period of time and reinforced by one's peers, to stop caring. In the absence of a major personal upheaval, vastly changed conditions on the job, or a concerted intervention, it can last forever.

HOPELESSNESS

Edelwich and Brodsky (1980) did not discuss hopelessness as a stage in the process of disillusionment; it is, however, implicitly evident in their stages of stagnation, frustration, and apathy. According to Horney (1967), hopelessness is the ultimate product of unresolved conflicts. It is looking forward to an event or an occurrence with the deeply held belief that the anticipated will not occur.

When hope is lost, a person may be in the stage of stagnation, frustration, or apathy. Hopelessness may fluctuate throughout the stages, diminishing at times and then returning full force to make the individual feel like giving up the role of helper. When the helper is experiencing hopelessness, he has a tendency to deny or to avoid revealing any personal thoughts or feelings that could be considered "unprofessional" and to behave instead as if he were in control of the situation and doing well. Failing to share true feelings with others leads to the erroneous assumption that he is the only one having such problems. This error is further enhanced by the fact that the individual who believes he is alone in having these feelings will be especially careful not to reveal this response to others and will maintain the façade of professionalism (McConnell, 1982).

Intervention

Intervention may be self-initiated, or it may occur in response to an immediate frustration or threat. It may be fueled in part by a person's own strength and in part by support and guidance from peers, supervisors, family and friends, or whoever else is important in his life. It may be a temporary stopgap or a real change. Intervention can and should occur at any of the four stages of disillusionment. One of the major tasks of trainers and supervisors should be to help staff members experience the four stages with greater awareness and thus be less subject to violent swings of emotion. In reality, however, intervention most often takes place at the stage of frustration, when it is almost too late. In the stage of enthusiasm, people are having too good a time to see any need for intervention. Stagnation does not usually provide the energy required to change course, although interventions in the areas of further education, skill development, and career advancement are sometimes initiated at this stage. As for apathy, that stage is already a long way toward disillusionment, and the road back up is a long, hard one that some individuals negotiate successfully but many never attempt.

More often, it is frustration that moves a person off center and impels changes. Frustration is not so bad when it gets people angry enough to break out of a bad situation instead of becoming apathetic.

Nothing is more important in handling burnout than to know what responsibilities the individual does and does not have. The professional is not responsible for clients or for the institution but is responsible for himself. This does not mean that the professional does not become involved with patients or does not try to change the way the institution is run. It simply means that he is responsible for his own actions, not theirs, and remains responsible for his actions regardless of what they do or do not do.

When other systems in life are strengthened, the individual gains strength for coping with work as well. The things people do to strengthen their outside lives and create a larger world to live in vary from individual to individual. An important first step is to make a clear separation between work and other areas of life by limiting off-hours socializing with co-workers or others in the same field and controlling the tendency toward extracurricular preoccupation with job-related issues. The number of hours required at work is usually set, but the rest of the day is controlled by the individual. The professional can, however, refuse to give friends and relatives free professional assistance with their personal problems. The benefits of giving a home telephone number to clients in order to be available to them in an emergency must be weighed against the costs.

Probably the most important way of enlarging a person's world is through close personal and family relationships. Developing and maintaining these relationships requires and, in turn, creates time commitments and emotional commitments that keep the person from being devoured by the job. It may take a lot of work to negotiate with family and close friends the space needed for commitment to the job and the space all concerned need to be together and to be away from constant reminders of the job, but by making this effort an identity independent of the job is created. There are, of course, many other reasons for wanting to have a fulfilling personal life. With regard to burnout, however, the importance of close personal ties is clear and crucial. When one is loved and appreciated by the family, whether one is loved and appreciated by clients or supervisors is no longer a life-or-death matter. When deep and constant support of family and friends is enjoyed, a person's whole self is not put on the line every morning.

Other interventions could include the technique of planned, temporary social isolation. At a minimum, professionals need times when they can get away from those who are often the direct source of job stress—the recipients and, in some cases, the administrators. This can be accomplished through physical and psychological withdrawals and long vacations (Edelwich and Brodsky, 1980).

Another alternative is a "decompression routine" between leaving work and arriving home, a time in which they can engage in some solitary activity, preferably physical and noncognitive, in order to unwind and relax. By being alone for a while, they are then more ready to be with people again, especially with those people who are close to them.

Some helping professionals deliberately use some of their off-duty hours to engage in activities with people who are normal, healthy, and functioning well. By having pleasant and successful interactions with these people, professionals can counteract the development of negative attitudes about clients and about their ability to work well with clients.

The following case study concerns the problems of a new trainee, Alan, who experienced burnout at a crisis center.

Case Study *Burnout*

ASSESSMENT OF THE INDIVIDUAL AND THE PROBLEM

Alan was a 24-year-old trainee in crisis intervention at a community mental health center. Alan was a graduate in psychology from a well-known university. At their first meeting, he impressed one of his supervisors with his solid theoretical background and his great enthusiasm at being accepted as an intern at the mental health center. He was attractive, tall, athletic in his physique, and very expressive. Because he was in that city for the first time, the supervisor questioned him about his living arrangements. He stated that he was sharing a townhouse with two other interns and that they were having "a ball."

Because the center is very busy, after their orientation the interns were immediately booked to see clients. Alan spent his time in supervision discussing his clients with great enthusiasm and discussing his plans for intervention in each case. For the first 3 months, everything went well. He was apparently functioning well as an effective therapist. He was able to glow with pride when he had successes and was able to accept that he could not "cure" everyone.

In the next 2 months, Alan began to show some psychological changes. His enthusiasm was beginning to diminish, and he appeared more concerned about his clients who were not responding to therapy—as *he* expected them to. When discussing this in his supervisory hour, he tried to pass over his concerns by saying, "I know I'm good. They won't do what I want because I'm too young." When questioned about what he did in his time off, he smiled ruefully and said, "What time off? I am here 5 days a week and I volunteered to be a coleader in four groups at another center every weekend." His supervisor asked why he believed he should "work" 7 days a week; he shrugged and said, "I feel it is a good learning experience working as a coleader." She continued to press the issue by saying, "Alan, when do you have fun? What about the girl you were dating and the sailing you used to do every weekend?" He said soberly, "Gone with the wind."

Alan appeared angry and bitter when the supervisor strongly suggested that he was jeopardizing his internship at the center by working on weekends and that he should terminate at the other center. He responded bitterly, "But they need me!" He was informed that he had no choice in the matter, that working with crisis clients was emotionally exhausting, and that all employees need time for themselves to recoup from the stress of being on call every night for their clients if needed. He very reluctantly agreed to stop working weekends. Over the next 2 months, Alan began to withdraw from his peers and seemed tired, pale, and thin. He appeared for supervision each week but had little enthusiasm and was poorly prepared to discuss the clients he was seeing. When this was pointed out to him, he merely replied flatly, "I try to help them, but if they don't want it, so what." He denied that he was working weekends. He was informed that his performance at the center was poor, and complaints had been received that he was not returning his clients' telephone calls. He responded by saying, "They are just neurotic and dependent."

He was told that a meeting was scheduled with his other supervisors the next week, and his presence would be required; he shrugged and agreed to be there.

Two days later, while in the main office where the switchboard is located, the supervisor was getting her mail when Alan walked in. The operator said, "Alan, I have a call for you. It's an emergency." Alan replied, "Just take a message." The supervisor turned to Alan and said firmly, "Alan, take that call at the other telephone." He sighed and agreed. He answered the telephone, listened for a few seconds, and then responded, "Oh my God! No!" and dropped the telephone. His supervisor picked it up and identified herself. On the line was a physician at a nearby emergency room; one of Alan's clients had committed suicide. In his hand was his appointment card with Alan's name and the center's emergency telephone number. The supervisor took Alan by the arm (he was pale, trembling, and crying) and led him to her office. She let him cry and ventilate his feelings over losing a client and gave him coffee and tissues until he was able to control himself. She told him that she believed there should be an emergency meeting with him and his other supervisors. He agreed, the appropriate contacts were made, and a conference room was scheduled.

All of his supervisors gave Alan great emotional support as he told them his feelings after losing a client. As a group, they all expressed to Alan how very much he needed a long vacation to recoup and to gain a different perspective on his role as a therapist. It was recommended that Alan return to his home in the east for a minimum of 3 months before resuming his internship at the center. He agreed that he would do as they asked.

Four months later, Alan returned to continue his internship at the center with a surprise—a bride! He appeared relaxed, happy, and very sound. His wife, Kay, was delightful; they had gone to school together, and they met again when he returned home.

The rest of Alan's internship went smoothly in every respect; he was more mature in his judgments, his enthusiasm was present, but, most important, he spent his time off with his wife, and they went sailing almost every weekend.

Alan apparently experienced burnout, from enthusiasm to frustration, hopelessness, and then apathy. Fortunately, after an enforced vacation, he was able to function again in a healthy manner as a therapist.

SUMMATION OF THE PARADIGM (Figure 9-1)

Intervention focused on helping Alan recognize that he had been overextending himself and had lost his sense of objectivity when working with his clients. He was living in a new environment and adjusting to a new role, that of a therapist. He became depressed when his clients did not respond as he believed they should; he truly believed he could "cure" everyone. He refused all situational support from his peers and supervisor. He had no previous experience or coping skills in his new role as a "helper," his depression increased, and he became apathetic, entering the fourth stage of burnout and then crisis. With the assistance of his supervisors and with peer support, he was finally able to accept the reality that a therapist can never become "all things to all people."

CASE STUDY: ALAN

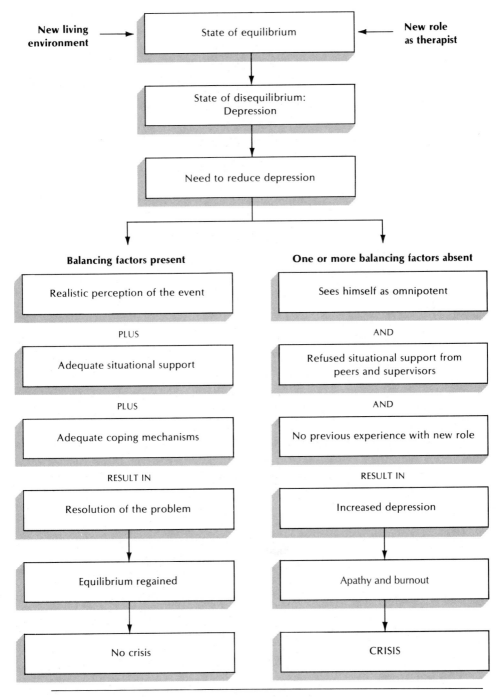

Figure 9-1

There are as many definitions of *burnout* as there are authors writing about it. Freudenberger (1974), an authority on burnout, says it is "a depletion of energy experienced by those in helping professions when they feel overwhelmed by other problems." Maslach's Burnout Inventory is an excellent verifiable instrument developed to test the degree of burnout that occurs when staff nurses show indications that they are suffering from the burnout syndrome. Nurses who work in high-stress areas such as the emergency room, intensive care unit, coronary care unit, AIDS wards, and hospice facilities should be very aware of their vulnerability (Raphael, 1983).

Freudenberger (1974) has identified personality types most prone to burnout.

- The dedicated and committed worker, who tends to take on too much for too long and too intensely
- The staff member who is overcommitted to work and whose outside life is unsatisfactory
- The authoritarian worker, who relies on authority and obedience to control others
- The administrator, who is usually genuinely overworked but begins to view himself as indispensable
- The professional, who tends to overidentify with those he is working with and for

Case Study — *Burnout*

ASSESSMENT OF THE INDIVIDUAL AND THE PROBLEM

Sabrina, a 34-year-old registered nurse, came to a community mental health center. She completed the brief chart and was told she would be able to see a therapist later that afternoon, in approximately 3 hours. Sabrina told the volunteer she would go out for coffee and come back later—maybe. The volunteer told the therapist assigned to Sabrina that she seemed "very angry."

Sabrina did return and leafed through every magazine, throwing them on the table carelessly; if they fell, she just let them lay. The therapist came out and called Sabrina. Sabrina stood up rather defiantly and looked at the therapist. The therapist introduced herself, and they shook hands. The therapist looked at the magazines on the floor and then at Sabrina, smiled, and asked, "Did you throw those magazines on the floor?" Sabrina put her chin up and said, "Yes, I did". The therapist smiled again and said firmly, "Then please pick them up and we can go to my office and begin therapy. We only have an hour and you are wasting my time." Sabrina looked slightly shocked and began to pick up the magazines. When she was through, she looked at the therapist, smiled slightly, and said, "My friends call me Bree. You can call me Bree." They walked to the therapist's office.

The therapist asked Bree to sit down, and she picked up her chart. The therapist had read Bree's chart. She knew that she was 34, married, had a 6-year-old son, Brian, and was a registered nurse. Until 3 days ago she had worked as a charge nurse at a hospice. She was of average height and weight and attractive, with large gray eyes and auburn hair. In answer to the question "Why are you here?" she had written on her chart, "*I can't take it anymore!!!*"

The therapist told Bree that she had read her chart and asked, "What can't you take anymore?" Bree looked up with tears in her eyes and said, "I can't take the dying . . . not anymore, I just can't!! The therapist asked Bree to tell her what had happened 3 days ago. Bree answered angrily, "It was more than 3 days ago. I don't *know* when it began, I just walked out 3 days ago and told them I would not be back!"

The therapist asked Bree how long she had worked at the hospice. Bree said that she had been the first nurse to go to the hospice when it had opened 3 years ago. The therapist asked her how she had liked working at the hospice. Bree answered, "It was wonderful. I really *felt* like a nurse, not just a paper pusher! It was so rewarding to be able to be in that lovely hospice. The rooms were just like a bedroom in a home, not at all like a cold, sterile hospital room! The families and friends, even pets, could visit any time they wanted to. I truly loved working there. It was sad when someone died, but all the staff supported each other; we never felt that we were grieving alone." She paused and then said, "I am a good nurse, a very good nurse. I honestly think no one is a better nurse than me." She started to cry. The therapist handed her a tissue and let her cry. She finally stopped and apologized for crying. The therapist said there was no need to apologize.

Bree looked at the therapist and began talking again. She said that she did not know what was wrong with her. Lately, she had been so irritable. She said that at home "she wasn't fit to live with" and that a week ago her husband asked her to take some time off so they could go away for a few days. She said that she had lost her temper and told him that she could not take any time off because she was needed. She said he became angry and said, "We need you, too. Do you realize that we haven't had a single day to ourselves since you started at the hospice?"

The therapist asked if this was true, and Bree reluctantly said that she had been too busy. There was so much to do at the hospice that a charge nurse was the only one who could do it.

The therapist asked Bree, "Why do you think you are the only nurse that can take care of *everything* at the hospice? Are you omnipotent? Everyone can be replaced in their job, even you or me. Don't you care about your family? Bree, surely you have heard of burnout. It sounds to me as if you are in burnout now. No job is worth the happiness and love you have with your husband and son."

Bree had listened to the therapist quietly and thoughtfully. She then said, "I know you are right. I am so exhausted, I've been having nightmares. I wonder if I gave Mr. A or Mrs. C their pain medication so I go back to the hospice to check, and I *had* given them their meds. It's just that I hate to fail! I have never failed before."

The therapist said, "Bree, you have not failed, I doubt if many nurses could work in a hospice as long as you did; 3 years is a long time. I know I couldn't. Bree, could you take a 3-month leave of absence from nursing, and that includes the hospice? You need a good rest, and you need to get to know your family. You are young, and you need to have some fun in your life. Would you go home and talk to your husband about it? Call me and let me know what he says, and I'll see you next week. Try taking a brisk 2-mile walk every day to relieve your excess energy."

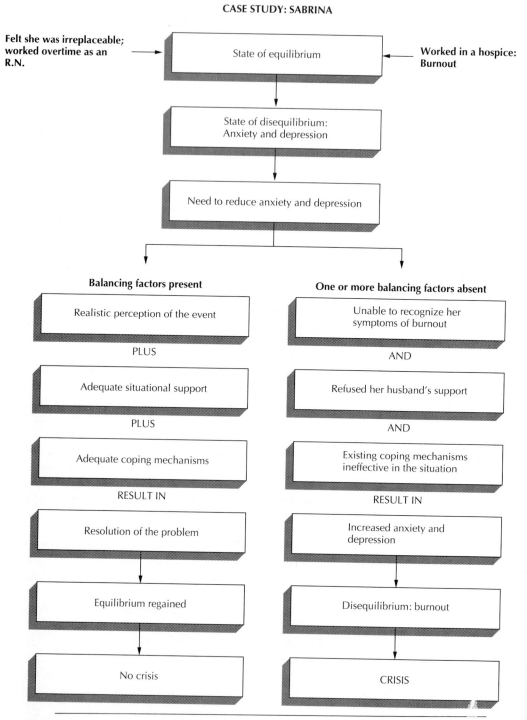

Figure 9-2

Bree said, "I don't know what I would do with 3 months off. I'll talk to Patrick and then call you." The therapist said, "Good, let's make an appointment for next week!"

They walked out of the office together, talking as they went, to schedule an appointment for Bree.

PLANNING THERAPEUTIC INTERVENTION

Bree was apparently suffering from burnout. She needed time off from the hospice and nursing. She was concerned that no one could take her place. It was felt that meeting and talking with her husband to get feedback from him was important. It was essential to find out how he felt about her taking a 3-month leave of absence.

INTERVENTION

Bree called the therapist and said that she had talked with Patrick and that he wanted to talk to the therapist. The therapist said, "Fine, Bree, put him on the telephone." Patrick took the phone and said hello to the therapist. He then said, "I can't believe that anyone could convince Bree that the hospice would not fall apart without her. I have got to meet you!" The therapist laughed and replied, "You read my mind. Could you come in with Bree next week?" Patrick said, "You can bet on it!"

The therapist continued to see Bree and Patrick together for the remaining sessions. Patrick had been very concerned about Bree and agreed with the therapist that she was suffering from burnout. Eventually, Bree began to relax. She began spending more time with their son, Brian, and he began to bloom with her attention, as did Patrick. At their last session, Bree said happily that they were booked on a cruise—a long one.

ANTICIPATORY PLANNING

Both Bree and Patrick were told that they could return to the center around any future crisis. The therapist cautioned Bree about becoming so involved with her work that it controlled her life completely. Bree agreed and said that when she did go back to work it would not be at the hospice. She was thinking of going into pediatrics. She was reminded to continue taking her 2-mile walks, as often as possible, to help her burn off her excess energy.

SUMMATION OF THE PARADIGM (Figure 9-2)

Bree did not recognize her symptoms of burnout. She refused the support of her husband. Her coping mechanisms were ineffective in this situation. Her anxiety and depression increased. She had burnout and went into a crisis.

REFERENCES

Edelwich J, Brodsky S: *Burn-out: stages of disillusionment in the helping professions,* New York, 1980, Human Sciences Press.
Ellison KW, Geng JL: The police officer as burned-out samaritan, *FBI Law Enforcement Bulletin,* March 1978.
Freudenberger HJ: Staff burn-out, *J Soc Issues* 30:159, 1974.
Friel M, Tehan C: Counteracting burn-out for the hospice care-giver, *Cancer Nurs* 3:258, 1980.

Fulton R, Fulton J: A psychosocial aspect of terminal care: anticipatory grief, *Omega* 2:91, 1971.

Hendrickson B: Teacher burn-out: how to recognize it; what to do about it, *Learning* 37, 1979.

Horney K: *Feminine psychology,* New York, 1967, W W Norton.

Knox LP, Knox MD: *Last wishes: a workbook for recording your funeral, memorial, and other final instructions,* Tampa, Florida, 1991, Applied Science Corp.

Larson C, Gilbertson D, Powell J: Therapist burn-out: perspectives on a critical issue, *Soc Casework* 59:563, 1978.

Maslach C, Jackson SE: Burned-out cops and their families, *Psychol Today* 12:59, 1979.

Maslach C, Pines A: The burn-out syndrome in the day care setting, *Child Care Q* 6:100, 1977.

McConnell E: *Burnout in the nursing profession,* St Louis, 1982, Mosby.

Miller EN, Selnes OA, McArthur JC, et al: Neuropsycological performance in HIV-1 infected homosexual men: the Multicenter AIDS Cohort Study (MACS), *Neurology,* 40:197, 1990.

Nichols SE: Psychological reactions of persons with the acquired immune deficiency syndrome, *Ann Intern Med* 103:765, 1985.

Parkes CM: Terminal care: evaluation of in-patient care at St. Christopher's Hospice, *Postgrad Med J* 55:517, 1979.

Parkes CM: Evaluation of a bereavement service, *J Prevent Psychiat* 1:179, 1981.

Pines A, Maslach C: Characteristics of staff burn-out in mental health settings, *Hosp Community Psychiatry* 29:233, 1978.

Rando T: A comprehensive analysis of anticipatory grief: In *Loss and anticipatory grief,* Lexington, MA. 1986, Heath.

Ransford E, Smith M: Grief resolution among the bereaved in hospice and hospital wards, *Soc Sci Med* 32:295, 1991.

Raphael B: *The anatomy of bereavement,* New York, 1983, Basic Books.

Salisbury DM: AIDS psychosocial implications, *J Psychosoc Nurs Mental Health Serv* 24:13, 1986.

Shubin S: Burn-out: the professional hazard you face in nursing, *Nursing* 8:22, 1978.

Stine G: *Acquired immune deficiency syndrome,* Englewood Cliffs, NJ, 1993, Prentice Hall.

Tighe, JB: Taking control, focus: A guide to AIDS research and counseling, *California Department of Health Services* 6:2, 1991.

ADDITIONAL READINGS

Ainsworth-Smith I, Speck P: *Letting go: caring for the dying and bereaved,* London, 1982, Anchor Press.

Ausfahl CB: Emergency nursing part time: answer to burnout? *JEN* 13:205, 1987 (letter).

Bartz C, Maloney JP: Burnout among intensive care nurses, *Res Nurs Health* 9:147, 1986.

Beaver RC, Sharp ES: Burnout experienced by nurse midwives, *J Nurse Midwifery* 31:3, 1986.

Bennett L, Michie P, Kippax S: Quantitative analysis of burnout and its associated factors in AIDS nursing, *AIDS Care* 3(2):181, 1991.

Blanks CD, Giovinco G: Stress/burnout indicators of concern across clinical areas of nursing, *Fla Nurse* 34:18, 1986.

Bruning-Nealia S: Gender differences in burnout: observations from an "unbiased" researcher, *Canadian Psychology* 32(4):575, 1991.

Cameron J, Parkes CM: Terminal care evaluation of effects on surviving care before and after bereavement, *Postgrad Med J* 59:73, 1983.

Cameron M: The moral and ethical component of nurse-burnout, *Nurs Manage* 17:42B, 1986.

Campbell RP: Does management style affect burnout? *Nurs Manage* 17:38A, 1986.

Capel SA: The incidence of and influences on stress and burnout in secondary school teachers, *Br J Educ Psychol* 57:279, 1987.

Cherniss C: Long-term consequences of burnout: an exploratory study, *J Organ Behav* 13(1):1, 1992.

Cherniss C: Observed supervisory behavior and teacher burnout in special education, *Except Child* 54:449, 1988.

Clark GH Jr, Vaccaro JV: Burnout among CMHC psychiatrists and the struggle to survive, *Hosp Community Psychiatry* 38:843, 1987.

Crotty M: "Burnout" and its implications for the continuing education of nurses, *Nurse Educ Today* 7:278, 1987.

Day HI, Chambers J: Empathy and burnout in rehabilitation counselors, *Can J Rehab* 5(1):33, 1991.

Dolan N: The relationship between burnout and job satisfaction in nurses, *J Adv Nurs* 12:3, 1987.

Dush DM: *Concepts and applications of bereavement programming.* In *Hospice handbook: a guide for managers and planners,* Rockville, Md 1985, Aspen.

Eichinger J, Heifetz LJ, Ingraham C: Situational shifts in sex role orientation: correlates of work satisfaction and burnout among women in special education, *Sex Roles* 25(7-8):425, 1991.

Ekberg JY, Griffith N: Spouse burnout syndrome, *J Adv Nurs* 11:161, 1986.

Firth H, McIntee J: Burnout and professional depression: related concepts? *J Adv Nurs* 11:633, 1986.

Firth H and others: Professional depression, "burnout" and personality in longstay nursing, *Int J Nurs Stud* 24:227, 1987.

Foster V: Supervisor impact on stress and burnout, *Today's OR Nurse* 9:24, 1987.

Green DE, Walkey FH, Taylor AJ: The three-factor structure of the Maslach Burnout Inventory: a multicultural, multinational confirmatory study, *J Soc Behav Pers* 6(3):453, 1991.

Greenglass BR: Burnout and gender: theoretical and organizational implications, *Canadian Psychology* 32(4):562, 1991.

Haack MR: Alcohol use and burnout among student nurses, *Nurs Health Care* 8:239, 1987.

Heine CA: Burnout among nursing home personnel, *J Gerontol Nurs* 12:14, 1986.

Horseman RE: Venture beyond burnout: the time is now, *Dent Manage* 27:18, 1987.

Horton K: International nursing: a cure for burnout, *J Pract Nurs* 36:38, 1986.

Hsia L: Burnout, *J Nurse Midwifery* 31:119, 1986.

Jayaratne S, Himle DP, Chess WA: Job satisfaction and burnout: is there a difference? *J Appl Soc Sci* 15(2):245, 1991.

Jenkins JF, Ostchega Y: Evaluation of burnout in oncology nurses, *Cancer Nurs* 9:108, 1986.

Jorgensen DM: Burnout in nurse faculty: relationships with management style, collegial support, and work load in collegiate programs, *J Prof Nurs* 2:252, 1986.

Kang R, Snyder C: Life without burnout: using consultation in community health nursing, *MCN* 12:301, 1987.

Korda L: Compassion, conviction, commitment: creed for quality hospice care, core of hospice burnout, *Am J Hosp Care* 4:39, 1987.

Kruger LJ, Botman HI, Goodenow C: An investigation of social support and burnout among residential counselors, *Child and Youth Care Forum* 20(5):335, 1991.

Lee RT, Ashforth BE: Work-unit structure and process and job-related stressors as predictors of managerial burnout, *J Appl Soc Psychol* 21(22):1831, 1991.

Leiter M: The dream denied: professional burnout and constraints of human service organizations, *Canadian Psychology* 32(4):547, 1991.

Levy JA, Gordon AK: Stress and burnout in the social world of hospice, *Hosp J* 3:29, 1987.

Martin CA, Julian RA: Causes of stress and burnout in physicians caring for the chronically and terminally ill, *Hosp J* 3: 121, 1987.

Mayou R: Burnout *Br Med J (Clin Res)* 295:284, 1987 (editorial).

McCranie EW, Lambert VA: Work stress, hardiness, and burnout among hospital staff nurses, *Nurs Res* 36:374, 1987.

Muller PA: Avoiding burnout through prevention, *J Post Anesth Nurs* 11:53, 1987.

Naisberg-Fennig S and others: Perosnality characteristics and proneness to burnout: a study among psychiatrists, *Stress Medicine* 7(4):201, 1991.

Pagel I, Wittman ME: Relationship of burnout to personal and job-related variables in acute-care pediatric settings, *Issues Compr Pediatr Nurs* 9:131, 1986.

Paradis LF, Miller B: Volunteer stress and burnout: issues for administrators, *Hosp J* 3:165, 1987.

Parham WD: Personal and professional issues for counseling center psychologists: 7-10 years postdoctorate, *Counsel Psych* 20(1):32, 1992.

Patrick PK: Hospice caregiving: strategies to avoid burnout and maintain self-preservation, *Hosp J* 3:223, 1987.

Purdy RR, Lemkau JP: Resident physicians in family practice: who's burned out and who knows? *Fam Med* 19:203, 1987.

Randolph GL, Price JL: The effects of burnout prevention training on burnout symptoms in nurses, *J Contin Educ Nurs* 17:43, 1986.

Ray EB, Nichols MR: A model of job stress and burnout, *Hosp J* 3:3, 1987.

Revenson TA, Cassel BJ: An exploration of leadership in a medical mutual help organization, *Am J Commun Psychol* 19(5):683, 1991.

Rich VL, Rich AR: Personality hardiness and burnout in female staff nurses, *Image J Nurs Sch* 19:63, 1987.

Rosse JG and others: Conceptualizing the role of self-esteem in the burnout process, *Group and Organization Studies* 16(4):428, 1991.

Russell DW, Altmaier E: Job-related stress, social support, and burnout among classroom teachers, *J Appl Psychol* 72:269, 1987.

Seidman SA, Zager J: A study of coping behaviours and teacher burnout, *Work and Stress* 5(3):205, 1991.

Shea ML: Burnout! *J Pract Nurs* 36:34, 1986.

Soupios MA, Lawry K: Stress on personnel working in a critical care unit, *Psychiatr Med* 5:187, 1987.

Stanek LM: An analysis of professional nurse burnout in two selected nursing care settings, *J Nurs Adm* 17:3, 1987.

Turnipseed DL Jr: Burnout among hospice nurses: an empirical assessment, *Hosp J* 3:105, 1987.

Turnipseed DL, Turnipseed PH: Personal coping resources and the burnout syndrome, *J Soc Behav Person* 6(3):473, 1991.

Vaccaro JV, Clark GH Jr: A profile of community mental health center psychiatrists: results of a national survey, *Community Ment Health J* 23:282, 1987.

Wadsworth NS, Clark NL: Managing organizational stress in nursing, *J Nurs Adm* 16:21, 1986.

Watkins EC: Early professional in counseling psychology: the academic setting, *Counseling Psychologist* 20(1):47, 1992.

Index

A

Abortion
  case study involving, 114-116, 117
  theoretical concepts of, 111-116
Abuse
  child
    case study involving, 96-105
    theoretical concepts of, 90-105
  cocaine, 169-182; *see also* Cocaine
  elder
    case study involving, 151-153,
     154
    theoretical concepts of, 147-153,
     154
  financial, indications of, 149
  marital; *see* Battered wife; Spouse
    abuse
  sexual, 91, 92; *see also* Child
    abuse; Rape
  spouse
    case study involving, 161-164,
     165
    theoretical concepts of, 159-164,
     165
  substance
    case study involving, 178-182
    theoretical concepts of, 169-182
Abuse-dynamic model of Kempe et
  al., 94
Abusive men, 159-160
Acquired immune deficiency syndrome, 257-291
  adolescent, case study involving,
    286-289
  common questions about, 271-276
  definition of, 271-272
  diagnosis of, 273-274
  disengaged family and, 261-262
  enmeshment in family with, 261

Acquired immune deficiency syndrome—cont'd
  fears of patients at risk for, 258
  health-care costs and, 266
  heterosexual, case study involving,
    277-281
  heterosexual female, case study in-
    volving, 289-291
  heterosexual transmission of, 269-
    270
  homosexual, case study involving,
    282-286
  opportunistic diseases in people
    with, 271-272
  population at risk for, 272-273
  precautions to prevent, 273-274
  role of therapist in, 260
  spread of, means of, 272, 275,
    276
  symptoms of, 271, 273
  teenage perceptions of, 270-271
  transmissibility of, 264, 265
  treatment of, 275-276
  in United States, 264-269
  in women, 274
Adaptation
  Hartmann's concepts of, 4
  Rado's concept of, 4
Adaptational psychodynamics, 4
Addiction to cocaine, 175-176; *see
  also* Cocaine
Addicts and AIDS, 264
Adolescence
  AIDS in, case study involving,
    286-289
  case study involving, 226-230
  pregnancy in, 113
  theoretical concepts of, 225-
    230